Political
Campaign
Communication

PRAEGER SERIES IN POLITICAL COMMUNICATION
Robert E. Denton, Jr., *General Editor*

Political Campaign Communication

Principles and Practices
Second Edition

Judith S. Trent
and Robert V. Friedenberg

Praeger Series in Political Communication

New York
Westport, Connecticut
London

Library of Congress Cataloging-in-Publication Data

Trent, Judith S.
    Political campaign communication : principles and practices /
    Judith S. Trent, Robert V. Friedenberg. — 2nd ed.
        p.   cm. — (Praeger series in political communication)
    Includes bibliographical references and index.
    ISBN 0–275–93400–4 (alk. paper). — ISBN 0–275–93401–2 (pbk. :
alk. paper)
    1. Electioneering. 2. Communication in politics.
I. Friedenberg, Robert V. II. Title. III. Series.
JF1001.T73   1991
324.7'0973—dc20   91–10610

British Library Cataloguing in Publication Data is available.

Library of Congress Catalog Card Number: 91–10610
ISBN: 0-275-93400-4 (hb)
      0-275-93401-2 (pb)

First published in 1991

Praeger Publishers, One Madison Avenue, New York, NY 10010
An imprint of Greenwood Publishing Group, Inc.

Printed in the United States of America

The paper used in this book complies with the
Permanent Paper Standard issued by the National
Information Standards Organization (Z39.48–1984).

10 9 8 7 6 5 4 3 2 1

To Jimmie D. Trent
and the memory of
Aaron Friedenberg

Contents

About the Series

Those of us from the discipline of communication studies have long believed that communication is prior to all other fields of inquiry. In several other forums I have argued that the essence of politics is "talk" or human interaction.[1] Such interaction may be formal or informal, verbal or nonverbal, public or private, but always persuasive, forcing us consciously or subconsciously to interpret, to evaluate, and to act. Communication is the vehicle for human action.

From this perspective, it is not surprising that Aristotle recognized the natural kinship of politics and communication in his *Politics* and *Rhetoric*. In the former, he establishes that humans are "political beings [who] alone of the animals [are] furnished with the faculty of language."[2] And in the latter, he begins his systematic analysis of discourse by proclaiming that "rhetorical study, in its strict sense, is concerned with the modes of persuasion."[3] Thus it was recognized over two thousand years ago that politics and communication go hand in hand because they are essential parts of human nature.

Back in 1981, Dan D. Nimmo and Keith R. Sanders proclaimed that political communication was an emerging field.[4] Although its origin, as noted, dates back centuries, a "self-consciously cross-disciplinary" focus began in the late 1950s. Thousands of books and articles later, colleges and universities offer a variety of graduate and undergraduate coursework in the area in such diverse departments as communication, mass communication, journalism, political science, and sociology.[5] In Nimmo and Sanders's early assessment, the "key areas of inquiry" included rhetorical analysis, propaganda analysis, attitude change studies, voting studies, government and the news media, functional and systems analyses, technological changes, media technologies, campaign techniques, and research techniques.[6] In a survey of the state of the field in 1983 by the same authors and Lynda Lee Kaid, they found additional, more specific areas of concern, such as the presidency, political polls, public opinion, debates, and advertising, to name a few.[7] Since the first study, they also noted a shift away from the rather strict behavioral approach. The 1983 edition of *Political Campaign Communication* was the first book-length study of political campaigns from a communication perspective. As such, it predated the series and addressed many of the concerns expressed by Nimmo, Sanders, and Kaid.

Today, Dan D. Nimmo and David L. Swanson assert that "political communication has developed some identity as a more or less distinct domain of scholarly work."[8] The scope and concerns of the area have further expanded to include critical theories and cultural studies. While there is no precise definition, method, or disciplinary home of the area of inquiry, its primary domain is the role, processes, and effects of communication within the context of politics broadly defined.

In 1985 the editors of *Political Communication Yearbook: 1984* noted that "more things are happening in the study, teaching, and practice of political communication than can be captured within the space limitations of the relatively few publications available."[9] In addition, they argued that the backgrounds of "those involved in the field [are] so varied and plurist in outlook and approach, . . . it [is] a mistake to adhere slavishly to any set format in shaping the content."[10] And more recently, Swanson and Nimmo call for "ways of overcoming the unhappy consequences of fragmentation within a framework that respects, encourages, and benefits from diverse scholarly commitments, agendas, and approaches."[11]

In agreement with these assessments of the area and with gentle encouragement, Praeger established in 1988 "Praeger Series in Political Communication." The series is open to all qualitative and quantitative methodologies as well as contemporary and historical studies. The key to characterizing the studies in the series is the focus on communication variables or activities within a political context or dimension. Scholars from the disciplines of communication, history, political science, and sociology have participated in the series.

I am, without shame or modesty, a fan of the series. The joy of serving as its editor is in participating in the dialogue of the field of political communication and in reading the contributors' works. I invite you to join me.

Robert E. Denton, Jr.

NOTES

1. See Robert E. Denton, Jr., *The Symbolic Dimensions of the American Presidency* (Prospect Heights, Il.: Waveland Press, 1982); Robert E. Denton, Jr., and Gary

Woodward, *Political Communication in America* (New York: Praeger, 1985, Second Edition, 1990); Robert E. Denton, Jr., and Dan F. Hahn, *Presidential Communication* (New York: Praeger, 1986); and Robert E. Denton, Jr., *The Primetime Presidency of Ronald Reagan* (New York: Praeger, 1988).

2. Aristotle, *The Politics of Aristotle*, trans. Ernest Barker (New York: Oxford University Press, 1970), p. 5.

3. Aristotle, *Rhetoric*, trans. Rhys Roberts (New York: The Modern Library, 1954), p. 22.

4. Dan D. Nimmo and Keith R. Sanders, "Introduction: The Emergence of Political Communication as a Field," in *Handbook of Political Communication*, ed. Dan D. Nimmo and Keith Sanders (Beverly Hills, Calif.: Sage, 1981), pp. 11–36.

5. Ibid., p. 15.

6. Ibid., pp. 17–27.

7. Keith R. Sanders, Lynda Lee Kaid, and Dan D. Nimmo, eds., *Political Communication Yearbook: 1984* (Carbondale and Edwardsville: Southern Illinois University: 1985), pp. 283–308.

8. Dan D. Nimmo and David L. Swanson, "The Field of Political Communication: Beyond the Voter Persuasion Paradigm" in *New Directions in Political Communication*, ed. David Swanson and Dan Nimmo (Beverly Hills, Calif.: Sage, 1990), p. 8.

9. Sanders, Kaid, and Nimmo, *Political Communication Yearbook*, p. xiv.

10. Ibid., p. xiv.

11. Nimmo and Swanson, "Field of Political Communication," p. 11.

Series Foreword

I had the pleasure of providing one of the early reviews of the first edition of *Political Campaign Communication: Principles and Practices* (1983). I noted that the book was "an important contribution to students and scholars in the growing area of 'political' communication" and that it was "the first book written on political campaigns from a speech communication perspective" (p. 303). To characterize *Political Campaign Communication* as a classic and a seminal work in the field is no exaggeration. Since the book appeared in 1983, research in the area has flourished, especially among communication scholars.[1] It is virtually impossible to pick up any contemporary work in the area of political communication and not find numerous references and citations from the first edition.

After every election, there appears to be a growing trend for journalists, academics, and the general public to call for sweeping reforms of the electoral process. The 1988 presidential campaign has been characterized as one of the meanest and less substantive races in American history. Journalists Jack Germond and Jules Witcover (1989) described the contest as a "trivial pursuit" where politics became open warfare. Kenneth Andersen (1989) argues that the campaign renewed concern for ethics and "will be remembered as one of negative advertising rather than positive advocacy, of sound bites rather than issues, of images rather than reality" (p. 479). According to Paul Taylor (1990), the "political dialogue is failing because the leading actors in the pageant of democracy—the politicians, the press, and the voters—are bringing out the least in one another" (p. 5). For Wilson McWilliams (1989), "the election of 1988 indicates the need for a new civility, and for the kinds of word and deed necessary to affirm, for the coming century, the dignity of self-government" (p. 200).

In light of such alarming reactions and the growing cynicism of campaigns, *Political Campaign Communication* offers a breath of fresh air, a hope, and a reaffirmation of the belief that political campaigns are essential and necessary to the functioning of democracy. This edition is written in the same belief and spirit that guided the first one. Judith S. Trent and Robert V. Friedenberg maintain their conviction that campaigns are essentially a communication phenomena where the utilization of the principles and practices of speech communication both informs and instructs our knowledge and appreciation of the electoral process.

This book remains an important contribution to the field of political campaign. It is a foundation text that addresses the concepts, theories, and concerns of communication scholars about the process and execution of political campaigns. With each election, campaigns transform into new electoral creatures. Of course principal actors and players change. But there is also the addition of new technologies, new rules, and new strategies. This updated edition provides the most comprehensive treatment of political campaigns in the field.

As with the first edition, this book is both theoretical and practical. It is useful to students, scholars, politicians, and practitioners of politics. By combining both theory and practice, the book provides a blueprint for improving our electoral process.

Politics is our national, collective conversation. Let's hope that it can become a genuine, an informative, and an intelligent one. Reading *Political Campaign Communication* is a step in the right direction.

Robert E. Denton, Jr.

NOTE

1. For a specific review of the growth of research in the area of political communication and for specific citations, see Keith R. Sanders, Lynda Lee Kaid, and Dan D. Nimmo, eds., *Political Communication Yearbook: 1984* (Carbondale and Edwardsville: Southern Illinois University Press, 1985) and David L. Swanson and Dan D. Nimmo, eds., *New Directions in Political Communication: A Resource Book* (Newbury Park, Calif.: Sage, 1990).

REFERENCES

Andersen, Kenneth. "The Politics of Ethics and the Ethics of Politics." *American Behavioral Scientist* 32, no. 4: 479–92.
Denton, Robert E., Jr. Review of *Political Campaign Communication: Principles and Practices*, by Judith S. Trent and Robert V. Friedenberg. New York: Praeger, 1983. *Presidential Studies Quarterly* 14, no. 2, 303–4.

Germond, Jack, and Jules Witcover. *Whose Broad Stripes and Bright Stars?* New York: Warner Books, 1989.

McWilliams, Wilson. "The Meaning of the Election." In Gerald M. Pomper et. al. *The Election of 1988*. Chatham, N.J.: Chatham House Publishers, 1989.

Taylor, Paul. *See How They Run*. New York: Alfred A. Knopf, 1990.

Preface

When this book was published in 1983 it was the first book-length study of election campaigns that utilized the principles and practices of speech communication to examine elective politics. While we certainly drew on other disciplines, and acknowledged the merit of much of the material they contributed to the study of election campaigns, we argued that communication was the epistemological base of political campaigns. Consequently we wrote from a speech communication perspective. We have been extremely gratified by the reception that our first edition received. We continue to believe the utilization of the principles and practices of speech communication as a means of examining elective politics contributes appreciably to our knowledge of the electoral process.

If there is any one theme of this book, it is that we view political campaigns as communication phenomena and in the following pages have examined those communication principles and practices central to election campaigns. We have sought to offer readers a realistic understanding of the strategic and tactical communication choices candidates and their managers must make as they wage the campaign. To that end all of the four original chapters in Part I have been substantially edited and updated to reflect changes since we first wrote. Additionally, a new chapter, "Communicative Types and Functions of Televised Political Advertising," has been added. Similarly, all of the four original chapters in Part II have been substantially edited and updated to reflect changes since we first wrote. Additionally, a new chapter, "Advertising in Political Campaigns," has been added.

This was a collaborative effort. We examined drafts of each chapter, shared equally in the writing of the epilogue and various editing chores. Chapters 1 to 5 were written primarily by Juddi, and chapters 6 to 10 were written primarily by Bob. We both share any of the successes or shortcomings of this volume.

We wish to acknowledge many people for their aid in producing this book. Particularly helpful to both authors were our colleagues, students, staff, and libraries of our home institutions, the University of Cincinnati, and Miami (Ohio) University. The staff at Praeger was uniformly helpful and pleasant. We also want to thank Ronald B. Cushing for preparing the index while under considerable time pressure.

In addition, Juddi would like to thank Carol Fathman for her professional and dedicated help in preparing the manuscript, Ronald B. Cushing for his consistently reliable research help and unfailingly good humor, the many University of Cincinnati students in her political communication classes, Communication Department colleagues (especially Teresa Sabourin who shares an interest in the communication strategies of candidates who are women), and political communication colleagues across the country who provided valuable comments about the first edition. And most important, she would like to thank Jimmie for his constant support throughout this and all other endeavors.

Moreover, Bob would like to acknowledge the consistently excellent support he has received from the Miami University libraries. Librarians Becky Zartner and Greg Carlson were particularly helpful in the preparation of this edition. He would also like to acknowledge the *Journal of the American Forensic Association* for permission to use portions of two articles he originally wrote for *JAFA*. Finally, he would like to acknowledge the wonderful support he received throughout the writing of both editions of this book from his mother, Florence, from his children, David and Laura, who were an unending source of delightful distraction whenever writing became difficult, and most of all from his wife, Emmy, for all of her support in so many ways.

PART I

PRINCIPLES OF POLITICAL CAMPAIGN COMMUNICATION

Chapter One

Communication and Political Campaigns: A Prologue

It has become fashionable to criticize our electoral system. Campaigns are too long and too expensive. Candidates are dishonest, concerned only with the image they project, and speak only in sound bites. Voters are bored with the process, distrustful of government and politicians, and frequently do not vote. Although we express these and other complaints, elections, and the political campaigns that are a part of them, are vital to us in at least three different but complementary senses.

IMPORTANCE OF POLITICAL CAMPAIGNS

Elections are important because they allow us freedom to actively participate in selecting our leaders. They are the core of democracy. Nowhere in the world are more people more freely engaged in active, responsible participation in the choice of leadership than in the United States. Whether the election will determine the occupants of two seats in city council or one chair in the Oval Office of the White House, the political election campaign is an essential element of a democratic system.

Elections provide us with the opportunity to determine how our own interests can best be served. We may, for example, try to decide which board of education candidate does not favor increasing our property taxes. We might also ask if the Republican candidate for governor sees the need to create jobs as the state's top priority or if the Democratic challenger running for Congress supports increasing money for education and public transportation. Once we feel enough questions have been answered, we must decide how actively to participate in the campaign. Will we try to ignore it? Will we work for the candidate or political party we favor? Will we vote? Any decision contributes to our self-development and expression.

Elections not only give opportunities for quiet decision making or overt participation in determining who will govern; they also provide the legitimacy with which to govern. The winners of elections receive a general acceptance of their right to power. No matter how large or small the margin of victory, the candidate who receives the necessary votes has been granted a legitimacy quite distinct from power. Any election can give the winner power. Only a democratic election will provide the sense of "rightness" or even "genuineness" necessary to govern or be governed. We may no longer "like" the president for whom we voted two years ago, but we recognize that he has a legitimate claim to the office until the next election. The president, like all other candidates we elect, can only be "overthrown" as a consequence of the next election.

Thus, in these pragmatic ways, our electoral system is important to us. No less significant are the symbolic aspects of election campaigns. The British historian J. H. Plumb maintained that there are two histories: the actual series of events that once occurred and the ideal series that we affirm and hold in memory. In other words, the past is composed not only of historical "fact" but of what is "made" of history. It is, in the largest sense, the collective memory—the national myth—that unites us as a people. Not only do elections provide leaders and grant them authority to govern, they also add to our memory or image of the electoral process and thus give proof that the system is a good one. The fact that we have elections, that leaders are not overthrown by revolution, that citizens freely discuss and participate in the selection process, or that the Constitution "worked" during the Watergate crisis of the 1970s grants support for the belief that the "American Dream" is real and that this country really is destined to be the mighty keeper of liberty. All the fanfare and excitement of the political campaign, be it bands and parades, buttons and billboards, speeches and rallies, or television ads and debates, is important for the reinforcement provided about the rightness of what we do and the way we do it.

Now, all of this is to tell you that the subject matter of this book is worthwhile. Although aspects of our electoral system may need repair from time to time, the process and the product are worth the effort. While the value of elections has remained constant, the manner in which they are conducted has changed enormously in recent years. As a matter of fact, the political campaign has undergone such a radical transformation that those principles and practices accepted by practitioners and theorists even 25 years ago are largely irrelevant today. Thus, before we can describe and analyze any of the dimensions of campaign communication in the chapters that follow, we must examine those changes that, to the greatest extent, comprise the essence of the new politics. There are four of them that will be discussed in the following order: (1) the decline in the influence of political parties; (2) electoral financing legislation; (3) political action committees; and (4) technological advancements.

CHANGES IN THE POLITICAL CAMPAIGN

The legendary party bosses once determined who would run for political office. In national and state politics, these people were often called kingmakers, who from the sanctity of the so-called smoke-filled rooms at nominating conventions handpicked "their" candidate to be the party nominee. In local politics, especially in the large cities, party bosses, through a system that combined the disposition of jobs with political favors, support, and even protection, controlled the votes, the party, and thus the selection of all candidates.

Decline of Political Parties

Undoubtedly, the most significant change in presidential politics occurred when in 1976 the reform rules, adopted by the Democratic party and, to a lesser extent, the Republican party, forced changes in state laws regarding delegate selection. Under the legislation adopted before the 1976 campaign, the caucus convention procedure was wide open for participation by everyone, and any candidate who could inspire a following had a chance to win delegates. By changing the process of delegate selection, political reformers aided in reshaping the presidential nominating system. In 1968 there were only 15 primaries, in which less than 40 percent of the delegates were chosen. In 1976, however, 77 percent of the delegates at the Democratic Convention had come from 30 primary states, reducing the strength of delegates from caucus states to 704 of the 3,008 delegates. By 1988 there were 36 primaries that determined the choices of 78 percent of the 4,162 delegates to the Democratic Convention and 77 percent of the 2,277 delegates to the Republican Convention. Finally, two years before the 1984 campaign, the Democratic party accepted a plan proposed by its Commission on Presidential Nominations to add 548 (or 14 percent) uncommitted members of Congress, governors, mayors, and party officials to its 3,675 delegates. By 1986, in preparation for the 1988 campaign, the Democratic party had increased the number of uncommitted delegates to 640. Although the proposals sought to return a little of the clout from citizen activists to elected officials, they simultaneously reaffirmed the 1976 commitment to reform, since 78 percent of the delegates to the convention would continue to be determined in state primaries and caucuses.

The result is that the change in rules and the proliferation of primaries have weakened political parties, the traditional vehicles for building coalitions and forging consensus. In the past, candidates had to work their way up through party ranks and appeal to party bosses, but in recent years successful candidates at all levels have often ignored the party regulars, built their own organizations, and taken their campaigns directly to the people. As presidential chronicler and political journalist Theodore H. White reflected, "The old bosses are long gone and with them the old parties. In their place has grown a new breed of young professionals whose working skills in the new politics would make the old boys look like stumblebums."[1]

While for our purposes it is unnecessary to trace the fall of the political bosses from "kingmaker" to "stumblebum," it is important to realize that citizens feel little allegiance to political parties. Each year since the mid–1960s, the results of the election studies conducted by the Center for Political Studies at the University of Michigan have shown that fewer and fewer voters identify themselves as Republicans or Democrats, while more and more call themselves Independents. In 1964 approximately 24 percent of the population eligible to vote labeled themselves as Independents, and 20 years later, in 1984, 32 percent claimed to be Independents. Furthermore, respect for the parties as institutions that represent the public has also decreased. The proportion of the "eligible electorate believing that political parties help a 'good deal' in making the government pay attention to what the people think, dropped from roughly 40 percent in 1964 to 29 percent in 1972 to 18 percent in 1976."[2]

Finance Reforms

The decline in party identification and influence is not the only element that has altered the nature of the election campaign. Closely related are the reforms in financing which, although initially affecting presidential candidates, have had some effect at all levels.

The Federal Election Campaign Act of 1974 and the amendment in 1976 changed much of the character of presidential campaigning, particularly in the early portion of the electoral process. The act provided for voluntary income tax checkoffs, and the money was used by the U.S. Treasury to provide matching grants to presidential candidates who had raised $5,000, in amounts of $250 or less, from citizens in at least 20 states. The maximum any individual could give a candidate was $1,000. But the Supreme Court ruled in 1976 that this ceiling could not prevent individuals or committees from spending unlimited amounts of money in support of a candidate so long as the effort was separate from the candidate's campaign, without any consultation or coordination. Suddenly, "running for president" became a possibility for people who were not wealthy. In fact, in the three elections immediately following the passage of the act, 36 people were serious enough as presidential contenders to have received federal matching funds (2 of the 36 candidates who qualified for matching funds, Marion G. (Pat) Robertson in 1988 and John Connally in 1980, refused to use the funds thereby freeing their campaigns from having to impose spending limits during the primary elections).

Not only has the finance law resulted in generating more participation, it has also forced presidential hopefuls to establish themselves among small donors in a number of states. Contenders can no longer rely on the traditional "fat cats" who financed "favored" candidates in the past.

In spite of the limits imposed by legislation, campaigns during the decade of the 1980s became more and more expensive. For example, in the 1980 election, candidates for Congress spent $228.8 million, which was well over the 1978 amount of $192.2 million; in the 1984 election, presidential hopefuls spent over $325 million, or double what was spent by those who sought the presidency in 1980; and spending on the total 1984 campaign (local, state, national) reached $1.8 billion, a 50 percent increase over that spent for the total campaign in 1980. By 1988, the Democratic and Republican candidates for president spent $227 million just on television advertising and the average cost of a successful United States Senate campaign was $3.1 million—or 33 percent more than a Senate race cost in 1982.

Not only do candidates continue to spend vast amounts of money, they find that they can raise it themselves, even for primary campaigns. For example, in anticipation of the 1988 primaries (particularly the Michigan multitiered delegate selection process that officially began in August 1986), Vice-President George Bush, with the help of his political action committee, the Fund for America's Future, was able to raise $3.9 million by early January 1986.

In Ohio, a state senator who ran for the Republican gubernatorial nomination raised $350,000 during the last three weeks of the primary. Thus for many who run even for governorships and Congress, the ability to raise money has been the most important effect of the reforms. It has widened the electoral process by bypassing the political parties. Candidates run their own campaigns and frequently hire their own professionals to raise funds—often completely independent of party support or discipline. In turn, raising money has become easier because individual voters who view themselves as political independents are contributing to specific candidates and causes and not to political parties. Therefore two factors—the decline of the influence of political parties and new campaign finance legislation—have combined to change contemporary political campaigns.

Political Action Committees

There is, however, a third and related element that has altered the way in which campaigns are waged; the political action committees (PACs) or single-issue groups.

Pressure groups have existed since the founding of the republic. Over the years, the efforts of some of these groups have brought about important changes, such as the abolitionists who helped eliminate slavery and the suffragettes who helped give women the right to vote. However, in recent years, pressure groups have become so powerful and so numerous that their efforts to influence legislation and elections have had a dramatic impact on electoral politics. Their campaigns for or against proposed legislation have often served to fragment the political system, and their efforts to affect the election of specific candidates have contributed to the declining influence of political parties.

Although by definition the single-issue or pressure groups are small, they have nonetheless become increasingly powerful. By the 1980 election, pollsters estimated that one in four voters was willing to vote against politicians for their position on a single issue, and the issues themselves affected 10 to 15 percent of the general electorate. While the issues around which the groups coalesce vary all the way from import quotas to environmental control, it is the so-called emotional or passionate issues (antiabortion, gun control, prayer in school, and sexual preference) that attract the most attention and motivate the groups to spring into action quickly if they feel that a proposed bill or even an individual legislator threatens their interests. They concentrate on the grass roots (pressuring city councils and state legislators), while simultaneously bombarding members of Congress with telephone calls, telegrams, letters, personal visits, heckling during public appearances, or letting them know that without support for the issue, the PAC will work to defeat them in the next election.

In 1950, there were fewer than 2,000 lobbyists in Washington. However, by the 1978 elections, pressure groups had proliferated to such an extent that there were 15,000 lobbyists based just on Capitol Hill to work for the interests of over 500 corporate lobbies, 53 minority group lobbies, 34 social welfare lobbies, 33 women's lobbies, 31 lobbies for environmental interests, 21 lobbies for religious interests, 15 lobbies for the aging, 6 for population control, 12 for guns (5 for weapon manufacturing, 4 proguns, and 3 for gun control), 61 working for Japan's interests, and 10 for Israel's.[3] Although some of these groups had been around a long time, by 1987 they had formed 4,165 political action committees and were much more aggressive in their attempts to influence legislation than they had been in the past. In fact, through the use of computerized mailing lists that identify supporters, many PACs have been able to raise large sums of money that is spent not only to lobby for their specific issue but to defeat legislators who do not support them and to elect others who do. The ability of the PACs to do this is directly related to the election law reforms we have already discussed. When Congress limited individual campaign donations to $1,000 per candidate per race, it simultaneously permitted corporations, unions, and other groups to become involved in making direct political contributions to candidates if they established political action committees. While companies are prohibited from contributing corporate funds, through their PACs they may solicit voluntary contributions from employees and stockholders and then give up to $5,000 to candidates in each of their primary and general election campaigns. Thus, for example, a congressional candidate who is oriented toward business can receive tens of thousands of dollars from dozens of corporate PACs, and a union-oriented candidate can receive tens of thousands of dollars from union PACs.

The ability of the PACs in raising money to contribute to the campaigns of "friendly" incumbents and "promising" challengers cannot be taken lightly. It is an ability that has been proven in every election since the election law reforms. For example, during the 1986 elections, PACs spent a record $338 million ($207 million more than they spent in 1980). Corporate PACs gave $79.6 million to candidates; labor PACs $58.3 million; and trade membership PACs $73.5 million. The biggest spenders were the National Congressional Club, which spent almost $16 million (twice the amount they spent in 1980), and the National Conservative Political Action Committee, "Nick-pack," which spent over $9 million during 1985 and 1986 (a $2 million increase from 1980).[4] And in the off-year elections of 1989, PACs contributed $57 million to candidates of their choice. The vast majority of this money flows to those who hold office. In 1988, PACs contributed $66 million to congressional incumbents and only $7 million to those who challenged their seats. In 1989 more than 90 percent of PAC donations went to incumbents. The reason for this obvious disparity is that PACs understand that incumbents are far more likely to win elections than are newcomers. The unfortunate result is that PAC money too frequently provides incumbents with what turns out to be a "lifetime appointment" to Congress.[5]

Just as the PACs work toward specific candidates' success, so can they work for their defeat. For example, in 1980 Nick-pack targeted five prominent liberal Democratic senators for defeat and ran an extensive media campaign against each. All five (George McGovern of South Dakota, Warren Magnuson of Washington, Frank Church of Idaho, Birch Bayh of Indiana, and John Culver of Iowa) were beaten, and Nick-pack, because of its financial involvement and the publicity generated by announcing its campaigns against the senators, received much of the credit (or blame).

Thus it would make little sense to discuss contemporary political campaigns without acknowledging the effect of the political action committees. They have become an important element because they breach party lines and make uncompromising, all-or-nothing demands on legislators and candidates. They care little for party loyalties, legislative voting records, or a candidate's overall philosophy or platform. They view every legislative roll call and every election as a major test of their cause. And, perhaps because of their zealotry, they have been highly successful in raising money. At any rate, the large-scale entrance of the single-issue groups into the electoral process has contributed mightily to the changed nature of the electoral process. (It is, however, important to remember that although PACs contribute a good deal of money to specific campaigns, the primary source of funds remains private citizens.)

Technology

Perhaps the most obvious transformation in political campaigns has been in the area of technology. Although the additions of radio in the 1920s and television in the 1950s brought with them a number of alterations to U.S. political campaigns, as technological advancements they were only the beginning. Today, campaigns from county to national level rely on a number of devices sophisticated enough to have hardly even been envisioned in a campaign as contemporary as John Kennedy's in 1960. In so doing, their nature as well as the people who run them have changed. For example, in statewide as well as presidential campaigns, the old electoral map on the headquarters wall showing in what districts the voters live has been supplemented with a map of the major media markets. The new map decides how and where the candidate travels, carves new political regions around the interstate television centers, and pinpoints, with the help of the computer, the exact demographic audiences who should serve as the targets of the candidate's campaign. Specialists, not county or state party leaders, now conduct campaigns for the candidates. The specialists who understand the media map can appreciate the intricacies of demographic target selection or the even newer zip code analysis. Today's candidates for state legislature, governor, Congress, and president pick their media consultant almost before they do anything else. In fact, as Sidney Blumenthal writes in his book *The Permanent Campaign*, early in the contest, candidates are often viewed as successful or not successful by the person they are able to hire to run their campaign. The bigger the name of the consultant, the more serious a contender the candidate is considered to be.

Not only have the media consultants taken over the modern political campaign, they are assisted by other specialists—in media advertising, in public opinion polling, in direct mail fund-raising, in street and telephone canvassing, and even in ethnic analysis. As White has written, everything has changed, including the vocabulary. Anyone who has the direct ear of the candidate is now called a "strategist," the old-fashioned hatchet man out on the hustings is now styled a "surrogate,"[6] and a sudden rise in the public opinion polls conducted by the candidate's polling specialist shows "momentum." Thus the sophisticated use of modern technology has brought significant alterations to political campaign communication. When these changes occurred is not really important. Whether they began in 1952 when Dwight Eisenhower first brought television commercial spots to presidential campaigns, in 1960 when John Kennedy became the first presidential candidate to use his own polling specialist, in 1972 when George McGovern pioneered mass direct mail fund-raising, in 1980 when Jimmy Carter campaigned by conference phone calls to voters in Iowa and New Hampshire, in 1984 when Ronald Reagan used satellite transmissions to appear at fund-raisers and rallies, or even in 1988 when a number of presidential hopefuls used video tapes to deliver their message to voters in the early primary states, the result is the same. Technology has changed the manner in which candidates run for office. A congressional contender may reject an appearance at the county fair in favor of a television interview that will be broadcast on the evening news in the major metropolitan area in the district. A candidate for the Democratic gubernatorial primary may not even publicly announce the intention to run until a direct mail specialist has raised enough money for the campaign. Presidential candidates may never set foot in a given city or state throughout the campaign but be seen by all in countless television spots or seen as they are talking with television reporters about issues of concern to voters in Yakima, Washington, even as they may be sitting in hotel rooms in Kansas City or Baltimore. In short, the advances in technology as well as the advent of the single-issue groups, the election law reforms, and the decline in the influence of political parties have combined to transform the nature and manner of our electoral system. Whether we like it or not, one significant result of these changes has been that we can scarcely avoid taking part in the campaign process. Those who choose not to participate directly become involved at some level even if it is only to explain to friends why they are not voting, or why they are throwing in the wastebasket personalized letters asking for contributions, refusing to respond to a candidate's telephone survey, or turning off the television to avoid political programs and advertisements. "We must actively choose not to be active; hence we are participating symbolically even if not actually" because the political campaign is ubiquitous.[7] Somebody is always seeking elective office and the "somebodies" are no longer strangers but your neighbor, the clerk in the store, or the mother of your best friend. The modern campaign knows no season. It seems that as one ends, another begins. Candidates start running for office months and even years in advance of the primary election.* Thus campaigns are now an unavoidable part of our environment, forcing us to become consumers of political communication.

COMMUNICATION AND POLITICAL CAMPAIGNS

The major argument of this book is that political election campaigns are campaigns of communication. Certainly, numerous forms or combinations of economic, sociological, psychological, and historical factors are crucial to or reflective of the electoral process. However, the core of each campaign is communication. This is not to argue that a variety of economic and situational needs, power relationships, and a whole host of additional elements and demands do not affect the campaign process or outcome, but rather to say that all of these other factors become important in the electoral system principally through the offices of communication. It is communication that occupies the area between the goals or aspirations of the candidate and the behavior of the electorate, just as it serves as the bridge between the dreams or hopes of the voter and the actions of the candidate. It is through communication that a political campaign begins. Individuals verbally announce their intention to run and posters/billboards announce nonverbally that election time has begun. During the campaign, candidates and their staffs debate, appear on television, prepare and present messages for media commercials, take part in parades and rallies, wear funny hats, submit to media interviews, write letters and position papers, and speak at all forms of public gatherings. They kiss babies, shake hands at factory gates and supermarkets, prepare and distribute literature, wear campaign buttons, and establish phone banks to solicit money, workers, and votes. In addition, countless hours are spent during the campaign trying to raise enough money to buy radio and television time or computerized lists of voters. All of this effort is for the single purpose of communicating with the electorate, the media, and each other. And when the time comes, it is through communication that the campaign draws to a close. Candidates verbally concede defeat or extol victory, and the posters/billboards are taken down announcing nonverbally that one campaign is over, even as another begins.

---

*Even the political parties are beginning to "run" early. In 1982 the Democratic party met in a miniconvention in Philadelphia to express their unity and opposition to the Republican administration by writing a 50,000-word position statement on foreign and defense policy, the economy, individual rights, energy, and federalism. The miniconvention was held two years in advance of the presidential nominating convention. And three years and a month before the 1992 presidential election, Governor Mario M. Cuomo invited prominent Democrats to New York for a round of national issue forums.

Hence, communication is the means by which the campaign begins, proceeds, and concludes. It is, as we suggested, the epistemological base. Without it, there is no political campaign. It is, therefore, not enough to approach the study of political campaign communication by analyzing the demographic characteristics or the attitudes of the electorate, although the information provided by such work is significant for our overall understanding of the phenomenon. It is also not enough to examine political campaign communication by studying only psychological construct theory or even the relationship and effect of the mass media on the campaign, in spite of the fact that each explains much about the contemporary electoral process. What is needed is a study that provides a communication perspective of a communication event or series of events—the political election campaign. Although you will find references to the works of political scientists, historians, and psychologists, as well as political journalists, we have drawn primarily on the work generated by scholars in communication.

In exploring such theoretical concerns as agenda setting, uses and gratifications, targeting, gatekeeping, information diffusion, positioning and repositioning, functionalism, legitimizing, or even in analyzing the pragmatic details of planning, organizing, and presenting speeches, television ads, debates, or fund-raising appeals, we have been guided by one question: What is it that we ought to study as political campaign communication? Our answers are contained in the subject areas we examine in the following chapters.

ORGANIZATION AND PREVIEW OF CHAPTERS

This book has two sections. Chapters 2 through 5 analyze important principles and theoretical concerns of political campaign communication, while Chapters 6 through 10 examine the crucial practices of contemporary political campaign communication. Although this distinction is designed to help you better understand the phenomenon, in the real world of political campaigns principles and practices blend. As you read the section on principles, keep in mind that in political campaigns, principles often generate practices and practices often generate principles. For example, in Chapter 2 when we discuss the principles involved in an individual's surfacing as a viable candidate, principles cannot be meaningfully presented without examining the practices of many individuals who have surfaced. In turn, those practices have subsequently generated many of the principles. Similarly, in Chapter 6 when we discuss the practice of political speechwriters, we cannot readily examine it without developing some of the principles that speechwriters utilize.

Thus, artificial as the distinction is, it does provide us with a pedagogically useful organizational framework from which to view political campaign communication.

Following this introductory chapter, the next four chapters focus on principles of political campaign communication. Political communication is a broad term. It has been used to describe the communication involved in winning elections, governing a nation, reporting on governmental activity, gathering and determining public opinion, lobbying, and socializing people into a nation. We have deliberately chosen to narrow the term and focus not on political communication, but rather on political campaign communication. We do not deny the validity of studying other forms of political communication. However, in a democratic society, to govern one must first win an election. To report governmental activity, there must first be an elected government about which to report. To lobby, there must first be elected officials to be persuaded. To gather and determine public opinion about candidates and their progress, there must first be a campaign. And to socialize people so that they accept cultural norms, elected officials must first help set the norms. In other words, we believe that political campaign communication is the root of all other forms of political communication. It is undoubtedly for this reason that political campaign communication has been the focus of far more scholarly and popular journalistic inquiry than any other form of political communication. In addition, the number of elaborately planned and professionally implemented campaigns is growing each election year. Thus it is particularly appropriate to limit our examination of political communication to political campaigns.

Chapter 2 examines the four stages of a political campaign, discussing the many pragmatic and symbolic functions provided by communicative acts to the electorate, the candidates, and the media.

Chapter 3 analyzes the communicative strategies and styles that incumbents and challengers have used in U.S. elections from 1789 to the present. In addition, a third style, one popularized by the two campaigns of Ronald Reagan, is examined.

Chapter 4 presents an examination of the means or channels used in contemporary political campaigns. Theoretical approaches used to study the effect of the mass media on political campaigns are discussed.

Chapter 5 discusses the communicative types and functions of televised political advertising. In addition, the way in which women appear to use televised attack advertising in their campaigns is examined.

At the conclusion of these four chapters, many of the principles associated with political campaign communication will have been explored. We hope that by the end of Part I, our readers will have an appreciation of the theoretical basis of campaign communication from the vantage point of a consumer, but we also hope that campaign communication principles will be understood from the vantage point of a user, one actively involved in campaigning for public office. We are aware that readers majoring in such fields as speech communication, mass communication, and public relations anticipate being involved in political campaigns professionally. Many other readers may also participate in campaigns, if not professionally, at least as highly interested citizens concerned with their communities. We believe that Part I can provide a valuable understanding of the principles of campaign communication from any vantage point that readers choose to follow in the future. Part II focuses on practices of political campaign communication. In this section, we will discuss five of the most common communication events in contemporary political campaigns.

Chapter 6 examines public speaking in campaigns. It explains how political candidates decide where and when to speak, how they develop speeches, and how they utilize speechwriters and surrogate speakers.

Chapter 7 also focuses on public speaking in political campaigns. But whereas Chapter 6 concentrates on the normal day-to-day public speaking that characterizes campaigns, Chapter 7 examines forms of speeches that occur in most campaigns, are unique unto themselves, and are not day-to-day occurrences. For example, portions of the chapter deal with announcement speeches, press conferences, speeches of apologia, and acceptance speeches, among others. Each of these forms takes place in virtually every campaign. The purposes and strategies involved in each genre are presented.

Chapter 8 deals with political debates. Debates are often the most anticipated and most publicized communication activity engaged in by candidates. The chapter presents a history of political debating and then discusses the factors that motivate candidates to accept or reject the opportunity to debate, the strategies that are used, and the effect of political debates.

Chapter 9 examines interpersonal communication in political campaign. Three interpersonal communication situations, typical of all campaigns, are analyzed in light of current interpersonal communication theory.

Chapter 10 concludes the section on practices by considering the advantages and disadvantages of a variety of media used for political advertising in campaigns. It also discusses the key players in political advertising, the consultants.

We find the study of political campaign communication to be fascinating and believe that some of our enthusiasm for the subject is apparent in the following pages. We hope readers come away from this book not only better informed, but also with renewed understanding and interest in a political system that, although abused and attacked in recent years, does not depend on coercion or force but derives its strength from the fact that it relies on human communication, largely as manifested in political campaigns, as a major means of decision making.

NOTES

1. Theodore H. White, "The Search for President," *Boston Globe*, February 24, 1980, p. A1.

2. Arthur H. Miller, "Partisanship Reinstated?" *British Journal of Political Science* 8 (1978): 133.

3. "Single-Issue Politics," *Newsweek*, November 6, 1978, p. 49.

4. Harold W. Stanley and Richard G. Niemi, *Vital Statistics on American Politics* (Washington, D.C.: Congressional Quarterly Books, 1988), pp. 143–48.

5. "The Price of Power," Christine Gorman, *Time*, October 31, 1988, pp. 44–45.

6. White, "Search for President," p. A1.

7. Bruce E. Gronbeck, "The Functions of Presidential Campaigning," *Communication Monographs* 45 (1978): 271.

Chapter Two

Communicative Functions of Political Campaigns

One of the ways to examine political campaigns is to analyze their communicative functions, that is, to investigate what functions the various forms or acts of campaign communication provide to the electorate and to the candidates themselves.[1] Many of these functions are instrumental or pragmatic in that they make specific tangible contributions. Others are consummatory or symbolic in nature; they fulfill ritualistic expectations or requirements. Both are discussed in this chapter.

The modern political campaign passes through relatively discrete stages, which can be categorized as preprimary, primary, convention, and general election. This chapter is organized and divided analogous to the campaign itself; the different functions are discussed in terms of these four specific stages. It is important to remember that each stage, although discrete, has a direct relationship to and bearing on all that follow. In other words, the functions of each stage affect the entire campaign.

FIRST POLITICAL STAGE: SURFACING

Although the first or preprimary stage has been called the "winnowing period,"[2] we have labeled it "surfacing" because this term more completely conceptualizes those communication activities that occur. Surfacing was originally labeled and defined as "the series of predictable and specifically timed rhetorical transactions which serve consummatory and instrumental functions during the preprimary phase of the campaign."[3] It would be difficult to set an exact time limit on the first stage because it can vary from candidate to candidate and election to election.

Political hopefuls must assess their visibility and credibility as well as determine their financial backing and organizational strength. Predictable rhetorical activities (the verbal and nonverbal communication acts)* during the surfacing stage include building a political organization in each city, district, state, or region (depending on the geographic scope encompassed by the office being sought), speaking to many different kinds of public gatherings in an attempt to capture attention (media attention for state and national campaigns), conducting public opinion polls to assess visibility or to determine potential issues for which stands will later have to be devised, putting together an organizational structure and campaign blueprint, and raising money. These activities take time whether an individual is running for mayor or for president. As one woman who was elected to a seat on her city council told us, "I didn't just start campaigning. I started planning in January for the November election. And this involved an organized plan—contracting for billboards, purchasing material for signs, mapping out financing and finding volunteers for sign lettering and door-to-door canvassing."[4] A gubernatorial contender, who announced his candidacy 13 months before the 1982 Democratic primary in Ohio, justified his early start by saying that his campaign could not be tied to traditional timetables because he had to let people know who he was and what his ideas were so that voters would know that alternatives existed to the "same old names."

If surfacing takes months for city council and gubernatorial candidates, it appears to take even longer for presidential contenders. For example, in October 1981, almost two and a half years before the first primary of the 1984 presidential campaign, former Vice-President Walter Mondale established a political action committee (to help him begin raising money in a sufficient number of states so that he would more rapidly qualify for federal matching funds) and announced on "Meet the Press" that he was considering running for president. Former Colorado Senator Gary Hart, who lost the 1984 Democratic presidential nomination to Mondale, never stopped campaigning after his defeat but just continued surfacing in anticipation of the 1988 election. He spent much of 1985 and 1986 putting together issue papers, writing a book on military reform, and forming a political "think-tank" called the "Center for a New Democracy." President George Bush was another early participant in the first stage of the 1988 presidential campaign. Thirty months, or two and a half years, before the New Hampshire primary, Bush announced the formation of a 476 member national steering committee composed of

---

*Forms of communication used in campaigns are virtually limitless. For a list of the most common verbal and nonverbal acts, see Chapter 1.

Republicans from all 50 states. And in 1990, two years and eight months before the 1992 presidential election, Georgia Senator Sam Nunn was certainly at least thinking about a run for the White House. He resigned from a golf club that does not allow women as members or even as guests and told friends that he would announce his decision about running two weeks after the 1990 congressional election.[5] Although it is impossible to place a definite time structure on the first stage, we have listed some of the important rhetorical activities the period demands. Thus surfacing begins with candidates' initial efforts to create an interest and image of themselves as candidates and extends through a variety of public rhetorical transactions prior to the first primary election.

But not only do we know what is typically demanded of the candidate during the first stage, we also have some idea of the characteristic functions served by the communication acts of the surfacing period. Although these can vary with the level of office sought (just as the time period does), we have observed seven functions that appear to be important in all political campaigns.

The first function is to provide an indication of a candidate's fitness for office—the "caliber" of the individual. During the campaign, especially the earliest portions when public images of potential candidates are beginning to be formed, the electorate draws inferences from campaign actions about how a particular contender would behave as mayor, or governor, or even president.

The electorate does not want elected officials who are viewed as dishonest, dull, unjust, immoral, corrupt, incompetent, or who are even the brunt of jokes such as television host Johnny Carson's labeling of Senator S. I. Hayakawa as "sleeping Sam" and the "Sominex kid." In other words, U.S. voters have some preconceptions about people who run for public office. Generally, successful candidates will be perceived as trustworthy, intelligent or competent enough to do the job, compassionate, articulate, poised, and honorable. The higher the office, the more judgmental voters become. For example, voters expect those candidates who run for or serve as our chief executive to be of "presidential timber"—to possess special qualities not always found in the same degree in all people. And although there is not a one-to-one relationship between the two, campaign actions are taken as symbolic of actions as president. We do not want presidents who hit their heads on helicopter doors, fall down steps, mispronounce words, or who are attacked by "killer rabbits." These are behaviors that cause a candidate to be characterized as "clumsy," "dumb," or "loser" as Gerald Ford and Jimmy Carter were labeled during the surfacing period of the 1976 and 1980 campaigns. As a matter of fact, perhaps conditioned by the negative perceptions of Ford and Carter's actions, voters' assessment of many of the 1980, 1984, and 1988 presidential hopefuls were sometimes harsh.

For example, former Texas Governor John Connally, a 1980 contender, was perceived as having charisma because of his tough-guy, macho image, but he was also viewed as arrogant and too tough to be president. He may have frightened voters with his hardline, two-fisted public speaking style, for as one person commented after hearing him, "He'd sure make a good dictator. I don't know that we need a dictator now, but he'd sure make a good one."[6] A 1984 hopeful, Senator John Glenn, was frequently termed as "too boring" to be president. In 1988, before his confrontation with CBS News anchor Dan Rather, then Vice-President George Bush was perceived as being a "wimp, a tinny-voiced preppy" who didn't possess the toughness to be president.[7]

Potential presidents are not supposed to frighten or bore people, but neither should reference to them produce laughter. This was the problem with the general perception of California Governor Edmund (Jerry) Brown, who during the 1980 presidential campaign was nicknamed "Governor Moonbeam" and was the object of countless one-liners depicting his visionary themes ("protect the earth," "serve the people," and "explore the universe"). Although Brown may have been a prophet of a new era of "holistic politics," real or successful presidential contenders are not the brunt of such jokes as "Do you realize that Jerry Brown is the only governor whose parents are trying to deprogram him?" Whatever the ultimate judgment, certainly one function of the preprimary period is to provide an indication of a candidate's fitness for office.

A second communication function of the surfacing stage is that it initiates the ritualistic activities important to our political system. In his book *The Symbolic Uses of Politics*, social scientist Murray Edelman discusses the idea of U.S. political campaigns as traditional, rule-governed rituals and then discusses ritual as a kind of motor activity that involves its participants symbolically in a common enterprise.[8] While each of the stages of the campaign demands certain rituals, none is more clearly defined than the activities surrounding the preprimary announcement speech. (Although the announcement speech itself will be discussed in Chapter 7, here we will consider its ritualistic aspects.)

When candidates decide to enter the political arena formally, there are certain protocols that must be performed because they are expected. For example, a press conference is called, the candidate is surrounded by family and friends while announcing the decision to run for office, and then embarks immediately on a campaign swing through the district, state, or nation. The candidate may only be announcing a campaign for the mayor's office, but there are expectations concerning how it is done. However, to capture the full flavor of the announcement ritual, it might be best to consider some of the presidential campaigns of the 1980s.

The 1988 ritual began on September 16, 1986, when Pierre Du Pont IV became the first officially announced candidate for the Republican presidential nomination. Du Pont, a former two-term governor of Delaware, made his announcement surrounded by his family and hundreds of supporters waving flags and banners in the ballroom of the Hotel Du Pont in the Du Pont Building that houses the Du Pont Company that had been founded two centuries earlier by the governor's French immigrant ancestors.

The Reverend Jesse Jackson, with his grandmother, his mother, his wife, Jacqueline, and the three oldest of his five children, announced his candidacy at the convention of the National Rainbow Coalition he had helped to establish following his 1984 presidential bid. He told a standing room only crowd at the Raleigh Civic Center that he was seeking the presidency "to bring justice in our land, mitigate misery in the world and bring peace on earth."[9] However, none of the candidates during the 1980s could match the detailed pageantry of Marion G. (Pat) Robertson's formal "beg me to run" announcement.

During the summer of 1985 Robertson let the media know that people were asking him to run for president. By October 1985 he allowed as how he was pondering a run for the presidency and was praying about it, seeking God's counsel. Apparently his prayers were answered a few weeks later when he formed an exploratory committee and founded a think-tank called the National Perspectives Institute. On September 17, 1986, Robertson went to Constitution Hall in Washington and on closed circuit television, in a three-hour production of trumpet fanfare and patriotic song, announced that if three million registered voters signed petitions "telling me that they will pray—that they will work—that they will give toward my election, then I will run." He set a deadline of one year for a show of support that would include the signatures of three million voters on petitions and raise three million dollars by mid-1987. Clearly, one communicative function of the surfacing stage is that it initiates the ritual vital to U.S. politics.

Thus far in discussing the preprimary period we have been focusing on what has been termed "consummatory functions of campaigning." These functions are essentially symbolic in nature—functions that seem to be rooted more deeply in the heart or soul rather than in the mind of the electorate. In other words, as communication scholar Bruce E. Gronbeck has written, "Campaigning creates second-level or metapolitical images, personae, myths, associations, and social-psychological reactions which may even be detached or at least distinct from particular candidates, issues, and offices."[10]

Thus communication during the first stage plays two symbolic but important roles: it provides an indication of a candidate's fitness for office and initiates the ritual we have come to expect in political campaigns. However, there are five additional contributions provided by the communication acts and symbols during the surfacing period. These functions are related to the pragmatic aspects of the campaign and have thus been labeled "instrumental."

The first of these functions is that the electorate begins to have some knowledge about a candidate's goals, potential programs, or initial stands on issues. During the surfacing period, in an attempt to determine if and with whom their campaign has any appeal, candidates must speak at countless neighborhood coffees, potluck dinners, and service club meetings. During these appearances, they often have to answer questions about why they are running for office as well as state their positions on specific issues important to those attending the gathering. Answers may at first be sketchy, but as the frequency of the speaking occasions and the perceived receptivity of the audiences increases, so does the candidate's confidence. Statements about political goals and aspirations as well as positions on issues become refined. What was in the beginning somewhat tentative now becomes more definite as the candidate proceeds to formulate statements of philosophy apparently acceptable to most potential constituents. For example, when Congresswoman Elizabeth Holtzman decided to enter the 1980 New York senatorial race, she began scheduling a number of appearances throughout the state months before the primary. Countless efforts were made to not only expand her visibility from one congressional district to the whole state, but also to let the electorate know what her positions were on issues wider than those facing her current constituents.

During the eight years in which Holtzman had been a member of the House of Representatives, she had demonstrated an ability to work for the fairly narrow concerns of her Kings County constituents. But with the decision to move from the House to the Senate, the congresswoman had to establish her understanding of and commitment to problems and issues facing a larger and more diverse audience. The surfacing period provided Holtzman the opportunity to not only determine what the issues were but to formulate positions that could be and were used during the second or primary stage of her campaign for the United States Senate.

Closely related is the second instrumental function—voter expectation regarding a candidate's administrative and personal style begins to be established. For example, candidates who have well-organized and disciplined staffs provide some knowledge about the kind of administration they might have if they are elected. Even in a campaign for a seat on the local school board, those candidates who right from the beginning appear to be operating from a precise plan or blueprint with regard to where and when they will canvass the district, or distribute literature, or speak at neighborhood coffees provide voters with information regarding the level of organization and efficiency it might be reasonable to expect if and when they are elected to the school board.

The personal style of a candidate is also revealed during the early days of a campaign. Perhaps one of the most interesting examples occurred during the preprimary period of the 1980 presidential campaign. Before Edward Kennedy began his pursuit of the presidency, he, like his brothers before him, had been perceived as an excellent speaker, a master of the art of campaigning and campaign rhetoric. Thus the expectations of the public were high—so high that it is unlikely that any candidate could have lived up to the dimensions of the Kennedy mystique. But in the first few ventures away from Washington and Boston, the senator fell far short. He read his speeches (he always had, but no one ever seemed to have noticed before), mispronounced words, seldom looked up from manuscripts to establish eye contact with his audience, stumbled frequently using vocal pauses or qualifiers such as "uh" or "ah," appeared confused in answers to questions on material and issues he should have known, rambled, and appeared unable to speak without constant reliance on manuscripts and especially prepared charts. Deficiencies were exaggerated because of high expectations, but the point is that the surfacing period is important for its revelations of a candidate's personal and administrative style.

The third instrumental function of surfacing is that it aids in determining what the dominant theme or issues of the campaign will be. The early candidates set the rhetorical agenda for the campaign. As they crisscross the country, state, congressional district, or even the city, they begin to come to grips with the issues on people's minds, begin to address themselves to those issues, and, as we noted earlier, begin to formulate "solutions" to problems that seem to be compatible with popular perception. In national or statewide elections, the media repeat a candidate's statements and thus aid in translating the problems and positions into national or state issues. In local campaigns, candidates often determine the problems by word of mouth rather than the media. A friend of ours who ran for a seat on city council had a fairly direct method for determining the issues on voters' minds. Instead of polling, which he could not afford, or public appearances before various groups, which he wished to avoid until the announcement of candidacy, he simply began attending weekly meetings of the city council nine months before the election. In this way, he had some guidance in selecting issues for his campaign because he was able to learn on a firsthand basis which issues were important or controversial enough to be discussed in council meetings. Thus the surfacing stage is important because the rhetorical agenda begins to be established. If these early concerns are widespread enough, they can become the dominant issues in succeeding stages of the campaign. And those candidates who surface early help determine what will be the agenda.

The first stage is also important because it begins the process of selecting front-runners or separating the serious contenders from the not so serious. Becoming a serious candidate during the surfacing period involves obtaining visibility. In even small races, much less in state or national contests, obtaining visibility requires persuading the media that one is a viable enough candidate to deserve attention.

Almost from the beginning, at least in state and national contests, the media strongly influence who will be considered a major candidate. Visibility during the surfacing period is often the initial reaction of the media to a candidate's past or present self. This has been illustrated a number of times when people who have achieved national recognition in the nonpolitical arena have decided to run for public office and the media have, in a relatively short period of time, turned them into serious candidates. Consider the cases of Senator John Glenn (one of the first U.S. astronauts), Governor J. Y. Brown (the Kentucky Fried Chicken "King" with a famous wife), Senator Bill Bradley (a former All American and All Pro basketball player, and a Rhodes scholar), or even the former governor of California, Ronald Reagan (a movie actor and television host). This was also demonstrated during the surfacing period of the 1988 presidential campaign when Gary Hart and Jesse Jackson, because of previous roles, were selected by the media as serious presidential contenders and thus accorded early and extensive coverage. To a lesser extent, this had also been a factor affecting Governor Jerry Brown and Senator Edward Kennedy during the surfacing period in 1980. However, in 1980, neither the past nor current positions of Brown and Kennedy were as important in generating visibility as was the fact that each was challenging his party's incumbent. Intraparty challenges such as theirs in 1980, Ronald Reagan's in 1976, and Eugene McCarthy's in 1968 normally attract media attention.

Who candidates are and their current position also aid in determining initial visibility. For example, George Bush and Robert Dole were considered the leading contenders during the early stage of the 1988 presidential campaign because of their positions as vice-president and Senate minority leader. The capability of some jobs to generate visibility was also demonstrated by two people who held powerful positions outside of the federal government during the surfacing period of 1988. In fact, Mario M. Cuomo, governor of New York, and Lee Iacocca, chairman of the board and chief executive officer of the Chrysler Corporation, received so much attention from the national media regarding their presidential prospects that each had to call a press conference to announce he was not then a candidate and would not be a presidential candidate.

Conversely, evangelist Pat Robertson, Alexander Haig, Bruce Babbitt, and Pierre Du Pont were not thought of as serious candidates by the media because they did not have current or powerful positions in government.

Quite apart from persuading the media that one is a front-runner based on roles and present positions, a candidate may also emerge from the surfacing period as a possible leading contender by successful grass roots organizing and fund-raising. Acquiring sufficient money to generate the momentum necessary to do well in the primary stage has always been and continues to be important for local, state, and congressional candidates. But with the advent of the campaign-financing laws, motivating enough support to raise the money to qualify for federal matching funds has become crucial to presidential contenders.

Becoming a front-runner because of early grass roots organizing and successful fund-raising helps explain the initial successes of presidential contenders such as Jimmy Carter in 1976, George Bush in 1980, and Michael Dukakis in 1988. Not one of them had been considered a serious candidate by the media prior to the first or second competition. Each used the surfacing period to gather the strength necessary to do well in the first contests (Iowa and New Hampshire) and thus forced the media to acknowledge them as serious presidential candidates.

The final communicative function of the surfacing stage is that the media and the candidate get to know each other. While this function is often not vital for local campaigns, it can be important in congressional and state races, and it is absolutely crucial in presidential campaigns. It is in these contests where we can most completely understand the sig-' nificance of the function to the entire campaign.

At each stage of the campaign, the relationships between candidates and the media who cover them are vital not only to the candidate but to the individual media representative. The candidate needs the visibility that only the media can provide and the media need information that only access to the candidate or immediate campaign staff can provide. It is not, especially in the preprimary period, the adversarial relationship as is commonly pictured. As one analyst who studied the media-press relations of the 1976 Carter campaign summarized:

A symbiosis of the goals of journalists and those who manage campaigns provides for a good deal of mutually beneficial interaction. On the one hand, news reporting organizations certainly define the presidential race as a story which must be covered . . . and are willing to expend considerable resources in news gathering. . . . Presidential candidate organizations, on the other hand, seek to use the news reporting process as a relatively inexpensive means of communicating with voters and political activists. Campaigns, therefore, are happy to facilitate journalists in the conduct of their work.[11]

Relationships can be established during the surfacing stage because there are few media representatives assigned to cover a specific candidate and because the candidate has a skeleton traveling staff—perhaps only the campaign director and candidate. Contact is informal; candidates and staff are accessible. It is a time for finding out details and learning enough about each other to know who can be counted on when or if the candidate's campaign begins to gather momentum. Conditions change from the first stage to the second, and it is the surfacing period that allows media and candidate to get to know each other. The importance of the relationship is first that it provides the opportunity for local media/candidate interaction, which is not always available after candidates find they can get national exposure, and second it gives both candidate and national media representatives a contact to be used later. In other words, the reporter soon discovers who on the staff will have the "real" story or lead and the candidate's people know not only who they can trust but which reporter has the best chance of getting stories in print or on the air. It is a reciprocal relationship and a significant function of surfacing.

These, then, are the necessary functions served by communicative acts during the first political stage. The period is crucial because of the functions it provides. Candidates who announce late (that is, later than other candidates) and thus do not participate in surfacing activities or those who fail to use the period wisely have little success and frequently do not even advance to the second stage.*

SECOND POLITICAL STAGE: PRIMARIES

Primary elections are, at any level, "America's most original contribution to the art of democracy."[12] Under the primary system, voters who make up the political party determine who the party's candidates will be. Although the system varies from state to state, generally, pri-

---

*In 1976, Frank Church and Jerry Brown did not even enter the race until the primary stage. After a few successes in individual primaries, they were out of the contest, having lost to the two major "surfacers" of 1976, Jimmy Carter and Morris Udall. In 1980 Howard Baker refused to leave his duties in the Senate until the primary stage had begun. Once again, it was too late. During the 1984 surfacing period, Senator Dale Bumpers of Arkansas began his short-lived campaign for the Democratic nomination in mid-January 1983. However, by his own estimation, a year before the first delegates would be chosen and a year and a half before the Democratic nomination, he had a late start and found his rivals already better organized and financed. Bumpers was out of the race before the primaries even began. In 1988, Senator Paul Simon was the latecomer. When he entered the race in April 1987, Democratic leaders in Iowa said that many of the people who would have worked for him were already working for and committed to other candidates who had entered earlier.

maries provide for a full-fledged intraparty election with the purpose of choosing a single candidate from each party to run in the general election. Direct primary elections, unlike the presidential primary, normally have a degree of finality in that the winning candidate is automatically placed on the November ballot. But in instances where there are a number of candidates competing for the same office, it is often necessary to have a second or run-off primary because one candidate usually does not capture a majority of votes in the first election. In the case of the presidential primary, even after all of the state elections have been held, the party nominees still have not been chosen. The national nominating convention (the third political stage) officially selects the candidate. Thus in presidential campaigns primary elections are only one phase of the nominating process, not the final act or choice.

There are almost as many variations of primaries as there are states. For example, Wisconsin for many years had what was known as the most "pure" of the open primaries because voters could vote in any primary (it was not necessary to be preregistered and vote as a Republican or as a Democrat and vote only in that party's primary) and have their vote remain secret. Registration took place on primary day and crossover voting was the norm. Connecticut, on the other extreme, only began holding full-fledged presidential preference primaries in the 1980s. For many years, the state allowed party leaders to choose its statewide candidates without fighting it out in primary elections.

Not only are there different forms of state primaries, some states do not even hold direct primaries but operate under the caucus system to determine nominees. To further complicate the process, the political parties within one state may vary in terms of their selection procedure. For example, in 1980 Michigan Republicans stayed with the direct primary, while Michigan Democrats switched to a caucus system after they were unsuccessful in their efforts to get the legislature to change the state's law to prevent or inhibit crossover voting. By the time of the 1988 presidential election, however, it was the Michigan Republicans who changed the process. In an attempt to play a significant role in determining the presidential nominee, Republicans established a multitiered delegate selection process that began with party precinct elections on August 5, 1986. Although Michigan Republicans were clearly hoping to replace Iowa's influence, Iowa remains one of the two best known caucuses or primaries because since 1976 it has been the first real presidential testing ground for candidates of both political parties. In 1988 the Iowa caucus began the night of February 8, in living rooms, schools, church basements, and firehouses. Democrats and Republicans gathered by precinct to elect delegates to county conventions who in turn chose delegates to state conventions and finally to the national conventions. The whole process took until June. Maine has essentially the same system, but timing and precedence has given the Iowa caucuses inordinate importance. In spite of the fact that local and state nominees are not selected at the precinct level and although proportionately fewer national nominating convention delegates for either party come from Iowa, the candidates who win the precinct caucuses receive enormous publicity boosts from the national media.*

Many professional politicians and party leaders hate the primary stage of a campaign because a genuine primary is a fight within the family of the party—a fight that can turn nasty as different factions within the family compete with each other to secure a place on the November ballot for their candidate. In addition, primaries can exhaust candidates, leaving them physically and emotionally drained just before the most important battle. Charges and countercharges of candidates and their staffs often provide the opposition party with ammunition they can use during the general election campaign. Moreover, beginning with the presidential primaries of 1980, another problem developed when the unit rule forced changes in strategy and thus made the presidential primary system even more detested by party leaders than it had been. Under the new rules, there could be no winner-take-all victory anywhere. Every state and every congressional district was forced to divide its delegates in proportion to the votes the candidates had won, and then candidates would "own" the delegate chosen in their name. In practical terms, it meant that no state was worth a candidate's full attention, and yet no state could really be ignored. Each candidate had to campaign everywhere in each primary because even in losing the state, the candidate could still get a substantial share of the delegates.

Finally, primaries use a lot of money—funds not only from contributors who might have been generous for the later campaign, but money that can be a drain on state and national resources in terms of matching funds. For example, because of the large number of people who ran in the 1982 New Jersey gubernatorial primary, the state had to spend over $13 million in matching funds. In Ohio, contenders for the 1982 gubernatorial primary spent as much as $2 million each for the Democratic primary. Moreover, the cost of the primaries continues to escalate. In 1984 the presidential candidates spent over $217 million during the primary campaigns, and by 1988 those candidates who received federal matching funds were allowed to spend $27 million each during the presidential primary season ($3 million more than they had been allowed to spend in 1984).

---

*Although Michigan Republicans did not generate the intense media scrutiny for their precinct elections that the Iowa caucus received in 1988, the Michigan GOP did achieve part of their goal. They, not Iowa, voted for George Bush as the party's nominee.

One reason inordinate amounts are spent on this stage of presidential campaigns is that there are so many primaries and they last so long. In 1988, for example, there were 36 primaries, which began on February 8 in Iowa and did not conclude until June 14 when voters in North Dakota went to the polls. While the 1988 schedule was as drawn out as those of the previous four, for the first time since 1976 Iowans did not have more influence in selecting the eventual nominees than larger states simply because their caucus was first.* Despite its size, Iowa had been able to exert an inordinate amount of influence because candidates used the win there to focus national attention on their campaigns and build a momentum that granted them front-runner status from the media. The idea was that the national surge of publicity would provide a substantial "bounce" toward the nomination so that before late spring when states with large numbers of delegates, such as California and Ohio, go to the polls, the race would effectively be over. In an effort to prevent this from recurring in 1988 and to try to ensure that a candidate less liberal and more to their liking than Walter Mondale was selected, Democrats in 14 Southern and border states expanded a regional primary begun in 1980 when Florida, Georgia, and Alabama voted on the same day. By March 8, 1988, voters in 20 states, in what became known as "Super Tuesday," rejected those candidates who had been the big winners in Iowa (Congressman Richard Gephardt and Senators Simon and Dole), and thereby turned the Iowa "bounce" into something more closely resembling a belly-flop.†

Yet for all of the problems with this second political stage, there are five functions that the communication acts and symbols of the period provide. While we do not want to suggest that primaries (particularly the presidential primary system) need no revision, we do believe these five functions are important to the entire political campaign process. The first relates directly to the candidates and the final four to the electorate.

For candidates, the primary season is a source of feedback from the voters about their campaigns, the organization they have put together,

---

*New Hampshire, however, held on to its record. In 1988, as in every presidential primary since 1952, New Hampshire voted for the candidate who eventually became president. In fact, in 1988 New Hampshire also voted for the candidate who became the Democratic nominee.

†It is important to note that although Senator Albert Gore won more votes on Super Tuesday than any of the other Democratic contenders, Dukakis carried enough to allow him to maintain his front-runner status as the next round of primaries in Illinois, Connecticut, Wisconsin, New York, and Pennsylvania began. He maintained his lead primarily because he had used the surfacing stage to raise enough money to mount a real campaign in each primary or caucus state. Although the 1988 primary period went from February to June, the elections were grouped too closely to allow candidates the luxury of "regrouping" between contests.

the competence of staffs, fund-raising efforts, physical stamina—in other words, their strengths and weaknesses as campaigners. During the surfacing period, the candidates' only measures of how they are doing are the comments of the media and, in some cases, the results of polls. But the primaries provide direct feedback from the voters and thus a chance for repositioning in terms of stands on issues, themes, images, and overall campaign strategies. Obviously, for those candidates who have only one primary in which to compete (most local, state, and congressional contenders), the feedback is either of no use (except as it may account for defeat), or it is used to plan for the general election. For example, feedback from the first campaign of candidates such as John Glenn of Ohio, Lee Dreyfus of Wisconsin, and S. I. Hayakawa of California allowed them to reposition their public images from astronaut or academician to senator or governor. For presidential candidates, the early contests are direct sources of feedback that can be used immediately as preparations are made for campaigning in subsequent states. There are times, of course, when repositioning does not work, as was the case in 1984 when John Glenn attempted to reposition his image from astronaut during the Iowa caucus to experienced statesman during the New Hampshire primary. But there are other times when it has. One of the most dramatic was the repositioning of Ronald Reagan's image and campaign strategy during the 1980 primaries.

As conceived originally by then campaign manager John Sears, Ronald Reagan's 1980 quest for the presidency was to be a regal campaign, one in which Reagan would slowly but surely win the delegates necessary to assure the nomination. The front-runner campaign conceptualized by Sears would be characterized by an "above-the-battle" posture in which Reagan would campaign leisurely in each state by making only one or two appearances in any one day, not appear on forums or debates with his Republican rivals, honor his own already famous "eleventh commandment" (Thou shall not speak ill of other Republicans), and be assisted with a well-planned and -financed media campaign.

The strategy was tested in Iowa, the birthplace of Reagan and the center of his so-called rural heartland. A week before the caucuses, Iowa newspapers talked about Reagan's failure to campaign in the state or to even appear with each of the other Republican candidates in the nationally televised forum sponsored by the *Des Moines Register*. Reagan's absence was noted throughout Iowa at countless fund-raising dinners, or as they are termed by politicians and the press, "cattle shows," where each of his Republican opponents made appearances and speeches. In fact, at some of these party functions there were not even any signs of a Reagan campaign in the state—no campaign buttons, no posters, no candidate. By the time of the caucus, Reagan had spent only 41 hours in the state, had avoided discussing the issues, and had made only one televised speech. It had been, as one newspaper headline proclaimed, a campaign that was "Invisible to Many." In defending this strategy, Sears said that "as a front-runner, Reagan could set the pace for the campaign, decide whether to give an event like the forum the prominence of his presence, and that the job of the other candidates was to make Reagan turn around and confront them."[13]

In contrast, one Republican, George Bush, had spent a full 59 days campaigning in Iowa and had thoroughly extended his campaign organization throughout Iowa months in advance of the caucus. On January 21 it was clear that the effort had paid off when Bush upset front-runner Reagan and finished first among the Republican candidates.

Although we do not know Reagan's immediate private reaction to his Iowa upset, we do know that he must have accepted the caucus result as instructive feedback about his campaign strategy or image. By the following week, a "new" Reagan was campaigning in New Hampshire. This Reagan was talking about issues, riding a press bus, speaking at rallies throughout the state, appearing at all multicandidate Republican gatherings, participating in (in fact, pursuing vigorously) all opportunities to debate his Republican rivals, and using an expanded media campaign to present his view to New Englanders. Perhaps the clearest indication that Reagan had used feedback from Iowa Republicans to reposition his campaign strategy and thus his image came on election day in New Hampshire when he fired his press secretary, his operations director, and his manager, John Sears.

Important also are the functions provided to the electorate. Just as the primary campaign is valuable in giving candidates the feedback necessary for repositioning, so too can it offer voters the information necessary for cognitive adjustment or readjustment.

Images are rather easily acquired by voters during primaries. As candidates crisscross the city or the state, speaking at all types of political receptions, coffees, rallies, or fund-raising events, voters have the opportunity to see and hear potential mayors, governors, or presidents. They can witness for themselves the candidate's habitual patterns of thinking and acting. They need no longer rely solely on earlier, perhaps inaccurate, accounts of a candidate's style or position on issues. A candidate for mayor does look and sound capable of coping with the city's striking sanitation and transportation workers. The Republican candidate for governor does have a plan for enticing major industry into the state. The nonincumbent candidate for city council is unable to answer a simple question about zoning ordinances. And the presidential candidate uses so many "ahs," "umhs," and "huhs" that it is impossible to understand responses to questions.

In other words, as the candidates seek all possible arenas of political talk during the primary stage of the campaign, voters can see on a firsthand basis just how candidates handle themselves verbally and non-verbally. The information they receive aids in determining or readjusting their opinions. As a matter of fact, political scientist Thomas E. Patterson has found that these early impressions gained during the primary stage tend to remain throughout the campaign.[14] From speeches and answers to audience questions, voters begin to have some information regarding the candidate's beliefs, attitudes, and value orientations. If Jerry Brown can only talk about protecting the earth and exploring the universe, how will he ever get the U.S. hostages home from Iran? If Edward Kennedy can only talk about spending more money on comprehensive health care insurance for everyone, how will he ever understand that most citizens are sick of federal government welfare programs? If George Bush is so proficient and experienced in so many different government and political roles, why is it that he has trouble answering questions about the home-less? Answers to these questions and countless others provide information about the candidates that allows voters to create what one communication theorist, Samuel L. Becker, has called a "mosaic model of communication," learning bits of information and then arranging those "bits" into a new or reinforced cognitive pattern.[15]

The third function of the primary period is that it involves many citizens in the democratic process. Involvement in the political process can take a number of different forms. For example, a person can engage in overt political action by participating in such activities as raising money for candidates, preparing placards, canvassing door to door for a party or for a candidate, attending a rally or a neighborhood coffee, distributing literature, licking envelopes, or voting. While there are, of course, many other activities possible for those engaging in overt political action, involvement can also be at the social interaction level. By this we mean simply that politics gives people a variety of topics or issues for discussion at work, parties, or anyplace where people interact with one another. Involvement may be no more than talking with a friend about whether or not a particular candidate believes in "pro choice" or "right to life," but social interaction is one form of involvement in the political process. A third form of involvement is parasocial interaction. This is interaction not with other people but interaction with the messages provided by radio, television, newspapers, brochures, and so on. In other words, it is arguing or agreeing with a negative political ad when it comes on your television set or a candidate's speech that you read in his literature or in the evening newspaper. Finally, involvement can be a matter of self-reflection—examination of your ideas or perceptions on economic or social priorities in light of the position or platform of a given candidate.[16]

Although the other political stages of the campaign do encourage forms of overt political action, social or parasocial interaction, and self-reflection, it is increasingly becoming the primary period where involvement is most intense because the sheer number of candidates and the attention given to the primaries by the media demand it. In his book on the role of the mass media in the 1976 presidential campaign, Patterson argues that one of the changes in contemporary campaigns is that public interest now peaks more quickly. In the election of 1940, for example, interest in the campaign did not peak until the general election stage, whereas interest in the 1976 campaign rose sharply in the early primaries. Patterson also found that interest in the campaign decreased during the later primaries, and so the overall interest of voters was no greater than it had been in 1940; it just peaked earlier.[17]

In 1988 the public was once again interested in the primary stage of the presidential campaign, and once again its interest peaked early and declined. The 1988 general election turnout (only 50.16 percent of the country's eligible voters cast ballots) was the lowest in 64 years, but the early primaries set voting records. In Iowa, for example, more than 233,000 people took part in the process of selecting a president. This figure was up from 200,000 in 1980, which was more than double the previous high of 88,000 set in 1968 when a desire to protest the Vietnam War drew thousands of supporters of former Senator Eugene McCarthy to attend caucus meetings. In New Hampshire, some 276,000 people cast ballots, surpassing the 1980 record of 261,000. And on Super Tuesday more than 13 million people took part in the process of selecting a president.

Why are citizens becoming involved in the primary stage of the campaign? Although there are no certain answers, participation has undoubtedly been strengthened for three important reasons. First, with the increased number of primaries, the public is growing more accustomed to them and the major changes they have contributed to the process of selecting a president over the last decade. People have discovered that presidential primaries are exciting, almost like a carnival, as 10 or 12 presidential hopefuls, each with family, large contingents of secret service, and hundreds of national media representatives, descend on a state for three or four weeks during the winter or spring every fourth year. Even states that had never had or rarely had presidential primaries joined the swelling list by 1988. Perhaps one reason for the excitement generated by the primaries is the direct personal contact with a potential president. Primary campaigning allows the candidate to meet individual voters. It is unlike the general election when the candidate is remote, isolated, and appears to be existing only for the national media. The primaries, like the surfacing stage, are a time for interpersonal communication as candidates and citizens interact at dozens of small group gatherings throughout an individual state.

A second reason for increased involvement may be that a larger number of presidential candidates are actively campaigning and spending extraordinary sums of money in the primary states. For example, in Iowa the major candidates in 1988 spent record amounts on television and radio advertising, with most media budgets running to six figures. Each commercial for a candidate was also an advertisement, in a sense, for the caucuses themselves. The increased publicity given the caucuses may have led a lot of Iowans to attend them out of curiosity. In Massachusetts, television spending in 1988 was even higher. Many commercials aimed at New Hampshire voters aired on Boston television, and candidates had to pay for large audiences, often including more Massachusetts residents than New Hampshire citizens.

Another explanation for the high levels of involvement in the second stage of the campaign is media coverage. The national media have also discovered the glamor, the excitement, the "gamelike" stakes of the presidential primary. Accordingly, each of the television networks's evening news programs devotes substantial amounts of time to covering the candidates in Iowa, New Hampshire, Florida, or wherever the primary or caucus happens to be that week. In addition to regular news features, the primaries are highlighted by special programs such as the Tuesday night telecasts of primary election returns and interview programs such as "Meet the Press." The media create "winners" and "losers" even though the "winner" may have won by only a few percentage points or maybe did not even win at all but did so much better than was expected or came so close to the "front-runner" that he is declared by the television commentators to have "won" the election. As Patterson argues, the media treat primary elections much as they do the general election—there must be a winner. Each primary is only incidentally treated as part of a larger nominating system.

There is, however, a fourth and closely related function of the primary period. As candidates campaign, regardless of what level of office is sought, they often make promises about what they will do if elected. Some promise little, others promise everything from lower taxes to increased morality, but few actually deliver once they take office. We believe that one of the important communication functions of primary campaigning is related to these promises made by candidates during the heat of the campaign. As we have already observed, one characteristic of primary campaigns is that they are normally more personalized than the general election stage. That is, voters have more of an opportunity for direct interaction with candidates. Campaigning is personally oriented as candidates attend countless events at which the relatively small number of people present familiarize them with the problems important primarily to their specific neighborhood, city, or state. The voters try to elicit promises of help and assistance from the candidates if they are elected. Once the promise is given, we believe that there is more likelihood of promises being kept after the election because of the physical proximity in which they were articulated and the fact that they are given to a specific individual or small groups of individuals, not an amorphous large audience or an impersonal camera.

Finally, we suggest that there is a fifth function performed by the primary stage of the campaign. The voters have a chance to determine the "real" front-runners or leading contenders for the nomination. Throughout the surfacing period, the media label candidates as "possible winner," or "dark horse," or "a favorite," or even "front-runner." With the primary, voters have the opportunity to go over and above the media and actually select the nominees or at least give true meaning to the term "front-runner." While we would not deny the influence the media have extended over the years in the self-fulfilling prophecy of their labels, there have still been a considerable number of instances when the voters, not the media, have determined the serious candidates. Consider the 1976 presidential campaign in which the media, overanxious perhaps because the surfacing period had been so long, had a whole string of candidates they labeled front-runners at one time or another. The list included senators Henry Jackson and Birch Bayh but never the former governor of Georgia Jimmy Carter. The voters from Iowa and New Hampshire determined that Jimmy Carter was a front-runner. The 1980 campaign was pretty much the same as the media labeled candidates such as John Connally and Senator Howard Baker serious enough contenders to defeat front-runner Ronald Reagan. As it worked out, of course, the only Republican candidate who ever defeated Reagan in a primary was George Bush. The media had not even considered Bush a serious candidate until the voters from Iowa determined his front-runner status. The reverse, of course, was true in the case of Senator Edward Kennedy. Prior to the first vote, the media gave the impression that Kennedy had already defeated President Carter. The voters, however, in Iowa and New Hampshire believed that the president was the Democratic front-runner and removed Kennedy from his preprimary position. In 1988, however, after Gary Hart withdrew from the race following the Donna Rice incident, the media were unable to decide on a serious Democratic candidate (calling the seven contenders "the seven dwarfs"). Apparently they decided to let voters determine who among the "dwarfs" was a front-runner. Voters in Iowa chose Gephardt; those in New Hampshire selected Dukakis; and the voters on Super Tuesday decided on Gore.

These then are the communication functions of the primary stage of the campaign. They are significant because the second stage is vital to our political system. The primary campaigns allow the people to determine who the candidates will be. During the primaries, the decision making is taken from the hands of political parties and media and given to the voters. The communication functions are crucial to the process.

THIRD POLITICAL STAGE: NOMINATING CONVENTIONS

Although a majority of citizens regularly tell pollsters that they would prefer some other method for nominating presidential candidates, the national party conventions remain as they have since their inception: the bodies that make official presidential and vice-presidential nominations for the Republican and Democratic parties.* However, just as the first two political stages of the modern campaign have changed, so has the third. Where instrumental or pragmatic communicative functions were once the primary reason for holding party conventions, now the symbolic or ritualistic functions are, in most instances, the chief purpose. In other words, the convention stage is an important and distinct period in the four-step process because of the symbolic functions it provides. From the time that the anti-Masons held the first national nominating convention in Baltimore in 1832 until the Democratic Convention in 1972, nominating conventions could be viewed as deliberate bodies—assemblies faced with difficult and important decisions to make in a few days. In addition to participating in the "required" political rituals of the day, delegates made decisions that often determined the success or failure of their political party during the coming election. In other words, the conventions served important pragmatic or instrumental functions in that the presidential and vice-presidential nominees were selected, the platforms were determined, and even the tone or "battle posture" for the general election campaigns were established. In short, the convention met to make party decisions. For many years, decisions were made and the conventions were controlled by bosses and special interests. Some of those conventions nominated candidates of top quality such as Abraham Lincoln and Woodrow Wilson, and other conventions tapped candidates of dubious quality such as Franklin Pierce and Warren Harding. Whatever the caliber of the candidates nominated or the platform written, it is important to remember that the nominating conventions actually made party decisions; in other words, they served instrumental functions.

However, beginning in 1952 and strengthened by action taken for the

---

*In many states and localities, parties also hold nominating conventions. However, since their structure, functions, and organization vary so much, it would serve little purpose to discuss them.

1972 Democratic Convention, at least three significant changes have occurred, thus shifting the communicative functions of conventions from instrumental to symbolic. While they have been discussed earlier, their impact on the third stage of the campaign has been so enormous that they should be understood with regard to the nominating conventions.

The first change was the introduction of television to the campaign. Although television did not bring the sights and sounds of the presidential contest to millions of people until the 1952 campaign, nonprint media had been involved in the nominating conventions for many years. In 1912 movies and phonograph records captured Woodrow Wilson's acceptance speech; in 1924 the acceptance speech of presidential nominee John Davis was broadcast over a network of 15 radio stations; and by 1928 the influence of the medium was so pervasive that the time and date of Alfred Smith's acceptance speech were determined by the network of the 104 radio stations that were to broadcast the speech.[18] However, when television was first used during the 1952 primary campaigns, the public apparently became more interested in the election battle than it had been in the past. Turnout jumped from less than 5 million primary voters in 1948 to almost 13 million in 1952. The new medium brought a different dimension first to the primaries and then to the conventions by dramatizing suspense, conflict, and excitement, as well as projecting a visual image of the candidates that had never before been possible. Television gave the public a sense of involvement in the conventions, and as many delegates and reporters covering the convention soon discovered, the television viewer could see more and know more of what was going on than the persons could who were on the floor of the convention hall.[19]

During the 1952 campaign, there were 108 television stations on the air, and as one study of the election showed, the impact of the new medium was significant:

The public went out of its way to watch the campaign on television. Only about 40 percent of the homes in the U.S. have television sets, but some 53 percent of the population saw TV programs on the campaign—a reflection of "television visiting." On the other hand, the campaign news and other material in newspapers, magazines and on the radio did not reach all of their respective audiences: more than 80 percent of the population take daily newspapers and have radios and more than 60 percent regularly read magazines, but in each case the number following the campaign in these media was smaller than the total audience. . . . In the nation as a whole, television, though available to only a minority of the people, led the other media in the number of persons who rated it most informative.[20]

As important as was television's influence in 1952, it can be seen as just a mere shadow of what it was to become in all stages of subsequent campaigns, including the nominating conventions. In fact, by 1976 when electorate interest in that year's presidential contest was studied, it was discovered that television coverage of the conventions boosted voter interest and attention to the campaign, especially among those who were not strong political partisans.[21] Perhaps in response to electorate interest, coverage of the 1980 conventions was increased to the point that media representatives outnumbered delegates by four and five to one at the Republican and Democratic Conventions. As a matter of fact, according to the *New York Times*, the Democratic Convention included 3,381 delegates and 11,500 reporters, editors, camera operators, and broadcasters. And although the public appeared as bored with the 1980 conventions as it had been interested in those of 1976 (network ratings showed a sharp drop in the number of people watching the 1980 conventions as compared with four years earlier), the presence of the networks has nonetheless had a profound effect on modern nominating conventions.

One reason is that the presence of the networks has restructured convention programming so that the party's "important" events occur during "prime time." To make certain that this happens, the convention chair often ignores the activities of the delegates on the convention floor and rushes through any official party business to make certain that those events planned to give the party the most favorable image (for example, ecumenical prayers, civic greetings, performances by show business personalities, keynote and acceptance speeches, and controlled and planned "spontaneous" demonstrations for candidates) will be seen during the hours in which most people watch television. Whether this strategy fails (as, for example, it did in 1972 when George McGovern's acceptance speech began hours after most people had gone to bed or in 1980 when Congressman Morris Udall's keynote address started as the delegates were leaving Madison Square Garden for the night) or is successful, the convention proceedings become ritual with little or no pragmatic value.

Another effect of the presence of the networks has been that convention participants have become almost more aware of media presence, particularly television cameras, than of convention business and thus alter their behavior and interaction. As one critic of the 1980 Democratic Convention wrote:

The omni-present camera eye contributed to the funny hat, placard, banner and button syndromes. . . . At times, the television camera introduced an almost schizophrenic atmosphere as speakers addressed themselves to an unlistening, often chaotic arena audience, while really hoping that their individual performance would coincide with network coverage.[22]

The last and undoubtedly most significant effect of the networks has been that television covers only those events it decides are important, thereby altering the shape, structure, and activities of the convention. There were times during the 1980 conventions, for example, when the networks conducted interviews with relatives of the candidates while prominent convention participants were debating platform positions. In fact, there was so much "gatekeeping" by the networks covering the Democratic Convention that one scholar estimated that television viewers saw less than half of the proceedings during those times when the networks were on the air. CBS, for example, made decisions about what to show or not to show viewers based on whether Walter Cronkite judged the event to be very exciting. And during the 1984 conventions, NBC did not go to the podium for nearly an hour, preferring to present its own interviews rather than an address by Congressman Jack Kemp. An 18-minute film introducing President Reagan was carefully inserted into the convention schedule to assure airtime. However, only NBC and CNN showed the film in full. Thus we believe communication analyst Gary Gumpert was correct when he wrote that television has helped to render the nominating conventions little more than "a series of arranged and controlled visual and auditory images."[23]

The second factor that has had a profound influence in changing the nature of the third political stage has been the reliance on primaries as the vehicle for selecting delegates to the national party conventions. As we discussed in the first chapter, the proliferation of primaries has contributed to the decline of the political parties, but now we want to emphasize that it has also changed the role of the national nominating convention from decision maker to "legitimizer." Perhaps this statement is explained best by taking a brief glance at the history of the presidential primary.

The presidential primary is a "uniquely American institution born, after decades of agitation, in the early twentieth century."[24] In the post–Civil War era, the party organizations in many states and cities came under the control of often corrupt political machines dominated by or allied with public utilities, railroads, and others who manipulated the convention system to suit their ends. In an effort to reform the system, the Populists and later the Progressives advocated the substitution of direct primary elections for party-nominating conventions. By 1917 all but four states had adopted the direct primary method of nomination for some or all offices filled by statewide election. However, the extension of primary elections from the local, state, and congressional levels to presidential politics was much more difficult.

In 1904 Florida held the first primary election for the choice of delegates to a national party convention, and by 1916 presidential primaries were held in 22 states amid speculation that within a few years the national convention would be only an ornament for making official those decisions already arrived at by the electorate. Calculations such as these, however, were a few years premature because two decades after the first presidential primary had taken place, the movement came to a halt with the number of states stabilized at around 15. Turnout remained low, and there was little popular interest in them until the 1952 campaign when the entrance of television into the primary elections renewed voter enthusiasm and then again in 1956 when Senator Estes Kefauver became the first candidate to use the New Hampshire primary as a way to call attention to his campaign. Although the outcomes did not determine the parties' ultimate choices, they generated more interest than they had at any time since 1912.

Twenty years later, in 1972, a major incentive for the adoption of presidential primaries was provided when the Democratic party's Commission on Party Structure and Delegate Selection to the Democratic National Committee, popularly known as the McGovern-Fraser Commission, sought to stop some of the injustices apparent to many liberals at the 1968 convention. The commission prepared 18 guidelines intended to ensure that the state Democratic parties' procedures for selecting delegates to the 1972 convention were open, fair, and timely. At least four other commissions followed McGovern-Fraser in the intervening years, and the guidelines have become so complex (to make certain that there is enough representation of minorities and women) that the state parties have found that they can best comply with them, and not disturb traditional ways of conducting other party business, by adopting a presidential primary law. Thus the number of presidential primaries has proliferated. As primaries grew, so did the number of delegates pledged to a specific candidate, and since 1972 everyone has known before the conventions begin who the candidates would be (except in 1976 at the Republican Convention when Ford and Reagan fought down to the wire). The conventions no longer determine the candidates. Voters in those states holding presidential primaries have decided who will be nominated. The convention meets to legitimize the earlier selection.

The third factor that has influenced the changing nature of the convention stage has been the emergence of the campaign specialists who, with the consent of the candidates for whom they work, determine important aspects of the convention that were once the domain of delegates and party leaders. The consultants have planned the candidate's strategies through the first two stages for the precise purpose of winning the nomination. With the nomination secured before the convention even begins, the specialists now turn to "putting on the best show" possible for the television-viewing audience. The party platform is negotiated in advance of the convention, with the staff of the candidate certain to be the nominee controlling the deliberations. If a spirited debate concerning a specific issue would enhance the "television show" or if, in the spirit of compromise, it becomes important to give the losing candidate and his supporters the chance to "air" a minority position, portions of the party's platform will be discussed during the convention itself. However, even when this has happened, as in the case of the "debate" on the MX missile at the 1980 Democratic convention, the vast majority of the delegates paid no attention to the debaters. In fact, as one communication analyst who attended the convention noted:

Signs against the MX popped up and down in the Garden: "X-rated Missiles Aren't Sexy," "NIX the MX," "MX-Missile Madness," "No MX-Nobody Wins World War III," "MX Says Have a Nice Doomsday," "Mighty Expensive," "MX Makes US the Target." Delegates wandered around talking to friends. There were many empty seats. The clear impression was of a ceremonial occasion rather than a deliberative one. . . . The debates served the symbolic function, though, of letting off steam for those who really did care.[25]

In other words, all real decisions regarding the convention are made by the candidate, based on the advice of consultants. The candidate, not the party leaders, determines the platform, the issues to be debated, the songs to be played, the identity of those who will speak from the podium during prime time, the name of the keynote speaker or speakers, and the content and length of the "spontaneous" demonstration. As one delegate to the 1980 Democratic Convention said: "We've turned over absolute control of the nominating process to the presidential candidates, and worse, to their staffs."[26]

Thus because of the influence generated by television coverage, presidential primaries, and campaign specialists, the overall function of the national nominating convention to the campaign has been altered. Gone is the once powerful role of decision maker. In its place is a new function. The primary significance of the modern nominating convention is symbolic—ritualistic—and as such, it serves four important communication functions.

The first function, and one of the most significant, is that convention rituals provide an opportunity for the legitimation and reaffirmation of the "rightness" of the American way or dream. The various communication acts and symbols of conventions (keynote speeches, nomination speeches, debates, demonstrations, state-by-state roll call balloting, official "greetings" from past party heroes, patriotic music, buttons, hats, placards, as well as nomination acceptance speeches) serve to renew our faith that U.S. citizens share not only a glorious tradition but a grand and proud future. In a sense, each convention can be viewed as a huge political rally where the candidate shares the spotlight with the democratic system that made his success possible. When, for example, the presidential and vice-presidential nominees make their triumphant entrance to the speaker's platform the last night of the convention, their appearance reinforces the belief that citizens are bound together in a noble tradition. There have been instances when nominees have acknowledged the reciprocity of the relationship during the nomination acceptance speech. For example, in 1988 Michael Dukakis said, "We are the party that believes in the American dream. A dream so powerful that no distance of ground, no expanse of ocean, no barrier of language, no distinction of race, or creed, or color can weaken its hold on the human heart. And I know, because my friends I'm a product of that dream, and I'm proud of it."

He reminisced that it was the American dream that brought his family to America 76 years earlier, unable to speak English, and only $25 in hand, but with a deep and abiding faith in the promise of America. Finally Dukakis, referring to himself, said: "Tonight, as a son of immigrants, and as a proud public servant who has cherished every minute of the last 16 months on the campaign trail, I accept your nomination for the Presidency of the United States."[27]

Certainly, conventions function to legitimize the selection of the candidates, the platform, and the unity of the party and its leaders. But in the largest sense, the communication rituals celebrate what is good about our system and thus ourselves. Convention sessions, for example, open and close with prayers (we are a spiritual and godly people). During the convention, former heroes are acknowledged (we have a sense of our roots), and countless speakers evoke selected elements of the "American dream" (we believe that the United States is destined to become a mighty empire of liberty where everyone can share in the prosperity of society). On the final night, the selected candidates articulate their visions of a grand and more noble country (we value the traditions of reform and progress), while national songs provide periodic emotional climaxes (we have pride in and deep-seated feelings about our country).[28] The convention rituals are, in short, a kind of emotional/spiritual/patriotic catharsis in which we can, if necessary, lament current shortcomings within the party or the country while remaining proud of and faithful to our legacy.

In writing about conventions as legitimation rituals, one communication scholar found that typically the ritual has three steps: it begins with a statement and demonstration of theme (traditionally the responsibility of keynote speakers); progresses to a clustering or gathering of stereotypical character types who are given convention time for speeches or "greetings" to the delegates (the hero or heroine, the also-rans or those who fought the good fight but lost in a noble cause and are now vindicated through history, and leaders representing the right and left and all divergent interest groups within the party); and culminates in the anointing of the nominee who symbolizes and enacts the convention's theme. However, not only are there identifiable steps or phases in the convention ritual, a variety of ritualistic forms are possible. For example, the 1984 Republican Convention explored the theme of "What's right with this country," by stressing that Americans were better off after four years of Republican control of the White House.[29]

Not only do the communicative acts of the convention serve to reaffirm our general commitment to the electoral process—there is a second and closely related function. The convention provides legitimation for the party's nominees. When the struggle for nomination is long and intense (as it has been for presidential nominees since 1972) or when the selection has gone to a relative newcomer (as it did when the Democrats nominated Jimmy Carter in 1976 or Michael Dukakis in 1988) or even when the convention nominates nontraditional candidates (as the Democrats did with Geraldine Ferraro on the ticket as the vice-presidential candidate in 1984), the ritual of the convention confirms or legitimizes the candidate as the party's nominee as a possible governor, senator, or even president of the United States. A person may have won primary after primary, but not until the convention delegates affirm selection through their votes at the convention can the candidate become the nominee. With the act of confirmation comes added prestige and respect. The person is no longer just a candidate, but the nominee of a political party.

The third function provided by the convention stage is that the party has a chance to show its unity. Whether the cohesion is more apparent than real, the convention is the time when wounds from the primary campaigns can be addressed and healed. Perhaps the importance of a unified party to the success of the approaching campaign can be understood by examining instances when the convention ritual has failed to produce cohesiveness. In 1964 the Republican Convention that nominated Barry Goldwater appeared to repudiate Republicans whose political philosophies were more liberal than those of the conservatives who dominated the convention. The governor of New York, Nelson Rockefeller, who had been a contender for the nomination, was booed and not given the opportunity to finish a speech. When Goldwater included an endorsement of extremism in his acceptance speech, many liberals walked out of the convention. The Republican party remained divided throughout the campaign, and Goldwater lost the election by one of the largest margins in the history of presidential politics. Similarly, in 1968 and again in 1972, the Democratic National Convention failed to unify and come together to support either Hubert Humphrey or George McGovern. Humphrey was tormented throughout the 1968 general election campaign by those in the Democratic party who felt his nomination was a betrayal of party principle and a disfranchisement for liberals. McGovern, on the other hand, was never able to unify the traditional or "old-line" party leaders with his more youthful and/or liberal insurgents. In each case, the Democrats remained divided throughout the convention and general election campaign and lost in November.

Thus even when tension below the surface is strained, the political parties strive for the appearance of unity during their conventions. At the 1976 Democratic Convention, for example, one communication analyst recalled that following Jimmy Carter's acceptance speech, party chairman Robert Strauss gathered all the party's candidates and factions on the speaker's platform as Martin Luther King, Sr., delivered the benediction to the convention:

King stunned the noisy delegates and galleries into silence, asking that they "cease walking, talking" and that "not a word be uttered unless that word is to God." In a rousing sermon that brought forth shouts of "Amen" from the audience, the father of Martin Luther King, Jr. cried: "Surely the Lord sent Jimmy Carter to come out and bring America back where she belongs.... As I close in prayer, let me tell you we must close ranks now. If there is any misunderstanding anywhere, if you haven't got a forgiving heart, get down on your knees. It is time for prayer." As Daddy King concluded, the delegates joined hands, linked arms, and slowly began to sing "We Shall Overcome Someday." The television cameras focused on the faces of the delegates, who wept and swayed as they achieved a cathartic moment of emotional release and affirmation.[30]

In a similar though less emotional manner, the Republicans and the Democrats in 1988 attempted to evoke images of unity in the closing moments of their conventions. Although the race for the 1988 Democratic nomination was filled with bitterness, particularly because of Jesse Jackson's feeling that neither the party nor the Dukakis staff was giving him the central role he felt he deserved, the victorious Michael Dukakis had Jackson join him at the speaker's podium after he had delivered his acceptance speech. Jackson was followed to the podium by contenders Albert Gore, Richard Gephardt, Bruce Babbitt, and Paul Simon, as well as Walter Mondale and former president Jimmy Carter. George Bush was joined at the podium following his address by those who had been opponents during the primary and caucus elections to sing "God Bless America." In each instance intraparty tensions were not erased because all factions of the party appeared together at the podium. However, the symbolic act of party leaders closing ranks around their nominees preserved the image of unity.

The fourth communication function served by nominating conventions is that they provide the public introduction of the candidate's rhetorical agenda for the general election campaign. Whether Republican or Democrat, the acceptance speeches of the nominees have frequently signaled the issues on which they plan to campaign (typically through the introduction of a specific slogan) and/or have announced an overall campaign style/plan they intend to follow (sometimes accomplished via a direct challenge to the opposition).

Franklin Roosevelt initiated the process of the nominee speaking to the delegates in person when in 1932 he flew to the Democratic Convention in Chicago. During his acceptance speech he introduced the phrase the "New Deal," which became the slogan for his campaign and subsequent administration. In 1948 Harry Truman not only announced that the central issue in his campaign would be the "do-nothing Congress," but he also explained that he was going to keep Congress in session during the summer to try and get some legislation from them. In 1960 Richard Nixon announced his intention to take the campaign to all 50 states, while John Kennedy introduced the "New Frontier" as the slogan/theme for those issues important to his campaign. In 1976 while accepting the Republican nomination, President Gerald Ford announced his intention to debate, virtually challenging his opponent to a face-to-face confrontation when he said: "This year the issues are on our side. I'm ready—I'm eager to go before the American People and debate the real issues face-to-face with Jimmy Carter."[31] Finally, in 1988 George Bush cited five major issues to draw a sharp distinction between his conservative agenda and Michael Dukakis's liberal agenda.[32]

These, then, are the communication functions served by the third political stage of the campaign. As we have pointed out throughout our discussion of this stage, though the nominating convention serves only ritualistic functions, it is no less critical to the overall campaign than are the other stages. In fact, as we suggested earlier, a campaign that fails to get the most out of the ritual demanded during the nominating convention will proceed to the fourth stage with a potentially fatal handicap.

FOURTH POLITICAL STAGE: THE GENERAL ELECTION

"Electing time"[33] means speeches, parades, debates, bumper stickers, media commercials, bandplaying, doorbell ringing, posters, billboards, polling, sound bites, direct mail fund-raising, and countless television spots. As we have discussed throughout this chapter, these acts and symbols are no longer reserved exclusively for the last stage, although they remain a significant and expected part. It is almost as if all has been in readiness—a type of dress rehearsal for this final and most important scene. Certainly, candidates may have been appearing and speaking at all manner of gatherings for many months. Thirty- and 60-second television spots may have been interfering with television viewing since the primaries. Citizens may have even voted for their candidate in a primary or watched a part of one of the conventions on television. However, once the final stage begins, the campaign communication is at once more intense, less interpersonal but more direct, and certainly more important because the candidate who emerges will be the new mayor, governor, legislator, or president. It is precisely because of the importance of the general election stage that we must discuss briefly three communicative functions, which although not unique to it, are nonetheless reflective of it.

The first function is cognitive. The electorate voluntarily seeks or involuntarily learns of information about some feature of the election and/or the candidates. News regarding the campaign is so widespread during the fourth stage that additional or restructured information may be gained from something as simple as talking with a friend, watching the evening news, or reading a newspaper or magazine. Because so much information permeates the environment during the general election, the majority of the electorate possess at least minimal knowledge about the election.

In recent years, people have been acquiring political knowledge from yet another source, the public opinion polls of the media. While syndicated polls during election years have been a regular feature of the press since the inception of modern public opinion polling in 1936, by the 1970s news organizations began to serve as their own polling agencies. News-gathering organizations were not simply printing or broadcasting the findings of others, they were creating news on their own initiative with their own polls—often extending opinion soundings down to the local level. The impact of this development is reflected in the results of a 1979 study by the National Research Council that showed that in two parallel surveys conducted during the heat of the 1976 campaign, only 16 percent of those interviewed failed to recall hearing something "in the news or in talking with friends" about "polls showing how candidates for office are doing."[34] By the time of the general election stage of the 1980 campaign, virtually every major news organization was conducting some poll each week, thus providing a constant stream of information regarding the election. Perhaps the most dramatic evidence of the importance of polls as a source of information was the continued candidacy of John Anderson during the fourth stage of the 1980 presidential campaign. As one writer suggested:

The primaries produced two presidential candidates, whose victories were ultimately certified by party conventions. They were joined by a maverick independent whose candidacy was buoyed up by the uncertainty or disappointment felt by an appreciable segment of voters over the choices confronting them. Rep. John Anderson, it was claimed during the primaries, was a serious candidate because he had demonstrated significant appeal to voters. But how had he done so? Not by his unimpressive vote totals in the few Republican primaries that he entered. Rather, it was the polls that initially documented his appeal to the satisfaction of leading media political correspondents, who confirmed his status in their reporting. And it was also the polls that were chosen by the League of

Women Voters to play a prime gatekeeping role in deciding that he could appear in the fall TV debates. Thus, unlike other "serious" independent candidates for the presidency in this century, who had established their claims by prior vote-getting, in 1980 an independent had his candidacy assessed as significant primarily by the results of opinion polls generated by or channeled through the mass media and widely accepted as accurate by strategic elements of the political system.[35]

Not only do communicative acts serve as cognitions during the general election stage of the campaign, there is a second function. The general election assigns legitimacy, the idea that the campaign process itself provides further proof that the system works.

In discussing the ritualistic functions of the nominating conventions, we discovered the importance of legitimation in affirming the candidate as the party's choice and the electoral system as superior. Legitimation is also an important function of the general election. As people stand in line to greet a candidate, put up posters for "their" candidate for city council, attend a rally, watch the presidential candidates debate, discuss with a friend the merits of one of the mayoral candidates, vote, or engage in any of the participatory activities typical of the final stage of the campaign, they symbolically reinforce the values for which the activities stand.[36] Thus campaigning becomes a self-justifying activity that perpetuates two primal U.S. myths, according to Bruce Gronbeck:

Acquiescence—providing a paradigmatic, "fail-safe" rationale for choosing leaders and fostering programs with particularly "American" bents, making it difficult for anyone to object to the process (for if you do, the system's ideological web reaches out, telling you to seek the desired change by participating—running for office, pressuring the parties, voicing your opinions in public forums); and, Quiescence—reasserting the values associated with campaigning and its outcomes (free-and-open decision-making, public accountability, habitual and even mandatory modes of campaigning, the two-party system), in order to remind a citizenry that it is "happy" and "content" with its electoral system; emphasizing the mores and ceremonial rituals associated with elections which make the country "devil-proof," invincible to attacks from within or without.[37]

Finally, the fourth stage of the political campaign contributes to fulfilling our expectations regarding campaign rituals. We expect candidates to address themselves to society's problems; we expect debates, rallies, door-to-door volunteers, bumper stickers, buttons, continuous election specials and advertisements over radio and television, polls, and all manner of drama, excitement, and even pageantry. In other words, we have any number of expectations regarding political campaigns. While the previous stages also function to fulfill our "demands," the directness, intensity, and finality of the fourth stage emphasize our pleasure or displeasure with the way in which a particular election has or has not met our pragmatic or ritualistic expectations. If during the general election stage the candidates fail to address those issues of paramount importance to us, fail to debate each other, or even fail to provide for us any of the excitement or drama we normally expect, we may feel cheated. It is, in short, the climax of a political season—a time for decision and participation. It is electing time.

CONCLUSIONS

With the changes in election campaigns in recent years, there have been countless proposals to modify or alter each of the four political stages. While many of the suggestions might well prove beneficial, we hope that you can now better appreciate that our system is far from purposeless. The various verbal and nonverbal acts of communication provide a full range of instrumental and consummatory functions for the candidate and the electorate in each political stage. While some of the functions are perhaps more significant than others, taken together, they are justification enough for the routines and rituals that in this country comprise the political election campaign.

NOTES

1. Bruce E. Gronbeck, "The Functions of Presidential Campaigning," *Communication Monographs* 45 (November 1978): 268–80.

2. Donald R. Matthews, "Winnowing: The New Media and the 1976 Presidential Nominations," in *Race for the Presidency*, ed. James David Barber (Englewood Cliffs, N.J.: Prentice-Hall, 1978), pp. 55–78.

3. Judith S. Trent, "Presidential Surfacing: The Ritualistic and Crucial First Act," *Communication Monographs* 45 (November 1978): 282.

4. The commentary is taken from an unpublished 1979 survey of all women officeholders in Ohio. Partial results of the survey were presented by Judith S. Trent at the 1979 convention in St. Louis of the Central States Communication Association.

5. Roland Evans and Robert Novak, "Sam Nunn Preparing to Run," *Cincinnati Enquirer*, April 10, 1990, p. A11.

6. This statement is attributed to a Conoco distributor from McAllen, Texas, who heard Connally speak in Dallas. See Tony Fuller, "Connally's Bitter End," *Newsweek*, March 24, 1980, p. 37.

7. Michael Oreskes, "He's a New Man Now, Thanks to the Press," *New York Times*, January 22, 1989, p. A1.

8. Murray Edelman, *The Symbolic Uses of Politics*, (Urbana and Chicago: University of Illinois Press, 1985).

9. David E. Rosenbaum, "Jackson Makes Formal Presidential Bid," *New York Times*, October 11, 1987, p. A1.

10. Gronbeck, "Presidential Campaigning," p. 271.

11. F. Christopher Arterton, "The Media Politics of Presidential Campaigns: A Study of the Carter Nomination Drive," in *Race for the Presidency*, ed. James David Barber (Englewood Cliffs, N.J.: Prentice-Hall, 1978), p. 26.

12. William R. Keech and Donald R. Matthews, *The Party's Choice* (Washington, D.C.: Brookings Institution, 1976), p. 91.

13. Adam Clymer, "Reagan's Fortunes in Iowa Caucuses Appear to Hang on His Organization," *New York Times*, January 13, 1980, p. A13.

14. In studying the effects of the media on the 1976 presidential campaign, Patterson found that even in the final stages of the campaign intense partisanship and overtly partisan media communication did not override early impressions. In fact, in 80 percent of the cases analyzed by Patterson, he found that any single impression of a candidate held during the general election was related more closely to earlier impressions of the candidate than to partisanship. Those people who thought favorably of a candidate's background, personality, leadership, or positions before the conventions also thought favorably about the candidate in these areas after the conventions, regardless of partisan leanings. See Thomas E. Patterson, *The Mass Media Election: How Americans Choose Their President* (New York: Praeger, 1980), pp. 133–52.

15. Samuel L. Becker, "Rhetorical Studies for the Contemporary World," in *The Prospect of Rhetoric: Report of the National Developmental Project*, ed. Lloyd F. Bitzer and Edwin Black (Englewood Cliffs, N.J.: Prentice-Hall, 1971), pp. 21–43.

16. Bruce E. Gronbeck talks about five classes of consummatory effects in "Presidential Campaigning," p. 272. See also Jay G. Blumer and Elihu Katz, eds., *The Uses of Mass Communication* (Beverly Hills: Sage, 1974). For further discussion of the uses and gratifications perspective, see Jay G. Blumler, "The Role of Theory in Uses and Gratifications Studies," *Communication Research* 6 (January 1979): 9–36.

17. Patterson, *The Mass Media Election*, pp. 67–75.

18. David B. Valley, "Significant Characteristics of Democratic Presidential Nomination Acceptance Speeches," *Central States Speech Journal* 25 (Spring 1974): 56–62.

19. Samuel L. Becker and Elmer W. Lower, "Broadcasting in Presidential Campaigns," in *The Great Debates*, ed. Sidney Kraus (Bloomington: Indiana University Press, 1962), pp. 25–55.

20. Ibid., p. 45.

21. Patterson, *The Mass Media Election*, pp. 71–75.

22. Gary Gumpert, "The Critic in Search of a Convention or Diogenes in Madison Square Garden," *Exetasis* 6 (October 1980): 5.

23. Ibid.

24. Keech and Matthews, *Party's Choice*, p. 92.

25. Kathleen Edgerton Kendall, "Fission and Fusion: Primaries and the Convention" (Paper presented at the Central State Speech Association, Chicago, 1981).

26. "Changing Times May Make Old-Style Conventions Obsolete," *Cincinnati Enquirer*, August 14, 1980, p. C3.

27. Michael Dukakis, Acceptance Address, Democratic National Convention, July 21, 1988, *New York Times*, July 22, 1988, p. A1.

28. Kurt W. Ritter, "American Political Rhetoric and the Jeremiad Tradition:

Presidential Nomination Acceptance Addresses, 1960–1976," *Central States Speech Journal* 31 (Fall 1980): 153–71.

29. Ann Devroy, " 'What's Right with This Country' Is GOP Theme," *Cincinnati Enquirer*, August 20, 1984, p. A1.

30. Ritter, "American Political Rhetoric," p. 170.

31. When Gerald Ford issued his challenge to Carter, he was trailing badly in the polls and needed something to give a boost to his campaign. As Bitzer and Rueter point out, Ford chose a prime moment at the convention to announce his intention to debate. In his speech accepting the nomination, Ford was aggressive and confident and when he challenged Carter to a debate, the convention audience gave sustained applause. See Lloyd F. Bitzer and Theodore Rueter, *Carter vs. Ford: The Counterfeit Debates of 1976* (Madison: University of Wisconsin Press, 1980).

32. George Bush, "Acceptance Address, Republican National Convention, August 18, 1988," *New York Times*, August 19, 1988, p. A14.

33. This phrase is borrowed from Edwin Black, "Electing Time," *Quarterly Journal of Speech* 58 (April 1973): 125–29.

34. Albert E. Gollin, "Exploring the Liaison Between Polling and the Press," *Public Opinion Quarterly* 44 (Winter 1980): 451.

35. Ibid., pp. 445–56.

36. Gronbeck, "Presidential Campaigning," p. 272.

37. Ibid., p. 273.

Chapter Three

Communicative Styles and Strategies of Political Campaigns

One of the central imperatives of political campaign communication is the whole notion of the manner in which incumbents seek reelection and their challengers seek to replace them, in other words, the style and strategies used by candidates as they campaign. Campaign styles have undergone significant changes over the years. There have been, for example, elections when candidates campaigned by staying home and saying nothing. There have been others when the contenders "swung around the circle" on anything from trains to jets to riverboats in an effort to draw attention to themselves and to be seen and heard by as many voters as possible. And we can each recall instances of campaigns that have been waged primarily by means of the mass media. In short, there has been no one way in which local, state, or national contenders have gone about the task of getting our vote. Strategies have been as varied and sometimes outrageous as those who have used them. Perhaps because of this there has been relatively little systematic investigation or analysis of the communicative strategies and styles that have been, and continue to be, used by all manner of incumbents and challengers.

Thus the subject of this chapter is the exploration of campaign styles. While it may be that readers are more interested in contemporary examples, the present is better understood when viewed from the perspective of the past. For this reason, examples from nineteenth- and early twentieth-century campaigns have been incorporated, thereby providing a more complete catalogue of the communication strategies important to all who have sought and those who will seek elective office.

Understanding of the material in this chapter will be enhanced by an examination of three preliminary considerations that are important to the way in which candidates campaign. A consideration of the term "style" is first. Second is a discussion of political image and its role in developing campaign styles. Third is an exploration of the relationship of technological advancements and styles of campaigning.

PRELIMINARY CONSIDERATIONS

Style

For many years, style has been studied by scholars who are interested in the customs and rules governing the use of language, including the choice of words (figures of speech) and the way the words are arranged (syntactical patterns) in oral and written communication. Although controversy over its meaning occurred historically because some believed style was divorced from content and only a frill or ornamentation, the conception of style as the peculiar manner in which people express themselves by means of language has been generally accepted. In other words, style traditionally has been the province of those concerned with the correctness, beauty, or even workability of language—the investigation or analysis of the words and arrangements a speaker or writer chooses in preparing a message. Thus one of the elements to be considered in the analysis of campaign style is the language that political candidates use as they campaign.

More recently, however, communication theorists have argued that style should not be limited to the study of language but ought to be considered a quality pervading all elements of an individual's communication. Considered in this way, style would include each of the nonverbal aspects of communication—including physical behavior, sound of the voice, body shape and movement, appearance, clothing, and choice of settings—that operate as symbols to create the meanings we infer from the transaction. In written messages, a number of symbols (in addition to language) create meaning, such as the quality, texture, size, and color of the paper and whether it is handwritten or typed for one particular person or printed and prepared for distribution to many. Thus, in election campaigns, style can be seen as a blend of what candidates say—in speeches, news conferences, interviews, advertisements, brochures, and so on—as well as their nonverbal political acts or behavior, such as kissing babies, wearing funny hats, shaking hands at rallies, waving at crowds from the motorcade, as well as their facial expressions and gestures while answering a question. It is what Bruce Gronbeck terms a question of "leadership style"—a combination of habitual modes of thought and action upon which individuals perceive or judge a candidate.[1]

What does any of this have to do with our analysis of campaign styles and strategies? In this chapter, style is a manner of campaigning that can be recognized by the characteristics defining it and giving it form. We have termed these characteristics "communication strategies" and the styles "incumbency," "challenger," and the combined "incumbent/challenger." Certainly, in describing each of the styles, we have been concerned with the traditional dimension of language; but as you have seen in the first two chapters, we believe strongly that political campaign communication is much more than just "talk." Thus as the styles are explored, it will become obvious that many of the characteristics deal with nonverbal political behaviors as well as verbal.

Image and Campaign Style

Imagery plays an important role in the consideration of style. All candidates, whether they campaign using the strategies of incumbency or those of the challenger, must do and say whatever it is that will enhance voter perception of them. They are concerned, in other words, about their image.

Although widespread awareness regarding the significance of image creation to the political campaign did not occur until the early 1970s, it had been used for years. The first major image campaign took place in the presidential campaign of 1840 when the Whigs, after searching for a candidate they thought could defeat Martin Van Buren, found no one. So they invented a national hero, gave him a slogan, said he was champion of the ordinary citizen as well as a giant of the frontier, and elected a president.[2]

When William Henry Harrison was "discovered" by the Whigs, he was 67 years old, a long retired army officer, and had spent four uneventful years as a senator from Ohio.

While military and legislative experience must be considered reasonable credentials for a presidential challenger, Harrison's career had been distinctly undistinguished. The Whigs, however, billed Harrison as a legendary Indian fighter and maintained that he was known widely and fondly as "Old Tippecanoe." The fact that Harrison's "glories" on the battlefield had been limited to one day, 30 years earlier, when he had repulsed a Shawnee attack at Tippecanoe on the banks of the Wabash River, did not stop his campaign managers from creating the image of a military hero. The Whig campaign ignored all issues, except those relating to the personality of their candidates, and gave image creation and "hype" a permanent place in presidential politics. When Democrats suggested that the aging Harrison might be content to spend his declining days in a log cabin "studying moral philosophy"—provided he had a barrel of hard cider at his side—the Whigs cleverly turned the attack into a reinforcement of Harrison's contrived image as a "common man."[3] From then on, every Whig rally sported cider barrels and miniature log cabins, and songs were written and sung celebrating Harrison's humble tastes (the idea being that if logs and liquor were good enough for the people, they were also good enough for the president). Lyrics from one of the campaign songs best describe the image created by the Whigs:

> No ruffled shirt, no silken hose,
> No airs does Tip display;
> But like the "pith of worth" he goes
> In homespun "hodding gray."
> Let Van from his coolers of silver drink wine
> And lounge on his cushioned setee,
> Our man on a buckeye bench can recline
> Content with hard cider is he![4]

Image campaigns did not end with the elevation of "Old Tippecanoe" to the presidency. Instead, the place of imagery became entrenched in elective politics, especially in the area of campaign style where specific strategies must be created and utilized to keep alive the perception of an incumbent or a challenger. The Harrison campaign's visual symbol of the log cabin represents what has come to be called "image" advertising in politics. As political analyst Wilcomb E. Washburn argues, "The modern-day equivalent would be the 30 second television spot commercial."[5]

The importance of imagery is evidenced each time we see yet another television commercial of a candidate surrounded by family, talking earnestly with a senior citizen, walking through a peanut field or standing in front of a sea of flags. Television commercials that present candidates in such situations are clearly designed to build or maintain certain perceptions of the candidate. Political images, however, are more complex than simply the strategies devised to present a candidate to voters. Images should also be considered in terms of the impressions voters have—what they believe to be true or untrue, desirable or undesirable about the candidates and the campaign. As Kenneth E. Boulding wrote in his classic book *The Image*, each of us possesses a store of subjective knowledge about the world, a collection of ideas we believe to be true. This knowledge constitutes our image.[6] While in recent years the work of a number of researchers has served to broaden the perspective by which scholars as well as practitioners view image, nonetheless, it is generally understood that the strategies candidates use to construct a public persona constitute an important area of political communication inquiry. We believe, however, that despite the importance of a candidate's role in the creation of a public perception, it is only part of the equation. In his doctoral dissertation on the construction of image in television spot commercials, Allan Dean Louden argues that image is "more than the message projected by a candidate or even a picture created by a voter. Image is an evaluation negotiated and constructed by candidates and voters in a cooperative venture."[7] In other words, beliefs voters have about candidates are based on the interaction or interdependence of what candidates do and the evaluative responses voters have to it: a "transaction between a candidate and voter."[8]

The view of image as a transaction, however, raises questions of balance or proportion between the strategies used by a candidate to create an image and the ideas already believed by the voter. Is one more important to the creation of persona than the other? Is one more likely to influence voter behavior than the other? Generally, researchers believe that one dimension does not necessarily play a more pivotal role than the other. People have some preconceived ideas regarding what a candidate's personal characteristics and behavior should be and these ideas are continually measured against the reality of what an actual candidate says and does during the campaign. In this way, voters define the campaign for themselves—sorting through competing or contradictory messages. However, there are circumstances in which the balance between the idealized and actual can be disrupted. For example, the context in which the campaign occurs can become the dominating force—as was the Great Depression during the 1932 presidential campaign and the Vietnam War during the 1972 election. In each instance, the images of the candidates were framed by an all-consuming event that in some instances overshadowed candidates' strategies to build an image and in others overcame voters' preconceptions of the "ideal" candidate. It is also possible that a single and dramatic campaign event can tip the scale one way or the other. During the surfacing period of the 1988 presidential campaign, Senator Gary Hart's alleged relationship with a Miami model, his challenge to the media to prove the relationship, the public accusation by reporters from the *Miami Herald*, and the subsequent intensity of national media attention completely overwhelmed anything else Hart said or did. No image strategies the senator might have utilized could have competed with public preconceptions about the ways in which candidates who would be president should behave and the contrast of this with Hart's alleged behavior. And in 1984 when Geraldine Ferraro was nominated by the Democratic party for vice-president, we believe that there was very little the congresswoman could have said or done to have created a public persona favorable enough to refute the preconceptions of some Americans regarding the personal characteristics or attributes vice-presidents are expected to possess. She, in fact, did not look or sound like—she did not resemble—a vice-presidential nominee.

Thus for some voters the fact of Ferraro's gender created an imbalance between imaging determinants.

Even though imbalance regarding the way in which people organize their thoughts about politics can occur, nonetheless, a consistent finding after years of research indicates that we share a lot of beliefs about the personal qualities candidates ought to possess—especially presidential candidates. Moreover, these characteristics are strongly associated with voting preferences and, in most cases, dominate ideas (cognitions) about the candidates and the campaign.[9] These personal qualities or attributes tend to cluster around such leadership characteristics as competency, experience, trustworthiness, ability to be calm, cautiousness, decisiveness, and boldness[10] and closely related personality characteristics such as strength, honesty, fairness, open-mindedness, reliability, energy, and some physical attractiveness.[11] Whether or not a candidate exists who embodies all of these attributes is almost immaterial in that we use the characteristics as a basis of comparison—a standard—by which to judge the acceptability of the flesh and blood women and men actually seeking our votes. As voters we may ask ourselves if the candidate campaigns as an incumbent should or if the challenger fulfills expectations. Viewed from this perspective, the reason for two common campaign activities becomes clear. First, one of the most crucial tasks facing candidates, especially during the surfacing stage, is to determine just what attributes voters believe are ideal for the office sought. Second, campaign activities in later stages are designed to attempt to illustrate that the candidate possesses these qualities.

Although we know that voter assessment of a candidate's image is a significant factor in voting behavior (far more important, for example, than party identification) and that voters have a mental picture of an ideal candidate that they use as a gauge in evaluating actual candidates, it is less clear if these characteristics vary among candidates and across election levels. In other words, are all candidates competing in the same race judged by the same preconceived attributes and are the dimensions of "idealness" the same for candidates running for local offices as they are for those campaigning for president? While scholars studying the political campaigns of the 1970s and 1980s have provided few absolutes, there has been some evidence to indicate that the relative importance of particular clusters of characteristics has varied from presidential election to election and that the level of a voter's own education plays a major role in determining which of the characteristics are most important.[12] In addition, it may be that questions regarding preconceived image characteristics are not particularly important in local races where the attributes and idiosyncrasies of the candidates as well as their positions on the relevant issues are well known.[13] However, there is nothing close to unanimity among scholars regarding the answers to these important questions. Obviously, further research is needed before we can say with any degree of certainty that voter expectations either do or do not vary across candidates and across election levels. One thing though is clear. The creation and maintenance of image, long a part of political campaigns, plays a dominant role because voters have a whole series of impressions regarding the behavior of those who seek elective office that they compare with a personal vision of an ideal candidate. And although other factors are important to the consideration of campaign style, it may well be that the extent to which a candidate is able to live up to these idealized expectations is the extent to which success can be achieved on election day.

Technology and Campaign Style

During the earliest period of our electoral system, the style of political campaigning was, at least in part, defined by the limits of our transportation system. This is one of the reasons that there were no national political campaigns as we think of them today. While it is true that in 1789 and again in 1792 George Washington had no opposition, it would have been difficult for him to have conducted a national campaign even had it been necessary for him to do so. Travel was difficult, uncomfortable, and time consuming. Even in 1800, when the Jeffersonian Democratic-Republicans launched the first activity that could be called a presidential campaign, it was not a national or even a regional effort. The rallies, parades, and leaflets were not nationally planned but the work of individual county and state political committees. The national road system, begun in Maryland in 1808, was the chief east-west artery, and it did not reach even the Ohio border until 1817. Commercial water travel started in 1807, but it took many days just to go from Pittsburgh to New York City. Therefore, the presidential election of 1824 was the first one in which any real mass campaigning took place. Friends of the three candidates (John Quincy Adams, Henry Clay, and Andrew Jackson) traveled within their own and neighboring states to campaign for the presidential contenders.

Although the Baltimore and Ohio Railroad began in 1829, it was 1853 before the tracks reached the Mississippi River and 1869 before the transcontinental railroad system was completed in Ogden, Utah. By 1854, although the transportation system had improved, it still took 30 hours to travel from Indianapolis to Cleveland by rail and 24 hours from Chicago to St. Louis. Thus it is small wonder that 1840 was the first time a political party conducted a national campaign by sending speakers to then all 26 states or that 1860 was the first time a presidential candidate traveled throughout the north campaigning for his own election. Moreover, it was not until 1896, after railroads serviced most of the nation and automobile production had begun, that a presidential challenger, William Jennings Bryan, was able to "whirl" through 21 states, give 600 speeches, and be seen by 5 million people.

Developments in the transportation network continued to affect the style of political campaigning. For example, the beginning of air travel in the 1920s allowed Franklin Roosevelt to fly to Chicago to accept the Democratic presidential nomination in 1932 just as the initiation of commercial jet service in 1959 afforded Richard Nixon and John Kennedy the opportunity to conduct "jet-stop" campaigns in 1960.

However, by the middle of the nineteenth century, a second factor had become important to the development of campaign style. With the invention of the telegraph in 1835, a communication network was able to transcend those of transportation because messages were able to move at the speed of electrical impulses rather than the speed of humans, horses, boats, or trains.[14] Moreover, the emergence of the telephone in 1876, wireless telegraph and the motion picture camera in 1895, commercial radio in 1920, and motion pictures with sound in 1927 allowed the public to "bypass the written word and extend communication senses and capabilities directly."[15] Communication scholar Frederick Williams has written "speech and images could now span distances, be preserved in time, and be multiplied almost infinitely."[16]

Even the first advances in the communication network began to influence political campaigning. For example, one of the primary issues of the 1848 presidential campaign was the almost two-year war with Mexico. The Whigs selected one of the war's heroes, General Zachary Taylor, as their candidate. The principal reason the war could become important to the campaign was that the initiation of commercial telegraph service in 1844 and the subsequent founding of the Associated Press Wire Service had provided far more rapid news than the country had ever known. Citizens were aware of specific battles and vigorously applauded each victory over the Mexicans. In other words, the telegraph was able to inject the war into the campaign with a realism not known before.

By the campaign of 1884, telegraph had so unified the nation's communication system that as James G. Blaine unwittingly discovered even one election eve gaffe could be telegraphed across the country and influence election returns. The day before the election, a Republican clergyman denounced the Democratic candidate, Grover Cleveland, by saying that his party was the party of "Rum, Romanism, and Rebellion." Republican candidate James G. Blaine failed to disavow the statement and therefore lost the support of Irish Catholic voters. A thousand more votes in New York, a stronghold of Irish Catholics, would have elected him.

Although each early communication development had some influence on political campaigning, certainly the most dramatic were the changes brought about by radio. Beginning in 1921, when President Warren Harding first used the new medium to talk with the public, the radio became the nation's most important means of political communication. It remained so until the widespread use of television in 1952.[17] Radio had a direct effect on campaign style because it made the personal appearances of candidates less necessary by providing an option. For the first time, candidates (even unknown ones) could become public personalities without campaigning around the country. In 1924 William McAdoo, a contender for the Democratic presidential nomination, hoped to establish a radio station powerful enough to reach all parts of the country so that he would not have to travel around the nation making speeches.[18] Although McAdoo never put his plan into action, losing the nomination to John W. Davis, subsequent candidates did. In 1928 Republican contender Herbert Hoover undertook only a few public appearances. Rather, he made seven radio speeches the focal point of his campaign. In 1936, 1940, and 1944, incumbent Franklin Roosevelt used radio extensively so that he could reach the entire nation without traveling.[19]

Thus the early achievements in electronic media had a profound effect on the manner of political campaigning. According to Joel L. Swerdlow, "political campaigns, whether at the presidential, state or local level, rarely involve new uses of communications technologies. What becomes 'new' in politics has long since been proved in the nonpolitical marketplace. As journalist James Perry noted in *The New Politics*, 'It's not show biz that's taking over in politics; it's industrial and business technology.' "[20] Although there have been many innovations, those that have had some direct effect on campaign style include: the beginning of scheduled television broadcasts in 1941; the first electronic computer in 1942; the beginning of color television in 1951; the introduction of portable video recorders in 1968; the widespread use of microelectronic chips in 1970; the perfected development of fiber optic signal transmission in 1975; the popularity of home computers in 1980; the use of cable television in 1984; and the widespread use of video cassettes and satellite transmissions in 1988.[21]

In the largest sense, television, as radio had done earlier, increased the number of campaign strategies available because candidates no longer had to be dependent on extensive national speaking tours to become well known to the public. A few nationwide television speeches, a series of well-executed and well-placed advertising spots, an appearance on one of the news/issues programs such as "Meet the Press," campaign coverage on the evening network news broadcasts, and perhaps a guest shot on one of the popular talk shows guaranteed public awareness. In addition, television, unlike radio, enhanced campaign swings by showing parts of them in evening news broadcasts. Although the candidate might go to one state or region of the country to campaign in person, millions of people across the country participated in the rally or parade by watching the pageantry from their own living rooms. Not only did a television campaign provide candidates with more exposure, it also allowed for more flexibility in the management of physical and financial resources. Perhaps the essence of the mass media strategy of the late 1960s and the 1970s is explained best in a memorandum written by H. R. Haldeman (and interpreted by Theodore White) in which he outlined the plan for Richard Nixon's 1968 presidential campaign:

Americans no longer gather in the streets to hear candidates; they gather at their television sets or where media assemble their attention. A candidate cannot storm the nation; at most he can see and let his voice be heard by no more than a million or two people in a Presidential year (the reach of the individual campaigner doesn't add up to diddly-squat in votes). One minute or thirty seconds on the evening news shows of Messrs. Cronkite or Huntley/Brinkley will reach more people than ten months of barnstorming. One important favorable Washington column is worth more than two dozen press releases or position papers. News magazines like *Time* or *Newsweek*, picture magazines like *Life* and *Look* are media giants worth a hundred outdoor rallies. Therefore the candidate must not waste time storming the country, personally pleading for votes—no matter what he does, he can appear in newsprint or on television only once a day. The inner strength and vitality of the candidate must not be wasted; if you do more than one thing a day, you make a mistake. If you test a man's physical strength too far, you push him beyond the realm of good judgment; both candidate and the following press must be given time to stop, rest, reflect and write. The importance of old-style-outdoor campaigning now lies less in what the candidate tells the people than in what he learns from them with the important secondary value that outdoor exertions do provide the vital raw stuff for television cameras.[22]

Although 1968 was not the first time television had been used extensively in a campaign, it was the first time that a presidential candidate had planned his entire candidacy around the medium. Richard Nixon not only used technology to help him win an election, he added an important dimension to campaign style—one that has extended far beyond his tenure as a political candidate.

In a similar fashion, the computer has made a profound impact on the manner of political campaigning. Its speed in information processing and its ability to interact intellectually with us and to automate many of our methods of information analysis have provided the candidate with an invaluable resource in such traditional tasks as identifying and communicating with specific publics or raising funds. It has also been enormously beneficial to the media. For example, on September 15, 1987,

"The Presidential Campaign Hotline" went on-line. The "Hotline" is a computer network that transmits campaign information each morning to subscribers (many of them are media outlets) for a monthly fee. The purpose of the service is to keep subscribers fully appraised of developments in the race for the White House such as: late-breaking news of events in the field; forwarding news stories, editorials and columns from influential periodicals and local newspapers in battleground states; and providing up-to-the-minute analysis from assorted campaign experts. Hotline's practice of carrying daily reports from each presidential campaign press secretary has also created a unique opportunity for each campaign to determine and circulate its own interpretation of events (spin control) before such events have had the chance to make an impact on their own.[23] Thus direct mail, instant voter prediction and analysis, and the campaign hotline are all part of the new politics facilitated by the computer.

But just as important as the past are the possibilities for the future. Such communication technologies as the computer, cable television service, push-button telephones, video cassettes, and video disks may completely change the nature of campaigns in the 1990s and beyond by allowing voters to interact with the candidate from their own living rooms. In other words, instead of a candidate simply stating a position on an issue to a mass audience during a television speech, debate, or interview, the candidate could ask a question or invite comments. Large numbers of viewers could press buttons on their television sets or on their phones and respond immediately to the candidate. This rapid and somewhat personal interaction might allow candidates the opportunity for repositioning their ideas and might also encourage voters to modify or change their beliefs regarding the candidate.[24]

Obviously, the effect on campaign style would be enormous. Incumbents and challengers alike could have the benefits of person-to-person campaigning without ever leaving the television studio. In addition, the determination of public opinion on a given issue would no longer be subject to the intervention of a third party (such as pollsters or the press). Mass media campaigning would, in effect, become true two-way communication.

Although interactive television has not yet been a part of a candidate's communication strategy, by the 1988 presidential election it had spilled over to elective politics. During the Democratic Iowa caucus debates, 87 participants were linked to a computer by a small box with a dial. As they watched the candidates' debate, participants were asked to continuously register their feelings about the speakers by moving the dial on a rising scale of one to seven on traits such as leadership, speaking ability, experience, and qualifications.[25]

The computer is not the only technology that has altered the nature of campaigns. During the 1982 elections, microwave transmission and cable television allowed Ronald Reagan to make a ten-state campaign swing, appearing at rallies for 14 Republican congressional candidates, without ever leaving the White House. And in March 1988 while sitting in a hotel room in Kansas City, presidential hopeful Congressman Richard Gephardt of Missouri responded to questions from television stations in Casper, Wyoming, West Palm Beach, Florida, Washington, D.C., and Spokane, Washington. He arrived in those communities via K–2, a satellite 22,300 miles above the equator. In addition, the potential for satellite campaigning is unlimited. Microwave transmissions can be received by broadcast outlets or cable systems and be sent to half of the homes in the United States with a television set. Cable is attractive to candidates because it is cheaper than network time, more selective in the geographic range it covers (there is no spillage or waste), and political programs or spot advertisements can be written and targeted for a specific city, congressional district, or even a particular group of citizens. In short, microwave transmission and cable television have the potential for creating almost personalized networks for candidates.

Another new technology that has made an impact on political campaigning is the proliferation of household video cassette recorders (VCRs). The practice of distributing campaign videos to provide primarily biographic information and to aid in fund-raising began with George Bush's 1980 presidential effort. By the time of the 1988 campaign, eight presidential hopefuls produced videos that were designed to introduce themselves to voters in the early primary and caucus states and to serve as vehicles for fund-raising. Just as videos can be used to build a candidate's public persona, so too can they undo or destroy an opponent's credibility. This power was graphically demonstrated during the 1988 surfacing period when Senator Joseph Biden of Delaware, a Democratic presidential contender, "borrowed" a stirring soliloquy from British Labor party leader Neil Kinnock without crediting him. Shortly after Biden gave the speech the New York Times received an "attack video" showing the Biden and the Kinnock speeches back-to-back. The Times ran the story on page one and the video was shown on the evening newscast. The video set in motion a chain of events that within 11 days drove Biden from the race.

Video disks are another technological innovation capable of influencing the way in which candidates campaign. For example, a disk can be used to supplement oral messages during a political debate. In 1988 a project called Disc Assisted Political Debate preselected visuals on a television screen that were designed to augment a candidate's verbal argument.[26]

While such disks have not made their way to presidential debates, the technology is available. Although it is impossible to know just what impact new technologies will ultimately have on political campaigns throughout the remainder of the 1990s, as we have seen before, innovations in transportation and communication have an infinite capacity to alter the strategies that candidates use to seek political office. As such, they are an important consideration in any examination of campaign style.

STYLES AND STRATEGIES OF CAMPAIGNS

Essentially, campaign styles are sets of communication strategies employed at times by all candidates, whether they run for president, mayor, governor, or legislator. Moreover, those who hold office may campaign in the manner of those who do not just as those who challenge may adopt strategies of incumbency. In other words, those candidates who are incumbents are not restricted to a specific set of incumbency strategies any more than challengers are confined to a particular set of challenger strategies. In fact, candidates frequently combine strategies of one style with strategies of another so that there are times during the course of one contest where an individual contender may assume a rhetorical posture normally associated with incumbency campaigning and at other times may appear to be campaigning as a challenger. This combination may well be a result of the seasonless electoral process discussed in the first and second chapters. As candidates extend the length of the campaign, no one style is likely to remain appropriate for the duration. New events, as well as changes in conditions, force modification in the manner of pursuit. While in February an attack on the incumbent's economic policy might be appropriate, by August the situation may be different enough to make attack an inappropriate strategy. As such, it would be misleading to try to analyze style by only examining the practice of one candidate or one campaign. Styles (incumbency, challenger, and incumbent/challenger) are a product of whatever candidates and their staffs believe is needed at a particular time within the context of their particular campaign. Therefore, the best way to understand them is to determine the composition of each, that is, to catalog their strategies.

Incumbency Style

Incumbency campaigning in the United States is almost as old as incumbents,* and its various strategies have been used by almost all who have sought election to any level of government.

---

*George Washington, the first presidential incumbent, was unopposed in the election of 1792.

Given its longevity and frequent use, one might assume it would have been defined long ago and its characteristics carefully delineated. While that is not the case, incumbency has been considered a "symbolic resource"[27] and the "Rose Garden Strategy."[28] Although each idea is useful in attempting to understand what it is that candidates do and say when they appear to be "running as an incumbent," each is nonetheless incomplete. Incumbency campaigning is a blend of both symbolic and pragmatic communication strategies designed to make any candidate appear as both good enough for the office sought and possessing the office (an assumed incumbency stance). This is not an easy task. We know that image creation and maintenance take significant amounts of skill, time, and money. But developing a credible incumbency style is well worth the effort. The results of countless elections indicate that incumbents tend to win. For example, during the twentieth century, only four presidents have lost their reelection bids, and congressional incumbents, especially those in the House of Representatives, almost always defeat their challengers. In 1990 only 16 incumbent congressmen of the over 400 who stood for reelection, about 4 percent, lost. Moreover, 74 of the House incumbents ran unopposed. Given this kind of success, it is not surprising that political scientist R. F. Fenno has suggested that incumbency is "a resource to be employed, an opportunity to be exploited."[29]

With this understanding, we now consider the specific strategies that candidates employ when they seek the advantages of incumbency. The first 4 are symbolic in nature and the remaining 11 are pragmatic or instrumental.

In exploring the symbolic characteristics of incumbency campaigning, we are, in essence, discussing presidential candidates because there is no other elective office for which the public has the same kind of feelings. In one sense the presidency can be thought of as a focus of impressions and beliefs that exist in our mind—a kind of "collage of images, hopes, habits, and intentions shared by the nation who legitimizes the office and reacts to its occupants."[30] Viewed from a related perspective, when we speak of the presidency, we are dealing with the myth of the office, the image we have possessed since childhood of the one institution that stands for truth, honor, justice, and integrity. We have a conception of an individual and an office that in ennobling each other, ennoble us. Perhaps Theodore White described it best when he wrote:

Somewhere in American life there is at least one man who stands for law, the President. That faith surmounts all daily cynicism, all evidence or suspicion of wrong-doing by lesser leaders, all corruptions, all vulgarities, all the ugly compromises of daily striving and ambition. That faith holds that all men are created equal before the law and protected by it; and that no matter how the faith may be betrayed elsewhere, at one particular point—the Presidency—justice will be done beyond prejudice, beyond rancor, beyond the possibilities of a fix.[31]

People may debate the character, quality, and personality of the men who have filled the office, and public opinion polls may indicate dissatisfaction with the performance of an incumbent, but the presidency is, for most citizens, an idealized institution, headed by a single visible individual through whom it is possible to grasp a "cognitive handle" or an understanding of "political goings on."[32]

In this context, then, the identity of a particular president is irrelevant; the concern is the office itself and the symbolic role it can play in a campaign.

Symbolic Trappings of the Office

The first strategy is the use of symbolic trappings to transmit the absolute strength and importance of the office. The presidency stands for power, and therefore incumbents take on the persona of the powerful. They are surrounded by large numbers of carefully trained and "important looking" bodyguards who appear to anticipate their every move; their song (played when they enter or leave a public ceremony) is "Hail to the Chief"; incumbents are addressed by title, never by name; when they travel a whole contingent of secret service, media reporters, technicians, and lesser governmental officials accompany them in a caravan of planes and limousines; their home, although the property of "the people," is heavily guarded and off-limits to all who have no official business to conduct with them or their staff; incumbents can be in instant communication with the leader of any other country of the world; they serve as commander in chief of all armed services; incumbents can command nationwide media time; and they are always close to a small black bag, the contents of which provide them the capability to blow up the world.

Thus it is little wonder that those who have campaigned against a president have objected to the continual and conscious use of devices that remind voters that they are seeing and hearing "the president," as opposed to "just another politician." For example, during the 1984 campaign President Ronald Reagan changed the location of his televised press conferences. He stood before an open doorway in the East Room of the White House that reveals a long, elegant corridor. The cameras recorded a majestic setting and a stately exit that dramatized the importance of the office, and served to remind the audience that they were listening to the president of the United States.

Legitimacy of the Office

The second strategy involves not so much what incumbents do, that is, the use of specific tangible symbols to remind voters of their power, but an intangible tool that only they possess and about which their challengers cannot even object. The presidency stands for legitimacy, and therefore the person who holds the office is perceived as the natural and logical leader. In other words, no matter who the incumbent may be (or regardless of the incumbent's current rating in the public opinion polls), the president is accorded a kind of sociopolitical legitimacy—a public trust. As one theorist has argued, we place our faith and trust in the hands of our leaders because they project an image that seduces us into participating in the comforting illusion that through rigid adherence to the constituted ideals of the society they can guide us through whatever possible troubles the future might present.[33] Moreover, their position provides automatic legitimacy during a campaign, in that they, unlike any of their opponents, are, from the beginning, considered legitimate candidates for the job.

Competency and the Office

The third strategy is also an intangible tool that comes with the office. The presidency stands for competency and therefore the person who holds the office can easily convey that impression. To trust in the president's competence is to accept the incumbent as a symbol "that problems can be solved without a basic restructuring of social institutions and without the threat a radical reordering poses both to the contented and to the anxious."[34] In other words, when we attribute a sense of competency to the president, it provides us with reassurance that all can be right. We want to believe that the person who is president is capable (after all, we elected the president in the first place).

As a matter of fact, our feelings about the office itself are so strong that whatever a specific president has done with regard to individual issues, a large number of people will always be supportive. For example, each year since World War II, every president has been ranked by U.S. citizens as one of the ten most admired persons in the world.[35] Perhaps a reason for this is, as Murray Edelman suggests, that "public issues fade from attention after a period in the limelight even when they are not 'solved' because they cannot remain dramatic and exciting for long and the media then have economic and psychological reasons to soft-pedal them."[36]

For whatever reasons or in whatever manner goodwill is retained, our point is simply that any president possesses a sense of competency that none of their rivals can share. It is, of course, a distinct advantage of the office.

Charisma and the Office

The finally symbolic strategy, like the first three, is dependent on the ability of the office to transfer its persona to the incumbent. However, this one is not an intangible resource in that it has had deliberate use since presidents began barnstorming the country for their own elections. The presidency stands for excitement, a kind of patriotic glamor, and therefore the person who holds the office takes on these characteristics. In no other way is the mystique of the presidency more visible than it is during a presidential campaign visit almost anywhere in the country. When the president comes to town (advance and security personnel have already been there for at least a week), roads are blocked, airports are closed, children are dismissed from school, bands play, television cameras and reporters are everywhere, hundreds or thousands of people converge along the streets or at the airport to greet the president; the very sight of the magnificent *Air Force I* produces a sense of awe, and for a while, we are participants in a warm and patriotic festival. It matters little whether or not we plan to vote for the incumbent; regardless of how dull and unimaginative the president may have been before living in the White House, once there, the office itself envelops the president in its aura or charisma.

Although campaign tours were not undertaken by incumbents (at least during the election period) until Herbert Hoover paved the way, their symbolic power has not been lost on any of the presidents who have succeeded him. The reasons for their trips have been as varied as have been their modes of transportation. For example, in 1948 Harry Truman whistle-stopped his way across 32,000 miles to blame what he termed the "do-nothing, good-for-nothing 80th Congress" for the nation's problems; in 1956 Dwight Eisenhower, in spite of two international crises, felt he had to undertake an extensive tour through the southern states to blunt his opponent's charges that he was too old and too sick to be president; in 1964 Lyndon Johnson barnstormed his way across the country, in part because he felt a psychological need to be "out with the people" and experience their warmth and acceptance of him; in 1980 Jimmy Carter boarded the Delta Queen and traveled the Ohio and Mississippi rivers, campaigning at each stop, in an almost frantic effort to restore his popularity with voters; and in 1984 Ronald Reagan whistle-stopped through several states riding the same presidential caboose Harry Truman rode in 1948. In Ohio, 80,000 people turned out to hear Reagan say that Truman was the last Democrat he voted for because unlike Walter Mondale, he did not intend to raise taxes. For the most part, other incumbents have used campaign trips for the same reasons. They have known that the glamor and excitement, the drama and pageantry of a presidential visit will, even if just for a short time, transfer the charisma of the office to them. As such, the trips are well worth the effort.

In turning to the pragmatic strategies of incumbency, it is important to note that they are more universal than are their symbolic counterparts because they can be and have been employed by candidates who are neither presidents or, in some cases, even incumbents. Certainly, there are those strategies which depend on the legitimate power that holding an office provides, but others have been used by candidates who only borrow the mantle or style of the incumbent.

Strategies that are examined in this section are:

1. Creating pseudoevents to attract and control media attention
2. Making appointments to state and federal jobs as well as appointments to state and national party committees
3. Creating special city, state, or national task forces to investigate areas of public concern
4. Appropriating federal funds/grants
5. Consulting or negotiating with world leaders
6. Manipulating the economy or other important domestic issues
7. Endorsements by party and other important leaders
8. Emphasizing accomplishments
9. Creating and maintaining an "above the political trenches" posture
10. Depending on surrogates for the campaign trail
11. Interpreting or intensifying a foreign policy problem so that it becomes an international crisis.

Creating pseudoevents. As the use of public relations experts and publicists has increased in political campaigns, so too has the frequency of hyped or manufactured news. Essentially, pseudoevents are defined as occurrences that differ from "real" events in that they are planned, planted, or incited for the primary purpose of being reported or reproduced.[37]

While all candidates use pseudoevents to try to capture media attention, incumbents have more success because they are in a better position to create them. For example, a governor or state senator may be featured on the evening television and radio news throughout the state because of an announced "major" initiative in attracting a specific corporation to the state and thus creating new jobs. A member of Congress may receive headlines from appointment to a special committee or commission created by the president. Moreover, incumbents have many opportunities for participation in ceremonious occasions—events that are sure to bring the local media. The ceremonies can be as different as the groundbreaking for a new government building to the announcement that a special day has been set aside to honor the city's firefighters. But each can be hyped up enough to guarantee publicity for the candidate. However, not only do incumbents have more opportunities to attract the attention of the media, they are better equipped to control the kind of coverage they receive. Perhaps a politician whose experience provides one of the best examples of what we mean is the ex-mayor of New York.

During his years as mayor, Edward I. Koch learned how to control the New York media. He was seen on television virtually every evening, most of the time it was as the leading participant in a special occasion or ceremony. (New York is a big city, and therefore many events can be important enough to make the mayor's attendance seem appropriate.) Equally important was the way in which Koch controlled the kind of coverage he received. During the 1985 Democratic mayoral primaries, the mayor's opponents issued frequent press statements attacking various administration programs. In response, Koch called press conferences on those days to announce new initiatives city government was taking in such areas as housing starts and education reforms, or even to announce park dedications. According to Koch, "My own comments were getting covered in long news stories, while the charges of my opponents were reduced to little metro briefs deep inside the paper. This is the power of incumbency."[38]

In short, incumbents such as Ed Koch have at their disposal the ability to create pseudoevents that not only guarantee media exposure but allow some measure of control over the coverage.

Making appointments to jobs and committees. One of the most common yet powerful incumbency strategies revolves around the ability to appoint personal or political friends—or potential friends—to local, state, and federal jobs or to give them key positions on party committees. Although patronage has been condemned by reformers in both political parties, it continues largely because it is so advantageous to everyone concerned. First, it allows candidates (and is not limited to incumbents in that all contenders can hold out the "promise" of appointment) to reward those who have helped them in the past. Second, it creates potential friends or at least puts people in a position of gratitude, and third, and undoubtedly most significant, it places supporters in key positions that may well be important in later stages of the campaign or even in subsequent elections. As such, few candidates, from county commissioner to governor to president, have failed to use this strategy.

Creating special task forces. Modern candidates understand the need to not only determine which issues are of concern to the voters in their city, district, or state but to speak to those concerns. One way to do this is to announce the formation of a special task force whose purpose is to investigate the issue/problem and make recommendations to the candidate regarding steps or actions to be taken in the future. The strategy is employed by incumbents as well as those who are not incumbents because the act of forming the task force is all that is really required to create the illusion that the candidate is concerned about the problem.

The primary advantage of the strategy is that the candidate is perceived as a person who understands and cares about those issues important to a particular constituency. However, a second benefit is that the candidate is in the position to postpone taking a stand on a controversial issue—one that might create as many enemies as supporters. Thus every election year seems to bring a plethora of specially created task forces composed of concerned community/state/national citizens who investigate topics as varied as mental health facilities and taxes for a new sewer system.

Appropriating funds/grants. Absolutely no incumbency strategy is less subtle or more powerful than appropriating special grants to "cooperative" (politically supportive) public officials for their cities and states. It is reserved only for incumbents (in that the strategy does not include promises for the future) and is viewed best at the presidential level, although it is certainly done at state and local levels as well.

Although every modern president since Franklin Roosevelt has had a prodigious amount of discretionary money to distribute in the form of federal grants, by the election of 1980 the amount totaled $80 billion. Like his predecessors, Jimmy Carter was determined to use it to aid him in the primaries—especially the early contests when the campaign of Edward Kennedy was still viewed as a threat. The money was employed to reward those public officials who announced their preference for the president, to gain a public endorsement where there had not been one, or to punish those who denied or withdrew support. For example, prior to the Illinois primary, Jane Byrne, mayor of Chicago, was told by the White House that U.S. Air Force facilities at O'Hare Field would be relocated to allow Chicago to expand its major airport. However, after the mayor announced her support of Senator Kennedy over the president, the secretary of transportation said that the cabinet had "lost confidence in Mayor Byrne, and would look for opportunities to deny transportation funds to Chicago and its mayor."[39]

Thus the Carter White House went into the 1980 campaign determined to "grease" its way through the primaries. Florida (in advance of the Democratic straw primary) received a $1.1 billion loan guarantee to an electric cooperative, $29.9 billion in grants for public housing in various counties, and $31 million for housing projects for the elderly throughout the state. Prior to its primary, New Hampshire received funds for such projects as a four-lane highway from Manchester to Portsmouth and a special commuter train from Concord to Boston.[40]

Is the appropriation of funds a successful incumbency strategy? While it is impossible to claim the effect of any one element in a phenomenon as complex as a primary election, the president soundly defeated Kennedy in New Hampshire and virtually annihilated him in the Florida and Illinois primaries.

Consultation with world leaders. While at first glance consultation with world leaders may appear to be a strategy possible for only presidential incumbents, the fact is that this strategy is employed by any number of governors and members of Congress as they attempt to build their credentials for reelection. Governors extend invitations to athletic teams or artists and may even negotiate with foreign business corporations and governments about the prospect of building a major factory in the state. Members of Congress take frequent junkets overseas in the effort to illustrate their power and importance to voters in their districts or states.

In addition to its use by incumbents, the strategy is employed by challengers who must also build credentials and convey a sense of their individual importance. Moreover, its use may be even more crucial for them because they do not possess the real authority or power of the incumbent. Thus a meeting with foreign governmental leaders grants at least a sense of legitimacy because it illustrates acknowledgement and a kind of acceptance into an important and official group of leaders.

While significant to congressional and gubernatorial candidates, a trip to Europe—better yet, the Soviet Union, China, or the Middle East—is virtually a prerequisite for potential presidential contenders, particularly those whose previous experiences have not included "official" foreign travel and consultation with government officials. At the very least, it allows them to work their trips into their discourse with such phrases as, "In my meeting with the prime minister, I was told that . . . " But even more important, the strategy provides those candidates who have absolutely no foreign policy experience the appearance of being a part of or involved in international affairs. As such, it is a useful strategy of the incumbency style.

Manipulation of important domestic issues. As a number of these strategies illustrate, incumbents have considerable power, which is, of course, one of the reasons they are difficult to defeat and challengers are so eager to assume their campaign style. However, the manipulation or management of important issues is one strategy that can be assumed only by the incumbent.

For example, throughout the years the economy has been a primary area of presidential management. One way this has been done is timing economic benefits to specific groups within the electorate to ensure their vote in the election. Political scientist Frank Kessler has pointed to the following Social Security incident during the 1972 presidential campaign as a case in point:

Checks went out in October 1972, one month before the elections, with the following memo enclosed and personally approved by President Nixon to each of the 24.7 million Social Security recipients: "Your social security payment has been increased by 20% starting with this month's check by a new statute enacted by Congress and signed into law by President Richard Nixon on July 1, 1972. The President also signed into a law a provision which will allow your social security benefits to increase automatically as the cost of living goes up."[41]

In using this strategy, presidents have not limited themselves to economic manipulation; other issues have been managed. For example, as Ronald Reagan's administration prepared for the 1982 congressional election, the president's Council on Environmental Quality prepared a report documenting improved air quality in 20 to 40 cities across the country. The report was prepared in the hope that it could refute environmentalists' charges by showing that although the administration had reduced the influence and number of personnel in the Environmental Protection Agency, air quality had not been adversely affected.

Thus the manipulation or management of important domestic issues is yet another strategy of incumbency.

Endorsements by other leaders. Although the growth of primaries has reduced their importance, endorsements are an attempt to identify and link the candidate with already established, highly respected, and generally acknowledged leaders. The idea is that endorsement by respected leaders signifies that the candidate is already part of their group and should therefore also be thought of as a leader; in other words, credibility by association. Obviously, this perception can be crucial for a nonincumbent who wishes to adopt the incumbency style. It is, of course, equally significant for the incumbent because continued acceptance by other governmental or political leaders is one way of advancing the perception of a successful term of office. Similarly, candidates hope they receive no endorsements from individuals or groups who are not perceived positively by large segments of society because negative association is also possible. For example, during the 1960 presidential campaign, Richard Nixon was endorsed by the president of the Teamsters Union, Jimmy Hoffa. Because Hoffa was already thought of as a "racketeer" or worse by many citizens, it was an endorsement that Nixon tried to ignore. When reporters questioned John Kennedy about his reaction to Hoffa's endorsement of Nixon rather than himself, Kennedy responded humorously that he guessed he was just lucky, which of course reinforces our point.

Emphasizing accomplishments. One of those strategies forming the core of the incumbency style is emphasizing accomplishments. Candidates must be able to demonstrate tangible accomplishments during their term of office if they are incumbents or in some related aspect of public service if they only assume the style. This is, of course, the reason that incumbents go to great lengths to list for voters all that they have done while in office. Thus the strategy is simple as long as the deeds exist. The difficulty occurs when there have been few accomplishments or when major problems have arisen that overshadow positive contributions (taxes are higher than they were before the incumbent took office, inflation is worse, unemployment has not been reduced). When this happens, the strategy becomes more complex in that the incumbent must either deny that the current problems are important ones (normally an impossible task for even the most persuasive) or blame them on someone else—even on uncontrollable forces. Blaming someone, scapegoating, is the path normally chosen. Examples are as numerous as candidates. State legislators blame the governor, governors blame the federal government (especially Congress), presidents blame Congress, and, surprisingly enough, members of Congress often blame other Congress members.

The practice of casting blame elsewhere is certainly not a new variation of the accomplishment strategy. However, its most interesting use is by members of Congress, especially those in the House.

Popular perceptions of Congress are not high. For example, in 1976 one public opinion poll revealed that citizens believed that Congress ranked low in ethics (of ten groups scaled, only corporation executives and labor leaders ranked lower), and in 1978 the results of another survey indicated that only 10 percent of the public had "a great deal of confidence" in the institution.[42] In 1984 one opinion poll revealed that 63 percent of the citizens did not trust the government to do what is right, and 40 percent believed politicians did not care what the people think.[43] However, despite these feelings, congressional incumbents win the overwhelming majority of their elections. One of the reasons for this paradox is that when individual representatives seek reelection, they disassociate themselves or even "run against" the institution of which they are a member. They talk about their accomplishments rather than those of Congress, and as two political communication scholars have noted, they play up the negative "myths" (Congress is a kind of shadow process in which sinister figures operate) while projecting themselves as hardworking and honest people who work against evil.[44] In this way, then, even when genuine accomplishments may be few, scapegoating makes the strategy possible.

Above the political trenches image. Another strategy that is at the center of incumbency style is the technique in which candidates try to create the image that they are somehow removed from politics. Essentially, the strategy is composed of any combination of the following three tactics (each designed to create the impression that the contender is a statesman rather than a politician):

1. Appear to be aloof from the hurly-burly of political battle—that the office has sought them and thus they run because of a sense of love of country and duty
2. Failure to publicly acknowledge the existence of any opponent—candidates may have opponents, but statesmen do not
3. Sustain political silence (absolutely refrain from any personal campaign trips or confrontations with opponents, including not answering any charges or attacks or discussing partisan issues).[45]

While portions of the strategy are used by contemporary candidates, it has been around for a long time. As a matter of fact, its progenitor was George Washington. He did not have to create a nonpolitical or statesman image because he was not a politician. He had been reluctant to become president and, once there, never campaigned for reelection. In spite of this, for candidates who were to follow (at least presidential candidates), he bequeathed a legacy of "being above politics," in a sense, conveying the attitude that being political would somehow "dirty" the office. Thus, for many years, the public picked presidents without ever seeing or hearing what their ideas or policies were—at least during the time in which they were candidates. With only two exceptions,* no major party candidates, even after formal nomination, personally solicited votes. They were not expected to (even after transportation networks improved) because the prevailing attitude was that the office must seek the person; that is, the appearance of modest reluctance—of being above politics—had to be maintained. Stephen Douglas was the first to break the taboo in 1860 when he shocked people with speaking tours on behalf of his own candidacy. Although other Democratic candidates followed his example, none were successful until Woodrow Wilson was elected in 1912. Republicans remembered Washington's example longer and eschewed mass campaigning until the 1932 campaign when an incumbent was faced with a problem of such magnitude that he felt he had to travel the country explaining why he should not be blamed for the Great Depression.

Thus this strategy has a long history, and its use, in combination with the next two strategies, continues to play a central role in the development and maintenance of incumbency style.

---

*William Henry Harrison in 1840 and General Winfield Scott in 1852 made, at the insistence of their managers, some speeches on their own behalf.

Use of surrogates on the campaign trail. This strategy is closely related to the last one in that it is possible for candidates to assume an above-politics posture because others are overtly campaigning for them while they stay home being nonpolitical. While the strategy is employed by a wide spectrum of candidates, it is the sophisticated use by presidential incumbents during the 1970s and 1980s that allows us to see most clearly the technique at work. For example, in 1972 Richard Nixon depended on the campaign tours of over 49 surrogates (including members of his family, cabinet officers, and other high-level government officials) while he stayed in the White House during most of the fall campaign against George McGovern. As a matter of fact, Nixon was so intent on creating the illusion of a hardworking, nonpolitical statesman that not only did he rarely take a political trip or make a speech in his own behalf, but when asked once by a reporter about his campaign, he cut off questioning with the remark, "Let the political people talk on that."[46]

The use of surrogates did not end with Richard Nixon's election. As a matter of fact, it became more pronounced, especially when the media dubbed it the "Rose Garden" strategy during the stay-at-home period of Gerald Ford's campaign in 1976. What they meant was that for weeks on end, as part of a specifically designed plan, Ford did not leave the White House to campaign for his reelection. Members of his family, his cabinet, and hundreds of Republican party faithful were out on the hustings for him as he stayed close to the White House and acted "presidential." In addition, as part of the plan, the media were alerted several times each day to witness pseudoevents (the president's welcome to visiting dignitaries or his signature on legislation), most of which occurred in the area adjacent to the Oval Office, the Rose Garden (thus the name). During the midterm elections of 1982, the Republican National Committee developed a program called "Surrogate 82" in which all cabinet members were required to devote 15 days to campaign activities.[47] But what is most interesting about surrogates and rose gardens is that the strategy is a direct descendant of the "Front Porch" campaigns used by Republicans many years earlier.

In 1888 the grandson of "Old Tippecanoe," Benjamin Harrison, was the Republican candidate for president. The party believed it had lost the 1884 election because of the mistakes their candidate made. Therefore, it was decided that Harrison would campaign from his home in Indianapolis against the Democratic incumbent, giving rehearsed and dignified speeches to delegations of visitors who were invited to hear him speak while other party leaders toured the country on his behalf. In other words, the challenger would not only appear presidential, he would have little opportunity to err. Thus, when Harrison won, the Front Porch or Rose Garden strategy was born.

As is the case with most campaign strategies, success means repetition. So in 1896 Republicans went back to the porch with a new candidate and increased zest for a campaign style that was in stark contrast to the "swing around the circle" effort of the Democrats.

Although William McKinley never left his porch in Canton, Ohio, he nonetheless was part of a far more vigorous campaign to return the White House to the Republicans than had been conducted for Harrison. Hundreds of visiting delegations were invited to visit his home and hear him speak. He gave as many as 12 carefully prepared speeches a day (each on a single issue specifically directed to the interests of the delegation), and copies were supplied to all major papers. Thus, while remaining at home, McKinley received daily nationwide press coverage—more, in fact, than did his opponent. In addition, 1,400 surrogates were sent out from party campaign headquarters to speak for him all across the country. With all this effort, McKinley defeated William Jennings Bryan.

In part because of their victories the first two times, Republicans returned to the porch for the 1920 election. While the Democratic candidate toured the country, the Republican managers sat Warren G. Harding on the front porch in Marion, Ohio (where day after day he delivered quiet and dignified platitudes about common sense and clean living) and then supplemented the porch performances with touring surrogates. Once again, the strategy worked as Democratic contender James Cox lost in the worst defeat a presidential candidate had known.

With this kind of success, it should now be easy to understand why front porches (currently called rose gardens) and surrogates have remained popular with modern presidential candidates.

Interpreting or intensifying foreign policy problems into international crises. Although variations of the strategy of interpreting or intensifying foreign policy problems into international crises are employed by incumbents at all levels, it is most completely studied as it has been used by presidents. Its purpose is simple: to create enough of a crisis situation so that voters (either because of patriotism or not wanting to change leaders at the time of an emergency) will be motivated to rally around the president. There have been many instances when the technique has been successful. In 1916 and again in 1940, presidents Woodrow Wilson and Franklin Roosevelt campaigned with the specter of war in Europe in the minds of the electorate. In 1964 when U.S. ships in the Gulf of Tonkin were fired upon, President Lyndon Johnson interrupted his "campaigning" to go on television where he pledged that the United States would take rigorous defensive measures. In 1975 when a U.S. merchant ship, the *Mayaguez*, was captured by Cambodian forces, President Gerald Ford (who was about to make official his bid for reelection) used the situation to build his leadership or command credentials by ordering marines to bomb Cambodia until the *Mayaguez* crew was released. However, one of the most adept uses of the strategy occurred in the surfacing and primary stages of the 1980 campaign when President Jimmy Carter (who had two genuine foreign policy problems with the seizure of the U.S. embassy in Iran and the Soviet advances into Afghanistan) combined the use of surrogates, a nonpolitical image, and international crises to promote his renomination campaign.

Prior to the Iowa caucus and continuing through the Maine and New Hampshire primaries, Carter pledged that he would not personally campaign until the hostages in Tehran were released. Later, when the Soviets marched into Afghanistan, the president reinforced his earlier vow when he announced that because "this is the most serious crisis since the last World War," he would be unable to leave the White House to campaign in person for reelection. In addition, when other candidates (notably Senator Edward Kennedy and Governor Jerry Brown) questioned the administration's handling of the "crisis," the president completed the strategy by suggesting that attacks on his policy were "damaging to our country and to the establishment of our principles and the maintenance of them, and the achievements of our goals to keep the peace and to get our hostages released."[48]

Until the very last round of the primaries, the president stuck to his pledge. He emerged only rarely from the White House or Camp David and left most comments on politics to his surrogates. Carter's use of incumbency strategies was eminently successful. While giving the appearance that he was too busy trying to solve the international crises to campaign for reelection, he was defeating his opponents in the Democratic primary elections.

These then are the strategies that comprise the incumbency style. There are, as we have seen, a large number of them—each somewhat different from, although often dependent on, the others and each potentially effective in the hands of candidates who understand and appreciate their power. Perhaps what is most startling about them is the extent to which they work. Normally, it takes enormous amounts of money, organization, and skill to defeat even somewhat inept incumbents. They have at their command not only the strategies we have examined, but whatever privileges the office itself provides—including public awareness (visibility) and the opportunity to perform various popular and noncontroversial services for constituents. These strategies have repeatedly enabled incumbents to overwhelmingly win reelections and win by larger margins than victorious nonincumbents. As we have said before, given all of the benefits, it is no wonder that candidates who are not incumbents often assume elements of the style.

But under what conditions can incumbents lose? In other words, are there burdens of the style as well as benefits? It seems to us that there are at least four major disadvantages of incumbency campaigning. First, and maybe most important, incumbents must run (at least in part) on their record. While they may cast blame elsewhere or minimize the scope or significance of problem areas within their administration, an effective challenger can make certain that the record of the incumbent (and short-comings can be found in virtually all records) forms the core of the campaign rhetoric. The incumbent can be kept in a position of having to defend, justify, explain—answering rather than charging, defending rather than attacking. Being forced to run on one's record can be a severe handicap, particularly in the hands of a skilled challenger.

The second and related burden faced by many incumbents is simply that the public may blame them for all problems—whether or not they were at fault. Incumbents are in the public eye and if the city sanitation workers refuse to pick up the garbage for a week or if the public trans-portation system is shut down because of weather, an accident, or strik-ing employees, they are held accountable. At the very least the question of competency or job effectiveness is raised in the public mind, waiting perhaps for the skilled challenger to capitalize on it.

The third disadvantage, although quite different from the first two, can be equally troublesome. The challenger is free to campaign, but incumbents must at least give the appearance of doing the job for which they have been elected. As campaign seasons become longer, this be-comes more difficult. Incumbents often find it unnerving to go about the day-to-day task of administering a city, state, or nation while their opponents spend countless hours out on the hustings—garnering media attention with attacks against them and their policies. If they respond by indulging in overt campaigning, they are criticized for not doing their job. If they ignore it, they may well be accused of having no defense and being afraid to go out and face voters. In other words, it is a real damned if you do and damned if you don't situation.

Finally, because incumbents are at the center of media/public attention far more than their opponents, expectations are great regarding their "front-runner" status. If those expectations are not met, the incumbent is in trouble. Nowhere has this been more thoroughly illustrated than in presidential primary campaigns. Even when incumbents win, if they fail to meet some preconceived percentage set by the media or even by their own staffs, they have, at least in terms of media publicity, lost.

Thus there are some burdens. Even the incumbency style does not guarantee election. With this in mind, we will now contrast the strategies of the incumbent style with those of the challenger, knowing that in each there are burdens as well as benefits.

Challenger Style

Challenger campaigning is not easy because the style demands a two-step process, the implementation of which requires not only a good deal of deliberate planning but equal portions of skill and even luck. The style can be defined as a series of communication strategies designed to persuade voters that change is needed and that the challenger is the best person to bring about the change. While the kind of change can vary all the way from shifts in a whole economic system to personality characteristics desired in the officeholder, challengers must convince the electorate that some kind of alteration is necessary if they stand any chance for success. However, the second part of the process is equally important; the voters must also be persuaded that the challenger is the candidate most likely to produce more desirable conditions or policies. Therefore, the complexity of the style is increased because not only must those who challenge call for change, they must simultaneously demonstrate their own capability in bringing about that change. As if all of this was not difficult enough, it is entirely possible that the success of the challenger may ultimately depend on the skill of the incumbent— whether or not the incumbent makes a major mistake in campaign strategy or becomes a victim of prevailing conditions. Thus it is no understatement to maintain that the task facing most challengers is formidable.

In spite of the potential hazards or burdens, advocating change—the challenger campaign style—is not new. As a matter of fact, it probably got its start in the presidential campaign of 1800 when Jeffersonians distributed leaflets that asked: "Is it not time for a change?" Whenever it began, it has been used by many candidates who have sought elective office. Moreover, elements of the style have even been employed by incumbents such as Harry Truman and Gerald Ford who felt it would be more beneficial to their candidacies to call for a change in Congress rather than only try to explain the present problems.

The strategies examined in this section include:

1. Attacking the record of opponents
2. Taking the offensive position on issues
3. Calling for a change
4. Emphasizing optimism for the future
5. Speaking to traditional values rather than calling for value changes
6. Appearing to represent the philosophical center of the political party
7. Delegating personal or harsh attacks in an effort to control demagogic rhetoric.

Attacking the record. Just as running on the record of their accomplishments is a central strategy of incumbency, so too is attacking that same record a prime characteristic of the challenger style. As a matter of fact, the ability to criticize freely (and often in exaggerated terms) may well be one of the most important benefits the challenger possesses.[49]

When there is no incumbent, candidates attack the record of the current administration (if they do not represent the same political party) or even an opponent's record in a previous position. Whatever becomes the focus of criticism, the object is to attack—to create doubt in voters' minds regarding the incumbent's/opponent's ability—to stimulate public awareness of any problems that exist, or to foster a sense of dissatisfaction and even unhappiness with the state of affairs generally.

In addition, a few challengers extend the attack strategy to demand publicly an investigation of some aspect of the incumbent's record or administration. This was the case, for example, during the 1989 Democratic mayoral primaries in New York. Ed Koch's challengers demanded that his record be investigated because of charges of widespread corruption during his tenure—charges and evidence of bribery and extortion that engulfed the mayor's most powerful allies and a few of his closest friends. Whether or not investigations such as these ever take place is almost unimportant. The tactic is to call attention to some alleged problem or instance of wrongdoing within the incumbent's administration and thus imply, at least indirectly, that the incumbent has some serious difficulties and therefore does not deserve another term.

Interestingly, attack is so much a part of challenger style that it frequently occurs even when the predominant public perception of the incumbent is that a credible job has been done. In this instance, the challengers may minimize the importance of the accomplishments, credit them to someone or something else (often another branch or level of government that happens to be controlled by their own party), never mention the accomplishments, or point out that in the years ahead accomplishments will be viewed as problems. However various challengers go about it, their ability to attack existing records or policies is a crucial tool and integral to the overall style.

Taking the offensive position on issues. Essentially, the strategy involves nothing more than taking the offensive position on issues important to the campaign—probing, questioning, challenging, attacking, but never presenting concrete solutions for problems. It is the incumbent who has to defend unworkable solutions to insolvable problems; the challenger can limit rhetoric to developing problems, keeping the incumbent in a position where all actions have to be defended.[50] In a sense, it is part of a challenger's expected role—to criticize, attack, point out needs—generally guiding voters to begin thinking that the incumbent has been ineffective. Challengers are not expected to solve problems (they have had no chance as officeholders to do so). This is, of course, a major advantage (one of the relatively few), and those who abandon it often lose the election. As a matter of fact, the more detailed challengers become in offering solutions, the more material they provide to be attacked themselves. In other words, when they drop the offensive, they have essentially traded places with incumbents, thus compounding their difficulties because unlike incumbents they lack the tools to solve problems. Thus the strategy is simply to talk about what is wrong without suggesting any precise ways in which conditions can be righted.

History is replete with examples of successful challengers who used this strategy and won. In 1932 Franklin Roosevelt never divulged the contents of his "New Deal"; in 1952 Dwight Eisenhower never suggested how he would deal with the Korean conflict except to promise that he would personally go there and look it over; in 1960 John Kennedy never shared the details of the "New Frontier"; in 1968 Richard Nixon only said he had a plan regarding the war in Vietnam but never provided any clues regarding it; in 1976 Jimmy Carter seldom offered solutions more substantive than his love and admiration for the people; and in 1980 Ronald Reagan never explained just how his supply-side economics would do all he claimed for it. In retrospect, it is unlikely that most of these challengers even knew how they might solve all of the problems they discussed once they were elected. Whether they did or not, solutions were not offered, and the candidates managed to keep their offensive position on the issues while forcing their opponents to defend, justify, and offer plans.

Conversely, in 1964 and again in 1972, two challengers never seemed to understand the essential nature of the strategy. Barry Goldwater and George McGovern thought they had to present specific proposals on topics as varied as welfare and the way to fight wars. As the details of their plans became known, they were subjected to intensive analysis, debated, refuted by opponents and media, and finally rejected as absurd. Goldwater and McGovern not only lost their credibility as serious presidential candidates, they lost an important advantage. Taking and keeping the right to attack without proposing solutions is a major challenger strategy that only the foolish abandon.

Calling for a change. From the beginning of each campaign season, it becomes clear that many candidates announce that they are "willing" to run for office because they believe that a change is necessary. Whether it involves specific programs and policies, philosophical assumptions regarding the nature of government, or even modification in administrative style, calling for a change has become the dominant characteristic of those who challenge.

There are various ways in which the strategy has been employed. For example, John Kennedy talked about the need to "get the country moving again"—a stylistic and substantive change from a passive attitude to aggressive, take-charge action. Jimmy Carter urged a moralistic change—a return to honest, decent, and compassionate government. Ronald Reagan argued for economic as well as philosophical change, while Edward Kennedy gave, as his only reason for an intraparty challenge, the need for a change in the manner and style of presidential leadership. Perhaps one of the most specific uses of the strategy was exemplified by Senator John Glenn, who in the early months of the surfacing stage of the 1984 presidential campaign, called for a change of direction in budgeting for basic research and technological development as well as a dramatic overhaul of the Social Security system. Conversely, the failure of Michael Dukakis to call for a change in 1988 was one of the reasons for his defeat. According to John Sasso, the chief strategist for Dukakis's presidential campaign, "the failure to establish a clear campaign theme and a compelling case for political change" was a mistake on their part.[51]

Thus regardless of how it is employed, the essence of challenger style must revolve around seeking change. If a change from existing conditions, incumbents, or administrations is unnecessary, then so too are challengers.

Emphasizing optimism for the future. While most candidates, regardless of the level of office sought, traditionally spend some time during their campaign talking about their vision or their optimism for the future, the strategy is particularly important for those who would challenge the status quo. After all, if existing conditions are so bad, can they ever be better? Thus the task of the challenger is not only to attack but to hold out the promise of a better tomorrow—a day when wrongs will be righted, when justice will prevail, and when health, wealth, and happiness will be more than just vague illusions. In other words, challengers must assume a "rhetoric of optimism" as opposed to a "rhetoric of despair."[52]

This is not to suggest that candidates who employ the strategy dismiss the nation's needs from their discourse; rather, it is a question of emphasis. For example, in 1932 Franklin Roosevelt obviously acknowledged the problems created by the severe economic depression, but the central focus of his campaign was hope for the future. John Kennedy talked about problems, but his emphasis was on the country's potential to get moving again; Ronald Reagan pledged that he would lead a crusade to make the United States great again; and the commitment of George Bush to the spirit of volunteerism as a substitute for federal government programs was embodied in the phrases first used in his nomination acceptance speech "kinder-gentler nation" and "a thousand points of light." In short, a part of the challenger style is reliance on the positive— emphasizing hope and faith in the future, an optimism that the nation's tomorrow will, in fact, be better than today.

Speaking to traditional values. Even though the overall challenger style is dominated by a call for redirection or change, it does not mean a redefinition of values. In fact, it is just the opposite. Successful challengers must reinforce majority values instead of attempting to forge new ones. In other words, they must have some understanding of the way in which people view themselves and their society—some understanding of the current tenets of the American Dream.

While this strategy has been understood by challengers such as Richard Nixon, Jimmy Carter, Ronald Reagan, and George Bush, it may be more interesting to explain it by the example of one who did not. In 1972 before suffering the worst defeat in the history of presidential politics, Democratic challenger George McGovern seemed to have little comprehension of what most citizens wanted. He talked about massive or radical changes in welfare and tax reform, military spending and inflation, school busing, amnesty for those who had left the country rather than participate in the Vietnam War, and the need for more civil rights legislation. What McGovern failed to understand was that most citizens "were tired of social reforms, tired of the 'good-cause' people; that the majority preferred to live their own lives privately, unplagued by moralities, or war, or riots, or violence."[53] Middle-class citizens viewed McGovern as a candidate of an elitist upper class whose values they did not understand except to know that they angered and frightened them. Through his failure to speak to the dreams or visions of the electorate, McGovern abandoned an important strategy of the challenger style.

Appearing to represent the philosophical center. Throughout our political history, successful challengers have been ideological representatives from the mainstream of the major parties, or they have tried to appear as though they were. While some may have been, on one or two issues, a bit to the right or left of the majority of the party, they have not been representatives of the outer or fringe groups. In most campaigns, the fringe groups eventually have compromised and supported their party's candidate, even though that candidate may have been more conservative or liberal than they would have preferred. In the presidential campaign of 1980 and even in 1984, Ronald Reagan, who had long been the champion of the ultraconservatives within the GOP, attempted to position himself closer to the ideological Republican middle once he had secured the nomination. In 1988 George Bush used the same strategy by repositioning himself on such issues as abortion.

The only two major exceptions in contemporary presidential politics have been Barry Goldwater and George McGovern, each of whom, as the candidate of fringe groups, did not try to reposition himself in the center of his respective party. Instead, each attempted to reform the ideological majority around the ideological minority. In so doing, they failed to employ a traditional challenger strategy.

While Goldwater and McGovern did not attempt to occupy a more central ideological ground, two nominees during the 1980s were blocked from using the strategy by their opponents. In 1984 Ronald Reagan was able to position Walter Mondale as a candidate of the Democratic fringe because of the former vice-president's stand on increased taxes, social welfare issues, defense spending and because of the endorsement of him by groups such as the National Organization of Women and the Gay Liberation Movement. Similarly, in 1988 George Bush, who for much of his political career had been perceived by conservative Republicans as too liberal, repositioned himself in the center and branded Michael Dukakis as a liberal even among Democrats. A liberal, according to the Bush definition, was someone who, like Governor Dukakis, was opposed to children saying the Pledge of Allegiance in school, was so soft on crime he let convicted murderers out of prison on weekend furloughs, and who did not support defense initiatives such as the MX missile. The label proved disastrous for Dukakis because the governor failed to reposition himself or to redefine the vice-president's interpretation of a liberal.

Delegating personal or harsh attacks. Although attack remains a central imperative of the challenger style, successful candidates (particularly in statewide or national races) do not themselves indulge in demagogic rhetoric. While smear tactics and political hatchet work have been a part of elective politics for years, wise challengers have left harsh or vitriolic language to running mates, surrogate speakers, or to their television advertising and printed materials. The reason for delegating this kind of attack is, at least in part, related to the symbolic nature of the campaign itself. As we have mentioned earlier, campaigns are a symbolic representation of what or how candidates might behave if elected—a kind of vignette from which voters are able to transfer campaign performance into performance as officeholders. Thus the challenger who likens the incumbent to Adolf Hitler, asserts that the president behaves like a reformed drunk, or argues that the incumbent is ignorant of foreign policy, as did George McGovern in 1972, Edward Kennedy in 1980, and Walter Mondale in 1984, is unwise.

Demagogy is never viewed as an asset and normally backfires for the challenger who employs it. In 1988 Michael Dukakis was attacked as being soft-on-defense, soft-on-crime, and soft-on-patriotism. However, George Bush was smart enough to leave direct attacks on his opponent to others and to his television advertising campaign.

These then are the strategies that comprise the challenger style. While there are fewer of them than there are incumbency strategies, they can also be powerful when used correctly. However, those who employ them, just as those who employ their counterparts, must understand the importance of image creation and maintenance. For example, it does little good if a candidate attacks the record of the incumbent but does so using demagogic language or leaves no outlet for the promise of a better tomorrow. In a similar manner, those who fail to understand the necessity of appearing to represent the values of the majority of the electorate as they call for a change in the course or direction of present policies will have little success. In short, challenger campaigning is difficult primarily because being a challenger is not nearly as advantageous as being an incumbent. Challengers win but not as often. Challengers have some advantages over incumbents but not very many. In the final analysis, challengers may be only as successful as incumbents are incompetent to employ the symbolic and pragmatic strategies their office provides.

Incumbent/Challenger: A Merger of Styles

As discussed earlier, the incumbent and challenger strategies are not absolute categories. Those candidates who are incumbents are not restricted to a specific set of incumbency strategies any more than challengers are confined to a particular set of challenger strategies. While the rhetoric of most candidates typically reflects their actual position in the race, there are instances wherein aspects of incumbency and challenger styles have been combined. It is not uncommon, for example, for challengers to assume the mantle of incumbency whenever and wherever possible; its advantages are well documented. Those who challenge must try to emphasize whatever accomplishments they have had in public life; must appear to be acquainted with other leaders; and they have a clear need to use whatever means are available to them to gain the attention of the media. Similarly, events may, from time to time, compel incumbents to borrow strategies more frequently associated with the challenger. While we consider it unlikely that any incumbent would ever find it advantageous to drop the symbolic strategies or to call for a change, an incumbent may well emphasize ideological centrality or rely on surrogate speakers for overt/direct personal attacks on opponents. Such rhetorical borrowing between categories, perhaps in response to changing conditions, is only part of what we mean by the incumbent/challenger style.

The most prominent characteristics of the combined style are abandonment of the essential purpose or thrust of incumbent or challenger rhetoric and abandonment of the responsibilities each has. If the challenger does not attack or at least question the policies and actions of the incumbent, no real campaign dialogue occurs. In a similar vein, if the incumbent will not acknowledge problems, defend current policies or programs, or even suggest/offer a future course of action, no real dialogue can occur. Perhaps the best way to understand the incumbent/challenger style is through an extended example from the 1984 presidential campaign.

In 1984 we had two challengers; one of whom was the president of the United States. Beginning with his nomination acceptance speech,

Ronald Reagan's rhetoric was heavily centered around two staples of the challenger style: attacking the policies of the opposition (in this case going back to the Carter-Mondale administration) while taking the offensive position on issues; and emphasizing optimism for the future. Incumbency strategies were used only to enhance his campaign as a challenger. While Reagan was not the first sitting president to try to campaign for reelection in this manner, he was the first one since Harry Truman to do so successfully.

Part of Reagan's success as an "incumbent challenger" was his ability to figuratively step out of office at crucial moments and reflect on problems—"posing as a commentator who happened to live on Pennsylvania Avenue"—never admitting that he, as the result of election, was currently more responsible than any other single individual for the federal government.[54] But there was another part to the strategy—painting the portrait of a future at once so uplifting and patriotic that all problems of the moment were dwarfed by it.

Americans are by nature optimists. We believe in people—especially heroes—and in happy endings. Successful candidates have long known that optimism is the way to the hearts of the American electorate. "At the worst of times, Franklin Roosevelt uplifted with a smile, while years later, Jimmy Carter guaranteed his fate by telling us that we were suffering from malaise."[55] What was so effective about Reagan's use of cheer was his own appearance of amiability, an understanding of the political fact that Americans want to hear good news as well as the way he managed to distance himself from responsibility when things went wrong. "It was as if he was a king who reigned but did not rule—a constitutional monarch whose performance was a symbol to his people while politicians did the dirty work of governing."[56] In 1984 he campaigned for reelection as a critic of federal budget deficits even while he had created the largest deficit in history.

In short, he offered voters—just as he had in 1980 when he had actually been a challenger—a picture of a future that did not include hard choices or sacrifices he might ask them to make after the election. However, a strategy of optimism is possible only if a candidate has managed to avoid the defensive position on issues. This was the second overt use of the challenger style employed by the incumbent president.

Throughout the campaign, it was as if there were two challengers—both attacking, probing, questioning, but the incumbent/challenger never defending his policies. In fact, by seizing the offensive on issues the president reduced his opponent to the most disadvantageous challenger posture, suggesting solutions for problems. Reagan did not have to make allowances for solving problems because he did not acknowledge the existence of problems. Unwilling to accept the issues presented by Mondale as problems, let alone acknowledging any responsibility for them, the president simply smiled and said that the trend is what was important and that things were getting better. When Mondale charged that the nuclear arms race had heated up between Washington and Moscow and that U.S.–Soviet relations were strained, the president responded by ignoring the issue and talked about America standing tall and looking to the 1980s with courage, confidence, and hope. Finally, in an absolute measure of desperation, Mondale outlined solutions—such as the inevitable raising of taxes to deal with the national deficit. When time after time Mondale tried to push Reagan on exactly what he was going to do about the deficit, the president only responded that it was a little scary to have a deficit of a $180 billion a year and that even if he had inherited the wreckage from the Democrats, he was willing to work with them to repair the problem.

From the beginning, it appeared that the challenger and the incumbent had reversed roles. The incumbent ran against "big spending demons in Washington," "puzzle-palaces on the Potomac" and whenever he left the White House, talked about what a pleasure it was to be out of Washington. The challenger sought to tie the incumbent to problems the country faced and when there was no response, created his own solutions. The Reagan staff had reasoned that it was unnecessary to speak to the specific issues raised by Mondale. They had determined before the campaign even began that the reelection effort would be concentrated on the president's leadership and the problems resulting from the Carter-Mondale past, without defending current programs or without proposing any new or specific programs for the future.[57] They believed their strategy would be successful because Reagan had been on the political stage for 30 years. His views were well known by the American people. As the press secretary for his reelection campaign, James Lake, said, "It would be foolish of us to let Ronald Reagan respond to Mr. Mondale . . . people don't care. They get his message. They see him on television and read the newspaper."[58] Thus the incumbent outlined scenes and evoked symbols, leaving details—particularly unpleasant details—for later. Patriotic slogans, such as "America is back," "America stands tall," "America is too great for small dreams," or "the opportunity society" combined with the persona of the incumbent himself and his stage-managed appearances drove the 1984 presidential campaign into what one political commentator called a "collage of manufactured happiness as in an infinitely extended television commercial."[59]

CONCLUSIONS

In this chapter, we have examined an important yet frequently overlooked element of elective politics—campaign style. In so doing, we considered style as sets of communication strategies that are employed by all candidates and noted the relationship of image and advancements in transportation and communication to their creation and maintenance.

The incumbency style was defined as a blend of symbolic and pragmatic communication strategies designed to make candidates be perceived by voters as not only good enough for the office sought but appear as if they already possessed the office. Fifteen different yet complementary strategies were examined. In a similar manner, we analyzed the challenger style, defining it as a series of communication strategies designed to persuade voters that change is needed and that the candidate is the best person to bring about change. Seven different yet complementary strategies were discussed.

Finally, we considered the incumbent/challenger style and noted that the combination of strategies which compose it, at least as illustrated during the 1984 presidential campaign, can play a major role in the creation of empty political rhetoric.

NOTES

1. Bruce E. Gronbeck, "The Functions of Presidential Campaigning," *Communication Monographs* 45 (November 1978): 268–80.

2. James Tobin, *The People's Choice* (Detroit: Detroit News, 1978), p. 3.

3. Ibid.

4. Irwin Silber, *Songs America Voted By* (New York: Stackpole Books, 1971), p. 34.

5. Kathleen Hall Jamieson, *Packaging the President: A History and Criticism of Presidential Campaign Advertising* (New York: Oxford University Press, 1984), p. 12.

6. Kenneth E. Boulding, *The Image* (Ann Arbor: University of Michigan Press, 1961), p. 6.

7. Allan Dean Louden, "Image Construction in Political Spot Advertising: The Hunt/Helms Senate Campaign 1984," (Ph.D. diss., University of Southern California, 1990), p. 1.

8. G. R. Pike, "Toward a Transactional Model of Political Images: Collective Images of the Candidates in the 1984 Elections" (Paper presented at the International Communication Association Convention, Honolulu, 1985). Quoted from Susan A. Hellweg et al., "Political Candidate Image: A State-of-the-Art Review," in *Progress in Communication Sciences* IX, eds. B. Dewin and M. J. Voigt (Norword, N.J.: Ablex Publishing, 1989), pp. 43–78.

9. Arthur H. Miller, Martin P. Wattenberg, and Oksana Malanchuk, "Schematic Assessments of Presidential Candidates," *American Political Science Review* 80 (June 1986): 521–40.

10. Dan D. Nimmo and Michael W. Mansfield, "Change and Persistence in Candidate Images: Presidential Debates Across 1976, 1980, and 1984" (Paper presented at the Speech Communication Association Convention, Chicago, 1986).

11. Hellweg et al., "A State-of-the-Art Review," esp. pp. 44–53.

12. Miller et al., "Schematic Assessments of Presidential Candidates," p. 533.

13. Susan A. Hellweg, Stephen W. King, and Steve E. Williams, "Comparative Candidate Evaluation as a Function of Election Level and Incumbency," *Communication Reports* 1 (Spring 1988): 76–85.

14. Frederick Williams, *The New Communications*, 2d ed. (Belmont, Calif.: Wadsworth Publishing Company, 1989).

15. Frederick Williams, *The Communications Revolution* (Beverly Hills: Sage, 1982), p. 37.

16. Ibid.

17. Edgar E. Willis, "Radio and Presidential Campaigning," *Central States Speech Journal* 20 (Fall 1969): 187.

18. Ibid., p. 191.

19. Ibid.

20. Joel L. Swerdlow, ed., *Media Technology and the Vote: A Source Book* (Boulder, Colo.: Westview Press, 1988), Introduction. See also James Perry, *The New Politics: The Expanding Technology of Political Manipulation* (New York: Potter, 1968).

21. Michael McCurry, "The New Electronic Politics," *Campaigns and Elections* (March/April 1989): 23–32. See also Williams, *Communications Revolution*, esp. pp. 17–39.

22. Theodore H. White, *The Making of the President 1968* (New York: Atheneum, 1969), p. 154.

23. Swerdlow, *Media Technology and the Vote*, pp. 6–7.

24. For a discussion of the potential of what he terms "push-button government," see Williams, *Communications Revolution*, pp. 183–99.

25. Mike Glover, "Survey Calls Dukakis Winner of TV Debate," *Cincinnati Enquirer*, January 21, 1988, p. A3.

26. M. Kate Sarles, "Disc Assisted Political Debate: A Rationale for Revitalizing Political Debate" (Paper presented at the *Eastern Communication Association*, May 7, 1989).

27. W. Lance Bennett, "The Ritualistic and Pragmatic Bases of Political Campaign Discourse," *Quarterly Journal of Speech* 63 (October 1977): 228.

28. Keith V. Erickson and Wallace V. Schmidt, "Presidential Political Silence: Rhetoric and the Rose Garden Strategy," *Southern Speech Communication Journal* 47 (Summer 1982): 402–21.

29. R. F. Fenno, Jr., *Home Style: House Members in Their Districts* (Boston: Little, Brown, 1978), p. 211.

30. Robert E. Denton, Jr., *The Symbolic Dimensions of the American Presidency* (Prospect Heights, Ill.: Waveland Press, 1982), p. 58.

31. Theodore H. White, *Breach of Faith* (New York: Atheneum, 1975), p. 322.

32. Dan D. Nimmo, *Popular Images of Politics* (Englewood Cliffs, N.J.: Prentice-Hall, 1974), p. 92.

33. John Louis Lucaites, "Rhetoric and the Problem of Legitimacy," in *Dimensions of Argument: Proceedings of the Second Summer Conference on Argumentation*, ed. George Ziegelmueller and Jack Rhodes (Annandale, Va.: Speech Communication Association), pp. 799–807.

34. Murray Edelman, "The Politics of Persuasion," in *Choosing the President*, ed. James David Barber (Englewood Cliffs, N.J.: Prentice-Hall, 1974), p. 171.

35. Denton, *Symbolic Dimensions*, p. 61.

36. Edelman, "Politics of Persuasion," p. 171.

37. William R. Brown, "Television and the Democratic National Convention of 1968," *Quarterly Journal of Speech* 55 (October 1969): 241. For a more extensive treatment of pseudoevents, see Daniel J. Boorstin's classic *The Image* (New York: Atheneum, 1980). Originally, the book was published under the title *The Image or What Happened to the American Dream* in 1961.

38. Edward I. Koch with William Rauch, *Politics* (New York: Simon and Schuster, 1985), p. 236.

39. Theodore H. White, *America in Search of Itself* (New York: Harper and Row, 1982), p. 296.

40. Ibid., p. 295.

41. Frank Kessler, *The Dilemmas of Presidential Leadership: Of Caretakers and Kings* (Englewood Cliffs, N.J.: Prentice-Hall, 1982), p. 313–14.

42. Dan D. Nimmo and James E. Combs, *Subliminal Politics: Myths & Mythmakers in America* (Englewood Cliffs, N.J.: Prentice-Hall, 1980), p. 78.

43. Harold W. Stanley and Richard G. Niemi, *Vital Statistics on American Politics* (Washington, D.C.: Congressional Quarterly Books, 1988), p. 138.

44. Nimmo and Combs, *Subliminal Politics*, p. 78.

45. Barry Brummett, "Towards a Theory of Silence as a Political Strategy," *Quarterly Journal of Speech* 66 (October 1980): 289–303.

46. "The President," *Newsweek*, August 28, 1972, p. 15. See also Judith S. Trent, "Image Building Strategies in the 1972 Presidential Campaign," *Speaker and Gavel* 10 (January 1973): 39–45; and for a discussion of the use of surrogate speakers, see Chapter 6.

47. Robert E. Denton, Jr., and Gary C. Woodward, *Political Communication in America* (New York: Praeger, 1985), p. 87.

48. Ellen Reid Gold and Judith S. Trent, "Campaigning for President in New Hampshire: 1980," *Exetasis* 6 (April 1980): 7.

49. Nelson W. Polsby and Aaron Wildavsky, *Presidential Elections* (New York: Charles Scribner's Sons, 1976), p. 165.

50. Judith S. Trent and Jimmie D. Trent, "The Rhetoric of the Challenger: George Stanley McGovern," *Central States Speech Journal* 25 (Spring 1974): 16.

51. David S. Broder, "The Lessons of Defeat," *Washington Post National Weekly Edition*, February 6–12, 1989, p. 4.

52. Trent and Trent, "Rhetoric of the Challenger," p. 17.

53. Ibid.

54. Francis X. Clines, "Friend and Foe Cite Reagan's 'Masterful' Use of Incumbency," *New York Times*, September 18, 1983, p. E5.

55. Anthony Lewis, "Dr. Pangloss Speaks," *New York Times*, October 14, 1984, p. E19.

56. Ibid.

57. Jane Mayer and Doyle McManus, *Landslide: The Unmaking of the President, 1984–1988* (Boston: Houghton Mifflin, 1988).

58. Howell Raines, "Reagan Appears to Succeed by Avoiding Specific Issues," *New York Times*, September 22, 1984, p. A14.

59. David Hoffman, "Accentuate the Positive, Put Off the Negative," *Washington Post National Weekly Edition*, March 26, 1984, p. 13.

Chapter Four

Communicative Mass Channels of Political Campaigning

No other nation in the world consumes so much mass communication. By the late 1980s we were buying more than 100 million daily newspapers and had 1,675 varieties from which to choose. Our radios were on over three hours a day, and we had more than 11,000 magazine titles available to us. However, the medium we devour to a greater extent than all others is television. More than 98 percent of all households have one television set, and approximately 50 percent have two or more, making television more plentiful than home telephones or automobiles.[1] More striking, however, than the number of television sets owned is the frequency of their use. Television is the major source of entertainment and information, the primary leisure time activity. We have our sets turned on more than seven hours every day and spend 40 percent of those hours watching it.[2] In other words, it is a dominant force in the lives and environments of most of the public, a fact that was called to our attention by political communication scholars Dan D. Nimmo and James E. Combs in 1990. In their book *Mediated Political Realities*, Nimmo and Combs claim that consistently since 1963 Americans have named television as their primary and most believable news medium.[3]

Not only is U.S. mass media consumption unequaled, in no other nation is it so inextricably linked to the electoral process. Mass communication has become the center stage for all major political events. For example, daily newspapers and weekly magazines keep political people and issues in our minds as they frequently report the result of the latest poll taken to measure how individuals feel about the president, governors, members of Congress, candidates, and specific issues and controversies. Radio programming is punctuated with five- and ten-minute news reports regarding some aspects of politics or with 30- and 60-second spot advertisements for candidates and local "vital" issues. But it is television that has most dramatically linked us to large-scale political campaign events such as presidential debates, national nominating conventions, primary victories and losses, candidates' gaffes, campaign trips, news conferences, election eve rituals and campaign speeches, biographies and negative commercials. It was television that brought Ronald Reagan to national political attention in 1964 as he delivered one of history's most financially successful speeches, just as 24 years later television announced his vice-president's election as his successor. In short, the mass media and particularly television have had a profound impact on the electoral process by connecting citizens and political campaigns.

In spite of this, the influence of mass communication on political behavior remains uncertain. Although media effect is one of the most studied areas in the social sciences, after almost 70 years of intense research there are relatively few absolutes, largely because the findings of one generation of scholars are frequently challenged by the next.

Thus the purpose of this chapter is to sort through the major theories, perspectives, hypotheses, and models that have been advanced regarding the media's role in or influence on political behavior and attempt to draw at least some general conclusions. In so doing it may be helpful to understand that for some scholars the "theories" are not theories at all because they are not all unambiguous, deductive, and interrelated structures from which empirically ascertained and consistent laws or general principles have been derived. For our purposes in this chapter, however, theories come in various packages. Although most have been empirically derived, not all are unambiguously and deductively determined. Moreover, if we insisted that the theories presented here must account for or predict general principles, there would be relatively little to discuss. Few of the perspectives or hypotheses have provided the consistency needed for determining general laws or principles. In other words, when it comes to the question of the role of media in determining political behavior, there is no one grand theory. There are a number of partial theories or what (in another context) communication scholar Frank E. X. Dance refers to as particularistic theoretical bits and pieces,[4] but no single theoretical development that can account for or predict related phenomena. It is for this reason that we discuss a number of the major perspectives and approaches that have generated research. Whether or not multitheoretical conceptualizations are desirable or undesirable, the fact is that seven decades of research have frequently led to conclusions that contrast with one another. This is one element to which we pay special attention as we proceed through the various theoretic approaches.

We define "mass" in a standard way as consisting of people representing all social, religious, and ethnic strata from all regions of the
country. Moreover, they are anonymous (do not necessarily know one
another) and therefore act not in concert but spontaneously as individuals. We use the terms "mass channels" and "mass media" inter-
changeably to refer to the primary means of mass communication (radio,
television, newspapers, and magazines). While we would not deny the
existence of other modes of mass communication such as books and
motion pictures in the political campaign any more than we would refuse
to recognize forms of "mini" communication such as posters, billboards,
and campaign literature, they are simply not as important. The major
perspectives have been generated from studies of radio, television,
newspapers, and magazines.

Finally, it is important to understand that the focus of this chapter is
not candidates and the campaign process but voters and the campaign
process. The principles that are analyzed center around the effect of
mass communication on the political behavior of citizens. As such, we
will be concerned with the way researchers have answered such questions as: (1) to what extent do the media influence cognitions and behavior? (2) what are the primary mass communication models that have
guided research? (3) what have been the effects of the media on the
electoral process itself? (4) how do people use the media in the political
process?

The chapter is organized chronologically in that the general conceptualizations from early and contemporary research compose separate
sections. Within each, major studies are examined and any specific hypotheses or models that have been derived from them will be discussed.
The conclusion focuses on a summary of principles regarding the influence of the media that are most important in understanding the nature
of political campaign communication.

EARLY STUDIES

The media's influence on political behavior has been a subject of scholarly investigation since the 1920s. Although readers might question the
need to be aware of anything other than the most recent research findings, many of the early studies have been of tremendous importance.
In fact, their impact has been so profound, they are considered "classics," and the conclusions they articulated as well as the methods they
employed influenced all who followed. Thus we will discuss each of the
major perspectives as well as the general models or hypotheses that
were derived from them during the 30-plus-year period in which they
dominated mass communication research.

Hypodermic Effect

The assumption that the press is a powerful force in shaping public opinion had been around for centuries. In 1529, 50 years after the printing press had been introduced to England, King Henry VIII seized control of the printing industry. Licensed printers held their patents only if what they printed pleased him.[5] In the mid–1600s the Puritan establishment in Massachusetts Bay Colony maintained strict control over printing because they feared that a free press might threaten the government and promote religious heresies.[6] In 1722 the founder and editor of a Boston newspaper, the *New England Courant*, was jailed for three weeks because of his attacks on the government.[7] Years later, the press was thought to have been a powerful force in creating revolutionary fervor in the United States, for providing passion and visibility to the abolitionist movement, and for provoking Congress to go to war with Spain.

However, it was not until the 1920s and 1930s that researchers actually tried to determine the power of mass communication in shaping values and behaviors of citizens. The motivation to learn more about the ways in which media could influence the public was provided, in large measure, by Adolf Hitler's propaganda machine, which seemed to have captured the minds of the German people, the brilliant yet frightening movies of the Nazi mass rallies, and the use of the radio by Benito Mussolini in Italy and Father Charles Coughlin in the United States to stir public support and sentiment for the fascists. The Information and Education Branch of the U.S. Army began recruiting social scientists to study the influence of media persuasion. As researchers analyzed the effects of propaganda films such as *The Battle of Britain* or the pro-German magazine the *Galilean*, they confirmed what had been assumed for centuries. The media really were powerful; they had the strength to not only change people's attitudes but to alter their behavior. And because citizens were often helpless to resist the persuasion of propaganda, they were easily "bamboozled." Moreover, according to the researchers, these effects occurred in all people because, despite individual attributes and characteristics, individuals responded in the same way when they received similar messages. Audiences were like mobs; there were no individual minds but only a group consciousness. Messages went directly from the media to the individuals where they were immediately assimilated. "Messages were literally conceived of as being 'injected' into the mind where they were 'stored' in the form of changes in feelings and attitudes. Eventually such feelings or attitudes produced the behavior desired by the message source."[8] This is, essentially, what researchers called the hypodermic effect or the hypodermic needle model.

Although it may be difficult for us to subscribe to specific aspects of the hypodermic model, it must be viewed in terms of the context in which it was developed. The 1920s through the early 1940s was a time of worldwide social, political, and economic unrest, passion, and violence. Economic depression, the rise of fascism and Hitler, and the domination of the Nazis throughout much of Europe suggested irrational yet somehow controlled mass group behavior. It seemed entirely likely that people's minds were being manipulated by powerful propaganda devices. In the view of many who were studying it, the "mass media loomed as agents of evil aiming at the total destruction of democratic society. First the newspaper and later the radio, were feared as powerful weapons able to rubber-stamp ideas upon the minds of defenseless readers and listeners."[9]

By the late 1930s, the hypodermic effect was widely enough accepted (even by those social scientists not involved in the government propaganda research program) to be applied specifically to the electoral process. One of the first systematic attempts to determine the political impact of the press was undertaken in 1937. Harold F. Gosnell studied the relationship of social and economic characteristics and newspaper-reading habits to election returns in several Chicago neighborhoods and found that the endorsements of newspapers could influence the way readers voted.[10] Thus social scientists were provided with additional proof of the seemingly unlimited power of the media to persuade.

Limited Effects or the Social Influence Model

Although the work of many of the army's psychologists and sociologists who were studying the effects of propaganda continued to reflect the hypodermic thesis, by the early 1940s the findings of some researchers began to challenge the idea that the media were so potent that the public was mesmerized by them. One of the most important challenges occurred when three social scientists from Columbia University's Bureau of Applied Social Research, Paul F. Lazarsfeld, Bernard Berelson, and Hazel Gaudet, studied the 1940 presidential campaign and discovered (much to their surprise) that campaign propaganda had little impact on the way the electorate had voted. This study and others that followed began to build a competing explanation for media influence, one that was in stark contrast to the presumption that people were unable to control their own destinies or the destiny of the nation. It was, of course, a much more comforting thought than the hypodermic thesis because it provided reassurance that in the United States individual rationality and society's sense of order could not be overthrown because of the seizure or control of the media by a demagogue or someone who had gone insane.

The 1940 study began to form what became known as the social influence model. Twenty years later, mass communication scholar Joseph Klapper, in summarizing the conclusions of the work done on the impact of the media during the 1940s and 1950s, concluded that media effects are limited and even in cases where they do occur, are mediated by other factors.[11] Thus he coined the term "limited effects model," a label that obviously stands in direct contrast with the earlier hypodermic perspective.

To understand this shift, it may be best to take a closer look at those studies that are regarded as the classics and that collectively influenced generations of mass communication scholars and their view of media and politics.

The first study by Lazarsfeld, Berelson, and Gaudet was conducted in Erie County, Ohio, a section of northern Ohio fairly equally divided between a city and farmland. Lazarsfeld and his colleagues wanted to measure the repercussions of campaign press coverage during a presidential election. At the outset they divided potential political effects into three categories: first, they believed the media could arouse public interest in the campaign and encourage voters to seek out more information about the candidates and issues; second, they reasoned that the press could reinforce existing political beliefs to make them stronger and more resistant to change; and third, they hypothesized that the media were powerful enough to convert attitudes, changing voters from supporting one candidate or party to supporting the opposition.

From May to November, a member of the research team interviewed someone each month in every 20th house or apartment in the county. In total, 600 people were questioned about political parties, candidates, issues, and the news. Interviewers kept carefully structured records of each talk, and from these records Lazarsfeld and his colleagues were able to reconstruct how Erie County citizens made their decision between Franklin Roosevelt and Wendell Wilkie. The results were published four years later in a book called *The People's Choice*.[12]

Although Lazarsfeld and his colleagues believed that their research would confirm the prevailing thesis that the media were capable of controlling individual thought processes, they instead found that very few people changed their vote in response to the campaign propaganda and that those who changed did not attribute their conversion to media information. Specifically, they learned that:

1. People who read or listened to a substantial amount of campaign media coverage were more likely to become more interested in the election

2. Their interest and activation were selective in that they tended to seek out stories that were consistent with prior political attitudes

3. Those relative few who did change their minds did so not because of attending to the media directly but by the filtering of information to them from people

in the community whom they respected. Such people were perceived to be highly active, highly informed, interested in politics, and therefore more likely than others to read or listen to media coverage of the campaign. These individuals were labeled "opinion leaders."

In the largest sense, the results of the Erie County study were not as important as the two explanations that Lazarsfeld and his colleagues offered for their findings. The explanations formed the cornerstone of the social influence theory. The researchers maintained that if a message presented by the media is in conflict with group norms it will be rejected. "Since groups have opinion leaders who transmit mass media information to individuals who do not attend to the media, these leaders influence whatever opinion change takes place in the followers; media messages do not have direct impact."[13] The second explanation given for their findings was that people are selective in those campaign messages to which they attend. They only listen to or read messages that are most consistent with their own beliefs, attitudes, and values. In other words, voters use the content of the media to support or reinforce the voting conclusions they would have reached because of their social predispositions. Interestingly, the concept of selective exposure was based on an analysis of only 122 persons who by August had not yet decided for which candidate they would vote. While 54 percent of those people with a Republican predisposition exposed themselves to Republican material and 61 percent with a Democratic predisposition exposed themselves to Democratic material, 35 percent of the Republicans and 22 percent of the Democrats did expose themselves to material from the other party—material that presumably was inconsistent with prior beliefs or social predispositions.

These percentages were never explained and the concept of selective exposure became a widely accepted phenomenon not only for the sociologically oriented voter studies but also by psychologists who eventually incorporated it into a series of studies regarding involuntary and voluntary exposure to information to reduce psychological dissonance.[14]

The second of the classic studies conducted by the Columbia group was also staged in a single location. In 1948 Paul Lazarsfeld, Bernard Berelson, and William McPhee went to Elmira, New York, to determine voter behavior during the presidential campaign. The Elmira results, published in 1954 in *Voting*, supported the Erie County findings that campaign press coverage converted few voters and that information was disseminated from opinion leaders.

The third single-location study was mounted in Decatur, Illinois, and was reported by Elihu Katz and Paul Lazarsfeld in the book *Personal Influence*. The researchers interviewed 800 women regarding "four arenas of everyday decision: marketing, fashions, public affairs, and movie-

going" and for each arena asked respondents "not only about themselves and their own behavior but about other people as well—people
who influence them, and people for whom they are influential."[15]

Essentially the results of the Decatur study confirmed the social influence model, although they also produced a more precise conceptualization of "the two-step flow of communication." The idea that had
been hypothesized from the Erie County data suggested that "ideas
often flow from radio and print to the opinion leaders and from them
to the less active sections of the population."[16] However, in Decatur,
the Columbia group wanted to compare the media behavior of opinion
leaders and nonleaders "to see whether the leaders tend to be the more
exposed, and the more responsive group when it comes to influence
stemming from the mass media."[17] They discovered that the women
they studied were willing to admit that they were influenced by other
women, that leadership varied by topic, that leaders for each topic had
different social and psychological characteristics, and that no single
leader exercised control over the political beliefs of others. However,
their most important finding, in terms of media impact on the electoral
process, was that "opinion leaders were not more likely than followers
to attribute influence upon their beliefs or opinions to the mass media."[18]
Thus as a result of the third Columbia study, the role of the media was
reduced even further in the minds of most social scientists. It appeared
as if no group sizable enough to be measured was persuaded by media
messages during a political campaign.

In 1952 another group of researchers began examining voters' behavior. Using the 1952 presidential election as their base, the University of
Michigan Survey Research Center, or SRC (now called the Center for
Political Studies, Institute for Social Research at the University of Michigan), soon replaced the Columbia group as the dominant research force
in large-scale voting studies. Methodologically as well as conceptually,
the work of the Michigan group represented a major shift in the effort
to examine voters and their behavior.[19] For example, the SRC relied on
panels of potential voters based on national probability samples rather
than a single community. In focusing on national behaviors, they moved
away from sociological explanations (the emphasis on traditions, structure, composition, and the sociological nature of major institutions
within single communities), which the Lazarsfeld group had presumed
were the reasons for voters' predispositions. Instead, the Michigan researchers sought cognitive and attitudinal reasons for voting decisions.
They asked citizens to indicate their party affiliation (Columbia had
studied parties only in terms of social predispositions that led voters to
choose one candidate over another). Thus with party identification as a
key factor in explaining voters' attitudes and evaluation of candidates,
the idea of interpersonal communication and the two-step flow concep-

tualization as the primary means of information diffusion was relegated to a "relatively unimportant position in the SRC model."[20]

However, in one important respect, the early SRC studies did not differ from their Columbia counterparts. Despite the fact that in 1952 television played a role in the presidential primaries, in the nominating conventions, and in the general advertising campaigns of at least one of the candidates, the Michigan researchers concluded that the impact of the mass media on the electoral process was minimal.[21] In fact, in *The American Voter* (a book based on the data collected in 1952 and 1956), the researchers indicated that it was party identification and not television that was the important factor in the development of political cognitions, attitudes, and behavior.[22]

Finally, in 1963, undoubtedly in an attempt to revitalize a theory that was being challenged by many, Lazarsfeld and his colleagues described a modification of the two-step flow. In the new conceptualization, information from the media was relayed from one opinion leader to another before it was passed on to followers. The revision became known as the "multistep flow" and because more people were added to the transmission process, the persuasive power of the media was viewed as even less significant than it had been before. Moreover, information not only traveled from opinion leader to opinion leader, any one of these people could act as a "gatekeeper" and thereby prevent a follower from even being exposed to part of the information. In other words, opinion leaders functioned not only as conveyers of information among each other and finally to their respective "audiences," they also determined just what information would be transmitted. Although gatekeeping was discussed by Lazarsfeld in relationship to the multistep flow in 1963, the idea was not new. As early as 1950 one study had examined the selection and rejection of messages by gatekeepers. One of the key findings mentioned in many studies that followed was that when media gatekeepers made decisions, they did not have the audience in mind.[23]

Essentially a gatekeeper is any person in the news gathering process with authority to make decisions affecting the flow of information to the public. "The image is precisely that of a turnstile gatekeeper at a sporting event—he examines the qualifications of each person in line, and decides whether or not to let him in. The difference is that what gets let in or left out is not a person, but a piece of news."[24] One of the reasons the gatekeeping function has received so much attention is that there are a variety of people in the media who must make decisions regarding the presentation of information and news. Examples include telegraph and wire service editors, reporters, film editors, headline writers, radio and television producers, news program anchors and commentators, and even other media (small newspapers and radio and television stations frequently take their news from the larger and more established media).

Thus given the wide spectrum of people who daily determine which of the many possible news items the public will be presented, it is little wonder that gatekeeping has been the subject of scholarly investigation as well as public consternation. Undoubtedly one of the most famous attacks against media gatekeepers was leveled in 1969 by Vice-President Spiro Agnew. One of the broad areas of his criticism concerned the similarities of the various media decision makers. In an address before the Midwest Regional Republican Committee in Des Moines, Iowa, Agnew charged that:

A small group of men, numbering perhaps no more than a dozen "anchormen," commentators and executive producers, settle upon the 20 minutes or so of film and commentary that is to reach the public. . . . We do know that, to a man, these commentators and producers live and work in the geographical and intellectual confines of Washington, D.C. or New York City—the latter of which James Reston terms the "most unrepresentative community in the entire United States." . . . We can deduce that these men thus read the same newspapers, and draw their political and social views from the same sources. . . . The upshot of all this controversy is that a narrow and distorted picture of America often emerges from the televised news.[25]

Whether or not Agnew's charges were true, they did provoke public discussion as well as a good deal of media response. In addition, gatekeeping continued to be a subject of scholarly investigation throughout the 1960s and 1970s.[26]

In summarizing the major ideas advanced by the early studies of media influence, it is tempting to conclude that in spite of the label of some of them as classics, almost four decades of investigation has had little relationship to contemporary theory. Researchers went from one extreme to the other; first media propaganda was the harbinger of all that was evil and then it had little impact at all. Effects were seen primarily on a one-dimensional level—persuasion. The informational or cognitive function was largely ignored because of the dominance of selective exposure, a concept with little empirical validation then and clearly inadequate now.[27] Moreover, investigators were so intent on confirming the basic tenets of the social influence model that they ignored media effect in such important areas as voter turnout, political activation, and information seeking. The studies were conducted at a time in which home television sets were far less plentiful than they are today, and so the medium was viewed as having little direct influence on political behavior. Radio and newspapers were important only in their role as reinforcers rather than opinion formers, thus suggesting that voters were limited perceptually by their past.

However, in spite of all this, the early studies remain an important part of our media research heritage for at least four reasons. First, they pointed the way toward research methodologies that were more so-phisticated than those that had been used. Moreover, the Columbia studies were the last massive single-community analysis for many years. And the Michigan studies of the national electorate continue to provide the most authoritative source of election data available. Second, the social influence model did rescue social scientists from the mass media hysteria symbolized by the hypodermic thesis. Third, although the Co-lumbia studies may have carried the sociological explanation of voters' behavior to the extreme, they did begin the path toward the study of mass media and interpersonal relationships, obviously an important area of political campaign communication. Finally, the limited effects theory served as a catalyst for later scholars who would challenge the idea that the mass media had little impact on voters' behavior or the electoral process. Indeed, the sheer attempt to disprove the theory may well have led to the multiperspectivism that characterizes contemporary mass com-munication research.

CONTEMPORARY STUDIES

Just as the hypodermic thesis reflected society's turmoil and the social influence model depicted a quiet, reflective people not swayed by cam-paign propaganda, the mass media research of the 1960s and 1970s was a product of or at least representative of its time. If the decade of the 1950s is described by such words as quiet, inactive, or dull, the following years can be characterized as disquieting, tumultuous, and wild. While the federal bureaucracy grew in size and influence, so did citizen in-volvement in public affairs. Beginning with the civil rights struggle, which brought local groups together to form national organizations, a number of large-scale political and social movements appeared on the national scene. Each of them demanded new social and economic leg-islation to ensure equality and to guarantee their rights as citizens to help formulate national and international policy. However, each of them also needed various forms of mass communication not only to recruit, organize, and maintain their movements but to publicize their demands by drastic and frequently passionate actions.

The changes in society and the escalation of the social movements corresponded to alterations in the mass media system. It too was grow-ing, largely because of the widespread use of television. More people owned television sets, and it was beginning to replace interpersonal conversations and meetings as a leisure time activity.[28] Television was becoming the most revolutionary branch of journalism. While in the 1950s television news was typically read by one person seated in front of a wall map, during the next 20 years it became a drama featuring live coverage of national and international events. The sit-ins and marches of the social movements, the urban riots and burning of U.S. cities, the funeral of a young president and the assassination of his alleged killer, the bloody battles of the war in Vietnam all contributed to the transformation of U.S. news-gathering and of those social scientists who studied it.[29]

It was in this atmosphere that many mass communication scholars began to question the basic tenets of the social influence model. Although they had no one holistic theory with which to replace it, maintaining that the media had little influence on or played no major role in the electoral process appeared a direct denial of what was happening all around them. A few researchers looked to the reigning paradigm for new explanations. For example, one study in 1962 indicated that uninvolved voters are susceptible to attitude change if any new information reaches them,[30] and another showed that under certain conditions it is possible for large audiences to get information directly from the media without the intervention of an opinion leader, suggesting that mass communication does not always work in a two-step flow.[31] However, the most important break with the social influence model occurred when social scientists Jay G. Blumler and Denis McQuail discovered in a study of the 1964 British parliamentary election that "regular viewers of television news developed significantly different perceptions of the Liberal and Conservative parties."[32] Clearly, it was possible for media to do more than simply reinforce the status quo.

Beginning roughly about the time that the work of Blumler and McQuail appeared to suggest a new perspective for viewing media influence in politics, other theories or quasi theories were being articulated. In the remainder of this section, we discuss the basic assumptions or tenets of four of the most important approaches undertaken during the 1960s and 1970s and reexamined, reformulated, or extended during the 1980s.

Diffusion of Information

One of the approaches that bridges the gap between the limited effects model and the contemporary conceptualizations is the diffusion of knowledge perspective. It is related to the research that characterizes social influence theory largely because it was initiated in that era and because it acknowledges the importance of interpersonal communication to the dissemination of information. However, it differs from that theory in at least two important respects. First, diffusion research maintains that under certain conditions media transmission of information will have a direct impact on individuals and can produce changes in their knowledge or even their behavior. Interpersonal communication occurs after the mass media transmit information about news events and is therefore only a response to media reports.[33] The second way in which diffusion research is distinct from social influence is that it does not study attitude change in voting behavior during political campaigns but focuses instead on the influence of the mass media on the acquisition of political cognitions. In other words, diffusion research is concerned with such topics as knowledge of campaign issues, candidates, and general public affairs. It is also used to investigate possible stages of information dissemination, how specific groups within society become aware of particular political matters, what factors contribute to the acceptance or rejection of political ideas, and what conditions mediate the flow of information about events.

Although diffusion has been defined in a variety of ways, generally conceptualizations of it in communication research capitalize on the idea of movement—the spread of adoption of new ideas (innovations) through time and space from one individual or group of people to another. In spite of the fact that diffusion research and the resulting diffusion model have roots in the physical sciences, it is employed by a number of disciplines within the social sciences. In the area of our interest, much of the early important work was done by Everett Rogers. In his 1961 book, *Diffusion of Innovations*, and in his later work with Floyd Shoemaker, Rogers discovered a multistage process of innovation diffusion. The four stages are: (1) information or knowledge; (2) persuasion; (3) decision or adoption; and (4) confirmation or reevaluation. In other words, new information is transmitted through society (or from person to person) in a particular sequential pattern. While it can be argued that these stages will not always be either separate or sequential under some conditions for some people, according to Rogers and Shoemaker, the media are important primarily in the first or information stage, where an interest in, awareness of, and understanding of the innovation can be created. Interpersonal communication is important during the last three stages as people seek confirmation or interpretation of the information they have received from the mass media.[34]

To support the view that the media were the predominant sources of information about political news events, early diffusion research in political communication was designed to measure the extent to which messages were transmitted. For example, it was discovered that the media informed most people about the death of Senator Robert Taft, President Dwight Eisenhower's decision to seek reelection, the dropping of Senator Thomas Eagleton as the Democratic vice-presidential candidate, and the assassination of John Kennedy.[35] To a large extent, much of the diffusion research even during the 1970s continued to be concentrated on the extent and veridicality of information flow. Thus researchers appeared to be more interested in the attention arousal and information-seeking characteristics of the first stage of the process rather than the later adoption or persuasion stages.[36] In fact, after reviewing the diffusion approach to political communication studies published during the 1970s, Robert L. Savage reported that with the exception of news dissemination studies very little use had been made of it. He urged scholars to investigate such questions as: Are diffusing messages causes or effects of human actions? What latent and/or dysfunctional consequences follow from existing diffusion patterns? He appeared to doubt that political communication scholars had used the approach for all relevant forms of political information.[37] In a similar vein, mass communication scholar Steven H. Chaffee acknowledged that the diffusion approach had not yet lived up to its potential when he called for research that would lead to the development of a universal scheme for categorizing different types of diffusion items according to the type of communication that transmits them, the type of person most receptive to them, and determining the way in which items are relevant from the perspective of the political system.[38] And authors Sidney Kraus and Dennis Davis suggested that the diffusion model be supplemented by stipulating specific patterns of media use and perception to understand better the conditions that mediate the flow of information.[39]

Unfortunately, those researchers who continued to use the diffusion perspective during the 1980s rarely broadened or extended the scope of the topics investigated or the ways in which human behavior was affected—especially political behavior. Studies continued to focus on crisis news events (such as the shootings of President Ronald Reagan and Pope John Paul II in 1981), the relative roles of interpersonal and mass communication in the dissemination process (which one is the primary source of information and under what conditions for what people), and the rate at which information is diffused through the population.[40] In short, the model was never really expanded as some political and mass communication scholars hoped that it would be.

Thus, while the diffusion of information perspective helped redirect the focus of media/political research away from the unidimensional thrust of the social influence model, its potential has yet to be realized.

Uses and Gratifications

A crucial assumption of the uses and gratifications perspective is that a wide range of motives exists for using the mass media and that individuals' media requirements are dictated by such factors as their social roles, situations, or personalities. In other words, media audiences should not be thought of as huge collectivities who watch television shows, attend movies, and read newspapers and magazines for the same reasons.[41]

In one sense, the uses and gratifications perspective is similar to some of the other research approaches discussed in this chapter in that there is really no single theory. We do not mean to imply that the perspective is atheoretical but simply that there are numerous theoretical bits and pieces that compose the perspective. However, as one of its principal advocates, Jay G. Blumler, has argued, the various theories about the phenomena "share a common field of concern, an elementary set of concepts indispensable for intelligibly carving up that terrain, and an identification of certain wider features of the mass communication process with which such core phenomena are presumed to be connected."[42]

Although a diverse range of research has been conducted under the uses and gratifications paradigm, essentially it has been concerned with determining those uses people make of the mass media in the circumstances of their own lives as well as the gratifications they seek and receive from such consumption.

To an extent, part of the popularity of the approach is that it has served as a means of integrating ideas of massive effects (the hypodermic thesis) with limited effects (the social influence model) to form a middle-ground position where the audience is viewed as active, thinking receivers who are neither susceptible to all persuasive media messages nor impervious to them. In fact, it has been argued that it is in this role as an integrative component in an effects model "that the uses and gratifications perspective offers its greatest promise to the study of political communication."[43]

Not only, however, is the approach used for its bridge between the effects models, it has the additional benefit of allowing researchers to study more than just effects—to get at the functions mass media may provide during a political campaign. While some of these functions may be obvious (we read a newspaper account of a candidate's speech to gain more information about the candidate and the campaign), others may be latent (we watch a television commercial about a candidate so that we have enough information about the campaign to maintain our social status as an informed citizen). In other words, the functions served by the media during a campaign are not necessarily what they appear to be. Information or cognitive gain may serve many important purposes for the individual and the uses/gratifications perspective provides a way to examine them.

Although the uses and gratifications paradigm began to be especially popular during the 1970s, research conducted under its label goes back as far as the beginning of World War II when studies were published that dealt with the use of radio for entertainment purposes. Similarly, during the following two decades when commercial television became important, the approach was used to generate data regarding entertainment programming. It was not until the landmark Blumler and McQuail study, published in 1969, that the perspective came into major use in examining political campaigns. In fact, it was this investigation of the 1964 British election that really spelled out the basic assumptions for researchers in political communication. Other studies followed, and in 1974 Blumler and Katz summarized much of the research the perspective had stimulated in *The Uses of Mass Communication*.

In spite of the fact that multiple studies have been conducted under the uses and gratifications paradigm, there is not only the lack of one unified theory, there is still some disagreement about such basic tenets of the perspective as the meaning of an "active audience" and if media gratifications differ in any important way from one set of ideological beliefs to another or from one culture to another—in other words, the relationship of social structure to the understanding individual citizens bring to political messages/events. The question of the socio/cultural bases upon which or through which the meanings of political messages are constructed and responded to was not clear in the original categorical scheme used by Blumler and McQuail. The five types of gratification orientations to political television programming employed in their study of the British national election were: using the political content of the media for vote guidance; reinforcement of decisions already made; general surveillance of the political environment; excitement; and anticipation of using the information in future interpersonal communication situations; and the three types of avoidance were: feelings of political alienation; partisanship; and relaxation.[44] However, in more recent years, some researchers—including Blumler—have emphasized the importance of the social structure, or the culture, in arriving at any understanding of the meaning people give to messages (or their motivation to use or avoid media). For example, in 1985 Blumler and his colleagues reported that they "never meant to talk about abstracted individuals, but about people in social situations that give rise to their needs. The individual is part of a social structure and his or her choices are less free and less random than a vulgar gratificationism would presume."[45] Whether or not Blumler and McQuail simply assumed the role of socio/cultural influence in their gratification and avoidance categories without specifically discussing it is not as important as the fact that in recent years researchers have begun to more clearly acknowledge the role played by social structure.

The second area of disagreement within the uses and gratification research is closely related to the first. Not only must the social-determinants of the audience's media needs and expectations be considered, so too must the idea or definition of an active audience be considered. As at least one theorist has argued:

If the uses and gratifications paradigm is truly to come to grips with the nature of the audience's media experience, it will have to give up the optimistic and simplistic notion that an active audience implies a powerful audience. It must be recognized that the concept of an active audience, as traditionally explicated in the literature, may in fact obscure the powerlessness of the audience. Certain audience media expectations are never voiced because they are perceived as inappropriate or as so unlikely as to make their articulation sound foolish or naive . . . Other expectations, for some individuals, when expressed, may be significantly modified or tempered due to the sense of powerlessness they feel with respect to the political and social system . . . In-depth probing of individual's media expectations may reveal more about the assumptions these individuals hold regarding their locations in the social and political system than about any true media needs. In-depth analysis of the meaning of a commonly expressed media expectation such as diversion may reveal the use of standard media fare not so much for polite relaxation but for opportunities to ridicule a presentation of reality which does not correspond to one's experience as opposed to mediated life.[46]

Thus, while the uses and gratifications perspective has been the focal point of a good deal of research and although the paradigm itself has served a useful function by illustrating that people pay attention to the political content of the media, it will begin to achieve its potential only when researchers who employ it give full attention to the social bases of message construction and response.[47]

Agenda-Setting Hypothesis

Undoubtedly the most popular contemporary approach for studying the relationship of media and politics is the agenda-setting hypothesis. It has generated more research than any of the others. It clearly separates the persuasive and informational communicative functions of the media. It comes closer than any of the other approaches to reaffirming the early basic assumption that the media do have a great deal of influence on politics; the media may not dominate, but they do have a significant impact on what we think about (our focus of attention). Finally, the perspective is important for another reason. The most frequent site for agenda-setting research has been election campaigns, and this has clearly not been the case with either the diffusion of information or uses and gratifications perspectives.

The underlying assumption of agenda-setting was first articulated by a political scientist, Bernard C. Cohen, in 1963. Cohen argued that the press may not be successful in telling its readers what to think but "it is stunningly successful in telling its readers what to think about. . . . The editor may believe he is only printing the things that people want to read, but he is thereby putting a claim on their attention, powerfully determining what they will be thinking about, and talking about, until the next wave laps their shore."[48]

Just two years later, empirical verification of Cohen's ideas began to appear. In a study of the 1964 presidential campaign, researcher Jack McLeod found that the stories from two newspapers revealed clear differences in their reports of two issues in the campaign, federal spending policies, and control of nuclear weapons. Specifically, the study revealed that respondents who read the paper that provided a good deal of coverage to nuclear control (the Democratic issue) ranked it higher than they did the economic issue. Correspondingly, those who read the paper that focused on spending policies (the Republican issue) ranked it higher than they did nuclear control.[49] In 1972 Maxwell E. McCombs and Donald L. Shaw explored the power of the press to set the agenda by studying the 1968 presidential campaign. Specifically, they hypothesized that "the mass media set the agenda for each political campaign, influencing the salience of attitudes toward the political issues."[50] Before the election, the researchers interviewed 100 people in five precincts in Chapel Hill, North Carolina, who had not yet decided whether they were going to vote for Hubert Humphrey, Richard Nixon, or George Wallace. The undecided voters were the only people interviewed on the presumption that they would be the most receptive to campaign information. McCombs and Shaw compared what voters said were the key issues in the campaign with the amount of space devoted to those issues in the particular medium used by the voters. They found a strong relationship between the emphasis given by the medium to specific campaign issues and the judgment of voters relating to the salience and importance of those issues. A third study, this time a national one conducted from 1964 to 1970, compared what people identified as the most important problems facing the United States (according to data from Gallup Polls) with listings of the content of news magazines. The researcher, G. Ray Funkhouser, concluded that "the average person takes the media's word for what the 'issues' are, whether or not he personally has any involvement or interest in them."[51]

In these three studies and many others that followed them during the 1970s, the agenda-setting functions of the mass media gained wide acceptance from social scientists. In part the perspective was well-received because it did not suggest that media have the all-powerful attributes envisioned by the hypodermic thesis. Instead the theme from the corpus of research undertaken was that the media set public priorities just by paying attention to some issues while ignoring others. They determine which issues are important and in this way play an important role in structuring our social reality. In other words, people not only learn about issues through the media, they learn how much importance to give them because of the emphasis placed on them by the mass media.

Throughout the 1970s and into the 1980s, the perspective remained significant because it illustrated "how significant communication variables" could be "operationalized and linked to concrete political processes such as election campaigns."[52] And it stimulated a good deal of research (although few consistent conclusions) on such important areas as the distinct agenda-setting roles of newspapers and television, the differences between the intrapersonal agenda (operationalized in most studies in terms of what each individual considers personally most important) and the interpersonal agenda (what each individual talks about most often with others), and the length of time required for agenda-setting to manifest themselves in the public agenda.[53] However, by 1982, perhaps in part because the campaign of 1980 and the subsequent election of Ronald Reagan reemphasized that television had become "the single greatest mediator of political outcomes in both everyday and campaign arenas,"[54] agenda-setting research suddenly was extended by some researchers to include evaluation. In other words, not only did the media tell us what to think about, it told us what to think about it. Evaluation was a major extension of the original formulation and, for those who subscribed to it, helped place in perspective the apparent power of such campaign tools as televised political advertising (the subject of the next chapter) during the political campaigns of the decade. Among other things, these researchers argued that news stories not only suggest the importance of the subject matter but the contextual cues or frames by which to evaluate the subject matter.[55] In one study, researchers found that when the media concentrate on a particular news story, not only do program viewers become convinced that the subject is important, through this process they become " 'primed' to evaluate the president, in part, by his apparent success in dealing with this issue."[56] And in a related study, published in 1983, scholars Gladys Engel Lang and Kurt Lang argued that Watergate never really became an issue in the 1972 presidential campaign (in spite of the extensive coverage of it) because it was framed as a partisan issue, just another example of election year politics.[57] The assertions of candidate George McGovern were "balanced" by denials from the Nixon White House. The Langs found that most people did not pay much attention to Watergate until Judge John Sirica was "presented by the media as a credible and presumably objective spokesperson for the cover-up scenario. Subsequently, the press abandoned its practice of balancing Watergate stories and printed news that was more or less exclusively supportive of the cover-up narrative."[58] They termed the "framing" and "balancing" media activities as agenda-building.

Without much question, the agenda-setting perspective has generated more research than the other approaches we have discussed. Its future looks bright because not only have scholars begun extending the approach in regard to the power of the media, they have also started investigating its use within specific political campaigns and the ability of televised political advertising to set issue agendas.[59] As such, it seems destined to remain an important perspective by which to explain the influence of the media in, at least, American politics and election campaigns.

Reconceptualization of the Classics

Although not a complete perspective like information diffusion, uses and gratifications, or agenda-setting, we nonetheless include in this section a brief summary of the major tenets of the 1976 study that, while modeled after those of the Columbia Bureau of Applied Social Research, came to opposite conclusions. We believe that one of the reasons the study is important is because it laid a foundation for research during the 1980s and beyond that explored the relationship between the media and political campaigns.

In an effort to provide a body of knowledge that would "contribute to an understanding of election coverage and the American voter,"[60] Thomas E. Patterson implemented the "most comprehensive panel survey ever conducted for the study of change during a presidential campaign."[61] The study and its results were described in the book *The Mass Media Election*.

Although the Patterson investigation resembled the earlier work of Lazarsfeld and Berelson, there were major differences that are important to our consideration of political campaign communication in two respects. The first concerns the overall design of the study, and the second relates to the conclusions. We will begin by comparing designs.

In each of the Columbia studies, respondents were interviewed a number of times to determine if their attitudes were changing as the presidential campaigns were proceeding. Panel surveys were the single source of data for findings. Moreover, each of the Columbia studies interviewed 600 to 800 potential voters, and each was conducted in a single community. By contrast, the design of the 1976 study was more comprehensive. First, more people were interviewed (1,236). Second, they were interviewed in seven waves (five face-to-face interviews and two over the telephone), which were timed to correspond with each of the important intervals and stages in the campaign (just before the New Hampshire primary, after the early primaries, after the final primaries, after the conventions, before the general election, after the first and second presidential debates, and after the election). Third, respondents represented two communities that had substantially different populations and media (Erie, Pennsylvania, and Los Angeles, California). Finally, data collected from repeated interviews represented only one of the sources of evidence. The other was a content analysis of election year political news stories that appeared on evening newscasts of the three major television networks, two news magazines, two national newspapers, and two local newspapers (one in each of the selected cities). The content analysis was conducted from January until after the general election in November, and the interviews began in February and also concluded when the election was over. In short, the Patterson study was not only a more ambitious undertaking than any of the Columbia efforts had been, it was the largest project attempted in the intervening years—years in which research regarding the influence of mass communications was beginning to illustrate that the media were not passive entities in the political process.

As we discussed earlier, the primary conclusion derived from the Lazarsfeld/Berelson work was that the media did not play a major role in determining voters' attitudes during a presidential campaign. In fact, media messages were far less important than the messages relayed through interpersonal communication channels. Political opinions were determined by party and social affiliations, and therefore if the media were not absolutely powerless they were of minor importance in influencing how people voted. However, in reporting the results of his 1976 investigation, Patterson argued that the presidential campaign is essentially a mass media campaign. He felt that for the "large majority of voters, the campaign has little reality apart from its media version."[62] In other words, far from being an unimportant factor, media are a significant part of the campaign process itself. As a matter of fact, virtually each of the conclusions from the 1976 study contradicted those articulated by the Columbia researchers. Among the conclusions Patterson discussed, the following three are particularly important for us:

1. Although the media do not change attitudes, they do influence because people rely on them for information, thereby placing media in a position to influence perceptions

2. The stories that voters see in newspapers and watch on television "affect what they perceive to be the important events, critical issues, and serious contenders; [media] will affect what they learn about the candidates' personalities and issue positions"[63]

3. Thus the power of the press "rests largely on its ability to select what will be covered and to decide the contest in which these events will be placed."[64]

Therefore the Patterson investigation of the ways in which voters were influenced by the media in 1976 is important. First, it firmly dispelled the long-term myths created by the Columbia studies and, second, it provided the comprehensive data necessary to begin updating and solidifying our knowledge of the ways in which voters, candidates, and the mass media interact with each other in contemporary political campaigns.

CONCLUSIONS

As we have seen, beliefs regarding the political influence and power of the mass media have come almost full circle during the almost 70 years researchers have been studying them. First, it was believed that the media were all-powerful. Then their power was seen as limited and of secondary or minor importance. In each instance, conclusions were frequently based on substantial evidence but gained prominence because they reinforced the dominant attitudes and context of the time in which they were articulated. The effective use of propaganda in the 1930s and the early 1940s convinced researchers that the power of the media was massive. Indeed, the media were virtually unlimited in the ways they could change attitudes and produce behavior modification or conformity. Whereas in the 1950s the opposite viewpoint was held because in the context of those years it seemed difficult to subscribe to the belief that U.S. citizens could be reduced to puppets who would follow the ravings of any demagogue. Moreover, it must be remembered that when the classic Columbia studies were undertaken (during the 1940 and 1948 presidential elections), television was not yet a real factor in politics or in the environment of voters. However, by the time of the 1960 presidential campaign, television was on its way to becoming a political force. Both candidates were using the medium for spot commercials, and their precedent-setting debates broke all previously established viewing records. When over 100 million people watched the debates and subsequently talked about their perceptions and reactions to the candidates, it became increasingly difficult for social scientists to deny that media, particularly television, had any impact.

Thus as the context/environment changed, some researchers began to question the limited effects model just as 20 years earlier they had challenged the validity of the hypodermic thesis. Eventually, most conceded that the media possessed some influence—even if it did not create massive changes in voting behavior. Some acknowledged the media's ability in the transmission and diffusion of information regarding candidates, issues, or the campaign itself. Other researchers suggested that people use the media for a variety of political reasons: for information, entertainment, increasing the range of topics for social exchange and acceptability, meeting expectations of peer groups, or for intrapersonal communication. And there were those who argued that the media are important because of their power to determine what information or news would be presented. Thus by the middle of the 1970s many social scientists had begun to believe that media influence in the electoral process could not be ignored. Finally, in 1976 a study was undertaken that provided enough data to confirm many of the trends evident since 1960.

But the pendulum continued to swing. During the 1980s, when every election year appeared to bring with it an ever increasing reliance on television to frame candidates' rhetorical and visual messages, some researchers once again worried about the omnipotence of the media.

Thus when we asserted at other points in this chapter that beliefs regarding the influence of the media had come full circle, we were not exaggerating. But do these perspectives from mass media research contribute to the understanding of campaign communication? We think they can and suggest seven principles of campaign communication that can be drawn from them.

The first of these principles is that the most important effect of media influence is seldom direct persuasion but providing information that affects perception and may ultimately persuade. Persuasion theorists have consistently determined that a "one-shot" persuasive effort or message does not change attitudes—at least does not change attitudes from one extreme to the other. There may be behavior modification or conformity when conditions include threat, punishment, or even reward, but not internalized attitude change. And it is naive to assume that it is any different in the context of a political campaign. Instead, persuasive information about a candidate, about the issues for which the candidate stands, even negative information regarding the candidate's opponent will affect perception and thus help to draw attention to the candidate and campaign and may even influence later perception. Therefore, we conclude that the media are important to and powerful in a political campaign not in necessarily changing votes because of a single message but in drawing attention to candidates and thereby providing information for a full range of attitude formulations (including reinforcement, reformulation, and repositioning).

The second principle is simply that the contemporary candidate needs the mass media, in part because voters have expectations regarding the media's role in providing information about the candidates and the campaign. Citizens rely on newspapers, newscasts, and televised political advertising to tell them about candidates, issues, and the campaign itself. Moreover, candidates have found that they can efficiently reach potential voters only through the mass media.

The third principle is that the media have tremendous power in determining which news events, which candidates, and which issues are to be covered in any given day. Thus a candidate's campaign must be focused, in large measure, around those sorts of issues, photographic opportunities, and events that will draw media attention and provide "sound bites" for the evening television newscasts. Whether these are pseudoevents or real, pseudoissues or real, modern candidates do those things that will "play" to the media—that will call attention to themselves and their campaigns. Perhaps more important, because of the media, candidates do not do some things and do not discuss some issues. Often what they fail to do is just as important as what they do.

The fourth principle may be less obvious. Although candidates attempt to use the media for their own purposes, they are not always able to control it. While a candidate can send a press release, its use is not guaranteed. Although an appearance at the state fair is planned, there is no assurance the event will be used in the evening newscasts. It may well be that election coverage will focus on an opponent or on yesterday's gaffe. Moreover, media have the power to penetrate even the most expertly contrived image—the newspaper reporter catches the wording of the answer to a question, or the television camera records unplanned nonverbal behavior. The point we make is simply that candidates may spend most of their campaign resources on the media, they may depend on them to present persuasive information regarding their candidacies, but with the exception of their own advertisements, they cannot control the media.

The fifth principle is that mass media influence is important to our knowledge or appreciation of the electoral process itself. The media allow us to witness political events, they teach and instruct, thereby adding to our expectations about the democratic process. Most of the crucial events of at least recent presidential elections in recent years have occurred on television. While this may increase or decrease our liking for particular candidates, issues, or campaigns, it does provide a sense of involvement as we affirm (or deny) our role as citizens.

The sixth principle regards how the mass media, primarily television, have changed the way in which candidates campaign for office. As we noted in an earlier chapter, we greet candidates in the living rooms of our homes via the television screen rather than at a political rally. Moreover, the candidates' television advertising and their nightly spots on evening news programs are the electronic age equivalent of the whistle stop tours.

Finally, we believe that the influence or power of the media has contributed mightily to the many changes in the electoral process. For example, the surfacing and primary stages of the campaign have become more important to the final outcome, receive more precise and planned attention by candidates, and generate more excitement and enthusiasm from the general public than before television entered the political arena. This has happened because the media treat these preliminary events in much the same manner as they treat the later stages. In fact, because of high media involvement, the first two stages have replaced not only the attention-getting power of the nominating conventions and the general election, they have also seized much of their legitimate power.

In the largest sense, we conclude this chapter as we began it—convinced that the mass media (especially television) have a tremendous impact on political campaign communication.

NOTES

1. Roy Eldon Hiebert, Donald F. Ungurait, and Thomas W. Bohn, *Mass Media V: An Introduction to Modern Communication* (New York: Longman, 1988), pp. 40, 54, 90, 148, 206–7.

2. Ibid., p. 213.

3. Dan D. Nimmo and James E. Combs, *Mediated Political Realities*, 2d ed. (New York: Longman, 1990), p. 25.

4. Frank E. X. Dance, "Human Communication Theory: A Highly Selective Review and Two Commentaries," in *Communication Yearbook II*, ed. Brent D. Ruben (New Brunswick, N.J.: Transaction Books, 1978), pp. 7–22.

5. Peter M. Sandman, David M. Rubin, and David B. Sachsman, *Media* (Englewood Cliffs, N.J.: Prentice-Hall, 1972), p. 20.

6. Ibid., p. 23.

7. Ibid., p. 25.

8. Sidney Kraus and Dennis Davis, *The Effects of Mass Communication on Political Behavior* (University Park: Pennsylvania State University Press, 1976), p. 117.

9. Elihu Katz and Paul F. Lazarsfeld, *Personal Influence* (New York: Free Press, 1955), p. 16.

10. Harold F. Gosnell, *Machine Politics Chicago Model* (Chicago: University of Chicago Press, 1937).

11. Garrett J. O'Keefe, "Political Campaigns and Mass Communication Research," in *Political Communication: Issues and Strategies for Research*, ed. Steven H. Chaffee (Beverly Hills: Sage, 1975), p. 133.

12. David Blomquist, *Elections and the Mass Media* (Washington, D.C.: American Political Science Association, 1981), pp. 4–6.

13. Kraus and Davis, *Effects of Mass Communication*, p. 117.

14. For a discussion of the methodological difficulties of the selective exposure concept, see, for example, Lee B. Becker, Maxwell E. McCombs, and Jack M. McLeod, "The Development of Political Cognitions," in *Political Communication: Issues and Strategies for Research*, ed. Steven H. Chaffee (Beverly Hills: Sage, 1975), pp. 28–31; Kraus and Davis, *Effects of Mass Communication*, pp. 51–54; and David Sears and Johnathan Freedman, "Selective Exposure to Information: A Critical Review," *Public Opinion Quarterly* 31 (Summer 1967): 194–213.

15. Katz and Lazarsfeld, *Personal Influence*, p. 138.

16. Ibid., p. 309.

17. Ibid.

18. Kraus and Davis, *Effects of Mass Communication*, p. 120.

19. Becker, McCombs, and McLeod, "Development of Political Cognitions," p. 32.

20. Ibid., p. 33.

21. Kraus and Davis, *Effects of Mass Communication*, p. 53.

22. Angus Campbell et al., *The American Voter* (New York: John Wiley and Sons, 1964).

23. David M. White, "The 'Gate Keeper': A Case Study in the Selection of News," *Journalism Quarterly* 27 (Fall 1950): 383–90.

24. Sandman, Rubin, and Sachsman, *Media*, p. 103.

25. Ibid., p. 109.

26. See, for example, Lewis Donohew, "Newspaper Gatekeepers and Forces in the News Channel," *Public Opinion Quarterly* 31 (Spring 1967): 62–66; Jean S. Kerrick et al., "Balance and the Writer's Attitude in News Stories and Editorials," *Journalism Quarterly* 41 (Spring 1964): 207–15; and G. A. Donohue, P. J. Tichenor, and C. N. Olien, "Gatekeeping: Mass Media Systems and Information Control," in *Current Perspectives in Mass Communication Research*, ed. F. G. Kline and P. J. Tichenor (Beverly Hills: Sage, 1972).

27. Studies in the late 1960s and in the 1970s have consistently indicated that voters use the media for purposes other than reinforcement of their views. Moreover, other studies have shown that there are cases wherein voters prefer messages that contradict their views. Finally, with the decline of party affiliation, there is reason to believe that voters are not holding onto preconceived political beliefs but enter a campaign season with a willingness to be persuaded on issues. Steven H. Chaffee and Michael Petrick call the concept of selective exposure "too simplistic." See their book *Using The Mass Media* (New York: McGraw-Hill, 1975), p. 141.

28. Kraus and Davis, *Effects of Mass Communication*, p. 123.

29. Blomquist, *Elections and the Mass Media*, p. 7.

30. Ibid.

31. Ibid.

32. Ibid., p. 8. See also Jay G. Blumler and Denis McQuail, *Television in Politics* (Chicago: University of Chicago Press, 1969).

33. Kraus and Davis, *Effects of Mass Communication*, p. 126.

34. Ibid., p. 128.

35. Ibid., p. 127.

36. Robert L. Savage, "The Diffusion of Information Approach," in *Handbook of Political Communication*, ed. Dan D. Nimmo and Keith R. Sanders (Beverly Hills: Sage, 1981), pp. 104–7.

37. Ibid., p. 115.

38. Steven H. Chaffee, "The Diffusion of Political Information," in *Political Communication: Issues and Strategies for Research*, ed. Steven H. Chaffee (Beverly Hills: Sage, 1975), p. 125.

39. Kraus and Davis, *Effects of Mass Communication*, p. 130.

40. See, for example, Walter Gantz, "The Diffusion of News About the Attempted Reagan Assassination," *Journal of Communication* 33 (Winter 1983): 56–66; Charles R. Bantz, Sandra G. Petronio, and David L. Rarick, "News Diffusion After the Reagan Shooting," *Quarterly Journal of Speech* 69 (August 1983): 317–27; and Ruth Ann Weaver-Tarisey, Barbara Sweeney, and Thomas Steinfatt, "Communication During Assassination Attempts: Diffusion of Information in Attacks on President Reagan and the Pope," *Southern Speech Communication Journal* 49 (Spring 1989): 258–76.

41. Jay G. Blumler, "The Role of Theory in Uses and Gratifications Studies," *Communication Research* 6 (January 1979): 21.

42. Ibid., 11–12.

43. Jack M. McLeod and Lee B. Becker, "The Uses and Gratifications Approach," in *Handbook of Political Communication*, ed. Dan D. Nimmo and Keith R. Sanders (Beverly Hills: Sage, 1975), p. 71.

44. Ibid., p. 87.

45. David L. Swanson and Dan D. Nimmo, eds. *New Directions in Political Communication Research: A Resource Book* (Newbury Park, Calif.: Sage Publications, 1990), p. 18.

46. Carl R. Bybee, "Uses and Gratifications Research and the Study of Social Change," in *Political Communication Research: Approaches, Studies, Assessments*, ed. David L. Paletz (Norwood, N.J.: Ablex Publishing, 1987), pp. 209–10.

47. While we have presented many of the major problems theorists have articulated regarding the uses and gratifications perspective, we have not discussed the charge that it is grounded in functionalism. For an excellent discussion of its functionalist roots and a critique of the approach itself, see David L. Swanson, "Political Communication Research and the Uses and Gratifications Model: A Critique," *Communication Research* 6 (January 1979): 37–53.

48. Bernard C. Cohen, *The Press and Foreign Policy* (Princeton: Princeton University Press, 1963), p. 13.

49. Kraus and Davis, *Effects of Mass Communication*, p. 216.

50. Maxwell E. McCombs and Donald L. Shaw, "The Agenda-Setting Function of Mass Media," *Public Opinion Quarterly* 36 (Summer 1972): 177.

51. G. Ray Funkhouser, "Trends in Media Coverage of the Issues of the '60s," *Journalism Quarterly* 50 (Autumn 1973): 538.

52. Kraus and Davis, *Effects of Mass Communication*, p. 214.

53. Maxwell E. McCombs, "The Agenda-Setting Approach," in *Handbook of Political Communication*, ed. Dan D. Nimmo and Keith R. Sanders (Beverly Hills: Sage, 1975), pp. 127–30.

54. Bruce E. Gronbeck, "Popular Culture, Media, and Political Communication," in *New Directions in Political Communication: A Resource Book*, ed. David L. Swanson and Dan D. Nimmo (Newbury Park, Calif.: Sage Publications, 1990), p. 85.

55. Anne Johnston, "Trends in Political Communication: A Selective Review of Research in the 1980s," in *New Directions in Political Communication: A Resource Book*, ed. David L. Swanson and Dan D. Nimmo (Newbury Park, Calif.: Sage Publications, 1990), pp. 336–38.

56. Ibid., p. 337.

57. Gladys Engel Lang and Kurt Lang, "The Media and Watergate," in *Media Power in Politics*, 2d ed., ed. Doris A. Graber (Washington, D.C.: Congressional Quarterly Books, 1990), pp. 255–62.

58. Dennis K. Davis, "Development of Research on News and Politics," in *New Directions in Political Communication: A Resource Book*, ed. David L. Swanson and Dan D. Nimmo (Newbury Park, Calif.: Sage Publications, 1990), p. 171.

59. Johnston, "Trends in Political Communication," p. 337.

60. Thomas E. Patterson, *The Mass Media Election: How Americans Choose Their President* (New York: Praeger, 1980), p. 8.

61. Ibid., p. viii.
62. Ibid., p. 3.
63. Ibid., p. 95.
64. Ibid., p. 53.

Chapter Five

Communicative Types and Functions of Televised Political Advertising

During the electoral campaigns of the 1980s, it became increasingly apparent that political advertising on television had become a central communication strategy for almost all who sought our vote. While during the previous two decades those who fancied themselves president had demonstrated a willingness to explore all manner of television commercials to champion the rightness of their cause, it was the 1980s that brought the television advertising attempts of all manner of candidates to our attention. Whether running for a seat in the U.S. Senate or for a chair on the Cincinnati city council, it seemed that every candidate was using television spot advertising. Political ads came to dominate whatever portion of public attention is reserved for things political. In fact, by 1990, during the first election of the new decade, there was at least as much discussion about the number and nature of the ads being used as there was about the candidates themselves. Voter or journalist, consultant or scholar, the central focus was television advertising. Criticism of the ads and their prominent role in the campaigns of 1988 and 1990 was broadbased. However, attention centered around what appeared to be a growing reliance on negative as opposed to positive ads, replacement of campaign dialogue with television commercials, the extraordinary cost of the spots, fear that the ads, especially those that were negative, determined electoral results, and the idea that television advertising had so "turned off" the public that in 1990 only 36 percent of the 186 million Americans eligible to vote did so.

Televised political advertising occupies a pivotal position within a candidate's campaign. Thus in this chapter, we will take a brief look at the development of television advertising in presidential politics, explore the principles underlying different types of political commercials, and then discuss some of the most important communicative functions they perform during the campaign. In so doing, we will examine the use of one kind of commercial, the attack or condemnation spot, by candidates who are women. We will conclude our discussion by reviewing the major question that has developed around the use of attack advertising. Because in Chapter 10 we examine all forms of media advertising, for now our consideration is limited to the ads candidates use on television.

HISTORICAL DEVELOPMENT

Televised political spots entered presidential politics in 1952 when the Republican nominee, General Dwight D. Eisenhower, filmed 40 commercials that were titled "Eisenhower Answers America." Although the 28 ads that were aired in 40 states revolutionized the way in which presidential candidates went about the job of getting elected, in terms of narrative and cinematography, the Eisenhower spots were but a primitive form of those we saw 36 years later when George Bush was the Republican nominee. The format for all of the spots was exactly the same: a male voice announced "Eisenhower Answers America." A regular citizen or "person-on-the-street" (actually from a line of people waiting to get into Radio City Music Hall in New York City) would ask Eisenhower a question and the general would respond with a one-or-two sentence answer that implied that it was time for a change. For example, "a man on the street" would say: "General, the Democrats are telling me I've never had it so good." Eisenhower would respond, "Can that be true when America is billions in debt, when prices have doubled, when taxes break our backs, and we are still fighting in Korea? It's tragic and it's time for a change."

The 1952 and 1988 spots did, however, have at least one common characteristic—each brought the techniques used in persuading Americans to buy commercial products to the front door of the White House. One of the most interesting aspects of the application of "Madison Avenue" strategy to the 1952 campaign was that it was totally unnecessary. Eisenhower, a genuine American hero, was, according to a 1952 Roper poll, the most admired living American. Although Eisenhower used the ads, his opponent, Illinois Governor Adlai Stevenson, rejected the idea of appearing in spot commercials—at least during the 1952 campaign. By 1956, when Governor Stevenson was again the Democratic nominee for president, he changed his mind about participating in spots—largely because the experts in both political parties believed television advertising had become a necessary part of the campaign effort. In fact, as political communication scholar Kathleen Hall Jamieson has written, "The major innovation of the '56 campaign was its increasing reliance on the five minute spot."[1] The ads in 1956 and the ones that followed in 1960 frequently consisted of the candidate talking directly to the television audience (the "talking head" ads) or those that made it seem as if "the viewing audience was eavesdropping on the candidate as he addressed a rally."[2] In spite of relatively minimal production techniques, by the time of the 1960 campaign it was clear that with the technology of television editing, ads could provide additional arguments for or against a candidate simply by juxtaposing a still photograph of the candidate, a name, or even part of a speech with specific visuals to create a whole range of image messages. Some of the images were positive (American flags, the Liberty Bell, waving fields of grain), others were negative (deserted factories, foreign demonstrators throwing rocks at cars, farmers standing in front of empty grain bins), but all were examples of arguments by visual association. As Jamieson noted in her chronology of the evolution of American political advertising, arguments by visual association (positive and negative) were used in the presidential campaigns of 1964 and again in 1968. Moreover, argument by positive association characterized the Ford and Carter campaigns of 1976, and remained a staple of political advertising through the early campaigns of the 1980s.[3] Although ads which utilized negative visual images (concepts) were used from at least the 1964 campaign forward, frequently those spots that directly attacked the opponent did not picture the candidate or the opponent. Attacks were left to running mates, other surrogates, or to unnamed, unknown voiceovers.

Without question, the best known of the negative concept ads aired only once (because of the legal and ethical questions it raised) and it never even mentioned the opponent's name. Nonetheless, the "Daisy Girl" ad so effectively cemented perception of the Republican nominee, Senator Barry Goldwater, as a warmonger—a man who could not be entrusted with our nation's national security—that he was never able to rid himself of the negative image. The force of the following ad was its ability to engage viewer's emotions and associate their negative response with Goldwater:

VIDEO	AUDIO
Camera up on little girl in field, picking petals off a daisy.	Little girl: "One, two, three, four, five, seven, six, six, eight, nine, nine—"
Girl looks up, startled; freeze frame on girl; move into her eye, until screen is black.	Man's voice, very loud as if heard over a loudspeaker at a test site: "Ten, nine, eight, seven, six, five, four, three, two, one—"
Cut to atom bomb exploding. Move into explosion.	Sound of explosion.

Johnson: "These are the stakes—to make a world in which all of God's children can live, or to go into the dark. We must either love each other, or we must die."

Cut to white letters on black background: "Vote for President Johnson on November 3."

Announcer: "Vote for President Johnson on November 3. The stakes are too high for you to stay home."[4]

In many instances, ads were targeted to appeal to voters in the opposition political party. For example, in 1964 several of Lyndon Johnson's spots openly called to Republicans "worried" about voting for Goldwater to join him. And in 1972 Richard Nixon used negative association or concept ads whose air time was paid for by an organization called Democrats for Nixon.

Typical of these ads was one titled the "McGovern Defense Plan:"

VIDEO	AUDIO
Camera up on toy soldiers.	Military drumbeat underneath.
	Announcer: "The McGovern defense plan.
Hand sweeps several away.	He would cut the Marines by one-third.
Cut to another group of toy soldiers; again, hand sweeps several away.	The Air Force by one-third.
Cut to another group of toy soldiers; again, hand sweeps several away.	He would cut the Navy personnel by one-fourth.
Cut to toy planes; hand removes several.	He would cut interceptor planes by one-half,
Cut to toy ships; hand removes several.	the Navy fleet by one-half, and
Cut to toy carriers. Hand removes several.	carriers from sixteen to six.
Cut to toys in jumble. Camera pans across.	"Senator Hubert Humphrey has this to say about the McGovern proposal: 'It isn't just cutting into manpower. It's cutting into the very security of this country.'
	[Music comes in: "Hail to the Chief."]
Cut to Nixon aboard naval ship.	"President Nixon doesn't believe we should play games with our national security. He believes in a strong America to negotiate for peace from strength."
Fade to slide, white letters on black background: "Democrats for Nixon."[5]	

Jamieson argued that in 1976 two new types of ads to attack opponents replaced the association or concept type—personal witness and neutral reporter. These ads featured ordinary Americans (not actors) expressing their beliefs about the opposing candidate (personal witness) or they presented a list of factual statements and invited people to make a judgment call (neutral reporter). As such, they appeared less harsh than the concepts ads and somewhat removed or apart from the candidate. Typical of these ads was the following example used by the Ford campaign:

VIDEO	AUDIO
Camera up on slide: white letters against black background. "Those who know Jimmy Carter best are from Georgia. That's why we thought you ought to know":	Sound of teletype underneath. Announcer reads script from slide and crawl.

Photo of Gerald Ford appears and holds underneath crawl: tough, unsmiling.

Script already on screen crawls upward, being replaced by new material:

"The Savannah, Georgia, *News* endorses Gerald Ford for President.

"The Augusta, Georgia, *Herald* endorses President Ford.

"The Atlanta, Georgia, *Daily World* endorses President Ford.

"The Marietta, Georgia, *Journal* endorses President Ford.

"The Albany, Georgia, *Herald* endorses President Ford.

"The Augusta, Georgia, *Chronicle* endorses President Ford.

"The Savannah, Georgia, *Press* endorses—"

The spot fades out midsentence, suggesting more papers to be named.[6]

In 1980 the personal witness or "man-in-the-street" ads were used once again. In addition, a longer ad, the documentary (spots designed to present a candidate's accomplishments) was utilized—especially by Ronald Reagan. But in the 1984 election, and again in 1988, the negative visual association or concept ad returned in such force that each was, at some point, termed the "year of the negative campaign."

Another element that has undergone change from campaign year to campaign year is the preferred length of commercials. There have been half-hour speeches or biographies; 4 or 5 minute documentaries or other special appeals squeezed between evening entertainment programs or right before or after the late night news; and there have been 20, 30, and 60 second segments. In other words, over the years, sandwiched in between programs and product commercials, political ads have taken a variety of time frames. However, during the decade of the 1980s, the 30 second spot became dominant—largely because research had documented that they were just as effective as longer spots in getting the message across. For the most part, campaigns have come to reserve longer ads, such as the 5 minute documentaries or biographies, for specific functions (introducing a new candidate, raising money, or an election eve message).

Thus, since their entrance into the presidential campaign arena, the form and style of televised political spots have, from election to election, undergone change. In some instances, stylistic changes were temporary and reappeared just four years later. In other cases, revisions or reformulations were more permanent. Over the years, however, political ads have reflected two patterns with some regularity. While neither is surprising, each is important enough to our understanding of televised ads as a critical tool of the campaign to spend some time discussing them. First, the style or form political ads take is frequently a reflection of the larger society of which they are a part. For example, in the two campaigns of the 1950s and even in 1960, the spots were neither hard-hitting nor very specific (particularly those in which the candidates themselves appeared) largely because Americans did not yet equate the techniques and manipulations of Madison Avenue advertising and public relations with their presidential candidates, and the candidates themselves were concerned that they not appear too "political" as opposed to "presidential." Between 1964 and 1972 we believe that the harshness of the negative associations used in commercials has to be seen within the context of the national anguish created by the escalating war in Vietnam and the civil rights movement. In the campaigns of 1976 and 1980, the number of positive ads and the "feel good" mood that was their theme, as well as the indirect and less attack-oriented negative spots, must be viewed as a reflection of public distrust and disillusionment with politics and politicians in the aftermath of Vietnam and Watergate. And the reemergence of strident and graphically explicit negative association or concept spots in 1984 and 1988 (whose meaning is perhaps less clearcut because of their relative proximity to us in time) may well have occurred because the campaigns did not generate any major issues or themes. From the surfacing through the general election stage, the focus was the character and image of the candidates rather than the identification and discussion of "burning issues" facing the electorate.

Not only, however, have political spots reflected broad societal problems/attitudes/preoccupations, they have also reflected the prevailing philosophical and stylistic "schools of thought" operant in commercial or product oriented advertising. While we would hesitate to contend that the process never works the other way, that is, particular strategies are used first in the political world and then by Madison Avenue, in general, those political consultants who work in most of the statewide to national races apply techniques that have been found successful in commercial advertising. In fact, after studying 669 political ads made in 1984 and 1986 for candidates on all levels, and after interviews with more than 800 campaign and media consultants, author Montague Kern wrote that during the 1980s the "world of political advertising absorbed its commercial counterpart and became as one."[7] Thus Kern argues that political spots in the campaigns of the 1980s were like their commercial counterparts in that they evoked feelings or experience, relied heavily on visual and aural effects, developed messages in which the candidate and a single issue were blended, and frequently attempted to associate a candidate with an affect-laden symbol that already had meaning for us.[8] While we do not intend to trace the historical development of commercial advertising, the ways in which its methods and techniques have been used by a variety of candidates will become obvious in the next sections as we explore the types and functions of televised political ads and the questions and controversies they have generated.

TYPES AND FUNCTIONS OF POLITICAL ADS

As the number of televised spots used during election campaigns have increased, so too have the number of people writing or talking about them. Whether the report of a practitioner or the analysis of a scholar, all seem to have contributed a name to describe the ads they have studied or those they have used. For example, in their book *The Spot*, authors Edwin Diamond and Stephen Bates argue that political advertising goes through four phases and thus produces four types of ads. Phase One brings ID Spots (ads that are biographical and are intended to introduce or identify the candidate—provide a sense of the candidate in the surfacing or primary stages of the campaign). Phase Two produces Argument Spots (ads that identify the candidate's causes, ideas, concerns— what the candidate stands for). Phase Three is the time for Attack Spots (ads that are direct and personal attacks meant to reduce the credibility of the opposing candidate—create doubt, stir fear, exploit anxiety, or motivate ridicule). Phase Four produces Visionary Spots (ads that are used as the campaign draws to a close to provide a reflective/thoughtful/ dignified view of the candidates—create the impression that the candidate has the leadership ability and the vision to move the country/ state/city forward).[9]

In his analysis of presidential television commercials used from 1952 through 1984, L. Patrick Devlin describes spots in terms of categories such as: talking head ads; negative ads (those spots that tear down the opponent); cinema verité ads (those in which the candidate is filmed in a real life setting interacting with people); documentary ads (spots that present the accomplishments of the candidate); man-in-the-street ads (those in which real people talk positively about the candidate or negatively about the opponent); testimonial ads (spots in which prominent people speak on behalf of the candidate); and independent ads (those that are sponsored by organizations separate from the candidate).[10] Montague Kern contributes two additional types of spots from her book *30-Second Politics: Political Advertising in the Eighties*. She defines platform ads as those that present a candidate's commitment to a position or to opposing the opponent's position and slogan ads as those that contain no policy statement, why statement, nor any answer.[11]

In a study of political advertising and its meaning in American elections, Richard Joslyn identified four different perspectives or approaches by which the contemporary election can be understood and argues that within each perspective, specific kinds of appeals are used in the television commercials. After examining 506 of these commercials, he found that the most prevalent type of appeal is one he labeled "benevolent leader." Benevolent leader ads, according to Joslyn, focus on a candidate's personality traits rather than programmatic actions, policy positions, or political values and "attempt to accomplish a correspondence between the role expectations for a public office and the persona of the candidate."[12] For example, the benevolent leader ads might focus on such traits as the candidate's courage, honesty, strength of character, sense of fairness and justice, or compassion. The ads can be in the form of biographies or documentaries in which the candidate is shown in situations wherein the traits discussed are evident, in testimonials in which a prominent person discusses a specific characteristic of the candidate, or even in a man-on-the-street format in which a number of people are featured as they remark on the candidate's virtues. Whatever form the benevolent leader ad might take, its focus is the candidate's personality or character strengths.

Not only have scholars offered a classification scheme for the variety of televised commercials, some have suggested that negative ads can be divided by specific types. As mentioned earlier in this chapter, Kathleen Hall Jamieson suggests there are three kinds of negative spots, which she terms concept ads (those that juxtapose unrelated visual images to suggest false inferences), personal witness ads (which feature regular citizens giving unscripted negative opinions about the opponent), and neutral reporter ads (those in which a series of informational statements are made and then the voter is invited to make a judgment or draw a conclusion about the opponent).[13] In 1985 Bruce E. Gronbeck identified negative ads as implicative (those that operate by innuendo without attacking directly), comparative (ads that juxtapose the opponent's record or positions on issues with those of the candidate), and assaultive (those that make direct and personal attacks on the opponent's motives, actions, and associations).[14] Although this summary is certainly not exhaustive, it may help you appreciate the complexity of trying to understand and distinguish among the types of televised commercials that have been used since 1952. However, we have no real desire to contribute either to the proliferation of ad types or to the difficulty of describing contemporary political advertising. Rather, our goal is to reduce ambiguity by classifying spots according to their primary rhetorical purpose. Within each category, we subdivide only in terms of videostyle factors (verbal content, nonverbal content, film/video production techniques)[15] that appear to have characteristics significant enough to distinguish them one from another. In some cases, you will see that at least one component of videostyle (usually film/video production techniques) overlaps from category to category, although the overall purpose of the ad is unchanged. You will also note that what we term videostyle factors, other theorists have classified as types of ads.

We suggest that the only important reason to categorize types of political commercials is to gain some understanding of their rhetorical purpose. While ads are used by candidates to fulfill a variety of functions (which we will discuss shortly), they have three primary rhetorical purposes: to praise the candidate; to condemn the opponent; or to respond to charges. Although from time to time these purposes may overlap, essentially ads can be understood in terms of their primary rhetorical purpose. Thus, we characterize televised political commercials and the communicative functions they perform in the following manner.

Ads Extolling the Candidate's Virtues

The videostyle factors available to be used in ads whose overall purpose is to praise the candidate are virtually unlimited. Over the years techniques such as testimony, documentary, talking head, cinema verité, man-on-the-street, slogan, platform, or benevolent leader have all been used. And although some election years and the campaigns of some candidates have made extensive use of a particular videostyle (for example, in 1980, 41 percent of the Reagan campaign's television commercials were documentaries)[16] most campaigns who have the financial resources to do so use a variety of the videostyles to promote the virtues/ strengths of their candidate. It is important, however, that the videostyle not detract from the ad's primary objective—extolling the candidate and ignoring the opponent.

The communicative functions performed by ads of this nature are as varied as the videostyles. Moreover, they are critical for both incumbents and challengers, although the extent to which they are used may vary in relationship to other conditions. For example, if the candidate is a relatively unknown challenger running against an entrenched incumbent, it is critically important that the campaign tell the candidate's "story." In other words, provide information on her background, accomplishments, positions on issues, strengths of character and personality, family and associates—define her. And television commercials can perform this function better and more rapidly than most other campaign tools available to the candidate and her staff. While there are countless examples of challengers running at all levels who have had some success in using commercials of this type to "define" themselves to the electorate, one who did not comes readily to mind. In the 1988 presidential campaign, challenger Michael Dukakis did not move rapidly enough after the Democratic Nominating Convention to tell the public who he was, what he stood for, what he had accomplished, and why he should be president. Consequently, the first series of ads aired by the Bush campaign immediately following the Republican Convention provided the missing definition of Dukakis. The problem for the Democratic nominee was, of course, that the Republican definition was not very flattering.

A second important function performed by these ads includes using commercials to develop and explain the candidate's stand or position on issues. Not only has television become the primary source of information, political commercials have become a significant source of voter information about all aspects of the campaign. As research has demonstrated, voters can learn more about a candidate's position or stand on an issue from a commercial than they can by watching the evening newscasts.[17] Moreover, ads have a cumulative effect in that their frequent repetition during the course of a campaign helps voters learn just where the candidate stands on a given issue.

Additional and related functions performed by spots that extol the candidate's virtues include: reinforcing the positive feelings of supporters and partisans (just watching the ad may strengthen conviction of the rightness of one's cause or choice of candidates); redefining or softening the candidate's image (in 1968 Richard Nixon's image as one of "life's losers" was redefined to "statesman," in part by his television commercials; and in 1976 Gerald Ford's image as a well-intentioned "buffoon" was redefined to "president" by the genius of the campaign's "I'm Feeling Good About America" spots); and raising money (in 1984 Democrats used a special five-minute commercial about Walter Mondale so that they could raise money from supporters to air future ads). In short, ads whose purpose is to praise the candidate can fulfill functions important to the success of the campaign.

Ads Condemning/Attacking/Questioning the Opponent

Just as a wide variety of videostyle factors can be used in ads that emphasize the virtues of the candidate, so too can a number of different techniques be utilized in spots that focus on the opponent. For example, contemporary campaigns have used techniques such as personal witness, comparison, negative association or concept, talking head, assaultive, or cinema verité. Although the videostyle factors can vary and, therefore, alter the directness and strength of the attack, the primary purpose can not. These are ads designed to place the opponent in an unfavorable light or in an uncomfortable position. They focus on the shortcomings (real or imagined) of the opponent rather than the attributes of the candidate. In the largest sense, the purpose of these kinds of ads—no matter the variability of techniques employed—is to increase the opponent's "negatives." As such, they have received a good deal of attention from the public, as well as from journalists and scholars.

Since the introduction of televised ads whose purpose was to attack the opponent, a wide variety of formats and strategies have been employed. Some commercials have utilized humor and ridicule, others have linked the opponent with unpopular issues, or negatively perceived people (guilt by association), some have fastened labels on their opponents and then defined those labels negatively, many have relied on fear appeals, and others have sought to create a suspicion or anxiety about the opponent's beliefs or previous actions. At times viewers are directed to make up their own minds, that is, the attack or condemnation is implied. For example, the records of the candidate and opponent are compared and the opponent appears to have no attributes. But direct charges or conclusionary statements are not made. In other instances, the attack is direct and overt. For example, either in the narrative or by use of visual or aural symbols, viewers are told of the opponent's shortcomings. Clearly, depending on the videostyle and, of course, the intent, the commercials in this category can vary a good deal. Montague Kern has given names to two of the hardest hitting spots and distinguished between them in terms of what we think of as their videostyle strategies—primarily format and production techniques. She calls them "soft-sell," ads that make "heavy use of lighter entertainment values, humor, self-depreciation, storytelling, or the unexpected turn of events," and "hard-sell," those which utilize "dark colors and threatening voices" and create "harsh reality advertising."[18] According to Kern, both were used in abundance in the campaigns of 1984 and 1986 and both relied on aural and visual symbols to create intense emotional reactions such as anger, fear, uncertainty, anxiety, or suspicion.[19]

Without question, the heavy use of emotionally laden attack or condemnation spots continued into the 1988 and 1990 campaigns. In fact, three particular ads used by George Bush in 1988 ("Harbor," "Revolving Door," and "Tank") were aired so frequently (the Bush campaign spent 40 percent of its budget "airing about a half-dozen of its best negative ads")[20] and had such an impact that much of the public/journalistic outcry against attack advertising may well have been fueled, at least initially, by them. An example of one of the ads, the "Revolving Door," is typical of each:

VIDEO	AUDIO
A guard with a rifle climbs the circular stairs of a prison watchtower. The words "The Dukakis Furlough Program" are superimposed on the bottom of the prison visual.	Dissonant sounds are heard: a drum . . . music . . . metal stairs. An announcer states, "As governor Michael Dukakis vetoed mandatory sentences for drug dealers.
A guard with a gun walks along a barbed wire fence.	"He vetoed the death penalty.
A revolving door formed by bars rotates as men in prison clothing walk in and back out the door in a long line. The words "268 Escaped" are superimposed.	"His revolving-door prison policy gave weekend furloughs to first-degree murderers not eligible for parole.
The camera comes in for a closer shot of the prisoners in slow motion revolving through the door.	"While out, many committed other crimes like kidnapping and rape.
The words "And Many Are Still At Large" are superimposed.	"And many are still at large.
The picture changes to a guard on a roof with a watchtower in the background.	"Now Michael Dukakis says he wants to do for America what he's done for Massachusetts.
A small color picture of Bush appears, and the words "Paid for by Bush/Quayle 88" appear in small print.[21]	"America can't afford that risk!"

When the 1988 election was over, many scholars and journalists believed that it had been the worst the country had ever experienced because of the harshness, lying, and distortion in the attack spots. Some argued that because advertising techniques during 1988 had built on the foundation established in the campaigns of 1984 and 1986, the public felt paralyzed about the election process and "turned out" the election. Others maintained that the press had become so caught up in the strategy of the ads that they never discussed content or analyzed them for accuracy and fairness. David Broder, a respected political journalist for the *Washington Post*, acknowledged that the press had not done its job in 1988 and challenged his colleagues to police the 1990 primaries and general election campaigns by scrutinizing attack ads for their truthfulness. He and others cautioned not to let the spots themselves serve as the news story (a practice that had occurred with much frequency in 1988). Thus in spite of the heavy use of attack ads by 1990 candidates, there were a number of attempts to monitor them. For example, newspapers such as the *Los Angeles Times*, the *Miami Herald*, and the *New York Times* experimented with ad critiques (in some cases, the text of the ad would be printed and the factual basis of the claims it made were probed as well as a judgment on its fairness), and another dozen or so newspapers ran what came to be known as "truth boxes." In addition, three major television stations ran commentaries on the visual images contained in the ads. While the effectiveness of the "ad cops" during the 1990 campaign continues to be debated, the fact is that it was the first time that a real effort had been made to monitor attack advertising, and many believe that just as these ads will continue to be used so too will the effort be expanded to monitor them during the remainder of the 1990s.

For the most part, the communicative functions of attack ads are pretty straightforward. If the candidate uses them early enough in the campaign and if they are aired frequently, they can set the rhetorical agenda for the opponent who will, in some fashion, have to respond. Perhaps there is no better example of attack ads that seized the agenda than those used by a college professor, Paul Wellstone, in his successful 1990 campaign for the seat of Minnesota incumbent Senator Rudy Boschwitz. In a series of spots designed to paint Boschwitz as an out-of-touch, "inside-the-Beltway politician," who was concerned only with his image, Wellstone simultaneously made himself a credible candidate and taught Minnesota voters to "read Boschwitz's polished TV blitz as cynical imagemaking."[22] The spots were simple in terms of production—just the candidate and a camera. In one of the early commercials, "Looking for Rudy," Wellstone was seen "searching" for his "invisible" opponent. First he looked at Boschwitz's St. Paul office where he asked to borrow a pen to leave his telephone number for the senator (one of the ideas being conveyed was the "rich" Boschwitz campaign versus the "bare-bones" Wellstone effort) and then he "searched" at the Boschwitz Minneapolis headquarters and was told by two big men in suits "that we don't like strangers walking around here."

To some extent, the Wellstone commercials had an even greater impact than they might have had in other campaign years. Not only did they attract attention because they were different than those used by other candidates, the press effort to scrutinize political messages resulted in media discussion of the ads and, consequently, of Wellstone's issues.

A second function of attack ads is that they may well cause a defensive posture—even in a challenger—and therefore reduce the time, thought, and money that can be allocated to presenting a positive image. Similarly, and perhaps most apparent in recent campaigns, the use of attack or condemnation ads (if the charges against the opponent take hold in the public mind) can make, by comparison, even a mediocre candidate look better than the opponent. In other words, in the parlance of the consultants, candidates attempt to reduce their negatives and build their positives by increasing their opponents' negatives. The use of attack spots can also aid candidates by contributing to the perception of them as strong or decisive. This, for example, was clearly part of the strategy designed to erase the image of George Bush as a wimp during the 1988 presidential campaign. Finally, employment of attack ads can function to divert public attention away from those issues which might threaten the incumbent or prove embarrassing for the challenger. In other words, they can serve to keep the focus of the campaign on areas of strength, avoiding areas of vulnerability. Clearly, many of these functions can block or prevent meaningful campaign dialogue.

Ads Responding to Attacks or Innuendos

Until recently, little has been written about this final category of televised advertising. But as is the case with the other two types, a wide variety of videostyles can be and has been employed by candidates as they attempt to answer charges or attacks that have been leveled against them. The only "rule" or "law" that appears to be consistent in regard to these ads is that they must occur and occur very rapidly, as well as repeatedly, after the initial attack. In fact, most media consultants believe that some kind of a response to a televised attack spot must be aired as soon as possible after the initial attack because people are influenced by them (many are disposed to believing the worst about politicians anyway). Some theorists believe that the only instance in which a candidate can get away without responding to an attack is when the attack has been made by a weak candidate (someone with "low name recognition, no prior electoral experience, inadequate funding").[23] Perhaps, however, it was the legacy of the 1984 senatorial campaign in Kentucky that made clear the immense peril of the unanswered charge. When the campaign began, incumbent Senator Walter Dee Huddleston's approval rating was 68 percent. His challenger, Mitch McConnell, was given no real prospect of winning. However, McConnell's media adviser, Roger Ailes, designed a series of humorous ads in which he used hound dogs searching for the missing Huddleston (the senator had missed some Senate votes while he was earning speaking honorariums). The ads were humorous but they focused attention on McConnell and his campaign. More important, Huddleston never responded to the allegation that he had a "sorry record."

While a response commercial may take a variety of forms, the most frequently used are those that employ a refutation strategy (a direct rebuttal to the attack), a counterattack strategy (instead of refuting the charge, the candidate launches an attack on the character/issue positions/ motives/actions of the attacker), or a humor/ridicule/absurdity strategy. For example, in 1982 a "Talking Cows" ad was used by Senator John Melcher to respond to charges that he was too liberal for Montana (Melcher was one of the incumbents the National Conservative Political Action Committee (NCPAC) had targeted for defeat). In one response, cows were talking and warned voters about outsiders in Montana who "have come to Montana to 'badmouth Doc Melcher' " and how the "cow pasture was full of material like NCPAC's."[24] There have been a number of successful response spots and with each election campaign their use becomes more frequent—growing, obviously, in direct proportion to the increasing use of attack spots.

During the 1990 election response ads not only became more plentiful, they were on the air more rapidly than they had ever been in the past. Consultants frequently created and broadcast them within six hours, hastening the process by beaming the ads off satellites and sending them into television stations in specifically targeted areas. In fact, "satelliting" became one of the "buzzwords" of the campaign. One of the reasons for focusing on a rapid response is that consultants fear the attack ads of the opponent will control the dialogue or even set the dialogue for the campaign. Although speeches given by candidates or written position papers were once the framework for dialogue, in recent years the source has frequently been the attack and response spot. No where was this more apparent than in the 1990 election in California between the former mayor of San Francisco, Democrat Dianne Feinstein and Republican Senator Pete Wilson. During August, Californians witnessed a month-long exchange of charges and countercharges between their two candidates for governor. He accused her of supporting quotas for appointments in state government; she denied the accusation in a counterattack. She accused him of being too close to the savings and loan industry; he countered with a charge of hypocrisy because of her husband's involvement in the industry. The only ads aired by either candidate for a solid month were attack or response.[25]

Without question, the most important communicative functions of response ads revolve around attempting to contain damage resulting from the attack. Specifically, the candidate's response must function to deflect attention away from the subject of the attack/charge and onto the candidate's own safe ground. Similarly, the ad should ideally function to put the candidate back in an offensive or "one-up" position. Candidates who must continually assume a defensive position rarely win the election.

One of the most interesting theses regarding the strategy and defense of attack advertising is offered by Michael Pfau and Henry C. Kenski in their book *Attack Politics: Strategy and Defense*. They argue that the most effective strategy candidates can use is to preempt attacks before opponents use them, "thus militating their effectiveness." Specifically, Pfau and Kenski contend that one kind of preemption, inoculation message strategy, is most effective because it not only anticipates and responds to an opponent's attack before it is initiated, it strengthens resistance to accepting or believing future attacks by exposing the voter to a "weak dose" of the attack. The "weak dose" is strong enough "to stimulate defenses but not strong enough to overwhelm him."[26]

Whether or not future candidates will take the advice of Pfau and Kenski in the use of response ads is difficult to forecast. In sum, we have attempted to present a complete yet uncomplicated view of the types of political commercials used by a wide variety of candidates in the television portion of their campaigns. We turn now to a consideration of one type of those commercials as they have been employed by one group of candidates.

TELEVISED ATTACK ADVERTISING WHEN THE CANDIDATE IS A WOMAN

One of the most interesting aspects of televised political advertising during the 1980s was the use of attack spots by female candidates. In some respects, the fact that women running for political office employed spots that condemned opponents is not surprising. As we discussed earlier, attack advertising was a prominent strategy for a wide variety of candidates in the last half of the decade (some researchers believe they were the dominant advertising type in the 1986 and 1988 election)[27] and many candidates who employed them won. Moreover, the phenomenon of increased numbers of women seeking and winning political office, a phenomenon which had begun in the 1970s, continued in the 1980s. In fact, the 1989 *National Directory of Women Elected Officials* documents that from 1970 through 1989, the percentage of women in the U.S. Congress increased from 1.8 to 5.2; the percentage holding seats in state legislatures jumped from 4.7 to 16.9; and the percentage serving as mayors of cities with populations over 30,000 increased from 1.0 to 12.7.[28] Although women continued to face fund-raising obstacles and a lack of party backing, more and more had enough support (frequently from organizations such as the National Women's Political Caucus or Emily's List) to begin running campaigns that employed media consultants and relied on television advertising as a major campaign option. Thus it is possible to view the use of attack commercials by female candidates as a natural progression in the evolution of their direct participation in elective politics.

On the other hand, there is at least one important reason why female candidates might hesitate before employing attack ads. In spite of the fact that published research does not unequivocally support the idea that distinct differences exist in the communication behavior of women and men, sex-role stereotypes continue to shape expectations regarding what is appropriate.[29] For example, traditional expectations regarding the communication behavior of men include characteristics such as toughness, argumentativeness, aggressiveness, and dominance. However, the expectation for the communication behavior of women is almost exactly a polar opposite. When women speak, they are expected to exhibit characteristics such as sensitivity to the needs of others, compassion, affection, politeness, and openness. They are not expected to employ harsh language or to be overtly assertive, either verbally or physically. Perhaps these stereotypes were summarized most clearly by Mary Anne Fitzpatrick when she argued that "masculine traits are instrumental and defined by competence, rationality, and assertiveness; whereas female traits are expressive and hence defined by warmth, expressiveness, and nurturance."[30]

While we do not contend that gender-based communication stereotypes are universally accepted, we do know that speakers who fail to conform to expected behavior risk audience rejection of their message. One of the ways in which the impact of gender expectations on perceptions of communication effectiveness can be explained is by using Michael Burgoon and Gerald R. Miller's idea of an "expectancy interpretation of language and persuasion." According to their theory, expectations about language behaviors influence the acceptance or rejection of persuasive messages. Language that negatively violates normative expectations decreases the effectiveness of persuasive attempts while language that conforms more closely to expectations than anticipated increases persuasive effectiveness.[31] Moreover, Burgoon and Miller maintain that "most people still accord the two sexes very different roles in the social structure."[32] Thus, for example, if we consider submissiveness as one of the prescriptive generalizations about appropriate language behavior for women, our expectation is that their language will be less intense than the language of males. In fact, one of the conclusions from Burgoon and Miller's research is that "females fared better when they used language of low intensity."[33]

While expectations based on gender create problems for all professional women, in elective politics, stereotypes are particularly troublesome because of the very real potential for a backlash effect on the campaign efforts of those women whose communication defies or even challenges normative standards. In other words, backlash may occur when a female candidate exhibits so-called masculine communication behavior and thereby violates the traditional view of women as deferential, soft, and feminine.[34]

In 1981 Ruth B. Mandel, author of *In the Running: The New Woman Candidate*, argued that the female candidate "still must cope with centuries-old biases with the perception that her image is wrong, that someone who looks like her was not made to lead a city, state, or nation or to decide questions of national well-being or international security."[35] One of the ways in which these biases are manifested is in the female candidate's communication behavior. If she does not employ the language expected, she will violate the "rules," the long-held perception of the way in which women traditionally communicate.

At first glance, it may appear that the biases or stereotypes regarding women are a concern of the past because the percentage of women holding elective office has increased in recent years. However, it is important to understand that the increased percentages do not tell the whole story. The fact is that the ratio of women to men remains small, especially as the level of office increases. For the most part, the higher the level, the less likely you are to find a woman as the elected official. And even after the 1990 midterm election in which a record number of women received major party nominations for state governorships and seats in the U.S. Senate, only three of the 50 states had women governors, only two of the 100 U.S. Senators were women, and only 29 of 435 members of the House of Representatives were women. Thus even with the increased percentage of women holding elective office, the ratio of men to women suggests that the biases Mandel documented in 1981 have not disappeared.

In 1984, for example, as the vice-presidential nominee of the Democratic Party, Geraldine Ferraro was questioned about her hair style and her recipes for baking pies. She was sometimes given a corsage to wear at rallies at which she was the principal speaker, and the size of her dress was apparently viewed as important enough to be included in a *Newsweek* story about her candidacy shortly after the Democratic Convention. Three years later, in recalling her brief campaign to "test the waters" during the surfacing stage of the 1988 presidential election, Congresswoman Patricia Schroeder noted that when she was talking about nuclear testing, the media asked if her "husband would donate his tuxedo to the Smithsonian Institution" and that judging from the kind of coverage the media gave her it was as if the "fate of all womanhood on the planet depended on whether I wore earrings."[36] Moreover, during the midterm election of 1990, the political reporters for *Newsweek* magazine, in an article entitled "Sex Still Matters," noted that although 1990 was supposed to be the "Year of the Woman," the "so-called women's issues have slipped and the macho issues are at the top of the list" and that with the "Persian Gulf crisis, there's this instinct—among men and among women—to leave it to the men."[37]

Thus given the continuing pervasiveness of gender-based expectations or biases as well as the increasing dominance of televised attack commercials, the task facing female candidates as they negotiate their way through a contemporary political campaign can be formidable. If they use attack advertising they run the risk of being viewed as too aggressive, shrill, vicious, nagging, and "bitchy"—in other words, unfeminine; thus losing the advantages of being perceived as nurturant, sensitive, and warm. On the other hand, the political danger in not using attack advertising, particularly in an environment in which attacks are being used by an opponent, has been well documented.

Most researchers believe that there are three campaign conditions that favor the use of condemnation spots: low budget campaigns; campaigns of challengers; and campaigns in which one candidate is way behind or has suddenly begun a precipitous decline in the polls. Because female candidates frequently find themselves in one or more of these conditions, they have been inclined to use attack spots. In fact, after examining 329 ads used by 25 female candidates running for the U.S. Congress or state governorships between 1982 and 1986, Judith S. Trent and Teresa Sabourin concluded that 20 percent or 65 of the 329 spots were attack commercials.[38]

Given the fact that female candidates are using attack advertising, three questions seem important. First, have they ignored gender-based expectations or biases regarding their communication behavior? Second, have they in some way attempted to accommodate normative expectations even as they use televised condemnation spots? Third, if they have chosen to employ both strategies how have their attack ads been packaged—that is, what have been their content and form? While the answers are incomplete, research done in recent years has provided some information.

In a study reported in 1985, James G. Benze and Eugene R. Declercq compared the television commercials of 23 males and 23 females who ran for elective office between 1980 and 1983. They learned that the females were slightly more likely than males to attack the issue stance of their opponents than to attack their opponent's character. They also discovered that the female candidates whose ads they examined did not use the ads to project an image of "toughness." Instead of toughness, there appeared to be a tendency for female "candidates to stress their strengths rather than counteract their weakness."[39] A second study, this one an examination of the "identity-building strategies" of the first two women in American history to oppose each other in a gubernatorial general election, drew a conclusion essentially similar to the one drawn by Benze and Declercq. After analyzing the television commercials used by Helen Boosalis and Kay Orr during the 1986 Nebraska gubernatorial campaign, researchers David E. Procter, Roger C. Aden, and Phyllis Japp concluded that both women attempted to "blend soft, 'womanly' images with more 'male' images of experience and leadership."[40] The authors argued that a major component of Kay Orr's victory was that even while using attack advertising, she was able to build an image that projected compassion as well as toughness, thereby avoiding the appearance of being too strident or abrasive. In other words, the 1986 Orr campaign sought the advantages of both feminine and masculine communication stereotypes.

The results of the third study, an examination of the content and form of 65 attack ads used by women competing for elective office between 1982 and 1986, reinforced the compassion/toughness theme. Researchers found a clear effort to use elements of stereotypical or expected feminine communication behavior within the confines of attack advertising. The candidates blended aspects of the female communication stereotype with masculine communication stereotypes to indicate that they were not too nurturing or too compassionate to be successful in the office sought. To project the masculine image of strength, competence, and qualifications, the ads are infused with male voiceovers, discussion of experience or competence, and the visual picture of a candidate dressed in a highly professional/business manner. However, to maintain the feminine image, and thus preserve at least some normative expectations, candidates used strategies such as attacking issues and not character, making comparisons as opposed to harsh attacks, talking about social welfare issues, using music, picturing children or senior citizens, or ending the ad with a positive discussion of the candidate rather than continuing the attack on the opponent. In other words, attacks on opponents were embedded within a set of secondary strategies designed to mitigate the potential negative impact of the ad on the candidate herself.[41]

Attack advertising is, of course, intended to weaken or damage an opponent. However, as we have seen in this section, when the candidate is a woman, her use of the strategy must be especially sensitive. "So, how do female candidates use negative advertising?" The answer appears to be "very carefully."[42]

Whether attack or condemnation advertising is used by male or female candidates, it, more than any other strategy in the contemporary campaign, seems to have captured public, media, and scholarly attention. In the final section of this chapter we will discuss the most frequently asked question regarding this option.

A FINAL QUESTION

Questions and concerns about the use of televised attack advertising in political campaigns have risen almost as dramatically in the last decade as has the employment of the genre itself. Out of all of the dialogue, whether from journalists, consultants, political communication scholars, or even the public, we believe one important question emerges that has not been specifically addressed in this chapter: Do televised attack ads work? Although there remain areas of uncertainty, we believe that the bulk of the information available indicates that the answer to the question is "yes." But explanation is clearly in order.

Do Televised Attack Ads Work?

The fact that since the 1984 election there has been a fairly consistent increase in the use of attack advertising by candidates at all levels suggests to us that political consultants who at least influence, if they do not make, the strategical choices in a campaign believe they are effective. Although consultants acknowledge the existence of some risks in using the option, clearly the frequency of their choice to "go on the attack" suggests more advantages than disadvantages.

One of the most discussed disadvantages in employing attack ads is that they will "turn voters off" or away from the election itself. However, in spite of the fact that voter turnout became progressively worse in almost every election in the 1980s, there is really no direct evidence to indicate that people are ignoring their voting responsibilities because candidates employ attack advertising. While we believe that attack advertising may be part of the reason a 1990 *New York Times*/CBS News survey found that 73 percent of Americans do not fully "trust the Government in Washington to do what is right,"[43] certainly it does not constitute the entire problem. And although voter turnout in the 1990 election was low, it was no lower than it had been in 1986, despite newspaper headlines such as "Voters Complain Negative Campaigns Are Driving Them Away."[44] Moreover, in 1990 voting was heaviest in North Carolina and other states that had hotly contested races in which attack spots were used.[45] Finally, the results of a study conducted, at least in part to test the effect of attack advertising on the political process, indicated that there was no real evidence that negative advertising had any effect on voter involvement. In fact, on the basis of their findings, the researchers observed that "perhaps negative advertising turns off some voters, yet motivates others to vote."[46]

The second concern regards what researchers and practitioners call the backlash effect.[47] Because consultants and candidates fear such an effect, attack ads are frequently sponsored by a group that is technically not a part of the campaign, frequently a political action committee.[48] However, in many of the campaigns since 1984, consultants and candidates appear to have decided that the risk of backlash is acceptable because of the research that indicates that "over time voters tend to forget the origins of political messages while retaining their content."[49]

In spite of the potential risks, most consultants believe that the advantages of using attack ads outweigh the disadvantages. And the preponderance of research suggests that voters are more influenced by attack ads than by non–attack ads, that they pay more attention to them, recall them more accurately and remember them for a longer period of time.[50] Thus we conclude that there is one very good reason for the increased use of attack commercials: They work.

CONCLUSIONS

In this chapter, we have examined an increasingly important element of contemporary campaigns, televised advertising commercials. In so doing, we have briefly discussed their historical development in presidential politics and defined three types of commercials in terms of the overall communication functions they perform.

Finally, we considered televised attack advertising by female candidates. We found that because stereotypes regarding the appropriate communication behavior of women and men still exist, a candidate who is a woman will frequently have to combine traits of "femininity" and traits of "masculinity" in her television advertising.

NOTES

1. Kathleen Hall Jamieson, *Packaging the President: A History and Criticism of Presidential Campaign Advertising* (New York: Oxford University Press, 1984), p. 97.

2. Kathleen Hall Jamieson, "The Evolution of Political Advertising in America," in Lynda Lee Kaid, Dan D. Nimmo, and Keith R. Sanders, *New Perspectives on Political Advertising* (Carbondale and Edwardsville: Southern Illinois University Press, 1986), p. 15.

3. Ibid., p. 17.

4. Edwin Diamond and Stephen Bates, *The Spot: The Rise of Political Advertising on Television*, rev. ed. (Cambridge: MIT Press, 1988), pp. 128–29.

5. Ibid., pp. 205–7.

6. Ibid., pp. 328–29.

7. Montague Kern, *30-Second Politics: Political Advertising in the Eighties* (New York: Praeger, 1989), pp. 23–24.

8. Ibid.

9. Diamond and Bates, *The Spot: The Rise of Political Advertising on Television*, pp. 293–345.

10. L. Patrick Devlin, "An Analysis of Presidential Television Commercials, 1952–1984," in Lynda Lee Kaid, Dan D. Nimmo, and Keith R. Sanders, *New Perspectives on Political Advertising* (Carbondale and Edwardsville: Southern Illinois University Press, 1986), pp. 21–54.

11. Kern, *30-Second Politics: Political Advertising in the Eighties*, pp. 51–54.

12. Richard Joslyn, "Political Advertising and the Meaning of Elections," in Lynda Lee Kaid, Dan D. Nimmo, and Keith R. Sanders, *New Perspectives on Political Advertising* (Carbondale and Edwardsville: Southern Illinois University Press, 1986), pp. 139–83.

13. Jamieson, "The Evolution of Political Advertising in America," pp. 17–19.

14. Bruce E. Gronbeck, "The Rhetoric of Negative Political Advertising: Thoughts on Senatorial Race Ads in 1984," (Paper presented at the Speech Communication Association Convention, Denver, 1985).

15. Lynda Lee Kaid and Dorothy K. Davidson, "Elements of Videostyle: Candidate Presentation Through Television Advertising," in Lynda Lee Kaid, Dan D. Nimmo, and Keith R. Sanders, *New Perspectives on Political Advertising* (Carbondale and Edwardsville: Southern Illinois University Press, 1986), pp. 184–209.

16. Devlin, "An Analysis of Presidential Television Commercials," p. 32.

17. Ibid., p. 23.

18. Kern, *30-Second Politics: Political Advertising in the Eighties*, p. 94.

19. Ibid., esp. pp. 93–106.

20. L. Patrick Devlin, "Contrasts in Presidential Campaign Commercials of 1988," *American Behavioral Scientist* 32 (March/April 1989): 406.

21. Ibid., p. 389.

22. Charles Trueheart, "The Incumbent Slayer from Minnesota," *Washington Post National Weekly Edition*, November 26–December 2, 1990, p. 10.

23. Michael Pfau and Henry C. Kenski, *Attack Politics: Strategy and Defense* (New York: Praeger, 1990), p. 36.

24. Ibid., p. 22.

25. Robin Toner, "90's Politics Seem Rough as Ever Despite Criticism of Negative Ads," *New York Times*, September 9, 1990, pp. A1 and A25.

26. Pfau and Kenski, *Attack Politics*, p. xiv.

27. Kern, *30-Second Politics: Political Advertising in the Eighties*. Also see Pfau and Kenski, *Attack Politics*, esp. pp. 27–38.

28. Marie Morse, *National Directory of Women Elected Officials 1989* (Washington, D.C.: National Women's Political Caucus, 1989), p. 12.

29. Constance Courtney Staley and Jerry L. Cohen, "Communicator Style and Social Style: Similarities and Differences Between the Sexes," *Communication Quarterly* 36 (Summer 1988): 192–202.

30. Mary Anne Fitzpatrick, *Between Husbands and Wives: Communication in Marriage* (Newbury Park, Calif.: Sage Publications, 1988), p. 93.

31. Michael Burgoon and Gerald R. Miller, "An Expectancy Interpretation of Language and Persuasion," in Howard Giles and Robert N. St. Clairs, *Recent Advances in Language, Communication, and Social Psychology* (London: Lawrence Erlbaum, 1985), pp. 199–229.

32. Ibid., p. 209.

33. Ibid., p. 210.

34. We would be remiss if we failed to note the very real "double bind" facing all female candidates. Not only must a woman avoid appearing "too tough,"

she must also avoid appearing "too soft" or "too caring" for fear that such emphasis will make her appear weak.

35. Ruth B. Mandel, *In the Running: The New Woman Candidate* (New Haven and New York: Ticknor and Fields, 1981), p. 62.

36. Nadine Brozan, "Schroeder and Politics: The Problems of Gender," *New York Times*, November 23, 1987, p. B12.

37. Eleanor Clift, John Taliaferro, John McCormick, Mark Starr, and Nonny de LaPena, "Sex Still Matters," *Newsweek*, October 29, 1990, p. 34.

38. Judith S. Trent and Teresa Sabourin, "When the Candidate Is a Woman: The Content and Form of Televised Negative Advertising" (Paper presented at the Organization for the Study of Communication Language and Gender Conference, Cincinnati, 1989).

39. James G. Benze and Eugene R. Declercq, "Content of Television Political Spot Ads for Female Candidate," *Journalism Quarterly* 62 (Summer 1985): 283.

40. David E. Procter, Roger C. Aden, and Phyllis Japp, "Gender/Issue Interaction in Political Identity Making: Nebraska's Woman vs. Woman Gubernatorial Campaign," *Central States Speech Journal* 39 (Fall/Winter 1988): 201.

41. Trent and Sabourin, "When the Candidate is a Woman: The Content and Form of Televised Negative Advertising."

42. Ibid. In some respects, a 1990 gubernatorial candidate, Ann Richards of Texas, defied the principle of blending feminine and masculine communication behavior to avoid appearing too aggressive. However, the Burgoon/Miller expectancy interpretation of language and persuasion provides another explanation. We have discussed the expectancy theory, which indicates that when violations of normative expectations occur, one of two responses happen: if the behavior represents a positive violation of expectations, the speaker's effectiveness can be enhanced; if, however, the speaker's performance falls short of expectations, a negative violation occurs and it will detract from perceptions of the speaker's effectiveness. However, determining expectations for male and female candidates involves issues other than gender; for example, the credibility of the speaker influences expectations. As such, although a female is expected to use less forceful language than a male, a high credible speaker is expected to use more intense language than a low credible speaker. As such, Ann Richards's use of unmitigated attack advertising may represent a positive violation of expectations. If in the "rough and tumble" of Texas politics she had exhibited stereotypically feminine communication behavior, she undoubtedly would have been perceived as ineffective (lacking credibility). By using tough/forceful ads, that is, in rising to the occasion and the norms for a credible Texas politician, she actually enhanced her effectiveness.

43. Randall Rothenberg, "Voters Complain Negative Campaigns Are Driving Them Away," *New York Times*, November 6, 1990, A11.

44. Ibid.

45. Phillip Shenon, "Turnout Is Again Low In Elections," *New York Times*, November 11, 1990, A15.

46. Gina M. Garramone, Charles K. Atkin, Bruce E. Pinkleton, and Richard T. Cole, "Effects of Negative Political Advertising on the Political Process," *Journal of Broadcasting and Electronic Media* 34 (Summer 1990): 308.

47. Gina M. Garramone, "Voter Responses to Negative Political Ads," *Jour-

nalism Quarterly 61 (Summer 1984): 250–59. Also see Gina M. Garramone, "Effects of Negative Political Advertising: The Roles of Sponsor and Rebuttal," *Journal of Broadcasting and Electronic Media* 29 (Spring 1985): 147–59. Also see Lynda Lee Kaid and John Boydston, "An Experimental Study of the Effectiveness of Negative Political Advertisements," *Communication Quarterly* 35 (Spring 1987): 193–201.

48. Ibid.

49. Pfau and Kenski, *Attack Politics*, p. 158.

50. Ibid., p. 4.

PART II

PRACTICES OF POLITICAL CAMPAIGN COMMUNICATION

Chapter Six

Public Speaking in Political Campaigns

This chapter will focus on what is perhaps the most fundamental communication practice in any campaign, public speaking. In the first section, we will examine the factors that enter into a candidate's decision to speak. Decisions on where and when to speak and what to say to a given audience are not made randomly but are often the result of considerable thought and planning on the part of candidates and their staffs. In the second section, we will inspect the use of stock or modular speeches. This practice is a common one utilized by candidates running for virtually every office. As we will see, it is an effective means of handling the massive speaking demands placed on candidates for public office. In the third section, we will discuss the practice of political speechwriting. Candidates are using speechwriters more today than ever before; any examination of public speaking practices in political campaigns must consider the use of speechwriters. Similarly, many candidates today are making extensive use of advocates or surrogates. These "substitutes" for the candidate may be heard in person by as many people, if not more, than those who actually hear the candidate. Hence, any examination of public speaking practices in contemporary campaigns that does not consider the use of surrogate speakers would be less than complete.

THE DECISION TO SPEAK

Perhaps the most important resource available to any campaign is the time of the candidate. That time must be used wisely. Decisions to use the candidates' time for public speeches are made out of self-interest, as the candidate attempts to influence the maximum number of voters. Hence, it is vital that candidates and their staffs do an effective job of analyzing voter audiences to best utilize the candidate's time. Essentially candidates face two tasks: first, to determine whom they should address and, second, to determine what messages should be presented to those they address.

Audiences

Since 1946 when Jacob Javits, then running for a seat in the House of Representatives, employed the Elmo Roper Organization to make opinion polls of his constituency to determine better what issues he should develop in his campaign,[1] political campaigns have increasingly relied on two tools to assist them in analyzing audiences. The first is studies of past voter statistics, and the second is the public opinion poll. As we have seen in earlier chapters, these tools have blossomed in recent years because of improvements in computer technology.

Local and national candidates make use of past voter statistics to analyze audiences. Yet these statistics play a more vital role in the campaigns of local candidates than they do in the campaign of national or major statewide contenders. Indeed, there is no more valuable campaign aid to the local candidate than accurate voter statistics. Though voter statistics may serve many potential purposes, their chief function is to pinpoint, on a precinct-by-precinct basis, where candidates should be concentrating their efforts. This knowledge enables candidates to determine what speaking invitations should be accepted and in what areas of the district their staffs should attempt to arrange speaking opportunities and otherwise concentrate.

Though the same principles apply for national figures and local figures, in practicality major national or statewide figures are rarely able to aim their speeches or campaign materials to a specific precinct. The size of their constituency and the extensive media coverage they receive often prohibit tailoring a given speech to a specific precinct, as can the local candidate dealing with a smaller constituency. The local candidate, far more than counterparts seeking national or statewide office, must know precisely, down to the precinct, the nature of the constituency. Because their constituencies are smaller, in many instances the local candidate can knock on every door in the district, or at least on every door in those precincts that are deemed most valuable. When a statewide candidate like "Walking Joe" Teasdale, former governor of Missouri, walks across the state, he is doing so primarily for media coverage.

Local candidates, however, will not receive the media exposure of the gubernatorial candidate. Rather, their walks in the district can put them face-to-face with a large percentage of their constituency. The act is real rather than symbolic. To be effective, the local candidate must know which areas of the district in which to walk, speak, and otherwise campaign. Accurate voter statistics are an acute concern for local candidates who can meet a substantial portion of their constituency, can express their concern for voter problems face-to-face, and whose limited financial resources must be used with maximum effect.

Typically, candidates direct their efforts primarily toward precincts where their party traditionally runs well, those where elections are likely to be close, and those where ticket-splitting commonly takes place. It is in these areas that candidates should concentrate the majority of their speaking efforts. That may even mean actively soliciting speaking engagements in these areas when none are forthcoming. It means consistently giving preference to these regions when simultaneous speaking opportunities arise in two or more sections of the district. Local candidates can think in precinct terms. National or statewide candidates use the same process but must think more in media market and electoral vote terms.

Utilizing past voter records and computers to help analyze the data, state and local political organizations will often provide candidates with a precinct-by-precinct breakdown of their district. The materials a candidate receives might be similar to the two examples shown in Table 1. These examples are modeled after materials available to Republican candidates in Cincinnati, Ohio, during the 1990 elections. Using the table provided, can you determine whether a Republican candidate should speak in these precincts?

The first precinct is one in which a Republican candidate should actively speak and campaign since it is a heavily Republican precinct. Note that ten of the eleven Republicans on the ballot in the last two elections have won. The only Republican who failed to win in this district was the 1988 U.S. Senate candidate. As you can see in column three, that candidate drew only 44 percent of the vote and lost by 54 votes. No other Republican candidate has received less than 57 percent of the vote and in 1988 the Republicans averaged 68.6 percent of the vote in this precinct, while two years earlier they averaged 70.4 percent of the vote. Among the 418 precincts in the city of Cincinnati, in 1988 this precinct had the 16th highest average Republican percentage, and in 1986 it had the 14th highest Republican percentage.

Moreover, Republicans in this district are not excessive ticket-splitters, although at first glance they may seem to be. In 1988 it ranked 59th of the 418 precincts in ticket-splitting. But notice, that was because of the senatorial candidate who lost, thus creating a ticket-splitting figure of 37.3 percent. Without that candidate on the ballot, only 15 percent of

Table 1
Prior Election Results

1988	U.S. Pres.	U.S. Sen.	U.S. Hse.	St. Sen.	St. Hse.	Cty Comm	1986 St. Gov.	St. AttG	St. Aud.	U.S. Hse.	St. Hse.	Avr. R.%	Rank	Total Vote	Rank	Tkt.Splt. R.%	Rank
SAMPLE PRECINCT 1: CITY OF CINCINNATI - WARD 1 PRECINCT E																	
Rep.	294	179	322	280	245	286	147	148	123	233	185						
Dem.	113	233	76	106	130	92	80	74	94	35	55						
Other	5																
Total	412	412	398	386	375	378	227	222	217	268	240	68.6	(1988) 16	423	107	37.3	59
R. pct.	72	44	81	73	66	76	64	67	57	87	77	70.4	(1986) 14	273	129	30.4	78
D. pct.	27	56	19	27	34	24	36	33	43	13	23						
Diff.	181	-54	246	174	115	194	67	74	29	198	130						
SAMPLE PRECINCT 2: CITY OF CINCINNATI - WARD 5 PRECINCT G																	
Rep.	213	175	212	192	169	191	130	137	117	153	112						
Dem.	162	205	141	172	162	173	114	96	109	90	99						
Other	4																
Total	379	380	353	364	331	364	244	233	230	243	211	53.1	(1988) 159	385	142	14.4	269
R. pct.	57	46	60	53	51	52	53	59	53	63	53	56.2	(1986) 134	258	138	10.1	272
D. pct.	43	54	40	47	49	48	47	41	47	37	47						
Diff.	51	-30	81	20	7	18	16	41	8	63	13						

TOTAL PRECINCTS - CITY OF CINCINNATI: 418

COLUMN 1

Rep.	The Republican vote in the precinct for a particular office.
Dem.	The Democratic vote in the precinct for a particular office.
Other	The vote for all other party votes in the precinct for a particular office.
Total	The total vote in the precinct for a particular office. Obtained by adding the Republican, Democratic, and other vote

150

R. pct.	The Republican percentage in the precinct for a particular office. Obtained by dividing the Republican vote by the total vote in the precinct.
D. pct.	The Democratic percentage in the precinct for a particular office. Obtained by dividing the Democratic vote by the total vote in the precinct.
Diff.	The difference between the Democratic and Republican vote for a particular office. A minus sign (-) indicates Republican vote less than Democratic vote.

COLUMNS 2-7
1988 Election Results

COLUMNS 8-13
1986 Election Results

COLUMN 14
Average R.%   This is the average Republican percent in the precinct.

COLUMN 15
Rank   This is the rank order number of the particular precinct in terms of Republican percentage in the total district. The precinct with the highest Republican % in the district is number 1.

COLUMN 16
Total Vote   This is the maximum number of votes cast in this precinct since 1980.

COLUMN 17
Rank   This is the rank order number of the precinct in the district in terms of total votes cast.

COLUMN 18
Ticket-Splitting R%   This is the percent of ticket splitting in the precinct. It was calculated by subtracting the lowest Republican percent from the highest Republican percent in the precinct.

COLUMN 19
Ticket-Splitting Rank This is the rank order number of the precinct in terms of ticket splitting. The precinct with the highest percentage of ticket splitting in the district is number 1.

Total Number of Precincts: City of Cincinnati Legislative Report - 418 the Republican voters would have been ticket-splitters. In 1986, when all eight Republicans won, the incredibly popular incumbent congressman drew a staggering 87 percent of the vote. This was 30.4 percent more than the lowest Republican, the state auditor candidate, who it should be remembered won with a solid 57 percent of the vote. If the incumbent congressman had not been on the ballot, only 20 percent of Republican voters would have been ticket-splitters. Thus, although on first glance it seems that this precinct is marked by a high incidence of ticket-splitting, a close examination of the figures indicates that the precinct is generally consistent in giving Republicans substantial victories of well over 60 percent, and the apparent high ticket-splitting is largely a function of aberrant races.

The second precinct is also one in which a Republican candidate should actively speak and otherwise campaign. It too is Republican, although not nearly so heavily as the first. Examining the difference figures indicates that although Republicans have consistently won this precinct, again losing only the 1988 Senate race, three of the 1988 races were won by 20 votes or less. Moreover, though all five Republicans won in 1986, three of them did so by less than 20 votes. This is clearly a precinct where close elections abound. A shift of only 11 votes would have changed the outcome of six of the last eleven elections in this precinct.

This precinct is not marked by excessive Republican ticket-splitting. In 1988 14.4 percent of the Republican voters split their ticket. In 1986 that figure was 10.1 percent. In both years this precinct was well within the bottom half of the district in ticket-splitting.

However, what might be disturbing to Republican candidates examining these figures is that Republican ticket-splitting does seem to be trending upward and the typical Republican vote seems to be trending downward. Between 1986 and 1988 Republican ticket-splitting increased by 4.3 percent. In the same period, the average Republican vote fell by 3.1 percent. Though these figures would have little effect on races in the first precinct examined, if this trend continued, by 1990 this could become a Democratic precinct. Hence, this is clearly a precinct where close elections might be expected.

Using figures such as these, local candidates determine where they wish to speak. Typically, they will write off about 30 percent of the district as hopeless. The first precinct we just analyzed, for example, would be targeted by Republicans, but ignored as a hopeless precinct by Democratic contenders. Candidates then target the remaining 70 percent, those precincts where their party runs strong, where a close election is likely, or where ticket-splitting is common. Precinct two, for example, might well have been targeted by both Republican and Democratic candidates during 1990. Though Republican, Democrats have frequently come within 11 votes of winning it, and both sides might reasonably expect close elections in this precinct. Additionally, both of these precincts are relatively large. The vote totals rank both precincts well into the top half of the district.

National and statewide candidates operate on the same premise. They too target about 70 percent of their constituency. Typically, presidential candidates target states and media markets within states, rather than precincts, and choose to speak and campaign accordingly.[2]

Messages

The second primary tool of audience analysis is the public opinion poll. Polls help candidates develop their messages. But polls are utilized differently by local and major candidates. Accurate voter statistics down to the precinct level are of acute concern to the local candidate but often of lesser concern to the major candidate. However, the public opinion poll is of more concern to major candidates but often of lesser concern to the local candidate. Typically, the explanation for this different emphasis on the use of polls involves two distinctions between local and major candidates. First, the major candidate can normally afford a polling service and may also be helped by national polls such as those of Gallup and Harris. Candidates for Congress and statewide and national offices all utilize polling services. Most state legislative candidates and contenders for local offices in larger urban districts also use polls. Candidates for lesser local offices, such as sheriff, county or city recorder, clerk, or engineer, particularly in less populated communities, cannot afford polling services.

Second, even if the local candidate could afford polls, the essentially administrative nature, rather than policy-making nature, of most local offices tends to minimize the distinctions between the viewpoints of local candidates. Issues of policy, which sharply divide candidates for major office, often are not at stake in local elections. This is not to say that there is no opportunity for policy making at the local level. Rather, it is to suggest that while major campaigns almost invariably involve clashes over policy issues, many local campaigns are waged for positions with comparatively little policy-making responsibilities. Hence, there is often little distinction between candidates on the basis of issues and less need for polls.

Issue polls are designed to determine what concerns are uppermost in the minds of the voters. They serve major candidates as a topoi, or topics, system. In addition to suggesting topics upon which to speak, they indicate voter opinions and beliefs. As we have noted earlier, candidates rely on polling services when they develop positions on issues.

Using polls to determine important issues makes good sense. Using polls, instead of solid study, research, and good judgement, to determine what to say about the public's concerns is a questionable procedure. Writing in 1954, when polling was first developing as a major campaign tool, former President Harry Truman asked:

I wonder how far Moses would have gone if he'd taken a poll in Egypt? What would Jesus Christ have preached if he'd taken a poll in Israel? Where would the Reformation have gone if Martin Luther had taken a poll? It isn't polls or public opinion of the moment that counts. It is right and wrong leadership—men with fortitude, honesty, and a belief in the right that makes epochs in the history of the world.[3]

Most political candidates agree with the implications of Truman's remark that although the polls can help determine what absorbs the public's attention, they should not be used to dictate the candidate's approach to an issue.

Typically, the candidate's polls will be able to rank issues of concern among specific constituencies such as older voters, women voters, or middle-income voters. The degree to which the polling data are broken down and analyzed depends on the candidate's needs and the finances available. A national campaign will break down the polling data extensively, determining, for example, what issues are of concern on such bases as geography, income, race, religion, and party. As candidates speak, they can vary their subject matter to insure they are addressing the major concerns of the groups to whom they are speaking.

Polls also provide candidates with indirect feedback on messages. Candidates often reposition their stands on issues as a consequence of that feedback.

Competency and Format

Most individuals who run for major public office feel comfortable in front of an audience.[4] Most have had extensive prior public speaking experience, and many have also had both formal and informal training.[5] If prospective candidates are apprehensive about the speaking demands of their races, they might well prepare by seeking the advice of competent professionals. Many candidates utilize the services of speech coaches. Both the Republican and Democratic national committees, as well as many state and local party committees, provide speech training in their candidates' schools.

If candidates are uncomfortable with some speaking formats, they and their staffs might attempt to place them in formats where they do not feel uncomfortable. If, for example, they are uneasy delivering formal speeches, perhaps their formal speeches could be kept brief and be followed by extensive question-and-answer periods. The type of training and formats utilized by candidates varies on an individual basis, but should not be ignored. A frank and realistic assessment of the candidate's speaking abilities, no less than assessments about where and when to talk and what to talk about must enter into the candidate's decisions to speak.

THE SPEECH

During the 1980 primaries, the *New York Times* wrote that the presidential candidates of both major parties

make hundreds of speeches in their campaigns, speeches that vary in content depending on where they are given and the audience addressed. But every candidate has a body of material, usually presented in every speech that varies little from audience to audience. This material represents the heart of his message to the voters as he moves around the country.[6]

The *Times* was describing what political speakers call their "stock speeches," and what their speechwriters might also call their "module speeches." The great demand to speak that is placed on contemporary political figures has caused most of them to resort to the use of stock or module speeches. The demand to speak is also one of the principal reasons used by candidates to justify the use of speechwriters. In this section, we will examine the use of stock speeches, and in the next section we will examine the practices of political speechwriters.

Need and Justification

Speechmaking is fundamental to political campaigning. The politician cannot reasonably expect to campaign without continually facing audiences. Even the candidate for city council in a small community must constantly speak. Typically, such a candidate is called upon to make several major speeches during the campaign, at such events as the local League of Women Voters "Meet The Candidates Nights," or at the Rotary Club's monthly meeting. Moreover, these candidates must be continually speaking, often three or more times an evening throughout the final weeks of the campaign, to smaller groups of citizens. Campaign coffees, teas, church socials, and similar activities crowd the calendars of most candidates. It is not unusual for local candidates to find themselves confronting the prospect of 100 or more speeches during the last four to six weeks of a campaign. Similarly, as we will see in the next section, candidates for more important local, state, and federal offices face situations where they must speak 30 or more times a week. Because of these demands, most candidates make use of a stock speech and if possible, the services of speechwriters.

Speech Modules

Although the phrase "stock speech" has entered the vocabulary of most politically aware citizens, it is a misnomer. We tend to think of it as a speech that is delivered time and time again with little change. We think of it as unvarying, set, well established. Yet if you read the *New York Times* description of stock speeches that opened this section carefully, you may recall that the *Times* noted that stock speeches "vary in content depending on where they are given and the audience addressed." They are not altogether set and established. Candidates do not give the identical speech time after time after time, regardless of the audience, occasion, or the actions of their opponents. Rather, they adapt to these factors.

How do the candidates adapt, given the heavy demands on time? They do so by making use of "speech modules." A speech module is a single unit of a speech. Typically, candidates will have a speech unit, or module, on each of the 10 to 20 issues on which they most frequently speak. Each module is an independent unit that can be delivered as a two-to-seven minute speech on the issue. The length of each can be varied simply by adding or subtracting examples, statistics, illustrations, or other support materials. Typically the organization of each module is similar and will be readily recognized by many students of public speaking.

Each module opens with some attention-gaining device, and then candidates quickly move to a discussion of a problem. Having sketched the problem, they then present their policies as an appropriate solution to the problem. If more time is available, they might then vividly describe or visualize what would happen if they are elected and their policies carried out. Thus the typical speech module is designed to: (1) gain attention, (2) describe a problem, (3) present a solution, and (4) visualize the solution. The first three of these steps are characteristic of virtually every speech module the candidate presents. The final step may not be necessary. It may be implicit from the discussion of the problem and the solution and hence not warrant explicit treatment. The following is an example of a speech module used by Ronald Reagan during the 1980 primaries.

Despite the protest about all the problems he inherited, Jimmy Carter came into office with the economy expanding, with inflation reduced to less than 5 percent, and with the dollar a relatively stable measure of value. In 36 months he has tripled the rate of inflation; the prime interest rate has risen to the highest level since the Civil War; the price of gold has risen from $125 an ounce to more than $600 and fluctuates up there to that level which measures the extent to which international confidence in the dollar has fallen. And that is the indication of the collapse of confidence of economic policies in the Carter Administration.

Attention: Startling statements used to (1) gain attention and (2) initially develop the problem

After last summer's Cabinet massacre, the departing Secretary of the Treasury confessed that the Carter Administration did not bring with it to Washington any economic philosophy of its own. So the President and his counselors embraced the only economic philosophy they could find at hand—the warmed-over McGovernism of the Democratic platform of 1976.

Problem: Developed in chronological order

Together Mr. Carter, his Democratic Congress and his first choice for chairman of the Federal Reserve proceeded on the premise of parallel lanes of national prosperity, Federal deficits and easy money. Pursuing this course together, they made a shambles of our national economy wiping out in three years' time tens of billions of dollars of value in our private pensions, savings, insurance, stocks and bonds.

I suggest that when one administration can give us the highest inflation since 1946, the highest interest rates since the Civil War, and the worst drop in value of the dollar against gold in history, it's time that administration was turned out of office and a new administration elected to repair the damage.[7]

Plan: Reject Carter and elect Reagan

Visualization: Not explicit

In this module, we see an independent speech unit or module on the Carter administration's conduct of economic affairs. The passage stands by itself. It also could be linked very easily into another module with a simple transition. In fact, this is precisely what Reagan did. Following the quoted passage he would normally add: "But when we consider what lies ahead in this new decade, the damage done to the national economy is insignificant alongside the damage done to our national security."[8] At this point he would present his module on national security.

Economy Module

Attention

Problem

Plan

Visualization

Transition

Security Module

Attention

Problem

Plan

Visualization

These happen to be the two modules Ronald Reagan used most frequently during the 1980 primaries. Because the economy and national security are issues that vitally affect all citizens, they were appropriate to use with most audiences. But let us imagine for a moment that Reagan was speaking to a group of voters during the New Hampshire primary. That primary was held in the dead of winter, in one of the coldest states in the union. He might reasonably expect that the high cost of energy and fuel oil was uppermost in the minds of his audience.

Having already prepared a module on energy, it would be a rather minor adjustment for Reagan to present his initial module, for New Hampshire like all the nation was suffering economically, and this was Reagan's major issue. Then, adapting to his audience and the occasion and timing of the speech, he might choose to speak about energy, not national defense. He could do so by:

Economy Module

Attention

Problem

Plan

Visualization

Transition

But when we consider what lies ahead in this new decade the damage done to the national economy is insignificant alongside the damage done to our energy programs

Energy Module

Attention

Problem

Plan

Visualization

Most candidates will develop key modules at the outset of the campaign, occasionally adjusting them as the need arises. Additionally, they will add modules as the need arises. Then, depending on the audience, the occasion, and any other relevant factors, they will determine what modules to use for a given speech. Often, as with Reagan and the national economy, the same module is used in many speeches. Yet each speech is in fact tailored to the specific audience and occasion.

Speechlike Opportunities and Modular Speeches

One of the principal advantages of developing a basic speech through modules is that the modules can then be used by the candidate in many speechlike situations. Often candidates desire to appear on interview shows such as "Meet the Press," or talk shows such as "Phil Donahue." Opportunities such as these must be weighed like any other opportunity to speak. However, because they do offer free exposure, many candidates, especially those operating on a limited budget, attempt to utilize them. Almost every media market has local radio talk shows and television shows, so that these decisions are not unique to national contenders.

If candidates have already prepared speech modules on most major topics, they are likely to do well on these shows. The module, which can be varied in length, lends itself to use in these formats. Candidates can accept such invitations with a minimum of preparation and be confident that they are unlikely to be caught ill-prepared. Moreover, they can be certain that their remarks will be consistent with those they have made throughout the campaign.

Occasionally, if a module is done especially well, it can also be turned into an effective television or radio spot. Since the module can stand alone and its length can be varied, it is easy to adapt to a commercial. Often media advisors wish to show their candidate in "the real world," talking to "real people." The speech module lets them do just that. Every Republican presidential candidate since Richard Nixon in 1968 has made use of modules excerpted from their acceptance address in precisely this fashion.

POLITICAL SPEECHWRITING

The use of speechwriters by political figures dates back to ancient Greece and Rome when men such as Julius Caesar and Nero received aid in preparing their speeches. In the United States, the use of speechwriters has been a feature of our politics since our nation's inception. George Washington had at least four different speechwriters, including Alexander Hamilton. Amos Kendell, a former editor of the *Kentucky Argus* newspaper and a close personal confidant of Andrew Jackson, was called by one of Jackson's critics, "the President's thinking machine, and his writing machine, ay, and his lying machine."[9]

Abraham Lincoln frequently called upon his secretary of state, William Seward, for advice on public speeches. Lincoln's successor, Andrew Johnson, had grown up on the frontier and did not learn to read and write until meeting and courting his wife, a teacher. Not surprisingly, he too sought a speechwriter. This rough-hewn president found his man in George Bancroft, perhaps the most erudite and distinguished historian of the day.

Although both presidents Calvin Coolidge and Herbert Hoover made use of the same speechwriter,[10] it was not until the administration of President Franklin Delano Roosevelt that the public at large became fully aware of the pervasive use of speechwriters by political figures. Roosevelt used a variety of individuals to provide him with aid in preparing speeches. Typically, Roosevelt drew upon both subject matter experts, often cabinet members, and stylists, such as authors Robert Sherwood and John Steinbeck. While the press on occasion reported on the use of speechwriters, it was not until Richard Nixon that an American president publicly acknowledged that individuals in his employ were in fact there primarily to help write speeches.[11]

Justification and Implications of Political Speechwriting

Since Roosevelt, the public has been aware that political figures often use speechwriters. Today no national or statewide campaign is run without them. The vast majority of candidates running for Congress utilize speechwriters, and so do many candidates running for lesser office.

Incumbents, whether presidents, members of Congress, mayors, state representatives, or town council members, almost invariably delegate some of their speechwriting chores to paid staff members. The staff members' title may be "assistant to," or "press secretary," but part of the job responsibility is speechwriting. Similarly, challenger candidates normally hire a "wordsmith" to help with speeches, press releases, and similar tasks right after hiring a campaign manager.

Though the public has accepted leaders who make use of speechwriters, somehow we remain vaguely troubled by the thought that those who aspire to lead us often do so by mouthing the words of others. Traditionally, there have been two basic justifications for using speechwriters.

First, candidates face such extensive demands on their time that it is impossible to fulfill those demands without speechwriters. In 1948 while governing the nation and running for reelection, President Harry Truman delivered 73 speeches in one 15-day period.[12] In 1952 during the final months of the campaign, the Republican and Democratic presidential and vice-presidential candidates delivered a combined total of nearly 1,000 speeches.[13] In 1960 John Kennedy delivered 64 speeches in the last 7 days of the campaign.[14] In 1976 Jimmy Carter delivered 2,100 speeches while running for president.[15]

These demands are not unique to presidential candidates. In 1954 Orville Freeman, running for governor of Minnesota, found himself facing over 120 speaking situations for which he felt the need for advanced preparation.[16] This number does not include the countless situations in which he spoke with little preparation. In 1970 Nelson Rockefeller delivered over 300 speeches in his campaign for the governorship of New York.[17] A recent survey of candidates for Congress indicates that they spoke approximately 4 times a day.[18] Thus candidates at all levels simply cannot prepare for the many speeches they must make, while simultaneously fulfilling other responsibilities as candidate, breadwinner, and family member, without the help of a speechwriter. This justification is a compelling one.

Though the public is aware of speechwriters and understands the time demands that justify their use, it remains slightly troubled by the practice of one person writing the words of another. A second reason candidates use speechwriters is because they believe the writer will produce a good speech. Speechwriters possess unique skills. If their skills can be marshalled on behalf of the candidate, the result will be a stronger speech, and to that extent, an increased likelihood of election. But this justification raises troubling questions.

One critic has suggested that "the essential question is how much borrowing is ethical?"[19] There is, he suggests, a continuum of help that one can provide to a speaker. On one end of the continuum, few people would find anything wrong if a candidate had a spouse or an aide listen to the rehearsal of a speech, or perhaps review drafts of a speech, in each instance making occasional suggestions to improve the language or organization. On the other end, most people might object to finding that speeches were written entirely by speechwriters who did not consult with the candidates, who in turn had no idea about what they were going to say until the moment they started to deliver the speeches that had been written for them. Where on this continuum does one draw the line between honest and dishonest borrowing and collaboration? This is an especially vexing question when speakers are using speeches to present themselves as competent to serve in a leadership position in their community, city, state, or nation.

Communication scholar Ernest Bormann finds that the point on the continuum where one must draw the line is

where the speech changes character. The language becomes different from what it would have been had the speaker prepared the speech for himself with some aid in gathering information and some advice from friends and associates about parts that he should consider revising. At some point the ideas are different, the structure of the speech is different, the nuances of meaning change from what they would have been had this speech really been his own.[20]

When this happens, the speech cannot achieve what should be one of its chief goals, portraying the speaker accurately to the audience, and the public clearly has reason to be troubled.

Thus voters accept the use of speechwriters. However, we remain vaguely troubled, because the speechwriter is a skilled artisan who produces a polished product, and this too causes the candidate to hire him. To the extent that the speech reflects the writer and not the speaker, the public has cause for concern.

The very nature of political speechwriting prevents us from knowing how often "the speech changes character," becoming more a creation of the speechwriter than of the candidate. However, an examination of the job demands imposed upon political speechwriters suggests that this is probably not a frequent occurrence. Fortunately for free societies, the demands of political speechwriting coincide with the needs of the public.

Job Demands

A veteran of over 25 years of political speechwriting for a wide variety of Democratic candidates, Josef Berger, claims that the most important part of a speechwriter's work is "to know his man, to know the man's ideas, not only his general philosophy and background but his thoughts on the issues that he's talking about if he's clear enough on them."[21]

Similarly, virtually every political speechwriter who has commented on the job reaffirms the absolutely critical importance of knowing the candidate for whom they are writing because they seek to create a speech that is essentially that of the candidate, accurately portraying the candidate to the audience. Speechwriters must be thoroughly acquainted with the candidate's value system. For speechwriters must not present what they believe is the best justification for the candidate's policy but must present the candidate's justification for a policy. William F. Gavin, a veteran political speechwriter currently on the staff of Representative Robert Michel, Minority Leader of the U.S. House of Representatives, has observed that a speechwriter should never "think he is writing speeches for himself. If you are doing that, then you're in the wrong business," he comments.[22] Moreover, speechwriters must use language with which the candidate will feel comfortable, language that is an accurate reflection of the candidate. Thus the primary demand placed on speechwriters is to gain an intimate familiarity with the candidate for whom they are working. That familiarity should include a thorough knowledge of the candidate's position on major questions, value systems, the way the candidate thinks through questions and makes decisions, as well as the candidate's manner of using language.

This information will enable the writer to produce a speech that accurately reflects the candidate. The speechwriter owes that to the public so that it might fairly judge the candidate. But what we often forget is that the speechwriter owes it to the candidate as well.

If the speechwriter does not accurately portray the candidate, the speech is likely to be a failure for several practical reasons. First, the candidate may choose to stray from the speech or ignore it altogether. In either case, the speechwriter will probably be fired for writing a speech with which the candidate felt uncomfortable or could not use. Second, if the candidate does choose to use a speech that is an inaccurate portrayal, there will likely be trouble in delivery. Unfamiliar with the basic lines of argument, the evidence, and the language, the candidate cannot be expected to do a good job in presenting the case. Third, candidates are likely to experience discomfort and nervousness in a public situation, where they are liable to make some type of error as a consequence of the discomfort. Fourth, they may repudiate parts of the speech in a question-and-answer session or in subsequent public appearances. This inconsistency could create an opening for criticism. Hence, the demands on the political speechwriter to produce a speech useful to the candidate create a speech that is an accurate reflection of the candidate's policies, thought processes, values, and language. In so doing, the interests of the speechwriter and candidate coincide with the interests of the public in securing accurate information about the candidate.

In addition to knowledge of the candidate, speechwriters need at least two other types of knowledge. First, they must know the subject. Occasionally, a political figure is concerned with a specific issue and calls on someone to help with speeches because of that individual's expertise on the issue. Throughout much of the 1980s Senator Jesse Helms has taken strong anticommunist positions on a host of foreign policy issues. Thus it is not surprising to find a foreign policy specialist with a highly conservative bent, Dr. James Lucier, on Senator Helm's staff. A U.S. senator, with a large staff, particularly concerned about one issue and perhaps having as many as six years before his next election can afford a subject-matter specialist. However, most political speechwriters are generalists because most candidates need generalists.

Campaign speechwriters must be versatile. The speechwriter for a Missouri congressional candidate in a recent election was asked to write speeches in a one-month period on such diverse topics as international terrorism, the importance of engineering technology to the St. Louis business community, abortion laws, a federally funded Lock and Dam Project on the Missouri River, Israel and Middle East affairs, and National Fire Prevention Week. Thus speechwriters invariably are widely read, often in literature as well as politics and current events. Moreover, they know how to do research. If they do not know about the topic, they know where to learn about it.

The final knowledge required by the good speechwriter is information regarding the audience and occasion. Speechwriters must know which audiences in the candidate's district are essential for victory. Moreover, they must know what message or impression the candidate wishes to leave with these target audiences. Is this speech being delivered exclusively to the audience in the room? If so, what is the nature of that audience? What are their interests? Is the immediate audience of secondary importance to the audience that will be reached by press accounts of his speech? How can the interest of those two audiences and the candidate be reconciled in an appropriate speech for this particular occasion? Answering these questions and then operationalizing the answers to produce a speech demand many kinds of information. It demands knowledge of the candidate's ideas, value system, reasoning process, and the use of language. It demands knowledge of the subject matter, the audience(s), and the occasion.

A final demand placed on speechwriters is the trying circumstances in which their knowledge must be utilized. As one speechwriter expressed it when commenting about the type of person hired to help, "We looked for the capacity to work under harsh and often preposterous time pressures. When a speech for a particular evening calling for a ban on leaded gasolines has been co-opted by your opponent that morning, swiftness, along with eloquence, is routinely expected of the writer in coming up with a substitute."[23]

Speechwriting Teams

As the previous section has indicated, the job demands of political speechwriting are formidable. These demands grow in proportion to the office contested. While the types of knowledge we have discussed are required by every political speechwriter, they are normally felt to a greater degree by the speechwriter working for a major national candidate because of such factors as the need to coordinate the candidate's speaking with the radio and television messages of the campaign, the need to respond to an opponent who is also constantly speaking and using media, and the constant interjection into the campaign of new issues. Hence, speechwriting in most major campaigns is done by speechwriting teams characterized by a sharper division of labor than is found in the small campaign. Additionally, the team may perform functions that are not performed in smaller campaigns.

Firsthand accounts by members of the campaign staffs of Franklin Roosevelt, Harry Truman, Adlai Stevenson, Orville Freeman, Nelson Rockefeller, John Kennedy, Richard Nixon, Robert Michel, Gerald Ford, Hubert Humphrey, George McGovern, Jimmy Carter, Ronald Reagan, Michael Dukakis, George Bush, and a wide variety of other gubernatorial, senatorial, and congressional candidates suggest that speechwriting teams exhibit a similar division of labor in most larger campaigns. Craig R. Smith, who has been a part of several such teams and has studied many others, finds that typically speechwriting teams in larger campaigns are composed of three groups: the researchers, the stylists, and the media or public relations advisors.[24]

All these individuals should be familiar with the policies, values, and decision-making processes of the candidate. In practicality it may not be possible for each member of these teams to acquire that knowledge. Rather, key figures in each group acquire it.

The research group does basic library research. This is a group that frequently employs college students who are familiar with library research techniques. Prelaw students, college debaters, or other students interested in campaigns and with good research backgrounds may get their first experience in larger campaigns as part of the research force.

The second group, the stylists, is normally composed of experienced speechwriters. They are often hired on the basis of recommendation and/or writing samples. These individuals must be able to write in an easy conversational style with which the candidate feels comfortable. They must be sensitive to the candidate's ability to tell a story, show righteous indignation, tell a joke, or use a particular jargon or group of metaphors. They use the materials presented by the researchers to produce a speech that meets high rhetorical standards and with which the candidate feels comfortable.[25]

The final group, the media and public relations consultants, are particularly concerned with the audience. More than the other groups, they tend to be familiar with survey research techniques. Their suggestions are designed to make the speeches consistent with the other messages the audience is receiving from the campaign, and given their surveys of the audience/public, to make sure that the candidate's speeches are perceived favorably by the audience.

Thus the demands put on speechwriters in large campaigns do not differ greatly from the demands put on speechwriters in smaller campaigns. The basic differences are not so much in the demands of the task, but rather in the division of labor employed to accomplish the task. Additionally, since a larger campaign is providing the audience/public with a great number of messages, most larger campaigns involve media and public relations consultants who focus on the speech from an audience's perspective, seeking to make the speech consistent with other messages the audience is receiving from the campaign.

Methods of Political Speechwriting

The literature of speech communication, as well as an examination of newspaper reports, biographies of the principals, and similar material indicate that most speechwriters and speechwriting teams operate in a similar manner.[26] In this section we will examine the basic steps involved in campaign speechwriting.

First, the speechwriter(s), the candidate, and in some instances subject matter experts will confer. In this initial conference, the purpose of the speech will be agreed upon. The candidate will indicate positions and rationales, "talking through" the speech. Many speechwriters have noted that often the conference will be taped, or a stenographer would be present. If not, the speechwriter would take copious notes. The record of the candidate's remarks would constitute a first rough draft. From the very inception, the ideas of the speech are those of the candidate. The justification and reasoning within the speech are those of the candidate. Often, some of the language used in these conferences by the candidate is worked into later drafts and remains intact in the final speech.

At this point the speechwriters, armed with a clear understanding of what the candidate wants, do their research. If the campaign has a research staff, it is brought into the development of the speech. If the campaign is small, the research is done by the speechwriter. One of the advantages of incumbency is that incumbent officeholders can often put the resources of government to work on their behalf. A speechwriter for the president might draw on the expertise of a cabinet member or someone in the appropriate department. Similarly, congressional speechwriters' efforts might be supplemented by the Legislative Reference Service of the Library of Congress, acting on a legislator's request.

At this point a draft is developed. In larger speechwriting teams this draft is typically done by one staff member whose work may be reviewed by other speechwriters, and altered. In a small operation, an equivalent process takes place as the speechwriter prepares a draft and then revises it, perhaps drawing on the suggestions of staff members or advisors who know the candidate well but have no responsibilities for speechwriting. It is not uncommon that the original draft undergoes three or more revisions as speechwriters revise their own work and incorporate the suggestions of others. If it is possible, the candidate is shown successive drafts for input. However, this is rarely possible with every draft in larger campaigns. Nevertheless, at some point the candidate is again brought back into the process.

Depending on the candidate's reaction, several actions can be taken with the version that the speechwriter believes to be close to final. Often the candidate accepts it as final, normally continuing to make minor changes, primarily stylistic, during free moments up until the time of delivery. If the speech is basically sound, but the candidate has more than stylistic concerns, these may be indicated in marginal notes or in a meeting. Subsequent drafts, better conforming to the candidate's wishes, can then be developed and resubmitted. The candidate may have an objection to one section of the speech or perhaps to some aspects of organization. Frequently when reading over the speech, the candidate may be concerned that the material will run too long or short for the allotted time. If the speech is to be delivered over the radio or television, the media consultants will normally enter the speechwriting process during the final few drafts. Their suggestions will be geared to insuring that the speech is appropriate for the allotted time and contains portions that can be used for a 20-to-30-second spot on the news shows. These spots normally contain vivid and startling language that exemplify the point the candidate wishes to make. In smaller campaigns, media consultants will not be available, but a conscientious speechwriter will strive to include potential media "spots" in the speech in case of press coverage. Additionally, such spots, even in smaller campaigns, might be submitted to the media in the hope they will be used.

With slight variations to accommodate their own circumstances, this process is an accurate characterization of speechwriting in the vast majority of political campaigns where speechwriters are employed.[27] Several key points result from this description.

First, throughout this process the candidate is a major writer/editor/collaborator in the creative process. The final speech is a clear reflection of the candidate. The candidate accepts responsibility for what is said. It is for this reason that, as one speechwriter has noted:

I don't think it occurs to the general public that a speech is ghostwritten. Even if someone in the audience has read somewhere that Congressman X has a ghostwriter and he knows it as the man speaks, he forgets it. He's listening to the man, and he's holding him responsible, and he's responding to him for everything that is said.[28]

Second, though the speechwriter has also contributed to the final product, the speech belongs to the person who utters it. It is the candidate, not the speechwriter, who will receive praise or blame for the speech. Thus it is easy to understand why one experienced political speechwriter has commented that "if there is any prerequisite to ghostwriting for political figures, I suggest that it is a willingness to sublimate one's self to the figure for whom one works."[29]

Third, major campaign addresses undergo many drafts. A recent study of Congressmembers indicates that they typically draft major campaign speeches at least three times.[30] New York Governor Nelson Rockefeller's speeches typically underwent six drafts during his campaigns for office.[31] Florida Governor Reubin Askew's major speeches are known to have undergone at least nine drafts.[32] Senator Henry "Scoop" Jackson of Washington routinely delivered speeches that were drafted and revised three or more times.[33] And though few presidents are as notorious for using the seven or more speech drafts that Franklin Roosevelt demanded for his major speeches, every president and presidential candidate of the last 50 years has made extensive use of draft speeches prior to delivering a major address.

SURROGATE SPEAKERS

Even though most candidates make use of speech modules and speechwriters to help them meet the demands on their time, inevitably they find that they simply cannot be in two places at once. Hence, even in smaller campaigns it is not unusual to see surrogate or substitute speakers filling in for an absent candidate. In large national campaigns, hundreds of people serve as surrogates for the candidate, many of whom have been trained by the campaign staff.

Selection of Surrogates

The selection of surrogate speakers is not left to chance. Candidates seek surrogates who meet these requirements: First, they should have a proven record of competence as a public speaker. In smaller campaigns, the skilled college debater, a lawyer, teacher, or anyone else with speaking experience may be called upon. In larger campaigns, public officials with extensive speaking experience might be used. In a governor's race, for example, members of the state legislature might serve as surrogates for their parties' nominee. At the presidential level, it is not uncommon to utilize cabinet members and members of Congress who are known for their ability as speakers.

Second, the surrogate should have some clearly identifiable connection to the candidate. It is for this reason that we so often see the relatives of candidates speaking. During the 1988 presidential race all of the adult children as well as the spouses of the four principal candidates—George Bush, Dan Quayle, Michael Dukakis, and Lloyd Bentsen—were on the campaign trail. Relatives are perceived as being close to the candidate, as are cabinet members and legislative allies.

If surrogate speakers do not have an obvious connection to the candidate, they should make their connection clear to the audience early in the speech. Perhaps they grew up with the candidate, previously worked with the candidate, or have simply been longtime supporters of the candidate. In 1976 Jimmy Carter made heavy use not only of his relatives, but of many other longtime supporters from Georgia, who became known as the "Peanut Brigade." In 1988 many of Bush's surrogates, members of the cabinet and Congress, could speak of their direct association with him as vice-president and their opportunity to witness his conduct in office.

Third, the surrogate should have some clearly identifiable connection to the audience. Since the substitute is just that, a substitute, the candidate or the staff should select a substitute who is appropriate for the audience. In local campaigns, the surrogate may be a member of the organization sponsoring the speech or a native of the geographic area. In national campaigns, the surrogate may be the cabinet member with responsibilities for the area of government that most affects the sponsoring group, as when the secretary of labor represents the president at union affairs. Again, surrogates should make clear reference to this connection early in their speeches if it is not obvious.

Since the candidate is not present, it is clear that whoever is speaking on the candidate's behalf is not the audience's first choice. Hence, that individual may have to overcome the resentment of the audience. It is for this reason that the speaker should be able to stress a connection to the candidate. In effect, the surrogate is saying "I'm the next best thing" and reminding the audience that, like Hallmark cards, this candidate cares enough to send the very best.

Utilization of Surrogates

Surrogates should have attempted to familiarize themselves with the candidate's positions. Indeed, one reason that some candidates like to use their speechwriters for surrogates is that they are uniquely adept at putting themselves in the candidate's shoes. Nevertheless, two rules should govern every presentation. First, surrogates must acknowledge why the candidate is not there. Most people understand the demands placed on a candidate, and a frank statement of where the candidate is will be better received than an attempt to hide the fact that the candidate has chosen to speak elsewhere. Depending on the audience being faced by the speaker, most surrogates can indicate why their principal is not present in a tactful or humorous way. One rather rotund surrogate we are acquainted with often opened his after-dinner or -luncheon addresses by saying that his candidate wanted to maintain his weight, and it was difficult to do so during the campaign when he was constantly attending breakfast meetings, luncheons, dinners, coffees, teas, beer busts, and the like.

So he's out rounding up some votes tonight in _____ where they are not serving food. Since I am the one member of the staff who clearly does not have a weight problem, he sent me here to guarantee that your food would be appreciated. Well, I certainly appreciated this fine meal, and I hope that when I am finished this evening you will have a better appreciation of why _____ ought to be elected to the congress.

An introduction like this one acknowledges that the candidate is campaigning elsewhere but does so in a humorous and tactful fashion, which reduces the audience's resentment.

Second, surrogates should not hesitate to remind the audience that they are not the candidate. Hence, they may not know all of the answers or precisely what the candidate thinks. If the surrogate is well prepared, there should not be many occasions for this to happen. However, the speaker may confront a difficult question. When this occurs the surrogate should simply acknowledge that to be the case rather than guess; arrangements should then be made for the candidate or staff to respond later.

Benefits of Surrogates

The use of surrogate speakers can provide a variety of benefits to campaigns. Martha Stout Kessler, who directed the Speakers Bureau of John Anderson's 1980 presidential race in New York, observed that in some instances surrogates may be more credible speakers for a given audience than the candidate. Moreover, she notes that surrogates also have the liberty to say things that the candidate might not wish to say, and they can also aid the candidate in fund-raising.[34]

Surrogates who have a unique connection to the audience may, on occasion, be more effective with that audience than the candidate. For example, in recent presidential elections, well known public officials of the Jewish faith were often used by the candidates to address predominantly Jewish audiences. In a Missouri congressional election, the candidate's college-age children spoke on the campuses in the district. These surrogates were well prepared on the issues that most concerned the audiences they addressed.

Frequently, candidates may wish to say something but find that it is not politically expedient. A surrogate may be able to make the statements for the candidate. For example, during most presidential elections the vice-presidential candidate, who is essentially a presidential surrogate, typically makes the harshest criticism of the opposing ticket. In 1988 surrogates like Jesse Jackson, Ann Richards, and Lee Atwater were among the harshest critics of their respective parties' foes. Surrogates can deliver the candidate's message, but they are not the candidate. Hence, surrogates may be able to make remarks that are not politically expedient for the candidate to make.

Finally, surrogates are often able to help candidates raise money. Maryanne Renz reports that from 1980 to 1983, while delivering over 200 speeches, James Watt raised over $3 million for the Republican party.[35] In many of these addresses, Watt, Reagan's secretary of interior during this period, was acting as, or was no doubt perceived by his audiences as, a surrogate for the president. Many political figures feel that it is unbecoming for them to personally ask for money. Surrogates are not embarrassed or compromised because the money is not for themselves.

In sum, the use of surrogate speakers can provide many benefits. Their primary function is to spread the candidate's messages to audiences that might otherwise not hear them. However, as Kessler stresses, this is by no means the only advantage to using surrogates. Indeed, the benefits of using surrogate speakers are so important in larger campaigns, where candidates cannot possibly address all the audiences that wish to hear them, that most national and many state and regional campaigns actively recruit surrogate speakers, provide them with training, and schedule them through a speaker's bureau.

CONCLUSIONS

Although, as we have seen in Chapter 4, the media have grown to play an increasingly important part in contemporary political campaigns, the public speaking of candidates and their surrogates nevertheless is at the core of any campaign. In small campaigns, public speaking may be virtually the only means of persuasion utilized. In this chapter, we have seen that the decisions to speak are not left to chance in well-managed campaigns. Rather, the campaign identifies the audiences to whom it wishes to speak and the messages it wishes to send and then arranges situations that conform to those wishes. Moreover, we have observed how candidates make use of speech modules to create a basic speech that can be used, with some variation, repeatedly during the campaign. Additionally, we have examined the reasons for the growing use of speechwriters, the demands placed on such individuals, and the methods they use to meet those demands. Finally, we have observed the use of surrogate speakers, focusing on the criteria for selecting such speakers, the techniques such speakers commonly employ, and the benefits surrogate speakers provide to a campaign. In spite of changes that have occurred in technology and the way campaigns are managed, all candidates, whether incumbents or challengers, whether they speak at a rally, a press conference, on television or radio, utilize the ideas we have discussed in this chapter. Clearly, public speaking remains a fundamental practice of political campaigns.

NOTES

1. Jacob Javits, "How I Used a Poll in Campaigning for Congress," *Public Opinion Quarterly* II (Summer 1947): 222–26.

2. See Martin Schramm, *Running for President: A Journal of the Carter Campaign* (New York: Pocket Books, 1977), pp. 428–31 for insight into a national campaign's targeting strategies.

3. Quoted in "Out of the Past," *People* 17 (February 16, 1981): 74.

4. Perry Sekus and Robert V. Friedenberg, "Public Speaking in the House of Representatives: The 97th Congress Speaks" (Unpublished study, Miami University, 1982), pp. 2–4.

5. Ibid.

6. *New York Times*, February 29, 1980, p. B4.

7. Ibid.

8. Ibid.

9. Quoted in William Norwood Brigance, "Ghostwriting Before Franklin D. Roosevelt and the Radio," *Today's Speech* 4 (September 1956): 11.

10. Robert Bishop, "Bruce Barton—Presidential Stage Manager," *Journalism Quarterly* 33 (Spring 1956): 85–89.

11. Bernard K. Duffy and Mark Royden Winchell, " 'Speak the Speech, I Pray You.' The Practice and Perils of Literary and Oratorical Ghostwriting," *Southern Speech Communication Journal* 55 (Fall 1989): 105.

12. Irwin Ross, *The Loneliest Campaign* (New York: New American Library, 1968), p. 89.

13. Walter J. Stelkovis, "Ghostwriting: Ancient and Honorable," *Today's Speech* 2 (January 1954): 17.

14. John F. Kennedy, *The Speeches of Senator John F. Kennedy: Presidential Campaign of 1960* (Washington, D.C.: Government Printing Office, 1961), pp. 840–1,267.

15. Jimmy Carter, *A Government as Good as Its People* (New York: Simon and Schuster, 1977), p. 7.

16. Donald K. Smith, "The Speech-Writing Team in a State Political Campaign," *Today's Speech* 4 (September 1956): 16.

17. Joseph Persico, "The Rockefeller Rhetoric: Writing Speeches for the 1970 Campaign," *Today's Speech* 20 (Spring 1972): 57.

18. Sekus and Friedenberg, "Public Speaking," p. 9.

19. Ernest Bormann, "Ethics of Ghostwritten Speeches," *Quarterly Journal of Speech* 47 (October 1961): 266.

20. Ibid., pp. 266–67.

21. Thomas Benson, "Conversations with a Ghost," *Today's Speech* 16 (November 1968): 73.

22. Quoted in Martin Medhurst and Gary C. Dreibelbis, "Building The Speechwriter-Principal Relationship: Minority Leader Robert Michel Confronts His Ghost," *Central States Speech Journal* 37 (Winter 1986): 242.

23. Persico, "Rockefeller Rhetoric," p. 58.

24. Craig R. Smith, "Contemporary Political Speech Writing," *Southern Speech Communication Journal* 42 (Fall 1976): 52–68; Craig R. Smith, "Addendum to Contemporary Political Speech Writing," *Southern Speech Communication Journal* 43 (Winter 1977): 191–94.

25. On the matter of candidate comfort with the writer and the speech, particularly see Medhurst and Dreibelbis, "Building the Speechwriter-Principal Relationship," pp. 242–46.

26. The speech communication literature utilized in this section includes Robert F. Ray, "Ghostwriting in Presidential Campaigns," *Central States Speech Journal* 8 (Fall 1956): 8–11; Benson, "Conversations with a Ghost," pp. 71–81; Persico, "Rockefeller Rhetoric," pp. 57–62; Howard Schwartz, "Senator 'Scoop' Jackson Speaks on Speaking," *Speaker and Gavel* 5 (November 1968): 21–31; Robert V. Friedenberg, "The Army of Invisible Men: Ghostwriting for Congressmen and Congressional Candidates," *Forensic* 62 (May 1977): 4–8; Sara Arendall Newell and Thomas King, "The Keynote Address of the Democratic National Convention, 1972: The Evolution of a Speech," *Southern Speech Communication Journal* 39 (Summer 1974): 346–58; Smith, "Political Speech Writing," pp. 52–68; Smith, "Addendum," pp. 191–94; Lois J. Einhorn, "The Ghosts Unmasked: A Review of Literature on Speechwriting," *Communication Quarterly* 30 (Winter 1981): 41–47; Medhurst and Dreibelbis, "Building the Speechwriter-Principal Relationship," pp. 239–47; Robert V. Friedenberg, "Jesse Alexander Helms: Secular Preacher of the Religious Right," *Speaker and Gavel* 24 (Fall/Winter/Spring 1987): 60–68; Lois J. Einhorn, "The Ghosts Talk: Personal Interviews with Three Former Speechwriters," *Communication Quarterly* 36 (Spring 1988): 94–108; Duffy and Winchell, " 'Speak the Speech, I Pray You,' " *Southern Speech Communication Journal* 55 (Fall 1989): 102–15.

27. An extremely brief description of the ghostwritiing process, which coincides with this one, can be found in Einhorn, "Ghosts Unmasked," p. 42. Also see Medhurst and Dreibelbis, "Building the Speechwriter-Principal Relationship," pp. 242–45.

28. Benson, "Conversations with a Ghost," pp. 79–80.

29. Friedenberg, "Army of Invisible Men," p. 4.

30. Sekus and Friedenberg, "Public Speaking," p. 6.

31. Persico, "Rockefeller Rhetoric," pp. 59–60.

32. Newell and King, "Keynote Address," p. 357.

33. Schwartz, "Senator 'Scoop' Jackson," p. 22.

34. Martha Stout Kessler, "The Role of Surrogate Speakers in the 1980 Presidential Campaign," *Quarterly Journal of Speech* 67 (May 1981): 148–50.

35. Maryanne Renz, "The Cabinet Member as a Representative of the President: The Case of James Watt," *Central States Speech Journal* 38 (Summer 1987): 107.

Chapter Seven

Recurring Forms of Political Campaign Communication

In his classic article "The Rhetorical Situation," Lloyd F. Bitzer defined a rhetorical situation as "a complex of persons, events, objects and relations presenting an actual or potential exigence which can be completely or partially removed if discourse, introduced into the situation, can so constrain human decision or action as to bring about the significant modification of the exigence."[1] Bitzer's work has served as the basis for many studies of rhetoric that are based on the premise that comparable rhetorical situations produce comparable rhetorical responses.[2] While such studies have been subject to criticism, we find that the basic premise that some rhetorical situations are relatively analogous and hence produce relatively analogous discourse is a valuable premise for the study of much political campaign communication. In this chapter, we shall suggest that most political campaigns tend to produce several similar, comparable, or analogous situations. Moreover, these situations tend to produce similar, comparable, or analogous discourse. Four such comparable situations, found in most campaigns, are the rhetorical situations created by:

1. The need of candidates to announce formally their candidacies to the public
2. The need of candidates to accept publicly the nomination of their party
3. The need of candidates to seek media coverage of their views
4. The need of candidates to make public apologies for their statements or behavior.

In this chapter, we will examine the discourse to which these situations traditionally give rise; announcement speeches, acceptance addresses, press conferences, and political apologies. We will study these recurring forms first by describing the situations that create the need or exigence for their use. Second, we will discuss the purposes that these four recurring forms of political campaign communication traditionally serve. Third, we will discuss the strategies most frequently and successfully employed by candidates delivering these four recurring forms of political campaign communication.

ANNOUNCEMENT SPEECHES

Candidates normally announce that they are seeking public office through a formal address to the public. However, this formal address is rarely the first act of the campaign. Rather, it has been preceded by considerable work. The effort that candidates and their associates have engaged in during the surfacing stage helps to shape the rhetorical situation in which the announcement address is made.[3]

Preannouncement Situation

At least three activities typically precede any announcement address, regardless of the office being sought or the candidate who is announcing. First, an assessment must be made of the likelihood of winning. This will include an assessment of the candidate's ability to attract sufficient voter support, sufficient financial support, and develop an organization capable of winning the office. The results of this analysis may enter into the announcement address itself. In any event, it gives the candidate a clearer understanding of the situation.

Second, most candidates tend to inform key individuals personally, prior to their public announcement. Typically these are politically, financially, or personally significant individuals whom the candidate wishes to flatter. If the office being contested is statewide or national in scope, often the candidate may inform a small group of individuals personally and then send a personal letter of announcement, in advance of the candidate's public statement, to several dozen, hundred, or even thousands of others. The point is that these individuals are significant, and the candidate wishes to flatter them.[4]

However, the advance announcement in person to a few figures fulfills a second purpose. It serves as a means of providing the candidate with feedback regarding the rhetorical situation to be faced. These key, well-placed individuals may be able to help shape strategy, better understand the concerns of the constituency, or identify possible obstacles. For example, a judge with a group of six family members and close friends decided to run for Congress. After having assessed his opportunity for winning, the judge personally set about contacting 25 key individuals whom he wanted to inform of his decision to run. He anticipated that all would be encouraging and would pledge their support. Among those contacted were three elected officials, several party leaders, five prospective financial contributors, the director of a prominent local political action committee, three journalists who were contacted entirely off the record, and officers of several organizations whose members the judge felt might be sympathetic to his candidacy. While those contacted pledged their support, over half indicated that they believed the incumbent would prove much more difficult to defeat than the judge's initial planning group had anticipated. Many pointed to aspects of the judge's record that might work against him in an election. Moreover, they pointed out characteristics of the incumbent that would make him much harder to defeat than he had been two years earlier, when he won election by under 5,000 votes. Thus, through a tentative exploration of candidacy with key individuals, the judge became more aware of the situation that confronted him.

Finally, the announcement should conform to any preconceived expectations that the public might have about it. Hence, the third preliminary activity of the candidate is to determine public expectations about the announcement. For example, have prior candidates conditioned the public to expect that an announcement of candidacy for the office sought should be made from the state capitol rather than from the candidate's home? Does the public have any expectations about what the candidate should say? Does the public have expectations about the qualifications necessary for this position, which might be mentioned in the announcement speech?

Clearly the rhetorical situation for every announcement address differs. Yet, typically, the candidate has first to analyze prospects for the campaign, second to share impending candidacy with a group of significant associates, and third to consider public expectations concerning the announcement address.

Purpose of Address

The announcement address should serve several purposes. Depending on the situation that the candidate confronts, one or more of the purposes discussed here may be minimized or underplayed, while others are stressed. Nevertheless, a sound announcement address may serve several purposes. First, it clearly signals the candidate's intention to run. Second, it may serve to discourage the competition. If the announcement address alludes to the candidate's strengths, such as the ability to articulate the issues, raise money, or wage an aggressive campaign, it may discourage other potential candidates from contesting for the party nomination or the office itself. As we will see in our discussion of strategies, typically the content of the address must be accompanied with actions that successfully discourage the competition. Nevertheless, one of the purposes of an announcement address, particularly if there is liable to be a primary, may be to discourage potential competition.

The third purpose announcement addresses often serve is to indicate why the candidate is running. Candidates may want to stress what they can bring to the office that others cannot—how they can uniquely serve the public.

A fourth purpose frequently served by the announcement address is to initiate the themes of the campaign. As the candidate's first major campaign address, it is appropriate to initiate any important themes that may run throughout the campaign. For example, Alan Cranston launched his 1984 presidential race by claiming that there would be one "dominating goal" for both his campaign and his subsequent presidency. That goal, claimed Cranston in his announcement address, was "to bring our selves and our children out from under the dark shadow of nuclear war." Cranston subordinated all other issues to this one overriding issue. "There can be no cure for growing unemployment, decreasing productivity, the diminishing opportunity for individual Americans to enhance their well-being," asserted Cranston, "if we continue to pour a mounting portion of our national resources—our money, our technological skills, the energies of our people and our government—into a race to build arms."[5] In sum, the announcement address may serve several purposes in addition to the obvious one of officially signaling the candidate's intent to run. It may serve to discourage possible competitors, indicate why the candidate has chosen to run, and initiate major campaign themes.

Strategies of Address

In preparing to announce their intention to run, a variety of choices confront candidates. They must consider the timing, location, who should be with them, speech content, and finally the means by which they follow up on their announcement.

Timing the announcement speech may be difficult. Often the first candidate to announce receives more coverage, and by virtue of being first, may be perceived as being more serious, credible, or legitimate. Though an early announcement may attract media coverage, content of the coverage might well focus on the candidate's potential to win, the funds raised, and the staff that has been recruited. Obviously, by announcing early to gain coverage, the candidate runs the risk that the announcement will not be taken seriously because there are few other overt trappings of a campaign.

Timing is also vital because of the effect that it may have on others who are politically important, both other candidates and potential supporters. There is evidence to suggest, for example, that Michael Dukakis was not anxious to run for the presidency in 1988, but was forced to do so because he feared that in 1992 Massachusetts Senator Edward Kennedy would be a presidential candidate.[6] By running in 1988, Dukakis could start with the support of his own home state, which could not be taken for granted if he delayed until 1992.

The importance of timing may have been best illustrated in 1976. Had either Governor Jerry Brown of California, the most populous state in the union, or Senator Frank Church of Idaho, chairman of the Senate Foreign Relations Committee, chosen to announce their campaigns much earlier, perhaps they would have attracted much of the early support that went to former Georgia Governor Jimmy Carter, the first Democratic candidate to announce his candidacy for president that year.[7] Rather, both Brown and Church delayed announcing their candidacies, allowing Carter to build a strong organization and raise funds without having to compete against them. In races for lesser offices, timing of the announcement can also be important. Obviously it may not receive the publicity that is associated with a presidential candidate's announcement, but it will be noticed and considered by other crucial decision makers in the constituency: potential opponents, potential contributors, volunteers, staff members, or supporters.

Where to deliver the announcement address is a second strategic consideration that candidates must confront. In so doing, they must consider voter expectations and tradition, as well as the issues they hope to develop in the upcoming campaign. For example, in 1984 Senator John Glenn positioned himself as a moderate, far less liberal than his principal rivals for the Democratic nomination, Walter Mondale, Gary Hart, and Jesse Jackson. In contrast to their liberal left leanings, Glenn claimed that his would be the campaign of the "sensible center," better reflecting traditional American values. To underscore this major thrust of his campaign, Glenn chose to announce his candidacy in his home town of New Concord, Ohio.

Visually, the town was ideal for both the media covering Glenn's announcement, and for Glenn himself. A town of approximately 1,800 people, with American flags flying everywhere in honor of its favorite son's announcement, New Concord seemed to be straight off a Norman Rockwell *Saturday Evening Post* cover. By announcing in New Concord, Glenn was encouraging the media to focus extensively on his small town, middle American roots and values, thus drawing attention to the very issues he hoped to emphasize in the campaign. Moreover, as Glenn rode down John Glenn Highway to the John Glenn High School where he delivered his speech and then moved on to the John Glenn Gymnasium on the campus of his alma mater, Muskingum College, to meet with old friends and supporters, the esteem and affection that his fellow citizens felt for him was readily evident. In sum the setting did much to reinforce public perception of John Glenn as a distinguished representative of small town, middle American values.[8]

Similarly, in 1988 the Reverend Marion G. (Pat) Robertson, founder of the Christian Broadcasting Network, wished to emphasize that he was not simply a religious leader, but also a highly successful businessman. Unlike his principal rivals for the Republican nomination, George Bush and Robert Dole, who had spent most of their lives in government service, Robertson had spent most of his life as a religious and business leader. Hence, he hoped to suggest that government programs had repeatedly failed to solve many national problems and it was time that the White House was occupied by a leader from the private sector, such as himself, with religious and business experience, not a career bureaucrat, such as his major rivals for the Republican nomination.

Robertson announced his candidacy in a speech delivered in the Bedford Stuyvesant section of Brooklyn, New York, one of the largest and most deteriorated inner-city neighborhoods in the country. He chose to initiate his campaign in Bedford Stuyvesant, he told his audience, for two reasons. First, because Bedford Stuyvesant was a symbol of America. It was, claimed Robertson, "strong at the foundation. Elegant. Proud. Crafted by workers who in their day were the very best in the world. There is beauty here." But, he continued, the many problems of the area, hunger, drugs, hopelessness, and despair, made the residents of Bedford Stuyvesant "living examples of the failure of the federal government, the failure of the bureaucracy, to solve the immediate problems of life in the modern world." Thus, Robertson used Bedford Stuyvesant to symbolize the failures of the very approaches to problems that his chief rivals could be expected to use.

Second, Robertson told his audience that Bedford Stuyvesant had a unique personal meaning to him. Twenty-seven years earlier he, his wife, and his three young children had lived on the third floor of the old brownstone at 33 Monroe Street, in front of which he stood. Recalling the brief ministry he had in Bedford Stuyvesant while still a student in seminary, Robertson claimed, "I moved here to begin a career of service. . . . For me it was a total commitment. Now, nearly 30 years later, I am prepared to make another commitment—a commitment to the nation."[9] Robertson's commitment to the private sector had resulted in his own success, and now he was committing himself to use the same methods of private industry to overcome national problems. The location of his announcement address did much to reinforce themes that Robertson hoped to make both in his announcement address and throughout the campaign.

Similarly, the location of the announcement address is important in lesser campaigns. The local candidate who is making improved road conditions a prominent issue might well deliver his announcement address from a major road repair site. Most communities have buildings and locations that have unique connotations. Candidates who announce their intention to run at such locations are at least symbolically identifying themselves with the persons or events that have given this location its uniqueness. Additionally, if the site is visually attractive, the candidate may be increasing the limited likelihood of receiving television coverage of the announcement address. Cincinnati city councilwoman Bobbie Stern announced her candidacy for reelection in 1982 while standing in front of the William Howard Taft statue in downtown Cincinnati's Lytle Park. Thus she associated herself with one of the city's most esteemed figures and assured herself of a stimulating visual background that enhanced the probability of television coverage.[10]

A third question candidates consider when making their announcement addresses is with whom they might wish to share the spotlight. That is, who else should be present and in a prominent position? Traditionally, most candidates have announced their candidacies while surrounded by family, close friends, admirers, and supporters. However, exactly who should be invited, who should sit with the candidates, and who might also make a few brief remarks are questions that must be answered by candidates as they plan their announcement event. Often the presence of prominent individuals in the community, city, or state, supportive remarks from party leaders, and similar visible signs of support for the candidate at the very outset of the campaign can help establish credibility and discourage potential competitors for the nomination or the office itself.

In 1960 John Kennedy's staff was in close contact with Ohio Governor Michael DiSalle. The Kennedy announcement was made with the full knowledge that immediately thereafter, Governor DiSalle would be the first governor to endorse Kennedy. In doing so, DiSalle could guarantee that the large Ohio delegation to the Democratic convention was committed to Kennedy.[11] DiSalle's actions, immediately after the Kennedy announcement, made it clear to prospective challengers that the Kennedy campaign was not to be underestimated and may well, as the Kennedys hoped, have slowed down or discouraged the challenges of other possible contenders.

The announcement address itself is yet a fourth strategic consideration with which candidates must deal. The content of this speech is, in part, dictated by its purposes. Typically, three themes are present in most announcement addresses. Candidates announce that they are, in fact, running. Additionally, they typically offer an explanation of why they are running. Finally, they also suggest the likelihood of their victory.

Unless candidates can provide some cogent reasons for running, their candidacy may end very early. Senator Edward Kennedy experienced this difficulty in 1980 when he announced his intention to run for the presidency. In his announcement speech and in the speeches and interviews that followed, he had difficulty in offering cogent reasons for running. He chose to challenge an incumbent president of his own party. Yet, analysis of his positions on major issues, compared to those of President Carter, revealed very few significant differences at the outset of the campaign.[12] Kennedy's failure to offer a clear explanation of why he was running hurt his candidacy. The public expects candidates to have rational reasons for running and to share those reasons at the outset of the campaign. Candidates who fail to provide them in the announcement speech, or very shortly thereafter, tend to generate public distrust of their motives.

In contrast to Kennedy, 1982 Ohio gubernatorial candidate Jerry Springer used his announcement address to claim that he was the one candidate who best knew "the people" and who could best work for their interests. Claiming he was the candidate of "the neighborhoods, the bowling lanes, and the plant gates," Springer asserted that as governor he would preside over an administration that would work for the average Ohioan.[13] "As long as there are folks out there hurting, we will share the pain and seek to reduce it. That is our reason for running," claimed Springer.[14]

In announcing candidacy, most office seekers also stress the likelihood of their victory. In so doing, they often focus on their strengths and on the weaknesses of potential opponents. Implicit in this discussion is their fitness for the office. The candidate claims to be better able to manage the office, better able to represent the constituency, and of course better able to attract funds and wage an effective campaign than anyone else.[15] In sum, the actual content of the candidate's announcement address varies with the situation. However, most candidates, perhaps conditioned in part by public expectations, will formally declare their candidacy, attempt to explain why they are running, and suggest that they will win.

The strategies involved in the announcement address must also include the immediate follow-up to the address. The candidate should not simply announce that he is running and then seemingly disappear from public view. Rather, the timing of the address, perhaps its location, the other people invited to the announcement, and the discourse itself might all contribute to and be climaxed by the means by which the candidate follows up on the announcement. For example, in recent years many cash starved candidates have followed up on their announcement addresses with a practice introduced by Florida Senator Richard Stone, but forever associated with Missouri governor "Walking Joe" Teasdale. Immediately upon concluding their announcement addresses these candidates start on a walking tour of their district or state. Such a method of following up may allow the candidate to stress key issues and begin to live up to announcement address promises. It enables the candidate to express concern for all constituencies within the district, evidencing ability to unify people. At various points in the walk, the candidate can be greeted by prominent supporters, discuss the campaign with them, and of course get extensive media coverage of all this.

Regardless of the specific method used, a walk, follow-up mailings, the endorsement of prominent citizens, announcing staff appointments, or the like, it is sound strategy to coordinate the announcement address with some type of follow-up activity illustrating that the candidate is serious about seeking office and is already gaining support.

In sum, the announcement address is not as simple as it may at first appear. Considerable thought must be given to the timing of the address, to its location, to the other parties who may share the spotlight with the candidate, to what the candidate will actually say, and to how the candidate will immediately follow-up on the announcement. The announcement address is the centerpiece of a rhetorical situation created by the candidate's need for formally announcing candidacy to the public. Though the address may be the first public indication of candidacy, it should not be the first political activity the candidate attempts. Rather, the announcement speech should be preceded by considerable thought and preparation to ensure that the candidate's campaign is opened effectively.

ACCEPTANCE ADDRESSES

In the 1830s national candidates nominated by the Democratic party began to respond to their nominations with letters of acceptance. By the 1850s Democratic candidates began to respond to their nominations with informal speeches. In 1868 Horatio Seymour delivered the first formal nomination acceptance address, but like most such addresses in the latter portion of the nineteenth century, it was a perfunctory speech indicating gratitude at receiving the nomination and promising a full formal letter of acceptance. It was not until 1892, when Grover Cleveland accepted his nomination for the presidency by speaking at a large public meeting in Madison Square Garden, that acceptance addresses began to assume their current importance. Cleveland, William Jennings Bryan in 1896, and subsequent national candidates have used acceptance addresses as means of thanking their supporters, seeking party unity, and dramatizing the issues. In 1932 Franklin Delano Roosevelt flew to the Democratic National Convention and became the first presidential candidate to accept personally his nomination at the convention.[16]

Situation During Address

The situations faced by candidates delivering acceptance addresses have often varied, but typically they share several key characteristics. Most important, candidates have successfully attained their party's nomination for office. This success may be the consequence of running in primaries throughout the nation, as it is with current presidential candidates. It may be the consequence of persuading a majority of party voters in a statewide or local primary. It may be a consequence of persuading a majority of key party officials in a local, regional, or state party caucus or committee. It may even be a consequence of default, because no one else chooses to run. Regardless of how it was achieved, the important point is that candidates have obtained the nomination of their party and the legitimacy and attention accompanying that nomination.

Acceptance addresses are given to audiences as varied as the massive television audience that watches the major party presidential nomination conventions, or a small group of highly partisan political activists who form the Republican, Democratic, or third party central or executive committee for a small town. The acceptance address may be given after a long, exhausting, and bitter fight, or it may be given after a placid and uncontested nomination. Clearly the nature of the audience and the nature of the struggle preceding the nomination are situational factors that must be accounted for in the candidate's acceptance address.

A final situational factor that heavily affects acceptance addresses is the fact that they must be considered as part of what a variety of scholars have called "a legitimation ritual."[17] In full view of those who have nominated them, candidates lay claim to their nomination and attempt to justify their supporters' faith and belief. Both their nominators and the public have come to expect such a ritual. Both nominators and the public will judge the candidate's effort and begin to accord the nominee legitimacy in part based on their judgments of the candidate's success at fulfilling the demands of acceptance address ritual.

Purpose of Address

Acceptance addresses should satisfy four closely related purposes. First, the address is the means through which the candidate publicly assumes the role of a candidate/leader of the party. Second, the address should generate a strong positive response from the immediate audience. Third, it should serve to unify the party. Finally, it is a partisan political address, which in some instances may be the most important such address the candidate makes throughout the campaign. Hence, it should also serve as a strong persuasive message.[18]

The candidate typically spends very little time formally assuming the role as a party leader. In their 1988 acceptance addresses to the Republican and Democratic National Conventions, George Bush and Michael Dukakis took 26 and 137 words respectively to acknowledge and accept their nominations. These perfunctory remarks, made at the outset of 5,000-word speeches, nevertheless, are vital.[19] The public has come to expect that candidates are grateful to be nominated and expects such ritualistic signs of that gratitude as acknowledgment and thanks. Convention delegates believe that they are doing an important job. They have come to expect that the candidate ritualistically acknowledge their efforts by formally accepting the fruit of their work, the nomination. Audiences would find something lacking, something incomplete, something unfulfilling if these rituals were not observed. The rhetorical situation demands that the candidate acknowledge obtaining the party's nomination.

The immediate audience for acceptance addresses is normally composed of those individuals who have affirmed the candidate's nomination. Hence, it is imperative that they respond positively to the candidate's remarks. These individuals, be they national, state, or local party officials, should constitute a nucleus of solid and vigorous support for the candidate in the forthcoming election. A second major purpose of the acceptance address is to arouse these individuals and properly motivate them for the responsibilities that will be falling upon them as the campaign progresses. This may be particularly difficult if large numbers of them have supported other candidates for the party nomination.

The third major purpose of acceptance addresses is to reaffirm and, if necessary, reestablish party unity. If most active members of the party, its delegates to local, state, and national nominating conventions, leave the proceedings divided and with mixed attitudes toward the candidate, the base that most candidates count on for election—their party's support—is of little value. In acceptance addresses that have been delivered by candidates who won bitterly contested nomination, it is not uncommon to see major segments of the acceptance address aimed at restoring party unity.

Finally, the acceptance address is a partisan political speech. David Valley has pointed out how each new advance in communications technology has brought national presidential acceptance addresses to larger and larger audiences.[20] Similarly, the acceptance addresses of state and local figures, delivered at state and local nominating proceedings, are often read or heard by a large portion of the public. Consequently, acceptance addresses present the candidate with a unique opportunity to speak not only to party partisans, but also to the general public. Valley concludes that as early as 1896 William Jennings Bryan was tailoring his acceptance address not to the immediate audience but to the hundreds of thousands of citizens who might read his speech.[21] Similarly, even state and local candidates must consider that their acceptance addresses may be carried in full, or quoted in part, by the newspapers. Moreover, segments of the address may be utilized in radio and television reports. Through such accounts and reports, even local acceptance addresses acquire broad audiences, while the audiences for the acceptance addresses of national figures number in the tens of millions. Hence, acceptance addresses serve partisan political purposes.

Strategies of the Address

A variety of strategies have been utilized by campaigners to satisfy the purposes associated with acceptance addresses. Commonly, acceptance addresses are characterized by:

1. Simplified partisan statements
2. Laments about the present and celebrations about the future
3. Stress on the crucial nature of this election
4. Attempts to seek support from the entire constituency.

Which of these strategies will dominate an acceptance address is largely a function of the specific situation in which that address is being delivered. However, all four strategies are common in current acceptance addresses.

In an attempt to attain a strong positive response from the immediate audience, as well as deliver a frankly partisan political address to the large secondary audience, candidates often use simplified partisan statements. Such statements characteristically suggest that the nominees and their parties are necessary to solve any problems confronting the constituency and/or that opponents and their parties will exacerbate any problems confronting the constituency. Typically, in harsh and uncompromisingly partisan language, candidates suggest that there is no real choice in this election, that their position and party are clearly right, and their opponents are clearly wrong. In his 1988 acceptance address George Bush examined the records of the two candidates and claimed that his own positions were based on "what's been tested and found to be true," while Dukakis's positions were "the imaginings of the social planners."[22] He then contrasted his own "tested and true positions" with Dukakis's "imaginings of the social planners" on a series of issues. On each issue—the death penalty, prayer in public schools, the right to own guns, abortion, and taxes—Bush drew a sharp and uncompromising distinction between himself and Dukakis, concluding his treatment of each issue with the simplified partisan statement that "my opponent says no—but I say yes."[23] Similarly in his 1988 acceptance address Michael Dukakis used harsh language and simplified partisan statements. "It's time to raise our sights—to look beyond the cramped ideals of the limited ambitions of the last eight years," claimed Dukakis, even finding fault with the ambitions of the Reagan/Bush administration.[24] Subsequently he found fault with their performance, claiming that the Republican administration had made the Justice Department "the laughing stock of the nation," had an Environmental Protection Agency that was more interested in protecting polluters than in stopping pollution, and had fought "a phony war against drugs."[25] Both Bush and Dukakis used harsh and uncompromising language to suggest that there was no real choice. Simplified partisan statements are so characteristic of acceptance addresses that at least one scholar has characterized acceptance addresses as the "apotheosis of political oratory."[26]

A second strategy characteristic of acceptance addresses is that they tend to lament the present, while celebrating the future. As Kurt W. Ritter has illustrated in his examination of the acceptance addresses of presidential nominees, challengers lament the present, claiming that incumbents have abandoned the abiding principles of the American Dream, and hence have contributed to the nation's problems. Challengers offer to lead the people back to fundamental American values, thereby resolving our problems, and thus giving rise to a bright future.[27] While this strategy seems uniquely suited to challenger nominees, Ritter points out that it is also used, with slight adaptation, by incumbents:

The "in-party" version of the acceptance speech places the speaker at the later stages in the sequence of the rhetorical form. Instead of citing immediate difficulties, the incumbent cites the national decline immediately prior to his arrival at the White House. The incumbent typically describes the sorry state of America when he took office and then points out how he has brought the nation back to its historic purpose. . . . Each incumbent is quick to add that our work is not yet done. In fact, the opposing party threatens the restoration.[28]

Hence, this strategy of lamenting the past and celebrating the future is one that incumbents may also utilize in their acceptance addresses. In his 1988 acceptance address to the Republican National Convention, George Bush lamented the past under President Carter, celebrated the past accomplishments of the Reagan/Bush administration, and then celebrated the future as it would exist in a Bush administration. "I will keep America moving forward, always forward—for a better America, for an endless enduring dream and a thousand points of light. That is my mission. And I will complete it."[29]

A third common strategy found in acceptance addresses is to stress the urgency and crucial nature of this election. Valley reports that 74 percent of all the words in the acceptance speeches of Democratic nominees he studied "have been used to discuss contemporary issues."[30] Ritter similarly concludes that "although incumbent and challenging candidates have found different lessons from the American past, they all find that their election represents a key moment in American history."[31] In his 1988 acceptance address, Michael Dukakis used the phrase "It's time" to start five successive paragraphs stressing the dramatic urgency of his election.[32] Dramatizing the importance of this election, whether it be for county sheriff, state senator, Congressmember, or president, is an acceptance address strategy designed to mobilize support.

A fourth strategy characteristic of acceptance addresses is to call on all audience members, immediate and secondary, to unify behind the nominee to secure victory in the upcoming general election. Calls of this sort may be exceptionally important if the nomination has been bitterly contested. In 1980 because of the highly divisive primary campaign between Senator Edward Kennedy and President Carter, the latter made a special point of including a passage in his acceptance address in which he addressed Kennedy by name:

Ted, your party needs—and I need—you and your idealism and dedication working for us. There is no doubt that even greater service lies ahead of you— and we are grateful to you and to have your strong partnership now in the larger cause to which your own life has been dedicated. I thank you for your support. We'll make great partners this fall in whipping the Republicans.[33]

Carter was trying to unify his party by beckoning to his Democratic opponent and inviting his support.

Candidates typically solicit not simply the support of their party colleagues, but also use their acceptance addresses to reach out beyond the immediate audience of party members, to solicit unity and support from others who might be listening, watching, or reading. Ronald Reagan implemented this strategy in his 1980 acceptance address when he stated:

More than anything else, I want my candidacy to unify our country, to renew the American spirit and sense of purpose. I want to carry our message to every American, regardless of party affiliation, who is a member of this community of shared values.[34]

In passages like this, candidates seek to move beyond their own party, which has already granted them the nomination, and establish identification and unity with other members of the village, city, state, or in the case of presidential candidates, nation.

In sum, acceptance addresses are often among the most important speeches of a campaign. They are responses to a unique rhetorical situation, which serve a variety of purposes beyond simply accepting a nomination, and which may utilize at least four common strategies to fulfill those purposes.

NEWS CONFERENCES

Candidates universally complain of their lack of media coverage. But some events or statements that occur during the campaign are perceived by candidates and their staffs as uniquely important and especially deserving of media coverage. Such occasions often cause the candidate to call a news conference.

Situation for News Conference

News conferences are normally occasioned by events or statements that the candidate feels warrant special attention. Ostensibly, they provide a means of making statements that will be passed on through the media, to the public at large. Though the public is one audience in the news conference situation, we should not ignore the fact that at least four other audiences also exist: the candidates' rivals, their own staffs, political elites, and journalists. These five potential audiences exist for every news conference.[35] Moreover, on occasion, the candidate's remarks at a news conference are not meant primarily for the general public but for one or more of the other four audiences. It is through a news conference, ostensibly held for the public, that the candidate may also choose to address these other audiences.

News conferences are an exceptionally effective means of addressing an opponent. Candidates can exchange challenges, promises, or threats in private and by using third parties. But if such messages are conveyed through a news conference, they take on a different dimension. A message to one's rival, made publicly in the midst of a news conference, clearly implies a degree of commitment, which the same message conveyed privately lacks. By deliberately going on public record and calling unusual attention to the message, the candidate is telling the opponent that this is no idle challenge, promise, or threat, but rather a deadly serious message. The use of a news conference, more than virtually any other form of communication, conveys that seriousness, and hence is occasionally used by candidates as a means of addressing one another.

Candidates may also use news conferences as a means of addressing their own staff. As political scientist Leon V. Sigal has observed, "Campaign organizations tend to combine decentralization at the bottom with inaccessibility at the top."[36] The decentralized group of supporters at the bottom of the campaign have infrequent and short contact with the candidate. A news conference presents the candidate with a forum to which the campaign organization will no doubt be attentive. Hence, messages aimed primarily at the candidate's organization may be transmitted through the news conference.

News conferences also serve the candidate by providing a means of addressing political elites. In prior years, as discussed in Chapter 1, campaign decisions were often made by relatively few individuals, often in private meetings to which the public had little access. The decline of political parties and changes in campaign financing have tended to increase the number of politically elite. In the past candidates might have used a few meetings and phone calls to put out the word that they needed money, had dramatically spurted in the last poll, or had found a new campaign issue. Today it would be difficult to contact all of those with whom a candidate might want to share this news. Hence, candidates may choose to use news conferences as a means of reaching political elites with information.

The use of news conferences to reach multiple audiences can be seen in the joint press conference held by George Bush and Dan Quayle on August 17, 1988, the day after Bush announced that Quayle was his choice for vice-president. Though many of the questions and answers were predictable in this exceptionally well attended and covered conference, the exchanges on campaign tactics suggest Bush and Quayle's awareness of multiple audiences.

Question: I'd like to ask both of you gentlemen about the growing speculation Senator Quayle that you are going to lead the charge against the Democrats. And words like pit bull have been used and so forth. Without using those words, is that true? Are you going to be leading the charge against the Democrats?

Quayle: Well, that's a new description. I am going to be working with the Vice President in campaigning and articulating a very positive agenda of the future of the family and preserving our freedoms and preserving our hope and opportunity. Now obviously I intend to point out what would happen if the party of McGovern, Carter, Mondale and Dukakis would somehow get back in power. I think it would be a disaster.

Bush: Let me add since you addressed it to both of us. We're going to tell the truth and it's going to seem like they've engaged a couple of pit bulls because that's the way it's going to be. . . . And we will be telling the truth about where we want to lead this country, spelling out my priorities and Dan speaking to the issues. And trying to challenge the Democrats to do the same thing. Competence is important but ideology is very important and we're going to be talking on both.[37]

In this exchange Quayle immediately links Dukakis to McGovern, Carter, and Mondale. This linking might well have helped to galvanize the Republican campaign staff and Republican political elites into action. Though Bush could have no doubt simply gone on to the next question, he also chose to respond to this question. Significantly, he picked up on Quayle's response and extended it, claiming that this campaign would involve not simply competence, as Dukakis had asserted in the Democratic convention several weeks earlier, but more importantly, ideology. Like Quayle, Bush may have been speaking not only to the public at large, but also to activist Republicans, and in this instance, perhaps to Dukakis as well. In their responses Quayle and Bush were serving notice that the Republican ticket would have a hand in framing the issues of this campaign, and that those issues would involve ideology as well as competency. Each time in this press conference that Bush or Quayle was asked about campaign tactics they invariably claimed that this was a campaign of issues and ideology. This emphasis on issues and ideology was important for the public, but Bush and Quayle surely recognized that in stressing it they were also sending a message to their staffs, other Republican political elites, such as large contributors, Republican candidates and campaign staffs, and perhaps to Dukakis as well.

Finally, candidates use news conferences as a means of influencing journalists. Those journalists who attend the news conference comprise the immediate audience. The candidate clearly seeks to influence what they disseminate, and by so doing influence the many secondary audiences already discussed. Additionally, many news organizations may choose not to be represented at the news conference and fail to cover it. If candidates are newsworthy at the conference and if their remarks get good play in the media that is represented at the conference, the likelihood of increased media coverage of their campaign will be enhanced.

In sum, rhetorical situations in which candidates perceive the need to seek media coverage of their views for the purpose of better expressing them to the public, to rivals, to their own staffs, to political elites, and to journalists may frequently give rise to news conferences.

Purposes of News Conferences

News conferences serve three basic purposes. First, they are an avenue by which the candidate can get the attention of a variety of audiences. News conferences often serve this purpose better than alternatives, such as news releases. However, they should not be abused. National candidates and major regional and state candidates can often be assured of reasonable media attendance at any news conference they call simply because of the importance of any statement being made by a potential president, senator, or governor. Incumbents also have an advantage in attracting the media simply because news organizations routinely assign someone to cover state senators, state representatives, members of city council, and administrative offices. Other candidates frequently have trouble getting media coverage of their campaigns. There are three reasons why properly used news conferences can increase coverage.

The first reason is novelty. The conference must be a reasonably unusual event. Candidates who are not overly newsworthy cannot expect the media to respond to daily announcements of press conferences. On the other hand, if they call conferences only a few times during the campaign, the very novelty may cause some news organizations to send representatives. Second, the conference should be called with a clear newsworthy issue in mind. News organizations should be made aware of what the candidate will discuss. Unless the candidate has hard news and hopefully the data to support statements, news organizations may choose to ignore the conference. But if candidates are prepared to really make news that will be of interest to the readers, listeners, and viewers of the news organizations in their area, the news conference may be well covered.

For example, a recent congressional candidate concerned about excessive government spending and what he believed to be unfair government intervention in strikes linked these two issues together when a major employer in his district was struck during the campaign. He pointed out that federal government benefits would be given to these strikers. He noted that the strikers all had well-paying skilled labor jobs and that they had voluntarily, by their own vote, given up those jobs to strike. The candidate questioned whether people who were voluntarily unemployed should be subsidized by the government. He cited federal employees and federal laws to explain in detail the benefits that these strikers would receive from the federal government, noting that it could well approach half a million dollars. This portion of his presentation was made with visually interesting aids for the benefit of television. He contrasted the government help that these strikers were receiving with the benefits received by people of his district who were physically disabled, could not work, and hence also received government aid. He claimed that the physically disabled should receive more money since they clearly needed it, while those who had voted to strike should not receive any government subsidy. Unlike the physically handicapped, they had well-paying jobs to which they could return at a moment's notice. He concluded by criticizing his opponent who had voted for much of the legislation that provided help to strikers.

This news conference was one of only three that the candidate called throughout the campaign. It was directly related to an important news story, a large strike that affected thousands of families in the district. It related this strike to a major difference in the position of the two candidates. Moreover, the candidate provided hard information by way of facts and figures on government programs, quotes from government officials, and the voting record of his opponent. The material was presented orally but also with an awareness of the needs of television. The novelty and newsworthiness of this conference resulted in extensive coverage for the candidate.

A final reason why news conferences can effectively serve to focus widespread attention on the candidate's message is that reporters consider them reliable. Reporters often express doubts about the reliability of press releases. But the reliability of news conferences, witnessed by many reporters, with the candidate's statements captured on both audio and video tape, cannot be doubted.

Thus the news conference can serve as an avenue through which the candidate is able to reach many audiences. Even candidates whom news-gathering organizations judge to be unworthy of much attention can gain some attention if they use news conferences properly.

A second important purpose served by news conferences is to allow the candidate to focus attention on one issue or a limited number of issues. As we discussed in Chapter 2, a major function of the press is to help set the campaign agenda. But the candidate also wants to help shape the agenda. By focusing remarks on one issue, the candidate is able to influence strongly what issue the media will cover. Using a press conference, but focusing the issues treated and stressed in that conference, is an effective means utilized by many candidates to help set the campaign agenda.

A final purpose served by news conferences is to establish and improve relationships between the candidate and individual members of the media. The more efficiently run the conference is, the more prepared and responsive the candidate is, the easier the job of the reporter becomes. Press conferences are one means by which candidates can make the job of reporters easier and in so doing improve relationships between themselves and the media. The chief purpose of news conferences—to allow candidates to bring their views to the attention of many audiences—may be readily apparent, but we should not ignore the other purposes served by press conferences: to allow the candidate to focus attention on one or a limited number of issues, presumably selected by the candidate to be of advantage to the candidate, and to enhance candidate-press relationships.

Strategies of News Conferences

Candidates attempt to use news conferences to their own advantage. One of the reasons they are used is to foster the illusion that the candidate is not in control. C. Jack Orr has suggested that presidential news conferences can be thought of as "counterpoised situations" in which the reporters have competing obligations. They must both confront the president, and they must give deference to him.[38] To a lesser extent, the same counterpoised situation exists when reporters interview any officeseeker. The candidate must be shown some deference as a responsible individual running for a responsible job. Moreover, the conference is, after all, the candidate's proceeding. Yet reporters also may seek to confront, challenge, and criticize.

The candidate's control extends beyond the deference that may be extended by reporters. The control is real. The candidate decides when and where to hold a news conference. The candidate decides what format will be used. The candidate decides who will ask questions, and of course the candidate provides the answers. Scholars who have examined news conferences, such as Robert E. Denton, Jr., and Dan F. Hahn, have concluded that while the situation may appear to be one in which the press has considerable control, ultimately it is the skilled respondent who controls the news conference.[39] Candidates exercise their control by utilizing one or more of at least ten common strategies.

Since it is the candidates who call news conferences, they will do so to suit their own needs. Decisions by the candidate about the timing of news conferences are important, and determining when to call a conference is the candidate's first strategic decision. As indicated earlier, typically the fewer conferences called, the more attention the press will extend to those that are called. Calling a news conference to deal with a topic is a clear means of signaling not only that the candidate attaches major importance to this topic, but of also increasing the treatment it receives in the media.

In addition, the candidate must consider the media that will attend and the deadlines with which they operate. Typically, candidates vary the time of day that they hold press conferences, so that they are not slighting any of the media organizations serving their constituency. However, this too is a strategic decision. The candidate, by determining the time of day to hold the conference, can play favorites with the media.

A second consideration is where to hold it. Candidates may make their conferences visually interesting to audiences and hence especially appealing to television news organizations by holding them in visually significant settings. The candidate who has promised to repair the roads and eliminate dangerous potholes might choose to hold the conference at the site of a recent fatal accident caused by poor roads.

Although George Bush held relatively few press conferences during the 1988 election, he used site selection to the utmost advantage when he attacked Michael Dukakis. For example, in his attempt to claim that Dukakis was weak on environmental issues, Bush visited the most polluted harbor in the nation, which just happened to be Boston Harbor, in Dukakis's home city. Similarly, Bush subsequently discussed the environment and pollution with the press while visiting the New Jersey coast, off of which Governor Dukakis had proposed dumping sewage from Massachusetts. By selecting these sites, Bush provided the media with visually significant settings, and focused the media's attention on the weaknesses of his opponent.

Candidates should keep in mind that sometimes a site might be highly visual, lending itself to television news, but it might be difficult and time consuming to reach. Such sites may cause radio and print media representatives to feel that a news conference is hardly worth their effort. Typically, candidates seek to balance their news conference site selections. Some are held with television in mind, while others are held in the campaign headquarters or some highly accessible central location. Whatever decision is made, the candidate can use the selection of a news conference site strategically to help fulfill overall purposes.

These first two strategic concerns involving news conferences, where and when to hold them, relate primarily to the candidate's goal of increasing news coverage. The second group of strategies can help focus the topic of the conference on the areas that the candidate wants covered and stressed in the media.

Candidates utilize at least five strategies to guarantee that the agenda-setting function of the media works in their favor when news organizations cover their press conferences. Perhaps the most commonly used of these strategies is to make an opening statement at the outset of the conference. Though this tactic seems commonplace today, as recently as 35 years ago it was not frequently used. Dwight Eisenhower was the first president who regularly made opening statements at his news conferences.[40] The opening statement should, in itself, be newsworthy. If it is, it will generally prompt questions on the issue it treats and be the focus of most reports of the news conference. Moreover, as Catherine Ann Collins has illustrated in her examination of Henry Kissinger's press conferences, if the interviewee assumes the role of the expert, defines the topic of immediate concern, develops a perspective from which events should be viewed, utilizes data to depict the event, and warns the media that other perspectives will not be considered acceptable, the chances are greatly increased that the interviewee's perspective will be reflected clearly in media accounts of the conference.[41]

Similarly, candidates may not only present opening statements, but they may also restructure questions. In restructuring a question, candidates are again generally attempting to focus attention onto key issues, from certain perspectives, in order to make their points better.

A third strategy frequently utilized by candidates to insure that news conferences focus on their agenda is to follow the advice of Republican political consultant Roger Ailes who recommends that candidates use the formula $Q = A + 1$ when responding to questions. Ailes explains that when asked a question (Q) his clients "reply briefly and directly with an answer (A). Then if it will help, add a point or points (+1) preferably from your agenda." One of his clients, Ailes continues,

a congressman, was asked by a reporter, "You were pressured by the big chemical companies not to introduce that legislation weren't you?" That's the question. The congressman answered, "I met with everyone involved in the issue, including the environmentalists, the consumer groups and the companies." Then he added (+1) "Based on these discussions, all the parties agreed that the industry would set new standards rather than Congress passing a law."[42]

A fourth strategy utilized to make sure candidates are able to focus the conference on their topics and from their perspective is to plant questions. This tactic was commonplace in the presidential press conferences of Eisenhower and Lyndon Johnson.[43] It has been used by many candidates for public office. Typically, a staff member approaches a reporter and suggests a question that might be asked, noting that it will no doubt produce a newsworthy response. Obviously, many reporters may not choose to be used in this fashion. But others will, perceiving the suggested question as a means of drawing attention to something that is newsworthy, which is just what the candidate also wants. The ethics of restructuring questions and planting questions is certainly open for debate. But clearly they are strategies that are utilized by many interviewees, including political candidates, who wish to limit the focus of news conferences.

The final strategy, utilized primarily to focus the news conference, is selective recognition of reporters. Candidates recognize those who question them, but they can fail to recognize those who wish to question them. Most of the time, recognition is haphazard. But it can also be done in a deliberate fashion. A survey of the White House press corps found that "the random selection of questioners by the President" was among the most serious problems associated with White House news conferences.[44] News conferences held by candidates for lesser office will not draw the massive number of reporters that a White House news conference attracts. But any conference that draws a reasonable sample of the media is one in which a candidate might selectively recognize reporters.

Candidates normally hold news conferences when they seek extensive coverage of their views. Typically, they have a limited number of issues on which they wish to focus in the news conference and that they hope the public will learn of through the efforts of the journalists in attendance. To insure that these topics are clearly the centerpieces of the news conference, candidates often assume the role of the expert, utilizing an opening statement that spells out their position on issues, and indicates the perspective on the issue that they find satisfactory. They may also choose to restructure questions, consistently add comments from their agenda to answers (Q = A + 1), plant questions, and selectively recognize reporters. All these strategies are done primarily to enable candidates to stress their issues and prevent the conference from dealing with other issues.

Three final strategies can be utilized by most candidates in news conferences. First is to prepare. Candidates differ in the manner of their preparation for news conferences. However, most attempt to anticipate questions that might be asked and prepare responses. Presidents such as Harry Truman and John Kennedy typically rehearsed for news conferences by reviewing 40 to 75 possible questions that might arise in their press conferences.[45] Most candidates follow similar procedures. They rely on their staffs to generate possible questions and then prepare responses.

Second, if the conference starts to go bad, the candidate can filibuster. Typically, press conferences are called for specific time periods. The press has deadlines and the candidate has a full schedule. Hence, if their conferences are going poorly, some candidates will take considerable time in answering questions, particularly those that they are comfortable with and deal with topics they wish to address. By so doing, they reduce the opportunity the press has for further questioning.

Finally, candidates often attempt to appear vulnerable in press conferences. Given the many controls and strategies available to candidates who utilize news conferences, it may be easy to forget that there are other actors in this situation. President Carter's television advisor noted that even though the news conference was in effect a theater in which the president called upon reporters to play their supporting roles, "it is important that the President appear vulnerable."[46] Similarly, most candidates wish to appear vulnerable in news conference situations. The desire to appear vulnerable often motivates the use of the news conference. It is one of the reasons why candidates will utilize "risky" news conferences, rather than safer press releases, audios, or other forms of communication with the public. The appearance that the candidate is taking a chance and is vulnerable is one that most candidates believe the public admires. The news conference situation suggests openness and honesty, as well as confidence in one's ability, that candidates are rarely able to attain through the use of other forms of communication.

The symbiotic relationship that exists between candidates and journalists is, perhaps, nowhere more evident than in the news conference. News conferences are called by candidates seeking widespread coverage of their views. They are attended by representatives of news organizations who sense that the conference may produce newsworthy material. Both the candidate and the reporter have an interest in aiding one another. But candidates are not only desirous of creating news, they are also desirous of influencing and persuading. Hence, most candidates utilize a variety of strategies, attempting to insure that their conferences are indeed covered and that the conferences focus on those issues that the candidates wish to focus upon. Moreover, though they prepare in order not to be vulnerable and weak, they recognize that a format that suggests their vulnerability may be desirable.

APOLOGIAS

An increasingly recurring form of speech that many candidates have recently found necessary to deliver is the apologia. In this section, we will examine the situations that create apologias and in so doing perhaps also gain an understanding of why they have been on the increase in recent years. We will also examine the major purposes of such speeches and the strategies utilized to attain those purposes.

Situation for Apologia

Apologias are speeches made by candidates who find it necessary to apologize for some statement or behavior. Typically, the statement or behavior implies a serious flaw in the candidate's character, one that if widely accepted by the public would prevent the candidate from winning office. In the 1982 Ohio Democratic party gubernatorial primary, it became common knowledge that years earlier, one of the candidates, Cincinnati City Councilman Gerald Springer, had consorted with a prostitute. This action was taken by many to suggest that Springer did not have the qualities of character and morality desired of a governor. In 1984 Jesse Jackson's anti-Semitic remarks, characterizing Jews as "Hymies" and New York City as "Hymietown," were offensive not simply to Jews, but also suggested that Jackson could not equitably and fairly govern a racially, ethnically, and religiously diverse nation such as the United States.

Similarly, by late 1987 and early 1988 Gary Hart had been the subject of repeated rumors that he was having affairs. When the *Miami Herald* broke the story that he was apparently having yet another affair, this one with model Donna Rice, Hart's campaign was in grave trouble. Not only did this affair suggest that he lacked the qualities of character and morality desired of a national leader, but given that Hart's sex life had been subject to constant question in the past, for him to have an affair while launching a presidential campaign raised serious questions about his maturity, judgment, and credibility.

Apologias have become an increasingly more common feature of recent campaigns for two reasons. First, the news media seem more prone then ever before to report on the candidate's weaknesses and flaws. Gone are the days when Franklin Delano Roosevelt could dictate that he never be photographed in leg braces or being carried by his aides. Gone are the days when the candidate's private life was not discussed. The press is far more unsparing of candidates today. Additionally, one of the legacies of Watergate has apparently been to sensitize the public to the personal integrity of candidates. More than ever before, candidates are finding the media inspecting their character closely, and the public concerned about the candidates' personal integrity and morality.

Purposes of Apologia

Apologias serve to enable the candidate to explain some statement or behavior that casts doubt on the candidate's suitability for office. To accomplish this explanation, with the least amount of damage to their image, candidates often have three purposes in mind when they deliver apologias.

First, they hope to explain the behavior or statement in a positive light. In so doing, they hope to minimize damage to their character and image. If the incident that triggered the need for the apologia cannot be explained positively, the second purpose of the apologia may be considered. The candidate can at least justify behavior. Again, by so doing, the candidate hopes to minimize damage to character and image.

The final purpose of an apologia is to remove the topic from public discussion. Ellen Reid Gold has pointed out that, at least with major national figures, frequently reporters repeat the charges against a candidate so often that it is difficult for the candidate not to appear guilty.[47] Day after day, the candidate is seen denying the charge. To the extent that an apologia can put an end to questioning and allow the campaign to move on to other issues, it has served a vital purpose.

Strategies of Apologia

Rhetoricians have identified six strategies commonly utilized by speakers delivering apologias. Not every strategy can be used in every apologia, but all six have been used frequently. First, apologias are often best delivered in settings where individuals other than the candidate seem in control.[48] Many early apologias were delivered in settings where the candidate seemed to be in complete control. For example, Richard Nixon's 1952 Checkers address, following charges that Nixon benefited from a slush fund set up by wealthy supporters, and Ted Kennedy's 1969 Address to the People of Massachusetts, following the incident at Chappaquiddick, were both made by men who had purchased air time and were in complete control of what was said. However, as Sherry

Devereaux Butler points out in contrasting these two addresses, by 1969 mass media viewers were "more sophisticated, less likely to place automatic belief in the magic power of the television tube, more likely to question."[49] Additionally, the legacies of Vietnam and Watergate include voter disenchantment with less than honest officials. Both of these facts, growing voter sophistication in using media and growing voter disenchantment with public figures, have contributed to changes in the early apologia, typified by Richard Nixon's Checkers address.

Rather than an address such as Nixon's in which the candidate is in complete control of the setting, candidates today often deliver their apologias in settings that appear to be controlled by others. For example, in 1980 President Carter found it necessary to apologize for the meanness he had exhibited in his criticisms of Ronald Reagan. Carter's image and character as a good, moral, nice man were called into question by his seemingly intemperate remarks that Ronald Reagan would divide the nation along economic, racial, and religious lines.[50] Rather than address this issue of meanness himself, Carter agreed to an interview with Barbara Walters. That Carter had deliberately chosen to make his apologia in a setting that he did not fully control was evident from Walters's first comment. "Mr. President, in recent days you have been characterized as mean, vindictive, hysterical, and on the point of desperation."[51] As Walters's interview with Carter illustrates,[52] the strategy of appearing in a setting where one does not have complete control involves risk. However, many contemporary candidates choose to take this risk, believing that public sophistication with media and alienation from leaders make this an acceptable risk that must be taken if their message is to be appreciated.

A second strategy utilized by candidates delivering apologias is to simply deny the "alleged facts, sentiments, objects, or relationships," that give rise to the charge.[53] If the candidate cannot deny the substance of the charge, one can deny the intent, arguing that the statement or action has been misunderstood.[54] In 1980 Jimmy Carter tried both approaches. In response to one question Walters asked, Carter noted, "I don't think I'm mean, Barbara." Moments later, asked how he could allow himself to engage in mudslinging, Carter noted, "It's not a deliberate thing."[55]

A third strategy frequently used in apologias is what B. L. Ware and Wil A. Linkugel characterize as "bolstering strategies." Bolstering strategies are attempts by the candidate to identify "with something viewed favorably by the audience."[56] In his Address to the People of Massachusetts, Senator Edward Kennedy repeatedly reminded his audience that he was a Kennedy, continually referring not simply to himself but to his highly popular family.

Similarly, in 1984 seven-term Idaho Congressman George Hansen, convicted of four felony counts for filing false financial disclosure records, claimed he was the victim of government persecution and attempted to identify himself as a crusader against big government. Hansen claimed that his repeated conservative stands and his earlier fights against the Internal Revenue Service and the Justice Department on behalf of his Idaho constituents had caused him to be singled out and prosecuted while Congresswoman Geraldine Ferraro and Attorney General Edwin Meese were not being prosecuted for similar offenses. Given the highly conservative, antigovernment attitudes of his audience, Hansen's attempt to bolster himself by associating himself with his constituent's conservative antigovernment attitudes made sense. It made sense at the ballot box as well, for Hansen, convicted and facing a prison term, nevertheless won a hotly contested primary and came within 133 votes, out of over 200,000 cast, of being reelected to his eighth term.[57]

A fourth strategy frequently used in political apologias is differentiation. Ware and Linkugel define differentiation strategies as "separating some fact, sentiment, object, or relationship from some larger context within which the audience presently views that attribute."[58] As Gold notes, "In political campaigns, the candidate may try not only to redefine the larger context for the audience, but to separate himself symbolically from the accusation by attacking the source."[59] In responding to Walters, Carter finds that his meanness should not be perceived simply as an aspect of his overall campaign style, as it was viewed. Rather, he finds that his meanness is in part a function of the failure of the press to treat substantive issues between the candidates but to focus instead on personal characteristics.[60]

The fifth type of strategy found in political apologias is what Ware and Linkugel have called the transcendental strategy. This kind of strategy "cognitively joins some fact, sentiment, object, or relationship with some larger context within which the audience does not presently view that attribute."[61] Such strategies "psychologically move the audience away from the particulars of the charge at hand in a direction toward some more abstract, general view of his character."[62] In 1980 Jimmy Carter engaged in this strategy when he attempted to move the audience away from the charge of meanness toward an understanding of his intensity over the issues. Twice in his interview with Barbara Walters, he linked his harsh attacks on Reagan with his own intense feelings about arms control, national defense, and the SALT talks.

The final strategy that political figures have utilized in their apologias is to confess. If the candidate is guilty a quick confession may put the unwinnable issue generating the apologia behind the candidate, and let the campaign progress to other issues. In 1984, Jesse Jackson's attitudes toward Jews became the focal point of 14 days worth of news coverage about his campaign, at the very outset of the critical first primary in

New Hampshire. Finally, on the 14th day, rejecting the advice of his staff, Jackson spoke to a Jewish audience at Temple Adath Yeshurun in Manchester, New Hampshire, confessed to making the derogatory statements that had given rise to the controversy, and observed that "however innocent and unintentional, it was insensitive and it was wrong. In part, I am to blame, and for that I am deeply distressed."[63] With that confession, Jackson was finally able to put the controversy behind him, and return to other issues. Moreover, the issue never surfaced in Jackson's 1988 campaign.

In 1988 Gary Hart used a variation of the confession strategy. Hart confessed to his affair with Donna Rice, but attempted to dismiss it as a minor aberration, a minor mistake. Had the issue been exclusively one of adultery, and the candidate someone other than Gary Hart, his gambit might have succeeded. But given the history of such allegations about Hart, his confession to having an affair while in the midst of a presidential campaign seemed only to reinforce the charges that he lacked the maturity, judgment, and credibility necessary to lead the nation.

In sum, apologias seem to be characterized by the use of one or more of six strategies. Increasingly, candidates are making their apologias in situations over which they do not have full control. Moreover, they are using denial, bolstering, differentiation, transcendental, and confessional strategies to carry out their apologias.

Apologias do not seem to have been a common form of political speech until relatively recently. Contemporary stress on the character of candidates and the aggressiveness of contemporary journalists seems, in recent years, to have created far more situations calling for apologias than ever before. It is likely that apologias will be a feature of American political rhetoric for years to come.

CONCLUSIONS

In this chapter, we have observed that most campaigns are marked by similar, comparable, or analogous situations that require a rhetorical response. The responses to four such situations take the form of announcement of candidacy speeches, nomination acceptance addresses, news conferences, and apologias. We have examined the situations that give rise to these types of presentations, the purposes of such presentations, and the major strategies employed in each type of presentation.

NOTES

1. Lloyd F. Bitzer, "The Rhetorical Situation," *Philosophy and Rhetoric* 1 (January 1968):6.
2. Karlyn Kohrs Campbell and Kathleen Hall Jamieson, "Form and Genre

in Rhetorical Criticism: An Introduction," in *Form and Genre: Shaping Rhetorical Action*, ed. Karlyn Kohrs Campbell and Kathleen Hall Jamieson (Falls Church, Va.: Speech Communication Association, 1977), p. 15.

3. Judith S. Trent, "Presidential Surfacing: The Ritualistic and Crucial First Act," *Communication Monographs* 45 (November 1978):281–92.

4. See, for example, Hamilton Jordan, "Memo of August 4, 1974, to Jimmy Carter," in *Running for President: A Journal of the Carter Campaign*, ed. Martin Schram (New York: Pocket Books, 1977), p. 416.

5. Quotations from Cranston's announcement address are drawn from the account of his announcement found in the *Cincinnati Enquirer*, February 3, 1983, p. A5.

6. Additionally, Dukakis had to consider the likelihood of John Kerry, the junior senator from Massachusetts, running in 1996. Shortly before Dukakis announced his 1988 candidacy, *Boston Globe* political columnist David Nyhan claimed that Kennedy might well be ready to run for the presidency again in 1992 and that Kerry was looking to 1996. If one believes this scenario, and certainly Dukakis and his advisors were aware of it, then 1988 loomed as the only year in which Dukakis could run and be assured of the unified support of the Massachusetts Democratic organization from the outset. See *The Winning of the White House*, ed. Donald Morrison (New York: Time, 1988), pp. 125–26.

7. Trent, "Presidential Surfacing," p. 284.

8. For a good flavor of the atmosphere surrounding Glenn's announcement see *Newsweek Election Extra*, November/December, 1984, p. 43.

9. For a description of the immediate circumstances surrounding Robertson's announcement see the *New York Times*, October 2, 1987, p. A16. The quotations to Robertson's speech found in these paragraphs are drawn from David Henry's excellent study of presidential announcement addresses, " 'Today, Surrounded by My Family and Friends': Rhetorical Dimensions of Presidential Announcement Speeches, 1988" (Paper presented at the Speech Communication Association National Convention, November 1988), p. 7. Henry indicates that he was provided a copy of the speech by Robertson's campaign staff. Robertson was heckled during his address and the *New York Times* account claims that he did depart from his prepared text. Also see Kim S. Phipps and Nancy E. Mitchell, "Pat Robertson's 1988 Campaign: Religion and Presidential Politics" (Paper presented at the Speech Communication Association National Convention, November 1988), p. 5 for an informative account of Robertson's announcement.

10. Robert V. Friedenberg interview with Dorothy Christenson, Administrative Assistant, Councilwoman Bobbie Stern, January 19, 1983.

11. Kenneth P. O'Donnell and David F. Powers, *Johnny, We Hardly Knew Ye* (New York: Pocket Books, 1977), p. 416.

12. See the Kennedy and Carter responses in *The Candidates 1980: Where They Stand* (Washington, D.C.: American Enterprise Institute, 1980). Also see Robert V. Friedenberg, "Why Teddy Wasn't Ready: An Examination of the Speaking of Senator Edward Moore Kennedy During the 1980 Presidential Primaries" (Paper presented at the Ohio Speech Association, October 1980), pp. 3–4.

13. Jerry Springer, "Announcement of Candidacy Address," February 1, 1982, p. 1. Springer provided one of the authors with a copy of his address.

14. Ibid., p. 5. In an interview with Friedenberg, January 20, 1982, Springer

stressed that his address was intended to reaffirm his campaign up to that point, which had consciously attempted to portray him as closer to the people of Ohio than any other candidate.

15. Perhaps because of a sense that the public expects modesty from candidates, often this theme is not as directly stated as the other two. Rather, candidates speak of "our administration," as though they have already been elected. They speak of the inspiration they have received from their families, their supporters, the people, and God. In so doing candidates obliquely suggest that no opponent could defeat them. See Robert V. Friedenberg, "Form and Genre in Announcement of Candidacy Addresses" (Paper presented at the Temple University Fourth Annual Conference on Discourse Analysis: Form and Genre in Political Discourse," March 1983), pp. 13–14.

16. For a thorough history of Democratic acceptance addresses, see chapters 2 and 3 of David B. Valley, *A History and Analysis of Democratic Presidential Nomination Acceptance Speeches to 1968* (Lanham, Md.: University Press of America, 1988). A more concise history can be found in Valley's "Significant Characteristics of Democratic Presidential Nomination Acceptance Speeches," *Central States Speech Journal* 25 (Spring 1974):56–60.

17. Thomas B. Farrell, "Political Conventions as Legitimation Ritual," *Communication Monographs* 45 (November 1978): 293–305; and Kurt W. Ritter, "American Political Rhetoric and the Jeremiad Tradition: Presidential Nomination Acceptance Addresses, 1960–1976," *Central States Speech Journal* 31 (Fall 1980):153–71.

18. For discussions of these purposes see Robert O. Nordvold, "Rhetoric as Ritual: Hubert H. Humphrey's Acceptance Address at the 1968 Democratic National Convention," *Today's Speech* 18 (Winter 1970): 34; Valley, "Nomination Acceptance Speeches," p. 60; and Ritter, "American Political Rhetoric," p. 155.

19. See George Bush, "Acceptance Address, Republican National Convention, August 18, 1988," the *New York Times*, August 19, 1988, p. A14; Michael Dukakis, "Acceptance Address, Democratic National Convention, July 21, 1988," the *New York Times*, July 22, 1988, p. A10.

20. Valley, "Nomination Acceptance Speeches," p. 61.

21. Ibid.

22. Bush, "Acceptance Address," p. A14.

23. Ibid.

24. Michael Dukakis, "Acceptance Address," p. A10.

25. Ibid.

26. Nordvold, "Rhetoric as Ritual," p. 34.

27. Ritter, "American Political Rhetoric," p. 157–64.

28. Ibid., pp. 161–62.

29. This quoted passage is the conclusion of Bush's actual speech text. Upon completing his speech, Bush immediately asked his audience to rise and pledge allegiance to the flag, thus celebrating the future by reaffirmation of our basic creed. See Elizabeth Drew, *Election Journal: Political Events of 1987–1988* (New York: William Morrow, 1989), pp. 258–60.

30. Valley, "Nomination Acceptance Speeches," p. 60.

31. Ritter, "American Political Rhetoric," p. 162.

32. Dukakis, "Acceptance Address," p. A–10.

33. Jimmy Carter, "Acceptance Speech, Democratic National Convention, August 14, 1980," in *The Pursuit of the Presidency 1980*, ed. Richard Harwood (New York: Berkley Books, 1980), p. 402.

34. Ronald Reagan, "Acceptance Speech, Republican National Convention, July 17, 1980," in *The Pursuit of the Presidency 1980*, ed. Richard Harwood (New York: Berkley Books, 1980), p. 416.

35. This analysis of news conference audiences is adapted from Leon V. Sigal, "Newsmen and Campaigners: Organization Men Make the News," *Political Science Quarterly* 93 (Fall 1978):466–67.

36. Ibid., p. 466.

37. "Transcript of Debut News Conference by Bush-Quayle Ticket," *New York Times*, August 18, 1988, p. A22.

38. C. Jack Orr, "Reporters Confront the President: Sustaining a Counterpoised Situation," *Quarterly Journal of Speech* 66 (February 1980): 17–21.

39. Most such examinations have focused on presidential news conferences, but the rationales for the conclusions, as well as the conclusions themselves, seem appropriate for most political candidates. See Robert E. Denton, Jr., and Dan F. Hahn, *Presidential Communication* (New York: Praeger, 1986), p. 252; Michael Grossman and Martha Kumar, *Portraying the President: The White House and the News Media* (Baltimore: Johns Hopkins University Press, 1981), pp. 243–44; Orr, "Reporters Confront the President," pp. 31–32; and Delbert McQuire, "Democracy's Confrontation: The Presidential Press Conference," *Journalism Quarterly* 44 (Winter 1967):638–44.

40. Peter M. Sandman, David M. Rubin, and David B. Sachsman, *Media: An Introductory Analysis of American Mass Communications* (Englewood Cliffs, N.J.: Prentice-Hall, 1972), p. 344.

41. Catherine Ann Collins, "Kissinger's Press Conferences, 1972–1974: An Exploration of Form and Role Relationship on News Management," *Central States Speech Journal* 28 (Fall 1977): 190–93.

42. Roger Ailes, *You Are The Message: Secrets of the Master Communicators* (Homewood, Ill.: Dow Jones–Irwin, 1988), pp. 154–55.

43. Grossman and Kumar, *Portraying the President*, p. 248.

44. McQuire, "Democracy's Confrontation," p. 640.

45. A. L. Lorenze, Jr., "Truman and the Press Conference," *Journalism Quarterly* 43 (Winter 1966): 673–75; and Harry P. Kerr, "The President and the Press," *Western Speech* 27 (Fall 1963): 220–21.

46. Barry Jogoda quoted in Grossman and Kumar, *Portraying the President*, p. 243.

47. Ellen Reid Gold, "Political Apologia: The Ritual of Self Defense," *Communication Monographs* 45 (November 1978): 311–12.

48. Ibid., p. 311.

49. Sherry Devereaux Butler, "The Apologia, 1971 Genre," *Southern Speech Communication Journal* 37 (Spring 1972): 283.

50. Jack W. Germond and Jules Witcover, *Blue Smoke and Mirrors: How Reagan Won and Why Carter Lost the Election of 1980* (New York: Viking Press, 1981), pp. 255–60.

51. Ibid., p. 262.

52. See Germond and Witcover, *Blue Smoke and Mirrors*, p. 262–65, for an analysis of the negative effects of Walters's interview with Carter.

53. B. L. Ware and Wil A. Linkugel, "They Spoke in Defense of Themselves: On the General Criticism of Apologia," *Quarterly Journal of Speech* 59 (October 1973):25.

54. Gold, "Political Apologia," p. 308.

55. Germond and Witcover, *Blue Smoke and Mirrors*, p. 256.

56. Ware and Linkugel, "General Criticism of Apologia," p. 277.

57. For an excellent study of apologia as utilized by Hansen in 1984, see Brant Short, "Comic Book Apologia: The 'Paranoid' Rhetoric of Congressman George Hansen," *Western Journal of Speech Communication* 51 (Spring 1987): 189–203. Colleen E. Kelley, "The 1984 Campaign Rhetoric of Representative George Hansen: A Pentadic Analysis," *Western Journal of Speech Communication* 51 (Spring 1987): 204–7 is also informative, though written from a different critical perspective.

58. Ware and Linkugel, "General Criticism of Apologia," p. 278.

59. Gold, "Political Apologia," p. 308.

60. Germond and Witcover, *Blue Smoke and Mirrors*, p. 262–63.

61. Ware and Linkugel, "General Criticism of Apologia," p. 280.

62. Ibid.

63. Quoted in Jack Germond and Jules Witcover, *Wake Us When It's Over: Presidential Politics of 1984* (New York: Macmillan, 1985), p. 159.

Chapter Eight

Debates in Political Campaigns

In the summer of 1858, one of the most remarkable local political campaigns in U.S. history was being waged on the plains of Illinois. The 1858 Illinois Senate race was remarkable for many reasons. Few races, regardless of office, bring together two such outstanding public servants as those competing for the Senate seat from Illinois in 1858. Few races, regardless of office, have had as profound an impact on our national history as did the race for the Illinois Senate seat in 1858. Few races have produced such masterpieces of campaign oratory as those produced on the plains of Illinois in the summer of 1858. For in that year, Abraham Lincoln and Stephen Douglas vied for the Senate seat from Illinois.

On July 24, Lincoln challenged Douglas to a series of debates. Douglas accepted. As the front-runner in what was anticipated to be a close election, Douglas dictated the terms. He suggested seven debates and demanded the opportunity to both open and close four of the debates. Lincoln would open and close only three. Lincoln accepted, and thus ensued what the *New York Tribune* called "a mode of discussing political questions which might well be more generally adopted."[1]

Though the Lincoln-Douglas debates were the first significant political campaign debates in U.S. history, as Kathleen Hall Jamieson and David S. Birdsell remind us, they were not the first American political campaign debates.[2] Moreover, unlike their successors, they were real debates rather than joint speeches or joint press conferences. Most authorities would agree with J. Jeffery Auer when he argues that there are five essential elements for a true debate. "A debate," claims Auer, "is (1) a confrontation, (2) in equal and adequate time, (3) of matched contestants, (4) on a stated proposition, (5) to gain an audience decision."[3] Auer points out that "each of these elements is essential if we are to have true debate. Insistence upon their recognition is more than mere pedantry, for each one has contributed to the vitality of the debate tradition."[4]

The Lincoln-Douglas debates were not followed by many other debates. It was not until a century later, in 1960, that we next had "Great Debates" of comparable significance. However, the 1960 presidential debates between Senator John F. Kennedy and Vice-President Richard M. Nixon gave rise to political debating as we now know it in the media age.

Yet most contemporary political debaters, including Presidents Jimmy Carter, Ronald Reagan, and George Bush have not engaged in political debates. Based primarily on the Kennedy-Nixon model of 1960, most contemporary political debates can be characterized as "counterfeit debates."[5] This is not to say that contemporary political debating is, like a counterfeit bill, of little value. As we will see later, contemporary political debates are extremely valuable. But in large part because of the influence of media, they involve different formats and strategies than those of the Lincoln-Douglas era.

Perhaps the counterfeit nature of contemporary political debates can best be understood by using Auer's five essentials of debate to compare the Lincoln-Douglas debate with the prototypic contemporary media political debate, that of Kennedy and Nixon in 1960.

First, the Kennedy-Nixon debate and most political debates since do not involve direct confrontation. Lincoln and Douglas confronted one another. They met on the same platform, questioned one another, and refuted one another. Indeed, the highlight of the seven debates came in the second debate, at Freeport, when Lincoln confronted Douglas with a series of four questions to set up what became known as "The Freeport Dilemma."

Lincoln claimed that Douglas had to repudiate the Supreme Court's Dred Scott decision (which made it illegal for voters to prohibit slavery in the territories and hence was enormously popular in the South) or repudiate his own program of popular sovereignty. As chairman of the Senate Committee on Territories, Douglas had argued that each of the western territories should be allowed to choose by popular vote if it would enter the Union free or slave. Repeatedly in the debates after Freeport, Lincoln confronted Douglas with this dilemma. Lincoln demanded that Douglas choose between a fundamental tenet of U.S. democracy—the sanctity of Supreme Court decisions—or his own proposal. If Douglas supported the Dred Scott decision, he was admitting that he had labored in the Senate on behalf of a policy that was illegal. If he supported popular sovereignty, he was admitting Supreme Court decisions were not the highest law of the land and was isolating himself from the Southern wing of the Democratic party. Lincoln confronted, questioned, followed up, and harangued Douglas. Douglas responded, claimed the dilemma was false, and argued that Lincoln ignored a third alternative.

In contrast, it was not Richard Nixon but a journalist who suggested to John Kennedy that "you are naive and at times immature." Nor was it John Kennedy but rather a journalist who suggested to Richard Nixon that his experience as vice-president was as an observer not as a participant or initiator of policy.[6] Kennedy and Nixon did not talk to each other, as did Lincoln and Douglas. Kennedy and Nixon did not question and pursue one another, nor did they respond to one another. Rather, if Kennedy, Nixon, and most political debaters since are confronted at all, it is by the media and not by one another.[7]

Second, the Kennedy-Nixon debate, and most political debates since, did not involve equal and adequate time. The key, of course, is adequate time. Lincoln and Douglas dealt almost exclusively with one issue, the future of slavery in the territories. Each man spoke for one and a half hours in each of seven debates. Kennedy and Nixon each spoke half an hour in each of four debates. The subject matter for the first Kennedy-Nixon debate was domestic affairs, for the last foreign affairs, and no restrictions whatsoever existed for the middle two debates. It is entirely fair to say that Lincoln and Douglas spent up to 21 hours debating one issue, while Kennedy and Nixon spent eight minutes on any one issue. Formats like those used by Kennedy-Nixon typically allow candidates three to five minutes to deal with an issue.[8] Kennedy and Nixon, and most political debaters since, did not have adequate time to deal with major public issues.

Political debates do typically meet the third criteria for debates. The contestants are closely matched. If one contestant is vastly brighter, more fluent, more poised, more knowledgeable, and better prepared, no real debate can take place. Typically, this is not the case in political debates, where both candidates must agree to debate and hence are probably able debaters, having merit enough to secure major party nominations to the office.

However, political debates frequently do not meet the fourth criteria of debates. The Kennedy-Nixon debate and most political debates since did not involve one stated proposition. Rather, depending on format, ten or more topics are discussed in a single debate. In the first Kennedy-Nixon debate, the two men dealt with such diverse questions as who was most fit and prepared to lead the country, how would each man handle the farm subsidy programs, what policies each would advocate for reducing the federal debt, what would each man do about improving the nation's schools, what policies would each pursue with respect to medical aid to the aged and with respect to a comprehensive minimum hourly wage program. Moreover, each was asked how serious a threat to national security he believed communist subversive activity in the United States was and how he would finance public school construction. In sum, Kennedy and Nixon had under an hour to deal with nine totally diverse topic areas.

Finally, the Kennedy-Nixon debates did not really gain an audience decision of the issues. Debates, as Auer suggests, are "clashes of ideas, assumptions, evidence, and argument."[9] They secure from audiences a decision of the issues. In 1858 the Lincoln-Douglas debates revealed the inadequacies of Douglas's program of popular sovereignty for the territories and the inconsistency of that program with existing institutions. It was because he illustrated the inadequacies and inconsistencies of Douglas's position, while justifying and defending his own belief in restricting slavery's spread into the territories, that Lincoln emerged from the debates a national figure, and Douglas's national aspirations were shattered. Those debates were a true clash of ideas, assumptions, evidence, and argument. In 1960 the Kennedy and Nixon debates did not facilitate the audience's making a decision about the issues. Contemporary political debates that are heavily oriented toward the broadcast media audience are not in the tradition of issue-oriented debates.

Political debating is widespread in this country. It is almost a ritualistic aspect of campaigns for one candidate to challenge the other to a debate. Yet, as we have seen, contemporary media-oriented debates, regardless of what office is sought, are vastly different from the first significant political debates in our nation's history. Though they typically involve matched candidates, they rarely if ever entail direct confrontation, equal and adequate time, one stated proposition, and a clear decision on the issues. In the next section, we will trace how political debates evolved from the Lincoln-Douglas debates to the media-oriented debates we have today.

HISTORY OF POLITICAL DEBATES

During the 19th century, debating was an important aspect of campaigning, though perhaps not as widespread as it is today. However, a few debates of local or statewide interest did take place.[10] Although Lincoln and Douglas had gained national attention, figures of comparable stature did not engage in campaign debates in the years that followed. Rather than debating their opponents, in the 19th century many candidates utilized surrogate debaters. This practice was especially widespread in 19th-century presidential elections.[11] Nevertheless, relatively few 19th-century debates received attention beyond their own constituencies, and none attained national prominence.[12]

By the mid–1920s, due to the growth of radio, national debates began to seem feasible. In 1924 testifying before a congressional committee investigating broadcast regulations, William Harkness, an executive of the American Telephone and Telegraph Company, made what is generally believed to be the first suggestion for broadcasting political debates.[13] At the time of Harkness's suggestion, such a broadcast would have probably been local or regional in scope, but within two years, with the birth of the National Broadcasting Company in 1926, nationwide political broadcasts became feasible. NBC's first programs were carried over a 24-station hookup serving 21 cities from the East Coast to as far west as Kansas City. Other networks soon followed.

The implication of national radio networks for political campaigns was not lost on Congress. In 1927 Congress included a section in its radio broadcast regulations dealing with political broadcasts. Those regulations were modified in 1934, and section 315 of the Communications Act of 1934 affected political broadcasts for years. This "equal time" provision required that if any licensed radio or television station allows a legally qualified candidate for any public office to use its station, it must "afford equal opportunities to all other such candidates for that office in the use of such broadcasting station."[14] This provision, designed to provide equal access to the public's airwaves to all candidates, tended to inhibit political debates. It required that if major party candidates received airtime from a station, that station would have to provide airtime to every other candidate, regardless of the extent of their following. Few broadcasters were willing to make time for the many minor party candidates, and hence little time went to any campaign activities. Although this act was modified in 1959 to insure that broadcasters could cover the normal newsworthy activities of political candidates without being subject to harassment by other candidates,[15] throughout the period of 1934 to 1976 section 315 inhibited political debates in any race where more than two candidates were involved.

Nevertheless, political debating did not come to a complete standstill during this period. On October 17, 1936, during the presidential election between Governor Alfred Landon and President Franklin Roosevelt, Republican Senator Arthur Vandenberg of Michigan produced a "fake" debate over the CBS network by editing recordings of Roosevelt's speeches. The live Vandenberg naturally bested the edited Roosevelt. The nature of this debate was not made clear to stations until shortly before the broadcast. Of the 66 stations scheduled to broadcast the debate, 23 did so without interruption. Clearly Vandenberg had edited Roosevelt's speeches to produce a partisan one-sided program. However, perhaps more than anything that had preceded it, this program focused attention on the possibilities of nationally broadcast political debates between major figures.[16] Four years later, in 1940, Republican Wendell Wilkie opened his campaign by challenging President Roosevelt to debate. Polls found the public almost evenly divided in their response to Wilkie's challenge; 49 percent opposed.[17] Apparently much of the opposition stemmed from the public's perceptions of the risks that might be involved in having an incumbent president debate. Roosevelt suffered no significant political consequences in declining to debate.

In 1948 the first broadcast debate between two major presidential candidates took place. The candidates were Governor Harold Stassen of Minnesota and Governor Thomas Dewey of New York. They were seeking the Republican nomination to challenge President Harry S. Truman. In the midst of the Oregon primary, Stassen challenged Dewey to debate. Dewey accepted but specified the terms. As Dewey wished, the debate was held in private, with only a small audience of journalists. Stassen had suggested that it might be held in a ballpark with a large public audience. Dewey spoke last as he wanted. Dewey selected the topic: that the Communist party should be outlawed in the United States. Moreover, Dewey chose to defend the negative. The debate was broadcast nationally by all four major radio networks and was well received by audiences and political observers.[18] Among the first suggestions that 1952 presidential candidates General Dwight David Eisenhower and Illinois Governor Adlai Stevenson engage in a televised debate were those made by Michigan Senator Blair Moody and Democratic media specialist J. Leonard Reinsch.[19] Both NBC and CBS immediately offered to provide the airtime, if Congress would suspend or revoke the equal time provision. However, nothing came of the network's offer, since both Eisenhower and Stevenson were reluctant to debate.[20] Not so reluctant were the two Massachusetts senatorial candidates, Henry Cabot Lodge and John F. Kennedy, who debated that year in Waltham, Massachusetts.

By 1956 virtually the entire country had access to television. Televised political programs of every sort were commonplace. Candidates at all levels—presidential, senatorial, congressional, as well as scores of local candidates—were routinely appearing on television. But with one significant exception, broadcast debates between political candidates were not seen on the nation's television screens.

In 1956 the contest for the Democratic presidential nomination became a fight between Tennessee Senator Estes Kefauver and Adlai Stevenson. Kefauver had become a well-known political figure in 1951 when, as chairman of the Senate Crime Investigating Committee, he had presided over nationally televised hearings investigating organized crime. Kefauver challenged Stevenson to debate during the primaries. Stevenson, reluctant to debate Eisenhower in 1952, was again reluctant. However, after losing the Minnesota primary, Stevenson agreed to debate Kefauver in the Florida primary. The debate was nationally televised, and though it apparently helped Stevenson he came away unimpressed with political debates.[21] As in 1952, in 1956 neither Stevenson nor Eisenhower wished to be involved in broadcast debates during the general election.

In 1960 John Kennedy was challenged to debate in the primaries by Senator Hubert Humphrey. During the West Virginia primary, both men agreed to a televised debate. Observers agreed that Kennedy did well in the debate, which was televised throughout the East Coast as well as throughout West Virginia. Perhaps this experience and his 1952 debate with Lodge contributed to Kennedy's acceptance of an NBC offer for free time during the general election if he would agree to a series of joint appearances with the Republican nominee. This offer had been made feasible by a joint resolution of Congress suspending the equal time law until after the election. Like Kennedy, Richard Nixon quickly accepted the NBC offer but noted that since the other networks had issued similar invitations the networks should coordinate their proposals. The networks had lobbied earlier in the year to suspend the equal time law for just this opportunity. They perceived televised presidential debates as providing them with enhanced credibility as a news medium. As we will see in more detail in the next section, 1960 was one of those years where the selfish interests of both candidates seemed best served by involvement in political debates. Hence, in 1960, for the first time since 1858, the United States was absorbed by a political debate or at least a joint appearance, national in scope and significance.

Political debates at the presidential level were not held for the 16 years following the Kennedy-Nixon debate for reasons that will be discussed in the next section. However, they became commonplace in campaigns for almost all other offices. In the years immediately following the Kennedy-Nixon debate, there were political debates between candidates for statewide office in Michigan, Massachusetts, Connecticut, Pennsylvania, and California. Races for lesser offices frequently included debates. Two short years after the Kennedy-Nixon debates, debates were held between the candidates for all six congressional seats in Connecticut.[22] Although presidential candidates frequently utilized debates during the primaries that were held after 1960, it was not until 1976 that presidential debates were held during the general election. However, unlike their presidential counterparts, local, regional, and statewide candidates made increasing use of debates during the 1960s and 1970s. One such debate, which took place between the two candidates for governor of Tennessee in 1970, indirectly led to the 1976 presidential debate between Governor Jimmy Carter and President Gerald Ford and resolution of the impediment to political debates caused by the equal time provision.

In 1970 Winfield Dunn, Republican, and John J. Hooker, Jr., his Democratic opponent for the governorship of Tennessee, decided to debate. Aiding Dunn was a University of Virginia law student, Stephen A.

Sharp, who found several Tennessee stations reluctant to carry the debates for fear that they would have to provide equal time to all other minor candidates for the governorship. Sharp's involvement in the Tennessee race caused him to prepare a law school paper on the history and interpretation of section 315. He found that political debates between major candidates might well be considered "bona fide" news events under the 1959 changes to section 315. If so, they could be reported on by stations as normal newsworthy activities, and those stations would not be subjected to providing equal time to all other candidates.

Sharp was subsequently hired by the Federal Communications Commission (FCC) where his work with section 315 became known. The FCC had previously ruled that candidate appearances not "incidental to" other news events were not newsworthy and hence not exempt from the equal opportunities requirement. Political debates by major candidates that were not incidental to any other activity were not exempt. But a political speech incidental to a rally or a dinner was exempt.

After considerable legal maneuvering by a variety of interested parties including the Aspen Program for Media and Society, the Columbia Broadcasting System, and others, the FCC ruled in 1975 that debates that were covered live and in their entirety and not sponsored by broadcasters (and hence presumably legitimate news events that would take place with or without the press) could be covered without fear of having to provide time to all minor candidates.[23]

This 1975 FCC ruling, known as the Aspen decision, made nationally televised presidential debates feasible from the network's standpoint. But debates do not take place without willing debaters. In 1960 Kennedy and Nixon had both been willing to debate for reasons that will become evident in the next section. Republicans and Democrats in Congress, following the lead indicated by their presidential candidates, had suspended section 315. After the Aspen decision, an act of Congress was no longer necessary for presidential debates, but willing debaters were.

The League of Women Voters, responding to the Aspen decision, took it upon itself to become the sponsoring organization for presidential debates in 1976. In 1976 both major candidates perceived that their own self-interest might be well served by political debates. We will examine in detail what motivates candidates to accept or reject an invitation to debate in the next section. However, in every election since 1976 both major presidential candidates were willing to debate. Today, political debates are widespread at all levels.

DECIDING WHETHER TO DEBATE

At every level of politics, candidates and their advisors strategically address themselves to six questions in determining whether to engage in political debates.[24]

1. *Is this likely to be a close election*? Expectations about the outcome of the election are vital to the decision to engage in debates. If the election seems as though it will be close and both candidates are in doubt about the outcome, the likelihood of political debates is greatly increased. If either candidate has a strong conviction that they can win the election without engaging in debates, the likelihood of debates taking place is dramatically reduced.

2. *Are advantages likely to accrue to me if I debate*? No candidate willingly engages in counterproductive activity. Consequently, both candidates must have good reason to expect that the debates will be advantageous to them. As we will see in the next sections, the advantages a candidate perceives may come as much from the act of debating as from the actual debates themselves. Nevertheless, unless both candidates can anticipate advantages, political debates are unlikely to be held.

3. *Am I a good debater*? No candidates willingly put themselves in a position where their foe will clearly appear to be stronger. Consequently, when measuring themselves against their opponent, each candidate must be confident about being a good debater.

4. *Are there only two major candidates running for the office*? Typically, our political system produces two serious candidates for each office. On those occasions where a third candidate seems to have a possibility of drawing a respectable share of the vote, it is highly unlikely that political debates will take place. Third party candidates are not predictable. They are not bound by the same "rules" as candidates who anticipate election. Often they speak to make a point, to dramatize an issue, rather than to win an election. Moreover, the presence of a third candidate provides the possibility that two candidates may "gang up" on one. These variables reduce the likelihood that political debates will take place in races where a third candidate is on the ballot and appears to have a possibility of drawing a respectable share of the vote.

5. *Do I have control of all the important variables in the debate situation*? Candidates cannot be expected to place themselves in positions where they cannot reasonably anticipate what will happen. Consequently, each candidate must feel comfortable with all the major variables in the debate situation: the dates, location, formats, topics, and other participants (moderators and questioners). Unless every candidate feels in control of all the major variables in the debate, they are unlikely to consent to debating.

6. *Is the field clear of incumbents*? If either candidate is an incumbent seeking reelection, the probability of debate taking place is reduced, especially for lower level races. Incumbency is a greater obstacle to political debating in lower lever races than it is in upper level races for at least four reasons.

First, most incumbents reason that their credibility is unquestioned by virtue of prior service. The credibility of their opponents is often an issue in the campaign. This is more apt to be true in lower level races where challengers may be virtually unknown, than in more prominent races where challengers have probably held other offices, or attained prominence in their chosen fields.

Second, incumbent officeholders are frequently better able than challengers to make their views known to the public. Hence, they are reluctant to provide their opponents with a platform from which to be heard. Again, this is more apt to be true in lower level races, where the overall press coverage of the race is not as great as the coverage for major races and challengers have an especially difficult time getting coverage.

Additionally, almost any incumbent will necessarily be placed on the defensive in a political debate. The incumbent's record will probably be a major topic of discussion. Typically, no incumbent will hand an opponent the opportunity to attack vigorously, much less in a well-publicized situation. Again, this is more apt to be true in a lower level race. In major races challenger candidates have generally held offices and established political records, which may lend themselves to attack by an incumbent. But in lower level races challengers may have not held office in the past and may not have an established political record for an incumbent to attack.

Finally, since 1976 when President Ford became the first incumbent president to engage in a debate, the public has grown to expect candidates for major office in engage in debates. By 1984 public expectations had grown so strong that some have argued that incumbent Ronald Reagan, holding a commanding lead in all the polls, nevertheless risked debating because he felt that not to do so would create a greater problem for him than any possible error he might make in debating.[25] In recent years incumbents have come to fear that their failure or obvious reluctance to debate will be interpreted extremely negatively by the public to mean that they are weak and unable to defend their own positions and policies.[26] Candidates for lower level offices do not generate quite the same expectations in the public and hence are unlikely to suffer as greatly if they fail to debate. The public is often unfamiliar with the positions and policies of such candidates, largely uninterested in them, and relatively unconcerned about debates between them.

APPLYING THE CONDITIONS REQUISITE FOR POLITICAL DEBATES

Few political debates will occur unless the conditions implicit in these questions exist to the satisfaction of both candidates. The importance of these conditions can be illustrated by analyzing virtually any campaign.

However, in the next few pages we will examine two presidential campaigns to better illustrate the ways in which candidates and their managers determine whether they should debate. We have chosen to focus on these two campaigns first because they are especially instructive and also because readers are probably more acquainted with the circumstances and events of presidential campaigns than with those of any other campaigns. However, keep in mind that these same principles are used by all candidates. Candidates do not choose to debate by chance; rather, their decisions are based on self-interest.

1960: Kennedy-Nixon Debates

From the outset, most observers expected a close election.[27] As the campaign progressed, public opinion polls confirmed expectations. Neither candidate ever led by more than six points in the major polls. Clearly, both camps anticipated a close election.

In 1952 vice-presidential candidate Richard Nixon gave one of the most successful political speeches in U.S. history. Using the new medium of television, he had saved his position on the ballot as Dwight Eisenhower's running mate with his Checkers speech. His 1960 advisors considered him a "master" of television.

His own extensive background as a college debater and his recent "kitchen" debates with Soviet Premier Nikita Khrushchev also contributed to Nixon's confidence in his ability to debate Kennedy. Nixon's strategists were so confident that their candidate would gain in the debates that they initially argued for only one debate. They believed that Nixon could virtually eliminate Kennedy in one debate and that it would be disadvantageous to give Kennedy any opportunity to recover. Clearly, Nixon's camp believed that advantages would accrue to him from debating and that he was a good debater.

Few 1960 observers recalled what most of Kennedy's inner circle best remembered about 1952. John Kennedy ran for the Senate against a heavily favored, vastly more experienced incumbent Republican, Senator Henry Cabot Lodge. Kennedy debated Lodge at Waltham, Massachusetts. From that point forward, Lodge's assertions about his superior experience, maturity, and judgment—the same issues Nixon was using in 1960—were no longer viable. At least two of Kennedy's inner circle, his brother Robert and close advisor Kenneth P. O'Donnell, anticipated that the Kennedy-Nixon debates might well be a "rerun" of the Lodge debate. Clearly, Kennedy's strategists felt that their man was an able speaker and that his presence on the same platform as Nixon, as well as what he said, would prove advantageous.

Kennedy and Nixon were the only major candidates for the presidency. After 15 negotiating sessions, which included discussions of virtually every detail of television production—camera angles, staging, lighting, and backdrops—both camps felt that no unexpected variable would confound the situation.

Thus Nixon and Kennedy had every reason to debate. It was not an accident that they became the first presidential candidates to engage in an extensive series of public debates. It was at their bidding that both Republican and Democratic members of Congress voted to suspend section 315 of the Communications Act of 1934 to allow national coverage of the debates.

1980: Reagan-Carter-Anderson Debates

From the outset, the presence of Illinois Republican Congressman John Anderson as a major independent candidate distinguished the 1980 election.[28] Anderson's presence clearly inhibited political debates and almost entirely prevented debate between the two major candidates. The presence of a third significant candidate, combined with the presence of an incumbent, makes the 1980 presidential election an unusually instructive one for examining how candidates determine whether they should debate.

As the general election opened, Congressman Anderson had left the Republican party, in whose primaries he had run and lost, to launch his own independent campaign for the presidency. Polls indicated that he and his vice-presidential running mate, Democratic former Wisconsin Governor Patrick Lucey, were favored by approximately 15 to 20 percent of the nation's prospective voters. Moreover, the vast majority of the public seemed disturbed with the two traditional choices. An exceptionally high percentage of voters were undecided.

Faced with this situation, the League of Women Voters had two choices. First, it could invite only the two major party candidates to debate. In 1976 the League had done just this, ignoring former Georgia Governor Lester Maddox and former Minnesota Senator Eugene McCarthy among others, while extending its invitation to debate only to President Gerald Ford and Governor Jimmy Carter. Second, the League could invite all three candidates. In doing so, the League would imply that it felt Anderson's candidacy was credible and that in fact there really were three major candidates. The League invited Anderson to debate.

By extending an invitation to Anderson, the League sharply diminished the prospects of a debate involving Carter and Reagan. Major party nominees cannot be expected to readily agree to participate when a third nominee is involved. President Carter immediately refused to debate. Patrick Caddell, the Carter campaign pollster, explained:

We just assume Anderson's presence helps him, makes him more legitimate, establishes him. Such added strength hurts Carter far more than Reagan since

Anderson has been getting most of his strength from disgruntled Democrats and this could give key states and the election to Reagan.[29]

By early September, based on Caddell's polls, the White House had concluded that Anderson's candidacy was going downhill and if left alone would soon be of little consequence. But the League would not leave it alone. Unwittingly or otherwise, by inviting Anderson the League had increased his legitimacy, thereby preserving his slim opportunity for victory and perhaps enhancing the likelihood of a Reagan victory.

Carter cited additional reasons for not appearing with Anderson and Reagan. The president noted that Anderson "ran as a Republican and he's still a Republican." The president constantly called the upcoming event "a Republican debate." Surrogates for President Carter repeated this theme, claiming that the two Republicans would gang up unfairly on the president in a debate. For highly predictable reasons, the president refused to participate in any debate with both Anderson and Reagan.

Similarly, for highly predictable reasons, Reagan accepted the League's invitation to join both John Anderson and Jimmy Carter in a debate. Reagan saw several advantages to debating. First, all the polls suggested that any improvement in Anderson's vote would hurt Carter more than Reagan. Second, the debate itself had become an issue. During the Iowa primary, Reagan had failed to appear in the Republican forum. This decision was subsequently believed to have hurt his Iowa campaign. By agreeing to appear with Anderson, Reagan was focusing attention on Carter's refusal. This strategy quickly proved effective against Carter, as it had in Iowa when other Republicans used it against Reagan. The Harris poll found that 69 percent of the public wanted Carter to debate. Finally, the debate with Anderson gave Reagan an opportunity to attack Carter in front of a large audience at no expense.

President Carter's refusal to participate in the September 22 debate between Anderson and Reagan reduced that event to little more than another Republican candidates' forum. One of the three major networks did not even bother televising the event, accurately anticipating that millions of voters would prefer to watch *Midnight Express*, a recent movie chronicling the adventures of a U.S. citizen convicted of drug dealing in Turkey. Newspapers the next morning also characterized the event as little more than another Republican candidates' forum.

Having effectively minimized the possibility of presidential debates by inviting John Anderson to their first debate, the League of Women Voters in mid-September sought a rationale for not inviting him to subsequent debates. Three weeks after finding him a viable choice for the presidency, league President Ruth Hinderfeld claimed that Anderson was "no longer the significant candidate he was." Anderson had fallen from the favorite of a "significant" 15 percent of the voters to the favorite of an "insignificant" 10 percent of the voters. Thus in mid-October the League of Women Voters issued an invitation to Carter and Reagan, but not to Anderson, to appear jointly in Cleveland for a presidential debate.

With only three weeks left in the campaign, and the League not having invited John Anderson, the conditions requisite for political debates now existed. In deciding to accept the League's invitation to debate without John Anderson, both Carter and Reagan had to evaluate the remaining conditions presented earlier.

First, each man had to conclude that this was likely to be a close election. Neither candidate could feel that he would be a sure winner without debating. Reagan had been consistently ahead of President Carter in virtually every poll taken since the general election campaign opened on Labor Day. However, by the last weeks of October, Carter had closed to within a few points of Reagan in most polls. Coupled with the large undecided vote, and the fading Anderson vote, which might not hold firm for the congressman, Carter's October surge had placed the election in doubt.

Second, each man perceived advantages likely to accrue to him if he debated. The *Cincinnati Enquirer* accurately summarized the situation confronting Reagan in mid-October. "There is widespread agreement among pollsters such as George Gallup and political operatives in both campaigns that the issue that is hurting Reagan most among women voters is the fear hammered on constantly by the Carter campaign that he might embroil the country in war." The *Enquirer* pointed out that among women voters Reagan was trailing Carter badly and that the vast preponderance of undecided voters were women. Reagan himself acknowledged that Carter's use of the war issue "has been effective in creating a stereotype of me." Reagan's pro-debate advisors perceived the debate as a means of dispelling fears of Reagan as a warmonger. James Baker spoke for many of Reagan's advisors when he commented about the Californian, "Is he dangerous? Any time anybody's exposed to him we dispel those doubts."

Moreover, Reagan was evidently concerned that Carter's use of foreign policy in the final days of the campaign was shifting voters. Indeed, as speculation concerning release of Americans taken hostage in Iran mounted in late October, the Reagan campaign was frustrated by its inability to respond or to even command press attention. Fear of an "October surprise" in the form of an administration foreign policy breakthrough clearly motivated Reagan's decision to debate.

Additionally, Reagan's advisors felt that by mid-October the campaign might have gotten almost all it could get from attacking Carter. The Reagan campaign was stagnating. Undecided voters, the Reagan team felt, were already disenchanted with Carter. That case had been made, but undecided voters were remaining undecided because they saw no reason to vote for Reagan. Observing Reagan side by side with President Carter would provide them with reasons to vote for Ronald Reagan and hence resolve their indecision.

President Carter also perceived advantages accruing to him from a debate. Carter the president, Carter the engineer, Carter the technician, Carter the manager might well overwhelm Reagan in a debate, thought many of his advisors. Carter's staff was reported to be "confident he can crush Reagan." A resounding debate victory late in the campaign might be just the impetus the fast closing campaign needed.

Moreover, as the election grew closer, many traditional Democratic voter blocs that had been displeased by Carter, particularly black, Hispanic, Jewish, and labor voters, seemed on the verge of returning to the president. A debate would give the president a huge audience at no cost. He could remind Democratic voters that he was a Democrat in the tradition of Roosevelt, Truman, Kennedy, and Johnson. This ploy had been effective in 1976. It might be even more effective in 1980 against an opponent who could be portrayed as the very antithesis of the Democratic tradition.

Finally, Carter had avoided debates with Massachusetts Senator Ted Kennedy and California Governor Jerry Brown during the primaries. He had avoided debating with John Anderson. He had defended these decisions, but the cumulative effect of his repeated refusals to debate, particularly in light of his eagerness to debate four years earlier, might be to signal the public that Carter was afraid to defend himself.

The third factor both candidates evaluated was their ability to debate. The Carter campaign seemed to perceive the president as far brighter, quicker, and better prepared than his opponent. In a remarkable speech delivered at Miami's Edison Senior High School, Carter spoke about his abilities vis-à-vis Reagan's to fulfill the demands of the presidency. He might equally have been speaking about the demands of a political debate. "Ronald Reagan is better at making speeches than I am . . . but in the oval office you can't rely on 3 by 5 cards and you can't rely on a teleprompter." Carter went on to claim that he was "prepared to deal with issues, think on my feet, and respond to questions," while Reagan was not.

Ronald Reagan was also confident of his ability. Reagan had been widely reported to favor debating Carter early in the campaign but to have acceded to the advice of his strategists who saw little point to debating. Many observers felt that Reagan's greatest attribute as a politician was his ability to communicate. His political career had begun with an impressive television address to the nation on behalf of Barry Goldwater in 1964. By late October, he too had endured repeated political debates and forums. Throughout 1980, including his most recent encounter with John Anderson, he had done well. A professional actor, Reagan seemed relaxed and poised in debate situations. Asked earlier in the year whether he ever got butterflies before debates, Reagan laughingly responded, "Debate butterflies? I've been on the same stage as John Wayne."

The fourth factor that both candidates had to evaluate was the variables associated with the debate situation: format, date, location, time limits, and similar questions. In 1960 representatives of Kennedy and Nixon discussed virtually every detail of their debates in 15 negotiating sessions. In 1980 almost all the details were resolved in six hours of discussion, which stretched over two days.

Thus by late October of 1980, five of the six conditions normally associated with fostering political debates were in place. The League of Women Voters had not invited John Anderson, and thus only two major candidates were involved. Second, the election appeared to be close. Third, both candidates could perceive advantages accruing to them from debate. Fourth, both candidates believed themselves to be good debaters. And fifth, both candidates were satisfied with the important variables in the debate situation.

Finally, earlier we noted that the presence of incumbents tends to reduce the likelihood of debate. In 1980 Carter was, of course, an incumbent. But he and Reagan were contesting for the highest office in the nation, and we have also noted that the presence of incumbents is more likely to deter debates for lower level offices than for higher level offices such as the presidency.

POLITICAL DEBATE STRATEGIES

Political debate strategies can best be understood if we recognize that they involve three stages. First are those strategies that take place prior to the debate itself. Second are those the candidate attempts to implement during the debate. Finally are those following the debate. Each is important. A political debate can be won or lost before it takes place, as it takes place, or after it is held. In this section, we will examine political debating strategies.

Predebate Strategies

The candidate who is perceived to have won the debate is often a function of what people expected. Hence, many candidates seek to lower public expectations of their performance. If prior expectations are low, then it may not take a strong effort on the part of the candidate to appear to have done well. Moreover, if a candidate is expected to be outclassed but does well, it may be perceived as a major victory.

Goodwin F. Berquist and James L. Golden have noted that the media tend to establish public expectations regarding the probable outcome of political debates.[30] Observing the 1980 Reagan-Carter debate, Berquist and Golden point out that prior to the debate the media alerted the public to what might take place by discussing expected candidate strategies, interviewing campaign staff, and presenting guidelines for successful debating to which the candidate might adhere.[31]

The interaction between the candidate and campaign staff on the one hand, and the media on the other, can be crucial during the predebate period. As the media go about their job, they will seek comments from the campaigners. Campaigners will normally tend to downplay the potential outcome of the debate. By minimizing expectations, campaigners feel they are putting themselves in the best possible position to capitalize on a strong performance and to rationalize for a weak one.

Typically, it is easier for a challenger to minimize expectations than it is for an incumbent. The incumbent already commands respect and has fulfilled the job responsibilities for several years. Incumbents may have debated about the demands of the very offices being contested just a few years earlier. To the extent that the debate contributed to that victory, incumbents are perceived as good debaters.

In their analysis of the 1984 presidential debates Craig Allen Smith and Kathy B. Smith observed that at the outset of the first debate expectations for incumbent Ronald Reagan were exceptionally high.[32] Much of his success in the 1980 election was attributed to his strong showing in his debate with President Carter. Moreover, throughout his Senate career challenger Walter Mondale had always been characterized as a relatively lethargic speaker who came across to audiences as rather boring. Expectations were extremely high for the incumbent president and extremely low for his challenger. However, Mondale exceeded all expectations, and Reagan failed to meet the expectations placed on him. Hence, Mondale was judged the winner, Reagan the loser.

Exactly two weeks later, when they debated a second time, the results of the first debate had contributed to reversing expectations. If the president had been overconfident and overrated prior to the first debate, reaction to that debate suggested that Reagan faced an uphill struggle in the second debate. It was widely speculated that his age was beginning to take its toll on his abilities. Moreover, Mondale was now perceived as a far more formidable debater than previously had been believed. Hence, public expectations for the second debate were far higher for Mondale and considerably reduced for Reagan. Facing far lower expectations, it was generally agreed that Reagan won the second debate. Facing far higher expectations, it was generally agreed that Mondale lost the second debate. Reagan had no difficulty in meeting the lowered expectations of his abilities, while Mondale was unable to match the inflated expectations of his abilities. As the 1984 presidential debates well illustrate, candidates, regardless of the office being contested, the size of the constituency, or the extensiveness of media coverage, have good reason to seek lower public expectations of their likely debate success.

Closely related to this first predebate strategy is the second—setting up an opponent. Again often utilizing the press to effect public perceptions, candidates typically take two themes in dealing with their opponents. First, they attempt to heighten expectations of their opponents. Lauding their opponent as an experienced debater and speaker, who may be quick on his/her feet (a skill not required for the office which demands considerable thought), candidates attempt to set difficult standards for their opponents to meet. The second theme a candidate will stress in setting up an opponent is to stress the anticipated shortcomings of that opponent, so that the press and public will be especially attentive. In predebate interviews, the candidate will ask if audiences might finally hear the opponent's plan to revitalize the economy, or conserve natural resources. A candidate will continually remind audiences prior to the debate of the opponent's penchant for talking in simple terms, or flip-flopping on issues, or failing to be specific. All of these remarks are meant to focus the public's attention on an opponent's anticipated weaknesses. Thus the second predebate strategy is to set up an opponent by heightening the expectations placed on the opponent and by alerting the press and public to the opponent's expected shortcomings and demanding that the opponent be held accountable.

The third predebate strategy is to determine clearly the target audience. Political debates, as will be illustrated in the next section, typically draw the largest audiences of any single communicative event of the campaign. The candidates must determine who their target audiences are for the debate. Typically, they will be the same as the normal campaign target audiences. However, due to the unusual size of the audience, it is possible that the candidate may choose to go after a new target group of voters during a debate. The debate may be the first time that this group has been exposed to the candidate. Most practitioners would not suggest using the debate to attract massive numbers of new and different voters to the candidate. But the unusual nature of debate audiences—their size, the presence of many adherents of the opponent, the propensity of both the college educated and women to attend debates—means that the candidates must clearly determine whether they wish to maintain their campaigns' targeted audiences for the debate or whether they wish to make some changes, normally in the form of adding a targeted group.

Finally, with a clear conception of targeted audiences in mind, candidates must work out answers to possible questions and practice them. This is the fourth predebate strategy. The firsthand reports of many participants in political debates suggest several successful approaches to practice.[33] First, in a relaxed atmosphere the candidate and a limited number of aides should work through possible questions and answers, consistently keeping in mind overall themes and target audiences. Second, the candidate should practice the answers in a situation as similar to the real one as possible. For nationally televised presidential debates, this has meant simulating the television studio or auditorium to be used and often utilizing a stand-in for the opponent. Some candidates have reviewed the speeches and tapes of their opponent's past performances. In the case of opponents who have debated in the past, an examination of their past debates has proven helpful.[34] Preparing for a debate may well mean curtailing other campaign activity for several days, but given the attention normally focused on debates, this sacrifice would seem worthwhile.

Debate Strategies

As the debate progresses, candidates must constantly respond to specific questions on the issues of the day. While those issues vary from campaign to campaign, most successful political debaters have been able to integrate the specific issues into an overall framework. For example, when Senators John Kennedy and Hubert Humphrey debated in the 1960 West Virginia primary, Kennedy developed the overall thesis, just as he did months later when debating Nixon, that while the United States was a great nation, it could and should be greater. As he dealt with specific issues concerning West Virginia and the nation, he integrated many of them into his overall thesis, that the United States could do better.[35] Similarly, in 1988 George Bush's overall thesis was that he was responsibly conservative whereas Michael Dukakis was too liberal for America. Repeatedly, his answers returned to this theme. Hence, the first debate strategy is to utilize issues by relating them to an overall theme.

The skilled political debater will first present his overall theme in his introductory statement, if the opportunity to make such a statement is allowed in the debate format being used. Then he will reinforce it with his answers to as many specific questions as possible. Finally, he will return to it in his concluding statement.

In the 1988 presidential debates the format did not include opening statements. However, George Bush concluded the first debate by observing that "it gets down to a question of values. . . . we've got a wide array of differences on those [values]. But in the final analysis, a person goes into that voting booth, they're going to say, who has the values I believe in?"[36] Bush felt his conservative values were more acceptable to the nation than Michael Dukakis's liberal values, and he used his concluding statement, as well as his responses to many questions, to emphasize this thesis. Similarly, in the final debate between the two men it was not an accident that Bush concluded by addressing three issues: taxes, crime, and military preparedness.[37] These issues were clearly among those that best distinguished Bush's conservative values from Dukakis's more liberal values.

Issues serve skilled debaters by allowing them to develop an overall thesis. We know that most people forget about half or more of what they hear in as little as 24 hours. Any response to an opponent or a panelist on a specific issue is liable to be forgotten by most of the audience. But by making the response to a specific issue part of a theme that is consistently repeated, issues can be used to the best advantage. Strategies on specific issues, of course, cannot be generalized. They vary depending on the candidate and the situation. But developing an overall thesis, which can be presented in opening and closing statements and repeatedly reinforced by the responses to many specific issues, is a highly effective strategy employed by many political debaters.

Issues are one of the two major concerns of the candidate during the debate. The other is image. As Robert O. Weiss has argued, in political debates "issues and images are in practical fact overlooked and . . . they intertwine in all manner of convolutions and mutually affect one another in countless ways."[38] Weiss calls this relationship the "issue-image interface."[39] Though issues and images are closely intertwined, there are several image strategies that can be employed in political debates.

The principal image strategies that can be utilized in political debating include the development of a leadership style, personification, and identification.[40] As Dan D. Nimmo points out, political figures can develop an activist leadership style or a passive leadership style. The activist is just that. In a debate, activists consistently refer to their actions, their initiatives, their effect on events. Passive leaders are cautious. They do not speak of their initiatives, but rather portray themselves as reacting to events.

Both Dukakis and Bush seemed to be seeking an activist image in 1988. Dukakis repeatedly used language such as "I brought to my state . . . I was a leader in. . . . I'm prepared to lead. . . . We ought to. . . ."[41] He continually spoke of himself as an activist who would tackle the hard problems that the United States confronted. Similarly, Bush's language conveyed the image of an activist as he claimed that "We are going to have . . . We are going to make . . . I see an involvement . . . I do strongly support . . ."[42] Like Dukakis, Bush's language was that of the activist, focusing attention upon himself and his actions.

The second image strategy that lends itself to political debating is personification, the effort of the candidate to play a definite role. For example, the candidate may work to be perceived as a nice guy or an efficient manager. In 1980 concerned about President Carter's attempts to characterize him as a warmonger who might have an itchy trigger finger on the nuclear button, Ronald Reagan worked to counter that image in the debate. For example, at various points in the debate he observed that "I believe with all my heart that our first priority must be world peace . . . I am a father of sons . . . I have a grandson . . . I'm going to continue praying that they'll come home [the Iranian hostages]."[43] In sum Reagan was attempting to personify himself, to play a role, as a kindly, statesmanlike, religious family man, seeking peace. This personification would be most distant from the image of warmonger.

The final image strategy is identification. Debaters attempt to symbolize what they believe are the principal aspirations of their audience. Vice-President George Bush was exceptionally effective at this throughout the 1988 campaign as he allied himself with President Reagan to identify himself with the nation's peace and prosperity, perhaps America's two principal aspirations. He concluded the second debate with a strong attempt to identify with the most potent of American aspirations, peace.

This election is about big things. And perhaps the biggest is world peace. And I asked you to consider the experience I have had in working with a President who has revolutionized the situation around the world. American stands tall again, as a result we are credible and we have now achieved a historic arms control agreement.

I want to build on that. I'd love to be able to say to my grandchildren four years after my first term, I'd like to say, "Your grandfather working with the leaders of the Soviet Union, working with the leaders of Europe, was able to ban chemical and biological weapons from the face of the earth."[44]

As these examples make clear, there is a close relationship between a candidate's response to specific issues and the image that the candidate projects. Nevertheless, as the debate is in progress the candidate should have a clear idea of an overall issue strategy or thesis to which specific answers can be related. Moreover, candidates should be cognizant of the image they may be projecting and develop appropriate strategies, such as a leadership style, personification, and identification, to create the persona they want.

Postdebate Strategies

Political debates are not over when the last word is uttered. Who won? Who made a grievous error? Who seemed best in control? Questions like these immediately follow the debate, and their answers are often as important as the debate itself. After all, it is what the audience perceives to have happened in the debate that is of consequence. Therefore, the well-prepared campaign will be ready to try to influence audience perceptions of the debate as soon as it concludes.

The importance of postdebate strategies was dramatized in the second Ford-Carter debate of 1976, perhaps best remembered because President Gerald Ford seemed to be unaware of the Soviet domination of Eastern Europe. Yet, at the time that Ford made his unfortunate statement, it was barely noticed. It was not until the next day, after continual publicity of his remark, that Ford was perceived as having erred badly. Frederick T. Steeper studied this debate and concluded:

The volunteered descriptions of the debate by the voters surveyed immediately after the debate included no mentions of Ford's statement on Eastern Europe. Not until the afternoon of the next day did such references appear, and by Thursday night they were the most frequent criticism given Ford's performance. Similarly, the panelists monitored during the debate gave no indication of an unfavorable reaction at the time they heard Ford's Eastern European remarks. The conclusion is that the preponderance of viewers of the second debate most likely were not certain of the true status of Eastern Europe, or less likely, did not consider Ford's error important. Given the amount of publicity given Ford's East European statements the next day by the news media and the concomitant change that took place it is concluded that this publicity caused the change.[45]

Most students of political debate believe that the effects often lag behind the debate itself. Often, audience members do not reach final judgment until they have discussed the debate with others and have observed the media reaction.[46] It is during these hours, when interpersonal influence and media influence are often operating, that the campaign engages in the postdebate strategy of favorably influencing perceptions of the debate.

The principal postdebate strategy is to provide a massive and well-coordinated surrogate effort. The *New York Times* illustrated the extent of these efforts of surrogates to affect the way people interpret the debates immediately after the first 1988 presidential debate.

The campaigns of the two Presidential candidates spent almost as much time and effort trying to influence what was said after the debate as they spent deciding what Vice President Bush and Michael S. Dukakis should say in the debate.

Their elaborate and carefully planned efforts marked a new level of "the spin," the attempt to shape the tone and content of news reports and through them the perception of the public.... As the two candidates were concluding their closing statements, the strategists of each campaign huddled and decided what their lines would be. Then they deployed, like an invasion landing force, following timetables and routes that had been arranged. Their mission: Get out to the world their view of why their man won and the other man lost.[47]

A massive and coordinated surrogate effort means that in the crucial postdebate hours, viewers and media representatives are hearing many respected figures present a cogent rationale of why their candidate did well in the debate. Often these interviews are widely reprinted and broadcast and may serve to influence audience perception of the debate. Learning from Ford's problem after the second debate in 1976, every major campaign since has made prominent spokespersons available to the media following their debate.

The use of prominent spokespersons to present a positive view of the debate is the most common postdebate strategy.[48] It is used in all levels of campaigns. Other strategies are less common and often depend on the circumstances and formats of the specific debate. Often, if an audience is present, campaign staff members will work to "load" the audience with partisans. Not only will they provide positive responses during the debate, but as they are interviewed later, they may well do the same thing. Community leaders, known to be sympathetic to the candidate, can be urged to write letters to the editors of local papers, commenting favorably upon the candidate's performance. In every instance, postdebate strategies such as the use of surrogates, audience members, and letters are designed to influence public perception in the crucial hours and days that immediately follow.

EFFECTS OF POLITICAL DEBATES

Any discussion of the effects of political debates must be tempered with an awareness that it is difficult to draw strong conclusions about them. This difficulty arises for several reasons. First, each debate is different. It involves different candidates, different offices, different issues, different audiences, different press coverage, different formats, and a host of other differences. Hence, to talk about the specific effects of debates is virtually impossible, for no two will be identical, nor will their effects be identical.

Second, debate effects cannot be isolated from the effects of all the other communication that voters receive during the campaign. Individuals may be exposed to a dozen messages about the candidates on the very day of the debate. Distinguishing the effects of the debate from all the others is difficult.

While there have been scores of political debates in the last 30 years, by and large, researchers have only studied the presidential debates in detail. Hence, our discussion of effects must necessarily be limited to a consideration of the effects of presidential debates. We cannot be certain that the effects of nationally televised political debates are similar to those of the vast majority of political debates held in campaigns for lesser offices. Most debates are not nationally televised. They are not well publicized in advance. They are not subjected to endless speculation, examination, and evaluation for days afterward. However, while findings concerning the effects of presidential debate are not necessarily valid for other debates, there is reason to suspect a broad similarity in the pattern of effects produced by political debates. But, we cannot be absolutely certain.

Finally, unlike laboratory experiments, scientists cannot control political debates. Hence, those debates that have been examined are often subject to studies that, of necessity, are prepared under less than ideal conditions, including little advance planning and an inability to control fully all of the variables in the study.

Despite each of the above problems, at this time there appear to be some striking findings about the effects of political debates, which are subject to revision as debating becomes an even more widely studied communication event.

Effect 1: Increased Audiences

Political debates, even at the local or state level, attract large audiences. Debates create conflict, the essence of drama. Hence, it should not surprise us that presidential debates attract huge audiences. Similarly, we might well hypothesize that debates attract larger audiences than virtually any other activity that takes place during the typical campaign. While research on audiences for nonpresidential debates is not yet widely available, the basic element of conflict exists and might operate as it evidently does in presidential debates—to attract a large audience.

In 1960 CBS estimated that over 100 million people in the United States watched at least part of the Kennedy-Nixon debates.[49] Numerous other surveys also suggested that the Kennedy-Nixon debates drew an immense national audience. In fact, the debates drew the largest audience for any speaking event in history, up to that time.[50] Similarly, every measure of audience size conducted in connection with the 1976 debates also suggests a massive audience. Most measures of the 1976 debates claim that over 70 percent of the nation watched at least part of the first Carter-Ford debate. While viewing fell off somewhat as the series of debates progressed, it never fell below 60 percent.[51] In 1960 and again in 1976 debates between presidential candidates were novelties. However, such debates have been a feature of every election since. Moreover, debates between the vice-presidential candidates have also become common. This may, in part, account for the fact that the audiences for national political debates are diminishing. In 1984, for the first time, slightly less than half the nation watched the presidential debates between Reagan and Mondale. By 1988 that figure is estimated to have shrunk to about 40%. Nevertheless, even the least watched of national political debates, the 1988 confrontation between vice-presidential candidates Dan Quayle and Lloyd Bentsen, drew an audience estimated at 60 million people.[52] Clearly, the first effect of political debates seems to be that they generate audiences far larger than those that are generated by any other communication activity during the campaign.

Effect 2: Audiences Reinforced

Comedian Lenny Bruce unwittingly summarized a host of research studies about the effects of political debates when he observed that

everybody hears what he wants to hear. Like when they were in the heat of the 1960 election campaign I was with a group who were watching the debate and all the Nixon fans were saying "Isn't he making Kennedy look like a jerk?"— and all the Kennedy fans were saying "Look at him make a jerk out of Nixon." Each group really feels that their man is up there making the other man look like an idiot.

So then I realized that a candidate would have had to have been that blatant— he would have had to look at his audience right in the camera and say, "I am corrupt. I am the worse choice you could ever have for President."

And even then his followers would say, "Boy there's an honest man. It takes a big guy to admit that. That's the kind of man we should have for a President."[53]

As Bruce's comment suggests, most research has concluded that political debates tend to reinforce the positions of a candidate's partisans. After the 1960 debates, most researchers did not find substantial shifts of voter opinion. Rather, they found that Kennedy and Nixon partisans became more strongly committed to their candidate. As *Newsweek* reported, the debates "merely stiffened attitudes."[54]

Research since the 1960 debates tends to confirm these early findings. Examining data pertinent to all of the presidential debates held prior to 1987, George Gallup, Jr., claims that "presidential debates in all years have tended to reinforce the convictions of voters who were already committed. They have caused few people to change their minds."[55] Similarly, the 1988 debates seem to have served primarily to reinforce existing attitudes.[56] The reason for this effect is explained by David O. Sears and Steven H. Chaffee, who claim that "the information flow stimulated by debates tends to be translated by voters into evaluations that coincide with prior political dispositions. They perceive their party's candidate as having 'won' and they discuss the outcome with like-minded people." Sears and Chaffee continue, noting that since the Democratic party is substantially larger than the Republican, the net effect of the cumulative reinforcement stimulated by the debates probably benefits Democratic candidates.[57] Sears and Chaffee's discussion is based on national audiences for presidential debates. The logical outgrowth of these conclusions, applied to local campaigns, would be that debates, because they tend to reinforce prior political dispositions, generally work to the advantage of the party that is dominant in the district, city, or state.[58]

Effect 3: Shifting Limited Numbers of Voters

Political debates do not normally result in massive shifts of votes. As indicated above, most audience members have their existing predispositions reinforced by the debate. However, some voters may shift. In a close election, the numbers who shift as a consequence of debates might be decisive.

The Kennedy-Nixon debates were widely perceived at the time as having affected massive numbers of voters. President Kennedy helped foster this impression by attributing his election to the debates. Yet evidence on this point suggests that while they may have been decisive due to the extremely close nature of the election, the debates did not shift massive numbers of votes. The highest estimate of voter shift is pollster Elmo Roper's guess that 4 million voters, about 6 percent of the vote, changed as a consequence of the debates.[59] However, most researchers are far more cautious. Elihu Katz and Jacob Feldman, after examining 31 studies of the 1960 debates, typify the conclusions of most when they write, "Did the debates really affect the final outcome? Apart from strengthening Democratic convictions about their candidate, it is very difficult to tell."[60] Evidence on the 1976 presidential debates,[61] as well as those of 1980, tends to confirm this limited effects paradigm.[62]

In their perceptive analysis of the effects of the 1984 presidential debates, Smith and Smith observe that although some polls reported that Walter Mondale had clearly beaten Ronald Reagan in their first debate, this victory did not translate into a shift in votes.[63] A Lou Harris Poll, for example, found that 61 percent of the respondents felt Mondale won the debate while only 19 percent felt that Reagan had won. Yet that same poll reported that President Reagan's support had only dropped from 54 percent prior to the debate to 53 percent after the debate, while Mondale's support had only risen from 42 percent prior to the debate to 44 percent after the debate. This degree of movement is negligible for such a one-sided victory, and given the amount of polling error reported, even this degree of movement is suspect.[64]

In 1988 Michael Dukakis was judged to have won a close debate in the first of his confrontations with George Bush.[65] However, as Elizabeth

Drew points out, "he was unable to capitalize on this victory."[66] Dukakis's debate victory did not seem to appreciably effect the preferences of many voters.

Effect 4: Debates Help Set Voters' Agenda

As we have discussed in Chapter 4, much recent research has stressed the importance of the agenda-setting function of mass communication. In essence, this research holds that "we judge as important what the media judge as important. Media priorities become our own."[67] If the considerable body of evidence that supports the agenda-setting function of mass media is correct, then it would stand to reason that those issues stressed in mass media political debates, and mass media coverage of those debates, should also become issues of high priority for voters who watch the debates and attend to the media coverage of them. Linda L. Swanson and David L. Swanson offer strong evidence in support of the agenda-setting function of political debates.[68] They attempted to determine whether those issues of primary concern to voters changed as a consequence of watching political debates. Based on research done at the University of Illinois during the 1976 campaign, they concluded that "the first Ford-Carter debate exerted an agenda-setting effect on our subjects who viewed it, although that effect was tempered by enduring personal priorities of subjects."[69] As Swanson and Swanson subsequently observed, "To the extent that citizens base their voting choices on their assessment of campaign issues, this is surely an effect of some political importance."[70] The agenda-setting function of political debates seems to remain strong. However, as campaigns become more and more sophisticated and candidates attempt to work into their debates the very lines that permeate their speeches and paid advertising, regardless of the questions asked by the panelists, it grows increasingly difficult to isolate the agenda-setting effects of political debate from the overall agenda-setting effects of media coverage of the entire campaign.

Effect 5: Debates Increase the Voters' Knowledge of Issues

A wide variety of studies have attempted to determine whether political debates increase the voters' knowledge of the issues. These studies seem to point to three conclusions. First, voters do seem more knowledgeable as a consequence of watching political debates. Second, debates are particularly helpful to voters in local elections. Tempering these conclusions is the final conclusion: often voters do not learn about the very issues that most concern them.

That voters clearly learn about the issues as a consequence of watching debates seems to have been well established by research.[71] Moreover, it would appear that debates serve as a more important source of information in local elections, which receive comparatively little media coverage, than for major national or statewide races. One study suggests that 80 percent of the viewers of debates between local candidates report that they had learned about the candidates by viewing the debates, whereas only 55 percent made the same claim about the presidential debates.[72]

Although voters apparently learn about issues by watching debates, often they do not learn about the issues that most concern them. Michael Pfau has cogently argued that "a political debate ought to match—to the extent possible—the agendas of the candidates and the public." However, after studying several presidential debates he concluded, "The journalists' questions have virtually ignored the public's agenda."[73] The problem is well illustrated in the remarks of one of the journalists who helped to set the agenda of the 1980 debates with her questions. She claimed that she "felt under enormous pressure to try forming a single question that would somehow catch the well-briefed candidates by surprise on a subject of importance."[74] More appropriately for the public, she might have attempted to ask a question dealing with those issues that were of greatest public concern. But far too often the public's concerns are not reflected in the journalists' questions.[75] Indeed, one critic of the 1988 debates has characterized many of the questions asked in that year's presidential debates as "trite."[76]

Significantly, virtually every program of reforms suggested for political debates includes a reduction or total elimination of the panel of journalists that helps to set the debate agenda.[77] Even the panelists themselves acknowledge that they are intrusive and the public might be better served by reducing the role of journalists or eliminating them altogether and having the candidates directly question one another without any third party intrusions.[78] It should be recalled that in 1960 when the precedents that have since been largely followed were established, the impetus for a panel of journalist/questioners came from the candidates, not the press.[79] Hence, for a variety of reasons, not the least of which is the intrusion of journalistic panels, the public agenda is frequently ignored in political debates.

In sum, while debates do increase the voters' knowledge of issues, particularly debates in local campaigns, their formats often prevent them from being as informative as the public might wish.

Effect 6: Debates Modify Candidate Images

Debates apparently affect the images of candidates. In their evaluation of the impact of the 1976 debates, Paul R. Hagner and Leroy N. Rieselbach suggest that debates affect candidate images primarily when the candidate is not well known and hence the candidate's public image is not well developed.[80] When the public is unfamiliar with the candidate, perception of the candidate's general character, personality attributes, and general competency seem to be affected by political debates and their subsequent media coverage.

Most accounts of the 1960 debates note that Kennedy, the comparative unknown, improved his image as a consequence of the debates. He was able to convey a sense of competency and familiarity with major issues, as well as a charming personality. Similarly, Sears and Chaffee summarize a number of studies of the 1976 debates and conclude that the public's image of the candidates was affected by the debates.[81]

In his perceptive study of the 1976 vice-presidential debates, Kevin Sauter observed that both Walter Mondale and Robert Dole hoped to impress the voters with their presidential potential. Sauter concluded that Mondale was successful in this effort and his strong image contributed appreciably to his subsequent nomination to the presidency. Conversely, Sauter finds that a variety of circumstances, many beyond his control, contributed to Dole's failure to impress the voters with his presidential potential. His failure in 1976, Sauter suggests, still remains a problem for Dole.[82] Dole's 1976 difficulties are suggestive of the current problems of Vice-President J. Danforth Quayle. In his 1988 debate with Lloyd Bentsen, Quayle did not create a presidential image.[83] Since the election he remains the subject of criticism and jokes concerning his lack of presidential stature.

In sum, debates can affect public perception of a candidate's image— general competency, personality attributes, and character traits. The potential for affecting image seems to be inversely related to public knowledge of the candidate. The better known the candidate, the less likely the debate will greatly affect that candidate's image. Hence, the potential for improving one's image is generally greater for the lesser-known candidate. Moreover, it is likely that in races for lesser offices, among lesser-known candidates, the impact of a debate on the image of the candidates is potentially great.

Effect 7: Debates Build Confidence in U.S. Democracy

A wide variety of studies have attempted to evaluate the effects of political debates on U.S. institutions. Do debates result in greater confidence and support of political institutions and officeholders? Do debates facilitate political socialization? While individual studies differ, and continued research will no doubt shed greater light on questions such as these, current research does offer some tentative answers.

First, as Sidney Kraus and Dennis Davis argue, debates are consistent with democratic theory, which stresses the importance of rational decision making by an informed electorate.[84] Second, as Samuel L. Becker, Robert Pepper, Lawrence Weiner, and Jin Keon Kim point out, debates provide voters with greater exposure to information about candidates, which "probably resulted in a certain degree of commitment to the election process and to the candidate selected through that process."[85] Third, as Chaffee illustrates, debates apparently have a positive impact on people's confidence in government institutions and play a positive role in political socialization or the recruitment of new members into the body politic.[86]

In sum, it appears as though political debates contribute to voter's satisfaction with the democratic process. Though much has been written about growing voter apathy, growing voter disenchantment with the political process, and growing voter skepticism of politicians, it would appear that this overall trend of disaffection with the political process is not fostered by debates. Quite to the contrary, as Sidney Kraus has claimed "televised presidential debates may be unparalleled in modern campaigning as an innovation that engages citizens in the political process."[87] Indeed, current research suggests that political debates might be a step in the direction of remedying current disaffection.

CONCLUSIONS

In sum, it would appear that political debates have at least seven distinct effects. Typically, they attract large audiences. Second, they seem to reinforce many of the preexisting attitudes and beliefs of audience members. Third, they seem to shift a limited number of voters. Though the number of voters whose opinions are shifted by the debates is limited, it should be kept in mind that, as discussed earlier in this chapter, debates are much more likely to be held in close elections, where the shift of a limited number of voters might well prove crucial to the outcome. Fourth, debates help to set the political agenda. Fifth, debates contribute to the education of audience members. Voters who watch the debates apparently are more knowledgeable as a consequence of their watching. This educational benefit of debates must be tempered somewhat by the recognition that current debate formats often preclude the viewers really learning about the issues that most concern them. Sixth, debates seem to affect the images of candidates. The image of the lesser-known participant is normally affected more by a political debate. Finally, debates seem to contribute to the public's confidence in government institutions and leaders.

NOTES

1. Quoted in *The Lincoln-Douglas Debates*, ed. Robert W. Johannsen (New York: Oxford University Press, 1965), p. 3.

2. Kathleen Hall Jamieson and David S. Birdsell note that as early as 1788 when two future presidents, James Madison and James Monroe, debated for a seat in the new House of Representatives, debates have been a part of American election campaigns. See their *Presidential Debates: The Challenge of Creating an Informed Electorate* (New York: Oxford University Press, 1988), p. 34.

3. J. Jeffery Auer, "The Counterfeit Debates," in *The Great Debates: Kennedy vs. Nixon, 1960*, ed. Sidney Kraus (Bloomington, Indiana University Press, 1962), p. 146.

4. Ibid.

5. This term was first used by Auer in his essay "The Counterfeit Debates" to describe the 1960 debates. It has since been used to describe many political debates, most notably by Lloyd F. Bitzer and Theodore Rueter in their work *Carter vs. Ford: The Counterfeit Debates of 1976* (Madison: University of Wisconsin Press, 1980).

6. The statements in this paragraph were made by panelists Robert Flemming and Stuart Novins during the opening minutes of the first Kennedy-Nixon debate. See *The Joint Appearances of Senator John F. Kennedy and Vice-President Richard M. Nixon: Presidential Campaign of 1960* (Washington, D.C.: Government Printing Office, 1961), p. 78.

7. See Bitzer and Rueter, *Carter vs. Ford*, esp. Chapter 3, for an excellent analysis of the adversary nature of the press in the 1976 debates. The adversary nature of the press remains a characteristic feature of campaign debates. Susan A. Hellweg and Anna M. Verhoye, "A Comparative Verbal Analysis of the Two 1988 Bush-Dukakis Presidential Debates" (Paper presented to the Speech Communication Association, November 1989), pp. 17–18 details the extent of adversary questioning in the 1988 presidential debates.

8. Formats of the presidential debates are fairly well known. For examinations of the formats used in recent presidential primary debates, see Susan A. Hellweg and Steven L. Phillips, "Form and Substance: A Comparative Analysis of Five Formats Used in the 1980 Presidential Debates," *Speaker and Gavel* 18 (Winter 1981): 67–76; Michael Pfau, "A Comparative Assessment of Intra-Party Debate Formats" (Paper presented at the Speech Communication Association Convention, Chicago, November 1984). Examinations of debate formats at the nonpresidential level can be found in Jack Kay, "Campaign Debate Formats: At the Non-Presidential Level" (Paper presented at the Speech Communication Association Convention, Anaheim, November 1981); and Michael Pfau, "Criteria and Format to Optimize Series" (Paper presented at the Speech Communication Association Convention, Anaheim, November 1981). Ironically, Patrick Caddell noted that the 1980 presidential debate format used by Reagan and Carter, which allowed for nine to ten minutes of discussion on a single topic, was "exhaustive." See his "Memo of October 21, 1980," reprinted in Elizabeth Drew, *Portrait of an Election: The 1980 Election* (New York: Simon and Schuster, 1981), p. 426.

9. Auer, "Counterfeit Debates," p. 148.

10. Perhaps the debate with the most significance for the subsequent development of political debating was the one held between the Tennessee gubernatorial candidates in 1886. For an explanation of the subsequent impact of this debate, see Herbert A. Terry and Sidney Kraus, "Legal and Political Aspects:

Was Section 315 Circumvented?," in *The Great Debates: Carter vs. Ford, 1976*, ed. Sidney Kraus (Bloomington: Indiana University Press, 1979), pp. 44–45.

11. See Jamieson and Birdsell, *Presidential Debates*, pp. 35–36 for a discussion of this feature of 19th-century campaigns.

12. When debates were held, they were frequently the centerpieces of the campaigns. For an especially informative example of this, see Cal M. Logue, "Gubernatorial Campaign in Georgia in 1880," *Southern Speech Communication Journal* 40 (Fall 1974): 12–32.

13. Samuel L. Becker and Elmer W. Lower, "Broadcasting in Presidential Campaigns," in *The Great Debates: Kennedy vs. Nixon, 1960*, ed. Sidney Kraus (Bloomington: Indiana University Press, 1962), p. 29.

14. Quoted in Sidney Head, *Broadcasting in America* (Boston: Houghton Mifflin, 1976), p. 331.

15. For a full discussion of these changes, see Edward W. Chester, *Radio, Television, and American Politics* (New York: Sheed and Ward, 1969), pp. 247–65. Also see Head, *Broadcasting in America*, pp. 330–32.

16. Chester, *Radio, Television and American Politics*, p. 37. Also see Becker and Lower, "Broadcasting in Presidential Campaigns," p. 35.

17. Chester, *Radio, Television, and American Politics*, p. 42.

18. An excellent description of this debate can be found in Robert F. Ray, "Thomas E. Dewey: The Great Oregon Debate of 1948," in *American Public Address: Studies in Honor of Albert Craig Baird*, ed. Loren Reid (Columbia: University of Missouri Press, 1961), pp. 245–70.

19. Lee M. Mitchell, *With the Nation Watching*, Lexington, Mass.: D. C. Heath, 1979), p. 28 claims that Moody made his suggestion while being interviewed on the CBS radio network show "The People's Platform," in July of 1952. J. Leonard Reinsch, a media consultant to Presidents Roosevelt and Truman, also made an early effort to get Stevenson and Eisenhower to debate. See Goodwin F. Berquist, "The 1976 Carter-Ford Presidential Debates," in *Rhetorical Studies of National Political Debates: 1960–1988*, ed. Robert V. Friedenberg (New York: Praeger, 1990), p. 29.

20. In 1952 neither man felt comfortable with the idea of televised debates. Both candidates were also advised not to debate.

21. Mitchell, *With the Nation Watching*, p. 30.

22. Chester, *Radio, Television and American Politics*, pp. 133–35, provides a brief account of the stimulus that the 1960 presidential debates had on political debating.

23. For a complete and far more thorough account of this change in the equal time provisions, see Terry and Kraus, "Legal and Political Aspects," pp. 41–49.

24. This section is based primarily on two articles by Robert V. Friedenberg. Full citations for all quoted material and fuller explanations of all major points can be found in those two articles. See Robert V. Friedenberg, " 'We Are Present Here Today for the Purpose of Having a Joint Discussion': The Conditions Requisite for Political Debates," *Journal of the American Forensic Association* 16 (Summer 1979): 1–9; Robert V. Friedenberg, " 'Selfish Interest,' or the Prerequisites for Political Debate: An Analysis of the 1980 Presidential Debate and Its Implications for Future Campaigns," *Journal of the American Forensic Association*

18 (Fall 1981): 91–98. The authors wish to thank the American Forensic Association for permission to use those articles.

25. Reagan's 1984 advisors have been quoted as claiming that "they did not think it would be politically acceptable" for the president to refuse to debate. Apparently well in command of the election, Reagan and his strategists nevertheless evidently feared the negative reaction his refusal to debate might prompt. See J. Jeffery Auer, "Presidential Debates: Public Understanding and Political Institutionalization," *Speaker and Gavel* 24 (Fall 1986): 5. Auer cites a conversation between Reagan advisors and reporter Elizabeth Drew. Similarly, see Craig Allen Smith and Kathy B. Smith, "The 1984 Reagan-Mondale Presidential Debates," in *Rhetorical Studies of National Political Debates: 1960–1988*, ed. Robert V. Friedenberg (New York: Praeger, 1990), p. 96.

26. On the evolution of public attitudes toward incumbent presidential debating see Robert V. Friedenberg, "Patterns and Trends in National Political Debates: 1960–1988," in *Rhetorical Studies of National Political Debates*, ed. Robert V. Friedenberg (New York: Praeger, 1990), pp. 188–191.

27. The following account of the 1960 debates is based primarily on Theodore White, *The Making of the President: 1960* (New York: Atheneum, 1961); Kenneth P. O'Donnell and David F. Powers, *Johnny, We Hardly Knew Ye* (New York: Pocket Books, 1973); and Friedenberg, "Conditions for Political Debates."

28. The following account of the 1980 debates is based primarily on *Time*, issues of September 15 to November 3, 1980, and *Cincinnati Enquirer*, September 11 to October 27, 1980. Also see Friedenberg, "Prerequisites for Political Debates."

29. Quoted in *Time*, September 22, 1980, p. 9.

30. Goodwin F. Berquist and James L. Golden, "Media Rhetoric, Criticism, and the Public Perception of the 1980 Presidential Debates," *Quarterly Journal of Speech* 67 (May 1981): 125–26.

31. Ibid., pp. 127–28.

32. This and the next paragraph are based heavily on Smith and Smith, "The 1984 Reagan-Mondale Presidential Debates," pp. 100–116, which focuses heavily upon the role of public expectations.

33. One of the authors, Friedenberg, has been involved in a variety of political debates. Also see, for examples, Dale Hardy-Short, "An Insider's View of the Constraints Affecting Geraldine Ferraro's Preparation for the 1984 Vice-Presidential Debate," *Speaker and Gavel* 24 (Fall 1986): 8–22; Myles Martel, "Debate Preparations in the Reagan Camp: An Insider's View," *Speaker and Gavel* 18 (Winter 1981): 34–46; Martin Schram, *Running for President* (New York: Pocket Books, 1977), pp. 326–31, 348–64, 370–89; Caddell, "Memo of October 21, 1980," pp. 410–39; White, *Making of the President 1960*, pp. 335–55; Theodore Otto Windt, "The 1960 Kennedy-Nixon Presidential Debates," in *Rhetorical Studies of National Political Debates: 1960–1988*, ed. Robert V. Friedenberg (New York: Praeger, 1990), pp. 9–10; and Judith S. Trent, "The 1984 Bush-Ferraro Vice Presidential Debate," also in *Rhetorical Studies of National Political Debates: 1960–1988*, pp. 135–36.

34. By all accounts, Ronald Reagan's preparation for his 1980 debates with John Anderson and Jimmy Carter was the most thorough in this regard. Reagan practiced in a garage converted to resemble the actual television studios used

in the debates. His staff went to great lengths to simulate and anticipate his opponents, including studying tapes of prior debates involving Anderson and Carter. Eventually David Stockman, a former administrative assistant to John Anderson, based in large part on his study of tapes, played both Anderson and Carter in Reagan's practices. The 1980s proliferation of candidate forums and candidate debates during the primary season has meant that by the general election, at least at the presidential level, candidates have been in a variety of debates or debatelike situations and an opponent will normally have access to tapes of their prior performances.

35. An informative account of this frequently overlooked precursor to the 1960 general election debates can be found in Goodwin F. Berquist, "The Kennedy-Humphrey Debate,' *Today's Speech* 7 (September 1960): 2–3.

36. "Transcript of the First TV Debate Between Bush and Dukakis," *New York Times,* September 26, 1988, p. A19.

37. See "Transcript of the Second TV Debate Between Bush and Dukakis," *New York Times,* October 14, 1988, p. A14.

38. Robert O. Weiss, "The Presidential Debates in Their Political Context: The Issue-Image Interface in the 1980 Campaign," *Speaker and Gavel* 18 (Winter 1981): 22–27.

39. Ibid., p. 22.

40. This threefold analysis of image strategies is based on Dan D. Nimmo's discussion of the techniques that can be used by a political figure. The terminology and definitions are Nimmo's. See Dan D. Nimmo, *Popular Images of Politics* (Englewood Cliffs, N.J.: Prentice-Hall, 1974), pp. 100–102.

41. "Transcript of the First TV Debate Between Bush and Dukakis," pp. A16–A19.

42. Ibid.

43. Quoted passages from the 1980 presidential debate are taken from the NBC-verified transcript record of the debate found in Richard Harwood, ed., *The Pursuit of the Presidency 1980* (New York: Berkley Books, 1980), pp. 359–400.

44. "Transcript of the Second Debate Between Bush and Dukakis," p. A17.

45. Frederick T. Steeper, "Public Response to Gerald Ford's Statements on Eastern Europe in the Second Debate," in *The Presidential Debates: Media, Electoral, and Policy Perspectives,* ed. George F. Bishop, Robert G. Meadow, and Marilyn Jackson-Beeck (New York: Praeger, 1978), p. 101.

46. Ibid. Also see Roger Desmond and Thomas Donohue, "The Role of the 1976 Televised Presidential Debates in the Political Socialization of Adolescents," *Communication Quarterly* 29 (Fall 1981): 306–8; and George A. Barnett, "A Multidimensional Analysis of the 1976 Presidential Campaign," *Communication Quarterly* 29 (Summer 1981): 156–65.

47. Michael Oreskes, "Both Parties Offer a Spin to the Event," *New York Times,* September 25, 1988, p. A1.

48. The use of this strategy is largely dependent upon the cooperation of the press, which must disseminate the views of the surrogate spokespersons. Steven R. Brydon's study of the network treatment of the 1988 presidential debates suggests that the networks are becoming sensitive to being "used" in this fashion. Negative network characterizations of candidate surrogates as "spin doctors," as well as the reduced time networks seem to be giving such

spokespersons, may ultimately reduce their effectiveness. See Steven R. Brydon, "Spinners on Patrol: Network Coverage in the Aftermath of Presidential and Vice-Presidential Debates" (Paper presented to the Speech Communication Association Convention, November 1989).

49. Cited in Harry P. Kerr, "The Great Debates in a New Perspective," *Today's Speech* 9 (November 1961): 11.

50. Susan A. Hellweg and Steven L. Phillips, "A Verbal and Visual Analysis of the 1980 Houston Republican Presidential Primary Debate," *Southern Speech Communication Journal* 47 (Fall 1981): 24.

51. John P. Robinson, "The Polls," in *The Great Debates: Carter vs. Ford, 1976*, ed. Sidney Kraus (Bloomington: Indiana University Press, 1979), pp. 262–63.

52. The preceding audience figures are all drawn from Warren Decker, "The 1988 Quayle-Bentsen Vice-Presidential Debates," in *Rhetorical Studies of National Political Debates: 1960–1988*, ed. Robert V. Friedenberg (New York: Praeger, 1990), p. 181. Decker cites a *Washington Post* article as the source of these figures.

53. Bruce is quoted in Kitty Bruce, *The Almost Unpublished Lenny Bruce* (Philadelphia: Running Press, 1984), p. 91.

54. *Newsweek*, October 17, p. 27.

55. George Gallup, Jr., "The Impact of Presidential Debates on the Vote and Turnout," in *Presidential Debates: 1988 and Beyond*, ed. Joel L. Swerdlow (Washington, D.C.: Congressional Quarterly Books, 1987), p. 34.

56. As we write in early 1990 few research studies concerning the 1988 debates are in print. However those available do conclude that the 1988 Bush-Dukakis debates did reinforce existing attitudes. See, for example, Michael Pfau and Jong Geun Kang, "The Impact of Relational and Nonverbal Communication in Political Debate Influence" (Paper presented to the Speech Communication Association Annual Conference, November 1989), p. 16.

57. David O. Sears and Steven H. Chaffee, "Uses and Effects of the 1976 Debates: An Overview of Empirical Studies," in *The Great Debates: Carter vs. Ford, 1976*, ed. Sidney Kraus (Bloomington: Indiana University Press, 1979), p. 255.

58. For a study of the 1980 debates that clearly supports these implications, see David Leuthold and David Valentine, "How Reagan Won the Cleveland Debate: Audience Predispositions and Presidential Debate Winners," *Speaker and Gavel* 18 (Winter 1981): 60–66, esp. pp. 65–66.

59. Elmo Roper, "Polling Post-Mortem," *Saturday Review*, November 1960, pp. 10–13.

60. Elihu Katz and Jacob Feldman, "The Debates in Light of Research: A Survey of Surveys," in *The Great Debates: Kennedy vs. Nixon, 1960*, ed. Sidney Kraus (Bloomington: Indiana University Press, 1962), p. 211.

61. Jack M. McLeod et al., "Reactions of Young and Older Voters: Expanding the Context of Effects," in *The Great Debates: Carter vs. Ford, 1976*, ed. Sidney Kraus (Bloomington: Indiana University Press, 1979), pp. 365–66; Paul R. Hagner and Leroy N. Rieselbach, "The Impact of the 1976 Presidential Debates: Conversion or Reinforcement?," in *The Presidential Debates: Media, Electoral, and Policy Perspectives*, ed. George F. Bishop, Robert G. Meadow, and Marilyn Jackson-Beeck (New York: Praeger, 1978), p. 178.

62. Leuthold and Valentine, "How Reagan Won," p. 62.

63. Smith and Smith, "The 1984 Reagan-Mondale Presidential Debates," p. 102.

64. Ibid.

65. For a summary of the findings of major polls taken after the first 1988 debate see Halford Ryan, "The 1988 Bush-Dukakis Presidential Debates," in *Rhetorical Studies of National Political Debates: 1960–1988*, ed. Robert V. Friedenberg (New York: Praeger, 1990), p. 159. *Time*, October 10, 1989, p. 27 summarized the findings of their poll, and illustrated part of Dukakis's difficulty in translating his debate victory into votes by observing that "although voters judged Dukakis the 'better debater,' they found Bush 'more presidential and more likeable'— qualities far more likely to guide them in the voting booth." Also see Pfau and Kang, "The Impact of Relational and Nonverbal Communication in Political Influence," p. 16.

66. Elizabeth Drew, *Election Journal: Political Events of 1987–1988* (New York: William Morrow, 1989), p. 291.

67. Maxwell McCombs, "Agenda Setting Research: A Bibliographic Essay," *Political Communication Review* 1 (Summer 1976): 3.

68. Linda L. Swanson and David L. Swanson, "The Agenda-Setting Function of the First Ford-Carter Debate," *Communication Monographs* 45 (November 1978): 347–53.

69. Ibid., p. 353.

70. Ibid.

71. Lee B. Becker et al., "Debates' Effects on Voter Understanding of Candidates and Issues," in *The Presidential Debates: Media, Electoral, and Policy Perspectives*, ed. George F. Bishop, Robert G. Meadow, and Marilyn Jackson-Beeck (New York: Praeger, 1978), pp. 137–38; Steven H. Chaffee, "Presidential Debates—Are They Helpful to Voters?," *Communication Monographs* 45 (November 1978): 336.

72. Allen Lichtenstein, "Differences in Impact Between Local and National Televised Political Candidates' Debates," *Western Journal of Speech Communication* 46 (Summer 1982): 296.

73. Pfau, "Criteria and Format," pp. 5–6.

74. Soma Golden, "Inside the Debate," *New York Times*, September 24, 1980, p. A30.

75. For an examination of the differing agenda of voters, reporters, and candidates, see Marilyn Jackson-Beeck and Robert G. Meadow, "The Triple Agenda of Presidential Debates," *Public Opinion Quarterly* 42 (Summer 1979): 173–80.

76. Ryan, "The 1988 Bush-Dukakis Presidential Debates," p. 160.

77. See for examples Stephen Mills, "Rebuilding Presidential Debates," *Speaker and Gavel* 24 (Fall 1986): 41–51; Jamieson and Birdsell, *Presidential Debates: The Challenge of Creating an Informed Electorate*, pp. 201–2; Sidney Kraus *Televised Presidential Debates and Public Policy* (Hillsdale, N.J.: Lawrence Erlbaum, 1988), pp. 144–45.

78. See J. Jeffery Auer, "Presidential Debates: Public Understanding and Political Institutionalization," *Speaker and Gavel* 24 (Fall 1986): 5–6. Auer cites a study of 11 journalists who served on debate panels and reports that 5 of them claimed such panels should be eliminated.

79. Windt, "The 1960 Kennedy-Nixon Presidential Debates," p. 4.

80. Hagner and Rieselbach, "Impact of 1976 Presidential Debates," p. 172.

81. Sears and Chaffee, "Uses and Effects of 1976 Debates," pp. 246–47.

82. Kevin Sauter, "The 1976 Mondale-Dole Vice Presidential Debate," in *Rhetorical Studies of National Political Debates: 1960–1988*, ed. Robert V. Friedenberg (New York: Praeger, 1990), pp. 45–68.

83. Decker, "The 1988 Quayle-Bentsen Vice-Presidential Debates," pp. 167–86.

84. Sidney Kraus and Dennis Davis, "Political Debates," in *Handbook of Political Communication*, ed. Dan D. Nimmo and Keith Sanders (Beverly Hills: Sage, 1981), pp. 273–98.

85. Samuel L. Becker et al., "Information Flow and the Shaping of Meanings," in *The Great Debates: Carter vs. Ford, 1976*, ed. Sidney Kraus (Bloomington: Indiana University Press, 1979), p. 396.

86. Chaffee, "Presidential Debates," pp. 343–45.

87. Sidney Kraus, *Televised Presidential Debates and Public Policy*, p. 123.

Chapter Nine

Interpersonal Communication in Political Campaigns

This chapter examines the place of interpersonal communication in political campaigns. We perceive interpersonal communication to be transactional. When people communicate they define themselves and simultaneously respond to their perceptions of the definitions being offered by others. This transactional perspective, which we share with most communication scholars, has several implications that have unusual importance for political communication.

First, interpersonal communication is contextual. Part of the context in which any communication takes place is the other person. You behave differently when you are with your children than when you are with your employer. Each participant affects the other. Similarly, candidates behave differently when they visit with a small group of bowlers in neighborhood bowling alleys than when they visit with a few large financial contributors in someone's home. The physical setting of the two transactions, the differences in background music and noise, the differences in clothing worn by the bowlers and the contributors, the differences in the language used by the two groups, and countless other stimuli help define the bowlers and the contributors to the candidate. Simultaneously, the presence of the candidate in the bowling alley or at a contributor's home, the clothing and language of the candidate, and countless other stimuli that the candidate emits enable the bowlers and the contributors to define the candidate. As each party to the transaction shapes and refines definitions of the other, their own behavior will be affected, thus continually changing the communication context.

Second, this perspective suggests that each party to the transaction is simultaneously both a sender and a receiver of verbal and nonverbal messages. When you meet the candidate at a neighborhood coffee and criticize a local bond issue that the candidate supports, you are simultaneously watching facial expressions, observing the tightening of the candidate's fist, and noting that the candidate's face is becoming flush. As candidates emit these communicative stimuli, they are defining themselves to you. You better sense the candidate's support for this bond issue and the irritation your criticism provokes, even though the candidate may have said nothing.

Clearly, as you observe candidates listening to your criticism, they appear affected by your statements. Similarly, as you see the candidate's face flush and fist tighten, you begin to temper your criticism. You gradually lower your voice and use more moderate language. You have been affected by this communication transaction, and so has the candidate. This is the third major implication that the transactional perspective has for political communication; each participant affects and is affected by the other.

As we discuss interpersonal communication in political campaigns, we will frequently note the importance of our transactional perspective. However, before beginning the discussion, we want to note two other characteristics of the interpersonal communication to be studied in this chapter. They deliberately narrow the expanse of interpersonal communication, limiting it to interpersonal communication utilized in political campaigns. First, one party to the interpersonal transactions discussed in this chapter is either a candidate or the surrogate/advocate of a candidate. The surrogate/advocate may be a formal representative of the candidate, such as a member of the campaign staff, or an informal representative, such as a voter who is not in any way affiliated with the candidate but nevertheless discusses the candidate. The final characteristic of the interpersonal transactions examined is that the overt, normally verbal, messages either directly or indirectly involve a campaign for public office.

In this chapter, we will discuss three crucial areas of interpersonal communication in political campaigns: interpersonal communication between the candidate and voters, interpersonal communication between the candidate and potential financial contributors, and interpersonal communication between voters.[1]

INTERPERSONAL COMMUNICATION BETWEEN CANDIDATES AND VOTERS

As indicated in Chapter 6, no resource is more vital to the campaign than the candidate's time. This is a finite resource. Once the time is lost, it cannot be replaced. Consequently, if candidates are spending time meeting individuals or small groups of individuals, they must be sure that there is an unusually high chance that these meetings will be productive. For candidates to spend three hours with two, four, or ten people and come away with nothing is a loss that cannot be recovered. More money cannot buy lost time, nor can more volunteers produce it. Hence, decisions on where the candidates should spend time and with whom they should meet are critical.

The use of the candidate's time is especially critical in local campaigns. Over 500,000 public offices in the United States, from president to the infamous dog catcher, are filled by election.[2] Lynda Lee Kaid points out that the tendency of researchers to study highly visible national and statewide campaigns has caused us often to neglect what is the most effective channel of political persuasion in vast numbers of races—the interpersonal communication of the candidate.[3] As Kaid notes, the channels of communication available to candidates in thousands of campaigns below the national and statewide levels are often severely limited.

In many campaigns, the geographic makeup of the district precludes the effective use of mass media such as radio and television. For example, the eighth congressional district of Ohio, located between Cincinnati and Dayton, includes about 95,000 residents of suburban Cincinnati. It also includes Hamilton (a town of 80,000), Middletown (a town of 60,000), all of Preble County (a prosperous agricultural county with no town over 15,000) and parts of Darke, Green, and Montgomery counties, including portions of suburban Dayton. To use television effectively in this district, the candidate would have to purchase time on both Dayton and Cincinnati stations. Yet the approximately 70 percent of the district receiving Cincinnati television constitutes less than 20 percent of the Cincinnati media market. The remaining 30 percent of this district, within the Dayton media market, constitutes less than 10 percent of the Dayton media market. To cover this district adequately with television, candidates would have to pay for an audience approximately ten times larger than the one they want.

Moreover, within this single congressional district, there are at least 500 other elected public officials; county commissioners in Butler, Preble, Darke, Green, and Montgomery counties, county prosecutors, treasurers, sheriffs, and the like in each county, city council members, mayors, and a variety of other officials in at least 40 communities. The point should be abundantly clear. Geographic and financial considerations make television, radio, and other mass media impractical for hundreds of races in this area alone and for hundreds of thousands of races nationally. Additionally, messages on behalf of most local candidates, delivered through the mass media, are liable to be ignored or ineffective when those media are saturated with information concerning the major contests for president, governor, or senator. As Kaid concludes, "The interplay of some or all of these limitations may create an environment

in which interpersonal communication, particularly communication between the candidate and the voters, may be a crucial factor in the outcome of an election."[4]

Given the importance of the candidate's time and given that in many
races its waste cannot be offset by purchasing media time, it is essential
that the candidate's interpersonal communication be utilized effectively.[5]
This means that candidates must know where to campaign. Consequently, and in local races especially, the most valuable materials that
a campaign can have are often the precinct analysis of recent voter
statistics, such as those illustrated in Chapter 6. The thoroughness of
such analysis is a direct function of the amounts of money spent on
obtaining them. In most states, local party organizations will prepare
voter statistics for candidates. Hence, even in areas where the local
organization is weak, candidates should not have trouble obtaining a
complete analysis of prior voting statistics for their district. Moreover,
if the various party organizations do not provide an analysis of statistics,
candidates can obtain the statistics themselves and perform their own
analysis, since all vote totals are a matter of public record and kept on
file by the appropriate election boards.

Once they have access to prior election results, particularly a precinct-
by-precinct analysis, candidates can determine which precincts are essentially Republican, Democratic, or marked by a high incidence of
ticket-splitting. As we observed in Chapter 6, the candidate should direct
the campaign primarily at those precincts where the party traditionally
runs well and those precincts where ticket-splitting commonly takes
place. It is in these precincts that most of the candidate's interpersonal
communication should take place.

Far more than national figures, local candidates must know precisely
where to spend their time. Because their constituencies are smaller, in
many instances local candidates can knock on every door in their district
or at least on every door in those precincts that are deemed most important. The door-to-door campaigning of candidates for major offices
is most often done for media coverage, rather than for any direct impact.
It allows the major candidate to appear in the media while walking
through a ghetto, or a cornfield, presumably illustrating concern for
blacks or farmers. Vice-President Spiro Agnew's widely repeated 1968
remark "When you've seen one ghetto you've seen them all," while
callous and insensitive, is nevertheless not far from the truth in describing the function that door-to-door campaigning serves for major figures.
Perhaps Agnew might have said, "When you've been seen in one ghetto,
it serves as though you've been seen in them all."

Local candidates will not receive media exposure of their door-to-door
campaigning. Rather, their efforts will put them face-to-face with a large
percentage of their constituency. Interpersonal campaigning is not sym-

bolic for the local candidate, as it is for the major candidate. Rather, it is often the major thrust of the campaign, an essential means of compensating for the lack of media exposure.

Though major candidates do not rely as extensively on interpersonal campaigning as do local candidates, it does often serve an important place in their campaigns. Clearly, because of the size of the constituency, the major candidate, as well as many local candidates, will utilize surrogate advocates to represent him in door-to-door canvasses of a community. The door-to-door canvass is often especially effective in the primary campaigns of major candidates. Such races typically involve substantially fewer voters than the general election. Candidates and their representatives can often reach a high percentage of those voters who are eligible to vote in the primary. George McGovern's effective use of the principles of interpersonal communication in door-to-door canvassing in small state primaries such as New Hampshire, Massachusetts, and Rhode Island, which occurred in early 1972, played a substantial role in his success that year and has created emulators in every primary season since.[6]

The most typical methods of interpersonal campaigning by candidates or their representatives are coffees and door-to-door canvasses. Each method allows the candidates or their representatives to interact for brief periods of time with a small number of voters. Done repeatedly, they may serve as an effective means of supplementing media campaigning or, as in the case of many local candidates, almost entirely replace it.

The Coffee

Keeping in mind the precinct analysis of voters, the campaign organization will arrange a schedule of coffees (in some areas, tea or beer might be the preferred beverage) for the candidate. The organization should arrange the coffees so that the candidate is able to meet with two groups. First, "those people residing in areas which are generally independent" and in which considerable ticket-splitting takes place. Second, "coffees should be scheduled in areas where the candidate and his party can be expected to run well."[7] In these areas, coffees give "the candidate an opportunity to pay personal attention to those who are working for him. It gives the campaign organization an opportunity to recruit new workers."

Keeping in mind our transactional viewpoint of interpersonal communication, we can readily see why campaigners seek to hold coffees and similar events that promote interpersonal transactions with neutral and friendly voters. Such events provide the candidate with much more than the opportunity simply to meet voters. They provide the candidate with the opportunity to establish a relationship, to affect the other parties in the transaction.

In virtually any election, but perhaps more so in local elections, candidates will often meet in countless small social gatherings early in the campaign. They can then follow up on the relationships initiated at these meetings by remaining in contact with short notes, letters, and calls. People are affected by the candidates they meet this way, and subsequently those people often prove helpful to the candidates.

Conversely, candidates are also affected by interpersonal transactions such as coffees. As we have seen in Chapter 2, promises made during the surfacing and primary stages of a campaign tend to be kept more than those made later. Part of the reason for this seems to be that promises made early in the campaign are frequently made in small interpersonal contexts, where the candidate is more prone to be affected by voters. Later in the campaign, crowded candidate schedules often prohibit the types of interpersonal transactions that frequently take place early in the campaign.

The candidate "should never attend the coffee by himself. He should always have with him another man (or woman if the candidate is a woman)." The function of this other individual is to get the candidate away from the coffee gracefully if the hostess fails to do so. The candidate's associate, not the candidate or the hostess, can take the blame for rushing the candidate away if that becomes necessary. The candidate should avoid making speeches at coffees. Rather, a candidate "need give only brief informal remarks." After the candidate's brief remarks, a short question-and-answer period is appropriate.

Four rules should govern every coffee. First, "optimum size of the gathering is twenty to thirty people." This includes the host and hostess, candidate, and those traveling with the candidate. Second, name tags should be provided for each guest. The affair is essentially social, and the candidate wants to establish a first name relationship with the guests, if possible. Third, the host or hostess should "never permit a guest to buttonhole the candidate or enter into arguments." Finally, it should always be remembered that the coffee "is an excuse for getting together, and the stress should be on easy informality and comfort."

This description of an ideal coffee clearly indicates that the simple act of being present and interacting with a number of voters is as important, if not more so, than what the candidate actually says. A well-run coffee maximizes the opportunities for fruitful interpersonal transactions. Time is devoted to establishing personal friendships. The group is small enough for the candidate to interact with everyone, and the candidate's aide as well as the host or hostess of the coffee facilitate the candidate's interaction with everyone.

Local candidates often run for administrative positions that do not involve issues of policy. The county recorder, engineer, or sheriff, for example, provide administrative services, but they rarely set policy. Hence, interpersonal communication opportunities, where candidates can establish relationships illustrating their concern, personality, and character, are vital. Given that many local races lack real issues between the candidates and that the candidates are relatively unknown, often the candidates who have met the most people, who are best known in the district, who have visited the neighborhood, who seem to make themselves available and accessible, and who have worked at establishing relationships are the candidates who most appeal to the voter.

Good campaigns can effectively arrange three coffees an evening for their candidates, several evenings a week, through the last months of the campaign. Such programs, particularly in local races, enable candidates to interact with a significant percentage of their constituency. Moreover, the candidate's presence in the neighborhood will be rapidly reported the next day over backyard fences, in beauty and barber shops, gas stations, and stores, as those invited to the coffee discuss their experience.

The Door-to-Door Canvass

The use of small social gatherings such as coffees serves primarily to foster interaction between the candidate and voters. A second major form of interpersonal communication between the candidate and voters, the door-to-door canvass, typically serves several additional purposes. Like the coffees, it should provide candidates and their representatives with an opportunity to deal personally with a large number of voters. Hopefully, as with the coffees, candidates will be perceived as accessible and concerned, leaving a positive image with the voters they meet. Presumably, the same impressions should be left with voters who meet the candidates' representatives.

The canvass can serve additional functions and is often utilized in major races, where coffees play a lesser role. When utilized in major races, most of the canvassing is done by representatives of the candidate. Regardless of who is canvassing, the canvass can identify voters who are favorable, neutral, or hostile to the candidate. Depending on their attitudes, these voters can subsequently be contacted. The canvass also is an excellent means of distributing information about the candidate. A conversation between the canvasser and the voter can provide information about the candidate. Additionally, the canvasser can leave materials and if the voter has a specific concern, the canvasser can arrange to have additional information sent later.[8]

Important principles of interpersonal communication should be implemented by canvassers if they are doing their jobs well. The instructions given to those who canvass on behalf of a candidate "will typically exhibit sensitivity to psychological principles important in interpersonal communication."[9] Instructions such as these are representative of what most campaigns will encourage.

1. Speak with enthusiasm and sincerity about the candidate.
2. Be a good listener. Let the voters speak. Do not interrupt or argue.
3. Be open-minded. Whenever possible, express your agreement with the voter.[10]

Canvassers who follow instructions such as these can accomplish much. They can leave literature, determine voting intentions, or question for other information that the campaign desires.[11] Additionally, when done by well-prepared canvassers, the door-to-door canvass leaves voters with a positive feeling about the candidate that will not be readily forgotten.

In sum, interpersonal communication between the candidate and the voter is, for most people, a unique event. The details of the coffee or the canvass meeting will no doubt fade from an individual's memory. But the fact that the candidate cared enough to come to the neighborhood or send a representative and followed up the initial coffee or canvass will often remain and loom far larger in the voter's mind than the specifics of what may have been said.

INTERPERSONAL COMMUNICATION BETWEEN THE CANDIDATE AND PROSPECTIVE FINANCIAL CONTRIBUTORS

Before examining interpersonal communication designed to solicit campaign contributions, we must first answer two fundamental questions about fund-raising. First, who currently contributes to political campaigns? Second, who is likely to contribute in the future?

In recent years, federal laws on campaign contributions have encouraged candidates for federal office to solicit relatively small contributions from large numbers of voters. As mentioned earlier, federal laws today place a $1,000 ceiling on the amount of money that a single individual can contribute to a candidate, and a $5,000 ceiling on the contributions of political action committees. Most individual states have also imposed ceilings on the amounts that can be given to candidates for state and local office.[12] Restrictions on state and local candidates are generally not as tight as those placed on candidates for federal office. Nonetheless, the effect of these relatively recent laws has been to reduce the number of large contributors and the size of their contributions, while increasing the total number of campaign contributors. Political scientist Larry Sabato summarizes the current situation when he observes that individual voters "still supply over three-fifths of all the money raised by House candidates and three-quarters of the campaign budgets of Senate contenders. Although the importance of PAC spending has grown, PACs clearly remain secondary to individuals as a source of election funding."[13]

Consequently, the largest single source of political contributions is the individual citizen donor. In recent years, a pattern of campaign giving seems to have emerged. Though this pattern varies for any individual campaign, generally speaking about 30 to 35 percent of the money raised for political campaigns comes from individual citizens contributing $100 or less. This percentage tends to be a little higher for lesser races and a little lower for major races. About 35 to 40 percent of the money raised for political campaigns comes from individual citizens contributing $100 to $1,000. Hence, in most elections approximately 65 to 75 percent of all contributed money comes in the form of individual citizen donations in relatively small amounts. The remaining money comes in the form of aid from political and special interest groups as well as loans.[14]

It is likely that the current pattern of campaign contributions will continue in the future. Surveys taken repeatedly over the last two decades indicate that in major election years 15 to 20 percent of the population is solicited for a political contribution. Of those solicited, slightly more than 40 percent make some type of contribution.[15] Currently, it is estimated that over 12 million U.S. citizens contribute to political campaigns.[16] Moreover, Gallup Poll figures suggest that about 40 percent of those not solicited for a political contribution would have made at least a $5 contribution to a political candidate if they had been asked.[17] The widespread success of direct mail—since 1972 when computer technology was brought to direct mail political solicitations—further suggests that in the future most money raised for political purposes will be raised through the relatively modest contributions of large numbers of individual citizens. Robert Agranoff summarizes the situation facing most political candidates when he concludes:

The campaigner is faced with having to raise most funds from individual contributions within a relatively narrow base of contributors that include family, friends, and associates of the candidate, plus other committed supporters, particularly partisans. On the other hand, there is a hint that the potential exists to broaden the financial base. The evidence also suggests that campaigners should not be deluded into expecting generous party and group financial support.[18]

People do not contribute to a political campaign unless they are attracted to the candidate. Political fund-raising is largely interpersonal in nature. Typically, the candidate, finance director, and members of the finance committee seek contributions from individuals they believe would be receptive to such an appeal. Similar in conception, though obviously less personal in execution, is direct mail fund-raising. Here again, the campaign seeks contributions from individuals believed to be receptive to the candidate. Invariably, the key is to determine who would be attracted to the candidate and thus receptive to financial appeals.

Students of interpersonal communication identify at least five principles of human attraction.[19] First, we are attracted to people who are in close physical proximity to us. Second, we are attracted to people who are similar to us. Third, we are attracted to people who provide us with positive feedback. Additionally, at least two situational factors tend to heighten the likelihood of our being attracted to other people. Fourth, if we find ourselves in an anxiety-producing situation, we tend to have a greater need for human interaction and hence are more prone to be attracted to other people. Fifth, if we have already extended some type of supportive behavior to an individual, we are more likely to be attracted to that individual than if we had never provided such behavior. Each of these five principles of human attraction has major implications for conducting political fund-raising.

The first determinant of attraction is proximity. That is, all things being equal, the more closely two people are located the more likely they are to be attracted to one another. Far too often, campaigns tend to neglect this simple fact. Rather than seek financial support from the most likely sources, people within the district, they seek financial support out of the district. Doing so creates two potential problems. First, and most serious, it rarely works. Just as charity begins at home, just as most of us contribute to our own United Way, our own church, our own civic groups, most of us will be more prone to contribute to candidates who will directly affect us.

This simple fact was illustrated by the efforts of a recent congressional candidate who was a Christian Scientist and a graduate of Principia College, the only Christian Science institution of higher education in the country. The candidate made an extensive fund-raising effort among Principia alumni. But he was running for a Missouri congressional seat and Principia is in Illinois. Additionally, as the only Christian Science school in the nation, Principia has a national flavor, attracting students from throughout the country, and its alumni have settled throughout the country. The candidate's efforts failed to produce any significant results because so few of those he contacted were located in close proximity to him and his district. Indeed, he received a number of responses indicating that some people were annoyed by his soliciting them, since they did not live in his district.

The importance of proximity is also illustrated by the guidelines both the Republican and Democratic national committees use to determine which candidates will receive their financial support. One of those guidelines is that candidates must demonstrate fund-raising ability *within* their district. The assumption is that if they cannot raise money among people in close proximity, they cannot raise money from anyone.[20]

The second determinant of human attraction that is of exceptional importance for political fund-raising is similarity. We are attracted to people who are similar to us. Potential donors should always be approached by people who are highly similar to them. A carefully selected and highly motivated fund-raising committee, working through their own social networks or precincts, the people with whom they are most similar, and drawing on the candidate's presence when necessary, is perhaps the most effective means of utilizing the concept of similarity. And for that reason, it is the most successful means of raising funds in most campaigns.

The recent fund-raising efforts of Minnesota Senator Rudy Boschwitz well illustrates the importance of similarity. Using himself, his family, and his friends, Boschwitz has been able to put together what he and his staff call "The Washington Club," a group of 850 supporters who contribute $1000 a year, payable in four equal installments, to his campaign: "The Lincoln Club," a group of supporters who contribute $100–250 a year to his campaign; and "The Skinnycats," a group of supporters who contribute under $100 a year to his campaign. Members of these groups receive appropriate certificates and buttons from Boschwitz, and no doubt have a strong feeling of being connected to him, though many of them were no doubt recruited by their friends, and have had little if any firsthand contact with Boschwitz. By utilizing the basic concept of similarity, Boschwitz has assembled a fund-raising organization that enabled him to open his most recent campaign with $1.5 million dollars in the bank earning interest.[21]

The third principle of attraction that has import for political fund-raising is that we are attracted to, and respond favorably to, people who like us and validate us with positive feedback. Candidates and their surrogates must keep this fact uppermost in their minds as they seek funds. This does not mean the fund-raiser must be overtly compliant. If fund-raisers feel compelled to do that, then they are not dealing with equals. They should not be attempting to get donations from persons with whom they do not feel similar and equal. Rather, it means that fund-raisers must do their research. They should be able, if the situation arises, to make reference to the potential contributors' family by name, to make reference to recent accomplishments of the potential contributors' businesses, etc. In many fund-raising meetings, it is fair to say that topics such as politics, current events, and making a political contribution do not take up more than 3 minutes of a 30-minute conversation. Fund-raising situations are so patently obvious that they do not need any belaboring. Rather, the meetings stress the similarities between the candidates, their supporters, and the prospective contributors, as the candidates or their supporters attempt to provide positive feedback to the prospective contributors. Often this is done by focusing comments on the contributor's role in mutual projects of a nonpolitical nature such as charitable, social, educational, or civic programs, as well as the political similarities between the candidate and prospective contributor.

A fourth principle of human attraction enters into political fund-raising. Research suggests that we experience a heightened need for human attraction during moments of anxiety.[22] This point should be noted by the competent political fund-raiser. As the campaign develops, the good fund-raiser will keep in mind who might be made anxious by current events. As opponents make statements and develop their campaigns, the good fund-raiser will follow them closely, seeking to determine who might be made anxious by the opponents' statements and positions. And as current events take place and receive publicity, the well-run campaign will have the appropriate person seeking funds from the individuals most likely to be made highly anxious by these events, at the very moment that they may be causing anxiety. For example, in a recent St. Louis area congressional race, one candidate announced that he was in favor of a controversial Army Corps of Engineers construction project that involved erecting several dams and flooding thousands of acres of lowland to create a large lake and recreational area to be utilized primarily by St. Louis residents. His opponent opposed this project as an unnecessarily wasteful and extravagant use of federal funds that would prove utterly disruptive to much of the Missouri environment and wildlife. Within three days of the first candidate's announcement, the second candidate or his representatives had contacted over 120 members of the St. Louis chapter of the Sierra Club, as well as similar environmental organizations. Within three days, this effort produced almost $8,000 of unexpected contributions and many new enthusiastic workers for the campaign.

The final basis of human attraction that warrants the attention of the political fund-raiser is the concept of supportive behavior. Research suggests that our own behavior greatly influences our perception of other people. If, for example, you perform a favor for another person, you tend to like that person better as a consequence.[23] Hence, good fund-raisers, if unsuccessful in getting what they want—large contributions— should always have backup requests. If the car dealer will not contribute $500, $100, or $25, maybe the dealer will let candidate Smith use that beautiful yellow car in the showroom for three hours during the Labor Day parade. If worse comes to worse, at least the car dealer can look over some of Smith's campaign literature.

The practice of consistently seeking some type of supportive behavior, minimal as it may be, has at least two beneficial effects. First, the tangible benefit requested will be honored. Candidate Smith does ride in the most attractive car in the parade. Second, now that the car dealer has provided some sort of supportive behavior to the candidate, the dealer is more likely to respond favorably to a second fund-raising appeal. Importantly, once people have made an initial contribution to the candidate, they are prone to make a second or third contribution. Notice, in the discussion of Senator Boschwitz's fund-raising group mentioned earlier, that those groups contributed money on a yearly basis, year after year after year. Effective fund-raisers are aware of the positive effect that supportive behavior has on subsequent behavior and consistently strive to obtain some type of supportive behavior from everyone they approach.

These principles of interpersonal communication should guide candidates and fund-raisers as they seek contributions. Moreover, they clearly have implications for other forms of fund-raising. They can help determine, for example, both the mailing list and the message content of direct mail solicitation on behalf of the candidate. In sum, candidates and fund-raisers who are skillful interpersonal communicators, clearly sensitive to and aware of the determinants of human attraction, are far more prone to achieve success than those who ignore these important variables of interpersonal communication.

INTERPERSONAL COMMUNICATION
BETWEEN VOTERS

Voters talk among themselves about politics, campaigns, and candidates. Interpersonal communication between voters is an important aspect of virtually every campaign. In this section, we will try to answer three questions about interpersonal communication between voters. First, in what campaigns is it likely to be of unusually high importance? Second, what do voters typically discuss? Third, what is the relationship between interpersonal communication and mass media in political campaigns?

Importance

Interpersonal communication between voters is normally of greatest importance in those campaigns that receive little media attention. When information about the campaign and the candidates is lacking in the media, voters rely more heavily on interpersonal communication. Consequently, several types of campaigns, characteristically lacking in media coverage, often must rely heavily on interpersonal communication. First are campaigns for lesser offices or local offices, second are primary campaigns. L. Erwin Atwood and Keith R. Sanders have found that communication with other people was the most credible source of information for 32 percent of the voters in a primary election, but that it was the most credible source of information for only 12 percent of the voters in a general election.[24] Often, as when three or more candidates seek a single office in a primary, the media coverage received by any single candidate tends to be more limited than in a general election. Moreover, the media budgets of most primary campaigns are lower than those of general elections. The reduced media coverage of individual candidates and campaigns in some primaries causes voters to rely much more heavily on interpersonal communication in these elections than in general elections.

The third group of campaigns where interpersonal communication between voters seems to play an unusually important role are those campaigns in which the constituency has a relatively high educational level. Research on this point is limited, and much of it has been done primarily on school-age populations. Nevertheless, it does tend to suggest that voters with good educational backgrounds are less affected by the media, more prone to discuss current events, and more prone to be influenced by those discussions.[25]

Discussion Topics

Voters discuss virtually everything that is pertinent to a campaign. However, three subjects tend to dominate their conversations. First, interpersonal communication is often the means by which people initially learn of a newsworthy development in the campaign. In one of the first studies to focus on how people learn about campaign events, Wayne A. Danielson found that knowledge of news events in a presidential campaign was most rapidly spread throughout the population by radio and interpersonal communication. Television and newspapers, according to Danielson, did not transmit knowledge of news events as rapidly.[26] Though Danielson's findings may have since been altered by the widespread growth of television, it nevertheless seems safe to conclude that people do frequently discuss and often first learn of news events through interaction with one another.

Second, William D. Kimsey and L. Erwin Atwood found that voters tend to "talk most about the things they like least about candidates."[27] Conversations between voters are not subject to libel laws, equal time laws, and the other legal constraints that may affect the various mass media. Media coverage of the negative aspects of a candidate may be tempered by considerations such as these, but interpersonal communication is not.

Additionally, Kimsey and Atwood found that voters tend to use interpersonal communication selectively to reinforce their vote decisions.[28] This finding makes good sense because of our tendency to be attracted and communicate primarily with those who are similar to us. Hence, we are prone to be exposed to messages congruent with our own ideas. Moreover, we do not equally attend to all the messages we receive. We tend to selectively attend to those messages that conform to our existing attitudes and beliefs. Kimsey and Atwood's findings, that we use interpersonal communication selectively to reinforce prior decisions, seems to be very much in accord with our existing knowledge of interpersonal communication.

In sum, interpersonal communication is used by voters to deal with virtually everything that happens in a campaign. However, in contrast to other forms of campaign communication, it may be especially important as a medium of news transmission, as a medium by which negative information about a candidate is transmitted, and as a medium that serves to reinforce attitudes and beliefs.

Interpersonal Communication Between Voters, Mass Media, and Voting Behavior

As early as 1948, students of mass media realized the relationship and importance of interpersonal communication. John P. Robinson provides us with a critique of the relationships between voting behavior, mass media, and interpersonal communication.[29] Robinson, like prior researchers, finds that when interpersonal communication is in conflict with media information "interpersonal sources wield greater influence."[30] The explanation for this no doubt rests in large part on the feedback and adaptation that one voter can provide to another as they discuss politics. Mass media messages cannot adapt and react to feedback, as can interpersonal communication. However, Robinson also finds that interpersonal influence attempts are not that pervasive in elections. More people seem to be exposed to media attempts to influence their votes than to interpersonal attempts to influence their votes.[31] Those people who receive media messages attempting to influence their votes, but no interpersonal messages, seem much more receptive to direct influence from the media.[32]

Robinson does find one situation in which the basic two-step flow scenario of a downward communication flow still takes place: when an individual attentive to the media exerts interpersonal influence on persons less attentive to the media. This pattern still seems to be common in nuclear families. Robinson found that husband-wife discussions are different from most other discussions. Husbands and wives seem to have more influence on each other's votes than do other conversational partners. Moreover, Robinson reports that generally the husband is more attentive to politics and plays the influential role in deliberations with his wife.[33]

Though most candidates make special efforts to facilitate interpersonal communication between themselves and voters, and between themselves and financial contributors, few candidates make concrete efforts to facilitate interpersonal communication between voters that might have a favorable impact on their candidacy. However, at least one nationally prominent political consultant has long attempted to stimulate interpersonal communication among voters to benefit his clients. Stephan C. Shadegg advises candidates to develop "social precincts" as crucial elements of their campaigns.[34] Social precincts, as Shadegg employs them, are simply enthusiastic and knowledgeable supporters of the candidate. They are not members of special organizations or groups, nor are they in any way prominent in their communities. Initially, members of social precincts are recruited from among friends and associates of the candidate, and gradually the number of members is increased. Many of these people may not even know the candidate well.

Members of social precincts are provided "inside" information. As the campaign progresses, they get key press releases a day in advance, and their opinion is solicited before the candidate makes a key speech. They are made to feel that they are insiders whose opinions and advice are valued by the candidate. And indeed, they are just that. By using the mail, the candidate is able to develop a large group of people who look upon the candidate as someone with whom they have a special relationship. Based on extensive experience with social precincts, Shadegg claims that if he can enlist 3 to 5 percent of the constituency in these social precincts, he will win the election. For if 3 to 5 percent of the constituency believe they have a special interest in a candidate, Shadegg feels that in their normal day-to-day social interactions they will prove influential.

Shadegg's approach is one of the few clear attempts to mobilize interpersonal communication among voters on behalf of a candidate. His success with social precincts, as well as research evidence on the relationship between voting behavior, mass communication, and interpersonal communication, speaks to the importance of interpersonal communication between voters.

CONCLUSIONS

In this chapter, we have examined interpersonal communication in political campaigns. We have found that interpersonal communication between the candidate and voters is exceptionally important in local campaigns, in campaigns where the use of media may not be feasible, and in primary campaigns. In such campaigns, the interpersonal communication between the candidate and voters, through programs of informal coffees and canvasses, can be extremely valuable. Moreover, we have found that political fund-raising lends itself to interpersonal communication and that current interpersonal communication research on attraction has major implications for interpersonal fund-raising by political candidates and their advocates. Finally, we have examined the often neglected interpersonal communication between voters. We have seen in which campaigns such communication is most important, what voters tend to discuss among themselves, and the relationships between voting behavior, media, and interpersonal communication.

NOTES

1. For a discussion of some of the mechanics involved in implementing the first two of these types of interpersonal communication, see Robert Agranoff, *The Management of Election Campaigns* (Boston: Holbrook Press, 1976), pp. 411–54.

2. Herbert E. Alexander, *Financing Politics: Money, Elections, and Political Reform* (Washington, D.C.: Congressional Quarterly Books, 1980), p. 1.

3. Lynda Lee Kaid, "The Neglected Candidate: Interpersonal Communication in Political Campaigns," *Western Journal of Speech Communication* 41 (Fall 1977): 245.

4. Ibid.

5. The following analysis of the importance of interpersonal campaigning in local political campaigns is based heavily on Robert V. Friedenberg, "Interpersonal Communication in Local Political Campaigns," *Ohio Speech Journal* 12 (1974): 19–27.

6. See L. Patrick Devlin, "The McGovern Canvass: A Study in Interpersonal Political Campaign Communication," *Central States Speech Journal* 24 (Summer 1973): 83–90 for an account of some of the McGovern techniques that have been widely copied.

7. This statement and all quotations in this section are drawn from "Coffee: The Campaign Beverage," a pamphlet issued by the Republican State Central and Executive Committee of Ohio to candidates for state and local offices. No date or place of publication.

8. See Patrick Devlin, "The McGovern Canvass," pp. 82–90 for an excellent description of a highly effective canvassing operation that served all of the functions described in these paragraphs.

9. Devlin, "McGovern Canvass," p. 89.

10. These instructions are typical of those provided canvassers today. They are modeled after those provided the McGovern campaign canvassers in the 1972 presidential primaries. See Devlin, "McGovern Canvass," p. 84–85.

11. See Agranoff, *Management of Election Campaigns*, pp. 411–54 for a discussion of the many purposes of canvasses as well as illustrations of the materials used in canvasses.

12. Alexander, *Financing Politics*, pp. 130–32.

13. Larry Sabato, "Real and Imagined Corruption in Campaign Financing,"

in *Elections American Style*, ed. A. James Reichley (Washington, D.C.: Brookings Institution, 1987), p. 157.

14. These figures are similar to those reported by Agranoff, *Management of Election Campaigns*, pp. 232–34 in his account of 1972 congressional races and by Sabato in his more recent studies of election financing. Moreover, Sabato notes that PACs have probably had their greatest influence on races for the U.S. Senate and House of Representatives. See Sabato, "Real and Imagined Corruption," p. 157. See also Alexander, *Financing Politics*, pp. 45–67 for a discussion of individual donors. Virtually all researchers, including those cited in this chapter, find that candidates for federal offices tend to raise a higher percentage of their funds from PACs than state and local candidates. Female candidates, regardless of office, have much more difficulty raising money from special interest groups, according to Ruth B. Mandel, *In the Running: The New Woman Candidate* (New Haven: Ticknor and Fields, 1981), pp. 191–94.

15. The best brief examinations of political campaign contributors can be found in Agranoff, *Management of Election Campaigns*, pp. 230–34; Alexander, *Financing Politics*, pp. 62–64; and Sabato, "Real and Imagined Corruption," pp. 157–59.

16. Alexander, *Financing Politics*, p. 64.

17. Ibid., p. 63.

18. Agranoff, *Management of Election Campaigns*, p. 234.

19. Many researchers have attempted to establish the major determinants of human attraction. Two of the better summaries of current research, upon which this analysis is based, are Stewart L. Tubbs and Sylvia Moss, *Human Communication* (New York: Random House, 1987), pp. 66–75; and William Wilmot, *Dyadic Communication: A Transactional Perspective* (Reading, Mass.: Addison-Wesley, 1975), pp. 68–74.

20. This guideline is a longstanding one, used by Republican and Democratic national committee field staff, to help determining which candidates are the most viable and hence warrant aid from their respective national committees.

21. For a description of Boschwitz's fund-raising efforts and his other suggestions about campaigning see "A Senator's Advice: Don't Give Consent to Reelection Debate," *Wall Street Journal*, May 2, 1985, p. A1.

22. Tubbs and Moss, *Human Communication*, pp. 72–73.

23. Wilmot, *Dyadic Communication*, pp. 73–74.

24. L. Erwin Atwood and Keith R. Sanders, "Information Sources and Voting in a Primary and General Election," *Journal of Broadcasting* 20 (Summer 1976): 298.

25. John P. Robinson, "Interpersonal Influence in Election Campaigns: Two-Step Flow Hypotheses," *Public Opinion Quarterly* 40 (Fall 1976): 312; and Marilyn Jackson-Beeck, "Interpersonal and Mass Communication in Children's Political Socialization," *Journalism Quarterly* 56 (Spring 1979): 53.

26. Wayne A. Danielson, "Eisenhower's February Decision: A Study of News Impact," *Journalism Quarterly* 33 (Fall 1956): 437.

27. William D. Kimsey and L. Erwin Atwood, "A Path Model of Political Cognitions and Attitudes, Communication and Voting Behavior in a Congressional Election," *Communication Monographs* 40 (August 1979): 429.

28. Ibid., p. 430.

29. Robinson, "Interpersonal Influence in Election Campaigns," pp. 304–19.

30. Ibid., p. 315.

31. Ibid.

32. Ibid., p. 316.

33. Ibid., p. 318.

34. This discussion of social precincts is based on Stephen C. Shadegg, *The New How to Win an Election* (New York: Tapplinger, 1976), pp. 103–19.

Chapter Ten

Advertising in Political Campaigns

Many campaigns are waged essentially through advertising, primarily over radio and television. These campaigns tend to be high profile races, such as those for national and statewide office. In many urban areas, races such as those for Congress or city offices are also waged heavily through the use of radio and television. However, in lower-level races, where budgets preclude the extensive use of radio and television, or where local demographic conditions make it impractical, other forms of advertising remain dominant. Moreover, even high profile media campaigns cannot forsake the more traditional, often pre-electric media, means of campaigning and advertising. If they do so, they run a serious risk of incurring consequences that so badly damage their efforts that even a highly effective media campaign cannot win the election.

The experiences of Harriet Woods in her two Missouri campaigns for U.S. Senate well illustrate the complexity and problems involved in using media in political campaigns. They provide us with three lessons that serve as background to understanding the practices commonly employed in using media in contemporary campaigns.

After a long career of public service in University City, a suburb of St. Louis, in 1976 Harriet Woods began to attract statewide notice by winning election to the Missouri Senate. Once established in the statehouse, in 1982 she waged an aggressive race for the U.S. Senate. A distinct underdog to Missouri's popular incumbent senator, Jack Danforth, Woods seemed on the verge of upsetting Danforth. Most statewide polls showed her ahead going into the last ten days of the campaign. At that point Senator Danforth launched an intensive statewide media blitz, which Woods did not have the finances to match, and Danforth won a narrow victory. Woods rebounded in 1984 running a successful race for lieutenant governor and becoming the first woman ever elected to statewide office in Missouri. Hence, in 1986 she and her advisors placed special emphasis on television advertising. Her 1982 experience led her 1986 campaign strategists to conclude that their number one priority in her race with two-time Missouri Governor Christopher "Kit" Bond would be to equal or exceed Bond's effort with paid television advertisements. She and her advisors were determined that she would not be beaten by television in 1986.[1] However, as the votes were tallied on election eve, it became apparent that Bond had beaten Woods. Ironically, Woods was beaten by television. However, unlike 1982, in 1986 she was beaten by her own use of television.

In 1982 Harriet Woods may well have lost because she could not mount sufficient advertising. Political advertising can be enormously expensive. Later in this chapter we will examine the expenses of advertising more closely; suffice to say at this point that for many candidates the major obstacle to successful political advertising is the lack of money. In 1986 the Harriet Woods campaign staff had estimated that to run successfully in the moderately populous state of Missouri, served by two major media markets, St. Louis and Kansas City, she would need to raise in excess of $4,600,000. As the campaign progressed that estimate was revised upward by approximately half-a-million dollars. Six years earlier, in 1980, Senator Thomas Eagleton had won reelection in Missouri, spending $800,000.[2] The single principal reason for this staggering increase was the increasing reliance of statewide candidates on increasingly costly television commercials.

The experience of Missouri candidates is typical of those throughout the country. The staggering increases in the costs of campaigning are primarily a consequence of increasing reliance on television. Thus, the first lesson that Harriet Woods's campaigns teach us about political advertising is that candidates who expect to use media, particularly television, must be prepared to raise substantial amounts of money. Harriet Woods found this out the hard way in 1982.

In 1986 Woods had a difficult time in raising money, but raise it she did. However, the principal student of Woods's 1986 campaign, participant/observer Deborah L. Chasteen has claimed that "although Woods was able to raise the millions of dollars necessary to remain competitive in the media, that success limited her ability to reach voters in other ways. She was unable to fund traditional voter appeals such as yard signs and bumper stickers, and had to restrict her public appearances to those which would yield either money or media coverage."[3] Chasteen notes that Woods curtailed virtually all other forms of advertising, and repeatedly passed up important speaking opportunities to facilitate her media campaign. Cumulatively, the effect of her decisions, claims Chasteen, was a "unidimensional campaign."[4]

In failing to engage in the traditional forms of advertising, and in failing to appear at a variety of locally important functions, often because she deemed her time better spent at fund-raising, or working on media, Woods cost her campaign the enthusiasm and energy of party workers and loyalists throughout Missouri. Understandably, though incorrectly, they often mistook her failures to appear at local events, or to provide them with such things as yard signs, bumper stickers, phone banks, and advertisements in the local press, as indicative of indifference. Different media as we will see in this chapter, serve different functions. Though Harriet Woods television commercials reached the public at large, the "unidimensional campaign" she waged made it difficult for Democratic party activists around the state to become enthused by her campaign. Some media serve not only to help persuade the public, but also to mobilize and encourage volunteers and staff. The second lesson that we learn from Harriet Woods campaigns is that most strong campaigns involve a mix of media to convey their messages.

The Woods campaign is instructive for yet a third reason. Preoccupied with getting her commercials on the air, Woods strategists failed to thoroughly consider the content and full implications of her commercials. Chasteen points out that Woods's most important decision in the campaign, to air a controversial series of advertisements that came to be known as the "crying farmer commercials," was conceived "hastily in reaction to an eight point shift in polling numbers," was "never tested," and represented a substantial shift from the campaign's original strategy for using television commercials, worked out in cooperation with media consultant Robert Squier.[5] Moreover, Chasteen observed that the Woods campaign "did not anticipate the types of responses Bond might have . . . did no contingency planning and had no strategy for extending their arguments."[6] In sum, Chasteen concludes of the Woods campaign that "the medium for conducting their ideas took precedence over the ideas they wanted to convey."[7] Thus, the final lesson of the Woods campaigns: Though the skillful use of the medium is critical, ultimately the medium serves only as a vehicle for presenting candidates and their messages. It is the images candidates present of themselves and of one another, and the ideas they express, that are of ultimate consequence.

With these three lessons in mind: (1) that political advertising is enormously costly, not only in dollars, but also in time and effort, (2) that appealing as television commercials may be, rarely can a campaign be waged successfully by relying exclusively on television, and (3) that advertising mediums are simply vehicles for conveying the images and ideas of candidates, which are ultimately of more consequence, let us now examine some of the major practices involved in political advertising. The remainder of this chapter will focus first on factors that affect the selection and use of various advertising media available to political campaigners. Second, we will focus on what have become key figures in many contemporary campaigns, the professional political consultant, with emphasis on those who specialize in media.

DEVELOPING A MASTER PLAN
FOR POLITICAL ADVERTISING

The array of advertising media that has been used in political campaigns is staggering. A partial listing includes brochures, newsletters, questionnaires, letters, billboards, yard signs, bumper stickers, newspaper advertisements, magazine advertisements, matchbooks, buttons, pencils, and, of course, radio and television commercials. This list does not even include one of the author's all time favorites, cans of GOLD WATER, the delightful drink for all right thinking supporters of the 1964 Republican standard bearer! Indeed, the list is endless. Political campaigners have used virtually every technological advance in communication to facilitate getting their messages to the public.

Among the first responsibilities of any campaign is to develop a master plan for the campaign's political advertising. This plan should serve to coordinate all of the paid media activities of the campaign. Obviously occasions will arise where events make it necessary to deviate from the overall plan. However, well-run campaigns plan their media activities early, and then stick as closely as possible to their overall plans, adjusting as events make it necessary.

The advantages of advance planning cannot be overestimated. Decisions that are made as the campaign is beginning tend to be made more dispassionately, and are typically based on greater objectivity, thought, and research. Decisions made on the spur of the moment, in response to campaign events, are typically subject to less thought, less research, less analysis, and hence are prone to be less successful. Notice, in the campaign discussed at the outset of this chapter, Harriet Woods's decision to run the controversial "crying farmer" commercials was made hastily, in response to a campaign development. It was a marked deviation from the campaign's previously well thought out plan, which involved using "soft" commercials, to develop a positive image for Woods at this early stage of the campaign rather than "hard" attack commercials, criticizing Bond.

The many advantages of advance planning can be best illustrated by example. Let us imagine that we are involved in planning a congressional primary race. Our candidate is only moderately known in the district.

However, our opponent is also known only moderately in the district. They are both vying for the nomination to succeed a popular incumbent who is retiring after 24 years in Congress. We will imagine that our candidate is a university professor who has served on local school boards and subsequently was elected mayor of a small college town of 21,000 within the district, a position he currently holds. He is also highly active in supporting the arts and has been a lifelong member of barbershop quartets. Our opponent is a young lawyer who just completed her second term in the state House of Representatives, representing a district of about 80,000 located in the suburbs of a large city. Her district comprises about one fourth of the congressional district, the town in which our candidate serves as mayor comprises only about 6 percent of the district. Another fourth of the district is comprised of suburbs such as that our opponent has represented, and about half the district is rural, though the rural area includes several towns of about 15,000 to 25,000 such as the one our candidate has served as mayor. For the sake of illustration we will imagine that traditionally candidates wait until January before announcing their candidacy for the May 1 primary.

Using the surfacing period during the summer of the year preceding the election, we draft our first master plan for advertising. We decide to run a series of radio and television commercials for ten days, immediately after declaring candidacy in January. Moreover, we decide to take out large advertisements in the three daily papers that serve the district and in each of the district's ten highest circulation weekly papers in the week immediately following our candidate's announcement. Our advertising master plan then calls for three direct mail efforts in February and March. The first two mailings, in February, are to target groups that may be expected to be highly supportive of the candidate. We might imagine a master plan that calls for a mailing on February 12 to individuals concerned with education, such as the members of teachers groups, PTA's, and similar organizations. The master plan then calls for a mailing on February 25 to members of a variety of groups concerned with culture and music, such as season ticket purchasers to local theater groups, supporters of the local symphony, ballet, and, of course, the Sweet Adelines and other groups who support barbershop quartets. The master plan we develop further calls for a mailing on March 25 to all voters eligible to participate in the primary. In addition to mailings, we develop a master plan that calls for the distribution of 300 yard signs during the first two weeks of March, and a major push to distribute 500 yard signs on each of the last two weekends of March.

Since the primary election is scheduled for May 1, we decide that our radio advertising should start on April 1, doubling in quantity every 10 days. That is, for every commercial run between April 1–10 two radio commercials will be run between April 11–20. For every commercial run between April 11–20 two radio commercials will be run between April 20–May 1. Moreover, we decide to use a second and final round of television commercials to start on April 1, and their number is to double on April 21. Additionally, the master plan calls for running large advertisements in each of the three daily papers and in each of the ten largest weekly papers in the district during the last phase of the campaign. Advertisements will be placed on each of the last three days in the three dailies, and in each of the last two editions for the ten weekly papers. Finally, the master plan calls for a final mailing to all eligible voters to be sent on April 25 so as to be received by voters within three days of the election.

Notice what developing this relatively simple advertising plan has forced us to do, and how it impacts upon and governs much of the rest of the campaign. The first advantage to developing this plan early is that it forces us to identify our basic goal in the campaign. In this example we have one basic goal, acquiring name recognition as a prominent member of our party. Since this is a primary there may not be major differences between the candidates. Moreover, since this district has been won by the candidate of our party for the last 24 years, securing the party nomination may in itself be the basic step necessary for our candidate's ultimate election. In most campaigns the first advantage to developing an initial advertising program is that it forces the campaign to develop and prioritize its overall objectives or goals for the campaign.

Since our goal is recognition, we have decided to campaign vigorously from the moment of our announcement. If we are going to use newspapers, radio, and television all in the first weeks of the campaign, as our plan calls for, then clearly we need money early in the campaign. Our master plan for advertising must be coordinated with our fundraising. For example, if we cannot raise money for ten days worth of radio and television at the outset of the campaign, what can we do? Perhaps we should curtail the radio and television and use yard signs earlier in the campaign. Yard signs, however, call for considerable use of volunteers. Yards have to be solicited, signs have to be made and distributed. We can estimate the cost of producing commercials and buying time. We can estimate the number of volunteers needed to produce and place yard signs. The second advantage to planning our advertising campaign early is that it forces us to work closely with those involved in fund-raising and volunteer efforts, making sure the entire campaign is well coordinated.

In this example we may conclude that since name recognition is clearly an early problem for us, we are best served, given our limited initial finances, by using radio, billboards, and yard signs early in the campaign. These forms of media can all be used effectively to help establish early name recognition. Moreover, they are typically less expensive than newspaper advertisements and television commercials. Hopefully, early in the campaign when we are laying out our positions we may be able to supplement advertising with free media: newspaper stories and stories and interviews on the local radio and television shows. Later in the campaign, when we have more money, and when we may need to communicate more than our name and party, billboards and yard signs will be of little help. Using them in March as we originally planned may not make as much sense as using them earlier, which also enables us to save money for newspaper and television advertisements that we might need later in the campaign to explain our positions. Moreover, if we use yard signs early, it forces our volunteer coordinators to amass a large number of volunteers early, and those people will be vital to our later efforts to put out a variety of mailings. Thus as we plan early we are able to refine our advertising program in those ways that best enable us to blend with the efforts of other elements of the campaign.

Additionally, as we begin to recognize our financial problems, we may choose to divert a greater effort in that area. We may be forced, as Harriet Woods was, to have our candidate spend a great percentage of his time on fund-raising. We may have to develop extra fund-raising activities. Regardless of our situation, by giving ourselves ample time to plan we can make the most of whatever resources we have available to us. Among the factors that our advance media planning should consider are:

- Relative costs in dollars of available media
- Relative costs in candidate time/volunteer effort or other campaign resources of available media
- Ability of media to target specific audiences
- Ability of various media to accomplish specific goals of advertising
- Sequential development of advertising
- Coordinating advertising with the remainder of the campaign

We can best understand the first four of these factors by examining the various media that campaigners can choose to employ.

BASIC CONSIDERATIONS IN THE SELECTION OF POLITICAL ADVERTISING MEDIA

Political campaigns make use of five types of advertising media; display graphics, direct mail, print, radio, and television. Each of these options has virtues, and each has liabilities. Those virtues and liabilities relate to the six factors listed above that enter into the advance planning of a campaign advertising program. Hence, this discussion will focus on each of the five types of advertising media in relation to the factors that must be considered as the campaign's advertising program is developed.

Display Graphics

Display advertising, also called graphic advertising, most commonly includes such items as billboards, posters, yard signs, bumper stickers, and buttons. Display advertising can be instrumental in helping (1) to create and reinforce name recognition, and (2) to give a very quick impression of the candidate. If these are among the goals of the advertising campaign, and often early in the campaign they are, the use of display advertising should be considered. Such advertising normally carries an exceedingly brief message, often no more than the candidate's name, or the name and a brief slogan. For example, in recent national elections billboards, posters, yard signs, bumper stickers, and buttons have carried such messages as: Forward with KENNEDY, Nixon Now, Reelect the President, PRESIDENT MUSKIE Don't You Feel Better Already?, Leaders for Change—CARTER Mondale, The Time is Now REAGAN & BUSH, Geraldine Ferraro America's First Woman Vice Pres., Reagan-Bush 84, For President 1988 George Bush, JACKSON For President—Follow the Rainbow.[8] Typical of the similarly brief messages used on display media in recent state and local campaigns are messages such as: VOINOVICH . . . Make the U.S. Senate Work for OHIO, ARONOFF Congress, I Gave A Buck for YOUNG for Congress, Run RABBITT Lt. Governor, ROCKY!, FRANKE for CONGRESS, Elect CASEY Congressman.[9]

Display advertising such as those cited above clearly contribute to enhancing name recognition. Additionally, as several of these examples illustrate, display advertising may reinforce a major campaign theme. For example, in 1972 Richard Nixon continually stressed his incumbency and experience, hence the theme of his campaign, Reelect the President. In the 1988 race for Ohio's U.S. Senate seat, Cleveland mayor George Voinovich argued that incumbent John Glenn was preoccupied with running for president, and had neglected Ohio. Hence, VOINOVICH . . . Make the U.S. Senate Work for OHIO.

Display graphics, the format of which does not allow for an extended message, can serve two additional important, yet often overlooked functions. They are particularly useful in reinforcing partisans who are already committed to the candidate. When distributed at campaign meetings, rallies, and similar activities they often enhance the spirit of the staff and volunteers, serving as a visible link between the candidate and the worker. Indeed, many campaigns will purchase a few hundred pins, bumper stickers, or yard signs simply to keep the morale of the staff up. One candidate of the author's acquaintance complained so badly about his lack of yard signs that the campaign manager assigned a volunteer to post 50 yard signs on the mile and a half route the candidate took into his headquarters every morning, and then to check once a week to replace any signs that had come down. The manager reported an immediate improvement in the candidate's outlook and performance! On occasion the cost for a small amount of display graphic advertising is well worth the improved staff and volunteer morale that it provides.

Finally, if handled well, display graphics can be used to impress voters with the candidate's strength and help to create a bandwagon effect. For example, most consultants would advise that yard signs or bumper stickers not be given out in a small trickle, a few every day. Rather, a well coordinated effort should be made to distribute a massive number of them simultaneously. So, for example, on day one there are virtually no yard signs in the district. All of a sudden, on day two, there seems to be one every block. Though there is not a sign in every block, the sudden appearance of many signs multiplies their effectiveness, making the casual voter highly aware of them, and often suggesting to that voter that the candidate must have a large organization behind him to get up so many signs so quickly. Putting up massive numbers of yard signs all at once makes their impact far stronger, suggests massive support for the candidate, and helps create a bandwagon effect among casual voters. A similar effect can be achieved by distributing bumper stickers throughout the district all at once. Many campaigns will post volunteers in every high school football parking lot one Friday night in early October, and in that fashion distribute thousands of bumper stickers simultaneously. The same effect can be achieved by using shopping mall parking lots.

In recent years the quantity and variety of display graphic advertising in political campaigns has been diminished. This is a direct function of cost. As recently as the early 1970s it was not uncommon for a voter to be able to walk into the campaign office of a candidate and be given pins, bumper stickers, and similar materials, not only of that candidate, but also of other candidates of the same party. Today, the voter seeking such material is often asked to leave a contribution of 50 cents or a dollar for every button or bumper sticker they take.

Display graphics are expensive, both in terms of dollars and in terms of time and effort. For example, while costs vary from community to community, the cost for 1,000 of the simplest standard 2 1/4 inch buttons (one color printing on standard background color) in a typical metropolitan area is $250. The cost for 1,000 of the simplest standard 3 inch by 11 1/2 inch bumper stickers, (one color printing on standard background color) is $260. The cost of pencils imprinted with the candidate's name and slogan vary between $150–190 per thousand, depending on the quality of the pencil.[10]

Larger forms of display advertising, such as billboards and yard signs are also costly. In Cincinnati, Ohio, the 28th largest media market in the nation, the 1990 cost of renting sufficient billboard space to provide that 25 percent of the Cincinnati population will see your message at least once daily was $8,800 a month. Additionally, the production cost for those boards will normally run between $800–1,000. Thus the total cost for a modest billboard effort running only one month in duration would be approximately $9,600–9,800.[11]

Yard signs are also costly. Their price will vary depending on such factors as the size and quality of paper. However, because they are designed to remain outside, the posterboard used must be of good quality. The typical cost for 1,000 professionally printed yard signs, measuring a standard 20 inch by 26 inch size, printed on 24 pt. stock, which is reasonably sturdy, will be about $745.[12] Though printing costs will vary, it should also be remembered that typically some expense will also be incurred in purchasing stakes for the signs and in transporting them throughout the district.

Moreover, the cost of some commonly used display graphic items such as yard signs and bumper stickers includes not only the production costs, but also the distribution costs, which must normally be measured in the time and effort of volunteers. Volunteers can serve a multitude of purposes in political campaigns. Nevertheless, their time must be used wisely. Volunteers can normally only give the campaign a limited amount of time. The use of volunteer time must be factored in as a cost when some types of display graphics are used.

Direct Mail

Direct mail advertising provides campaigns with one enormous advantage that cannot be readily duplicated by any other form of political advertising. It allows the campaign to be highly selective in targeting audiences. The wise use of radio and television commercials, or of newspaper and magazine advertisements, also allows for some degree of targeting. However, direct mail allows the campaign to target an audience more precisely than virtually any other form of advertising.

Unlike many other forms of campaign communication, direct mail can be considered "high interest, low backlash communication." That is, a direct mail piece can be tailored to reflect the interests of a specific constituency. For example, the candidate's views on recent changes in Soviet policy towards the nations of Eastern Europe might be featured in a mailing sent to a large section of the district where most residents are of Eastern European extraction. However, the candidate's views on Latin American policy can be featured in a mailing sent to an immediately adjacent few square blocks in the district where most residents are of Latin American extraction. Such mailings focus on topics of high interest to the recipient. However, they create low backlash. If the candidate spoke about Eastern Europe or Latin America on radio, television, or in the print media, it is likely that many viewers or readers would have little interest in these topics and hence react negatively to the candidate for boring them by failing to address their concerns.[13] By using direct mail to target audiences, the likelihood of high recipient interest is increased and the risk of backlash is largely eliminated.

Not only does direct mail allow for precise targeting of audiences, but it allows for an extended message. It is a vehicle that enables the candidate to fully express himself on a given issue. It is not uncommon for candidates to use letters and mailings that run four or more pages in length to treat one specific issue or a group of closely related issues. For example, a candidate may wish to fully explain his position on Social Security and compulsory health insurance, topics that are of special interest to older Americans. To do so might require considerable radio and television time, or considerable newspaper space, and hence be extremely expensive. However, by using a mailing piece directed at older voters, the candidate can explain his position more fully than would be possible by using other media, and actually save money.

Because it allows for precise targeting, and because it can be used to convey a long message, political campaigns have used direct mail for a wide variety of purposes. However, these two virtues make it an exceptionally useful fund-raising tool. In the 1970s direct mail became the principal means of fund-raising for a variety of candidates, most notably George McGovern who harnessed the direct mail team of Morris Dees and Tom Collins to find approximately 250,000 supporters who financed his presidential campaign.[14] Since that time direct mail has served as the principal means of fund-raising for at least two other presidential campaigns, the 1980 campaign of independent candidate John Anderson, and the 1980 Republican campaign of Congressman Philip Crane. It has been the principal means of fund-raising for a host of lesser candidates.[15]

The dollar costs of direct mail are difficult to talk about because mail pieces can be as simple as a mimeographed flyer or as elaborate as a multicolor, multipage letter and brochure, with pictures, produced on high quality stock. A recent examination of mailpieces that were deemed highly successful in the 1990 campaigns of Dianne Feinstein, Democratic candidate for governor of California, Jesse Helms, Republican candidate for the U.S. Senate from North Carolina, Sidney Yates, Democratic candidate for the House of Representatives from Illinois, and Claudine Schneider, Republican candidate for the U.S. Senate from Rhode Island, revealed that they ranged in cost from $240 per thousand mailpieces, or 24 cents each, for Feinstein's extensive letter, replete with four photographs and a separate donation card, to the $667 per thousand, or 67 cents each spent by Claudine Schneider on an impressive looking mailpiece inviting recipients to purchase tickets to a campaign dinner at which President Bush would speak on Schneider's behalf.[16] Costs for the mailing piece itself generally diminish as the number of pieces purchased increases. However, the larger the mailing the larger the costs of postage and the larger the costs in the use of volunteer time, or payment to a direct mail house that arranges the mailing.

Typical of the prices such firms charge are the 1990 prices of Below, Tobe, and Associates, perhaps the leading campaign computer services and direct mail house for Democratic candidates. In 1990 Below, Tobe, and Associates advertised that they would provide a normal 8 1/2 inch by 11 inch mailpiece, designed as a letter or self-mailer, with two color union printing on the piece itself and one color on the envelope, using an all laser process, multiple fonts, and postal sorting, for a fee of $145,000 per million pieces, or 14.5 cents per piece. The same mailpiece, purchased in the minimum quantity Below, Tobe, and Associates typically handled, 10,000 pieces, would cost $4,430, or 44.3 cents per piece.[17] None of the costs discussed in the preceding paragraphs include the actual cost of postage.

Because, as the figures in the preceding paragraphs suggest, the cost of the mail piece itself can generally be controlled to conform to the campaign's needs, and the size of the mailing can be controlled to accommodate the postage costs, most campaigns are able to use mailings. Direct mailings are the major form of campaign advertising in many lower-level races. Often, the advertisements that the lower-level campaign might use in newspapers or on radio and television are likely to be lost in the large number of political advertisements that flood those media in the weeks before election. Direct mail provides the likelihood that the targeted voters will at least see the message, something that cannot be guaranteed if other media, crowded with political advertisements, are used. Direct mail, which can be made to fit most campaign budgets, can be targeted to specific voter blocs, and can allow the candidates to explain themselves comparatively thoroughly, is often critical in lower-level races.

As with any form of campaign communication, there are principles that have proven successful in the use of direct mail. Hal Malchow, creative director of the November Group, a well-respected political direct mail firm, has recently suggested a variety of guidelines for designing direct mail. They include:

1. Throw Away the Envelopes. Malchow claims that envelopes cost extra money and serve no useful purpose. To gain immediate attention, he recommends using over-sized postcards, unusual shapes, and folded pieces that look nothing like either a letter or a traditional campaign brochure. Such a mailpiece gains immediate attention.

2. Give the voter a reason to read your mailing. Begin the mailpiece in a dramatic and compelling way. The opening panel of the mailpiece should be designed to attract attention through the use of a dramatic headline or an interesting photograph.

3. Localize your message. Because direct mail facilitates very precise targeting it should be used accordingly. If a neighborhood in your district is concerned about a school issue or a proposed highway be sure that the mail sent to that community reflects your interest in their concern, and does not ignore local issues in favor of simply treating issues of more general concern throughout your constituency.

4. Use the 20-second test. Malchow claims that the average voter will give a mailpiece between 20 and 60 seconds. "They will look at the cover, the headlines, the pictures, and often the captions under the photographs. But few people will actually read your literature." Thus he claims that "to be effective, you have to tell your story in a 20-second glance. Can someone in 20 seconds read the headlines, look at the pictures and maybe read the captions, and come away with the basic points of your message? If not, you have not designed a good piece of campaign literature."

5. Use a lettershop. Malchow is an advocate of using a professional mailing organization. He claims that "we all want to save money but don't be a dunce. A lettershop is cheaper than pizza and beer for your volunteers." Malchow has found that for two to five cents per piece, a lettershop will automatically label your pieces, sort and bag the mail, and fully prepare it for the post office in a manner that qualifies for full postal discounts for presorted mail. He claims that "even the poorest campaign should avoid" hand-labeling and sorting third-class mail. He finds such a task to be both so difficult and so time-consuming that the costs of having it done professionally are well worth the expense.[18]

Print Advertisements

Print advertisements in newspapers and magazines have been a part of American campaigns from our nation's inception.[19] Newspaper and magazine advertisements, the two types of print advertisements upon which this section will focus, offer political advertisers several advantages. First, they provide for timeliness. Not only can the campaign plan well in advance to determine precisely when they want an advertisement to run, but normally the campaign can make changes, both in the advertisement content and in the advertisement size, relatively quickly. Consequently, utilizing the daily paper may be an effective means of quickly countering an opposition argument.

Typically, if advertisement space has been purchased in advance, the copy can be changed on 48 hours notice in most metropolitan dailies. Additionally, a new advertisement can be purchased on 48 hours notice.[20] Since skilled writers can normally produce a political advertise-

ment extremely quickly, the daily paper is an efficient means of responding to opponents. Radio commercials offer a similar advantage,
but television is normally not as advantageous. Though television stations can accommodate changes in commercials, it normally takes a
considerably greater effort to produce a television commercial than to
produce a newspaper or radio spot, making it more difficult for the
candidate to respond rapidly through television. This is not to say that
television commercials cannot be changed, for frequently they are. However, typically the process is either slower, or works considerably more
hardship on the campaign.

Newspaper and magazine advertisements also offer the opportunity
for candidates to express themselves more fully than do most other types
of paid advertising. Candidates can present a considerable amount of
material about themselves in a full page, or even a half or quarter page
advertisement. Speaking at the normal rate of speed, a 60-second radio
or television commercial forces the campaign to reduce its message to
150 words or less.[21] By adjusting the size of both the advertisement and
the type used in the advertisement, candidates can easily present a print
message which is three times longer or more, and still create a physically
appealing advertisement. If the message being sent is complex and needs
considerable explanation, newspapers and magazines are often exceptionally good vehicles for getting the message to voters.

The liabilities of print advertising involve targeting and cost. First,
according to most estimates over 12 percent of adult Americans are
functional illiterates.[22] Clearly this substantial group of citizens cannot
be effectively reached by print media. Second, it is frequently difficult
to target specific audiences with newspaper and magazine advertisements.

However, in recent years targeting messages to specific magazine and
newspaper audiences has become easier. Many larger daily papers that
have readerships located in large geographic areas have special sections
or editions that are used in the appropriate geographic area. For example,
both of the daily papers in Cincinnati, Ohio, have special northern Kentucky editions. While the paper is largely the same, the northern Kentucky editions focus the local news coverage more heavily on northern
Kentucky than on Ohio. These editions are distributed to Kentucky
subscribers and used on newsstands in Kentucky, facilitating some geographic targeting. The use of special editions aimed at specific geographic segments of the market has become commonplace for many
larger metropolitan papers.

Smaller newspapers, because their circulation is limited, may also lend
themselves to targeting. Candidates running for offices that include the
entire voting populations of smaller towns may do well to advertise in
the weekly papers that service most smaller communities or suburban

communities. Candidates who have targeted a specific religious, ethnic, or occupational group might also do well to consider advertising in the smaller, often weekly, newspapers that are aimed at these audiences.

Additionally, today many magazine advertisements can also be bought on a regional, or even a zip code, basis. This type of magazine purchase facilitates rather precise targeting. For example, a congressional candidate might choose to advertise in a special interest magazine that she feels is read heavily by a group she has targeted. Moreover, the candidate can limit her purchase to subscribers who live in those zip codes within her congressional district.

An additional advantage to this type of purchase is that it may give a local, regional, or statewide candidate additional stature to be associated with a national publication. The degree to which specific magazines can accommodate this type of advertising varies, as, of course, does price. In recent years, primarily as a function of the growth of computerization within the newspaper and magazine industry, the use of magazines and newspapers for targeted audiences has become more feasible. However, they are still considered "mass media" and cannot be as narrowly focused as direct mail.

Precisely because they are "mass media," read by hundreds of thousands of people, newspaper and magazine costs are often high. For example, a full page weekday black and white advertisement in the *Cincinnati Enquirer*, the dominant daily paper in the 28th largest market in the country, costs $5,050.35. Smaller advertisements are sold at the rate of $39.15 per column inch and their costs are calculated using 129 column inches to the page. A similar ad, run on a Sunday, when the other daily paper in Cincinnati does not print, costs $8,017.35. The costs of smaller Sunday advertisements are calculated at the rate of $62.15 per column inch.[23]

Radio

Radio is an often underestimated vehicle for political advertisements. Surveys suggest that the typical American household has four radios, not including those in cars.[24] Radio also allows for a moderate degree of targeting. While not as precise as direct mail, the wide variety of radio stations found in most areas tends to segment the audience and provides campaigns with the means to target some audiences.

For much of the first half of the twentieth century radio was ranked with the print media as the dominant form of political advertising. However, beginning in the 1950s radio was utilized less and less frequently. The 1952 presidential campaign between General Dwight David Eisenhower and Governor Adlai Stevenson was the last national campaign in which expenditures on radio advertising were roughly equal to those on television.[25] Since 1952 television has superseded radio as the dominant electric media.

Nevertheless, radio retains an important place in the arsenal of political advertising weapons available to candidates. In 1968, after managing Richard Nixon's successful presidential campaign, John Mitchell claimed that if he were to manage the campaign over again the only significant change he would make would be to utilize more radio.[26] The reasons that radio retains considerable popularity among campaign professionals are at least three-fold.[27] First, radio lends itself to advertisements that can vary greatly in length and hence can serve a variety of functions. Second, radio can be targeted. Third, radio is not perceived as an expensive medium.

Radio commercials can be bought in a variety of time lengths, ranging from 10 or 15 seconds, through the more common 30- and 60-second spots, to longer time slots, such as 5 minutes, 15 minutes, or half an hour. Consequently radio can serve a variety of functions. For example, a 10-second spot might consist of nothing more than a brief jingle in which the candidate's name is repeated several times. Repeated use of this jingle can quickly help to establish name recognition. A five-minute commercial allows the candidate to present a reasonably complete analysis of one or perhaps more questions. Purchasing such time slots on television is often either costly or impractical.

Radio can be targeted because certain stations tend to attract certain demographic groups. Easy listening stations, religious stations, foreign language stations, hard rock stations, newstalk stations, oldies stations, all appeal to different demographic groups. Radio gives the campaign an opportunity to target specific audiences and prepare messages aimed at those audiences. It is impossible to say whether radio allows for better targeting than, for example, newspapers and magazines. Every campaign has to evaluate the media available to it and the audiences it wishes to target. Nevertheless, in many communities radio can be used to reach target audiences, and often lends itself to this use better than many other forms of advertising.

Radio is often perceived as an inexpensive advertising medium. Most political campaigns seek to advertise during drive times: 5 A.M. to 9 A.M. and 2 P.M. to 6 P.M. when commuters on their way to and from work help to create the largest radio audiences. During the 1990 elections, a 1-minute commercial, during drive time, on the station with the largest drive time audience in Cincinnati, Ohio, cost $175.[28] While the specific target audiences of a given campaign will help to dictate the choice of stations used, newstalk stations tend to be popular with political campaigns because of the perception that they attract knowledgeable audiences who are more likely to vote than the audiences attracted to many other types of stations. During 1990 a drive time 60-second spot on the highest rated newstalk station in Cincinnati cost $42.[29]

As will become evident in the next section, in some areas the cost of a single television commercial on a local nightly news program may be the equivalent of a week's worth of drive time radio advertising on a highly rated station, or two weeks or more of drive time advertising on a station that may not attract a broad audience, but that appeals to a group targeted by the campaign.

Radio is particularly popular among political advertisers who are campaigning in rural areas and those who are campaigning for lesser offices. Rural areas may be reliant upon papers from larger nearby cities, or on small town weekly papers. Similarly, they are normally reliant upon more urban areas for television. Advertising in the larger paper or on television forces the campaign to purchase an audience that cannot vote in its election and is often simply not cost effective for the rural election. Utilizing the small town paper provides an appropriate audience but that audience can only be addressed once per week. Hence, many rural campaigns find local small town radio stations an attractive option to include in their media mix. Similarly, lower-level elections, often poorly financed, and often covering a smaller geographic area than that serviced by television stations and large circulation metropolitan area papers, find radio a viable option.

Indeed, in some areas radio stations have been forced to put a limit on the number of political commercials they will accept. Typically, such stations limit political campaigns to two drive time advertisements each morning and two each afternoon during the work week, and eight weekend commercials.[30] Such limits are often necessary because the demand of political advertisers during the few weeks preceding the election are often so great that stations could not accommodate their normal advertisers and honor their long term advertising contracts to those advertisers if they accepted all of the political commercials that campaigns wish to air.

Though radio has many virtues as a vehicle for political commercials, it also has drawbacks. Chief among them is that of all of the major forms of media, radio demands the least amount of attention. Most radio is listened to by individuals simultaneously engaged in other activities. Consequently, campaigns are paying for audiences that are not giving them full attention.

Television

Television offers the political advertiser a variety of advantages. First, it is the only advertising medium that appeals to two of our senses, sight and hearing. As a consequence, television is able to convey more in a short time, and typically has a greater impact on the viewer who is getting "twice the message."

Second, of all the mass media, television is often able to produce the largest audiences. The viewership for a popular show often exceeds the readership for the largest circulation papers in a community. If the candidate seeks widespread exposure, television is unmatched as an advertising medium. However, many television programs attract audiences that are politically apathetic, thus somewhat diminishing their value. Because news programs tend to attract audiences that are attentive to current events and more prone to vote, political advertisers normally seek to place their advertisements on news programs and other shows such as "Donahue," "Today," and "Good Morning, America" that attract individuals with an interest in current events.

Somewhat related to the fact that television can provide a large audience is the third advantage of television. In our media oriented society, television lends a degree of credibility. Imagine, if you can, how serious a presidential candidate would be taken if he never used television. Indeed, this was one of the problems that Jesse Jackson faced in 1984. In part because his campaign did not make extensive use of television, he was not viewed as a viable candidate. The legitimacy that television conveys to a campaign has also been recognized by candidates running for lesser offices. Today, in many areas, it is not uncommon to see television commercials on behalf of candidates for every federal and statewide office, and for many local offices such as mayor, city councilman, county prosecutor, judge, or sheriff. Candidates for offices that voters have come to associate with television commercials run a real risk of losing credibility if they do not include television in their media mix. One big city mayor appropriately characterized the situation when he recently observed, "Unfortunately, you have to hit the tube to be considered a big-league candidate."[31]

A final advantage of television is that it does allow for some degree of targeting. As indicated above, certain shows tend to attract audiences composed of individuals who are concerned with current events and prone to vote. Other shows attract audiences that are heavily weighted towards a given demographic group which the campaign may have targeted. Shows like "The Golden Girls" tend to attract an older audience, while a sporting event is more prone to attract a male audience. Even local news shows attract audiences with different demographic appeals, often depending on the nature of the anchorpersons.

In sum, television has become the dominant media of political advertising for a variety of reasons. Because it allows the viewer to use two senses it often is able to convey more than other media. Television can provide wide exposure, helping the unknown candidate become known rapidly. Moreover, it lends a sense of credibility to candidates, and allows for some degree of targeting. However, like all political media, television is not without its liabilities.

The most obvious disadvantage of television is the enormous expense associated with it. In the growing number of campaigns that utilize television it almost invariably is the principal expense that the campaign incurs. Many campaigns budget 75 to 80 percent of their money for television.[32] In 1974 the average campaign for an incumbent U.S. senator cost $556,000. In 1988 to raise sufficient funds to finance an average $3.96 million race for the U.S. Senate, a senator had to raise $5,422 every day for two years. Similarly, in 1974 the average incumbent member of the U.S. House of Representatives spent $54,000 to win the election. In 1988 to raise sufficient funds to finance an average $380,000 race for the U.S. House of Representatives, a congressman had to raise $521 every day for two years.[33] Of course, to keep up, challenger candidates must raise similar amounts of money. Virtually every explanation for this staggering sevenfold increase in the cost of campaigning between 1974 and 1988 focuses primarily on the increased costs of television.[34]

Several examples will make clear how quickly television costs escalate. a single 30-second political spot on the top rated late evening news shows in markets such as Kansas City and Cincinnati ranged in cost from $1,300–1,800 during 1990.[35] An identical spot on the second rated late evening news shows in these markets would cost approximately $800. In 1990 a single 30-second political spot on highly rated newslike morning shows such as "Today," "Phil Donahue," or "Sally Jessie Raphael" cost between $400 to $450 in medium sized markets such as Cincinnati. A 30-second spot on syndicated game shows such as "Wheel of Fortune" and "Jeopardy," which are typically aired right after the local news and right before the start of the network prime time schedule, and hence often favored by campaigns, sold for $800 in the Cincinnati market during 1990. A single 30-second spot on a highly rated prime time show of the type favored by political campaigns, such as "60 Minutes," sold for $2,600 in the Cincinnati market in 1990. A single 30-second spot on other prime time shows favored by political candidates, such as "Monday Night Football," which is often used by political candidates who have targeted males because it is one of the few prime time shows that attracts a predominantly male audience, or "Roseanne," which consistently was rated among the five most popular shows, cost $3,000 or more in the Cincinnati market during 1990.[36]

Thus in 1990 a very limited television campaign consisting of a daily 30-second spot on one daytime show that political campaigns favor, such as "Donahue," plus a daily 30-second spot on one syndicated game show such as "Wheel of Fortune," plus a daily 30-second spot on a top rated late news show, costs a campaign almost $16,000 per week in a market like Cincinnati. Keep in mind, this very limited advertising campaign includes only three commercials a day, for a five-day week. Moreover, it does not include any prime time advertisements and Cincinnati is not among the largest 25 media markets in the nation. A campaign that included an occasional prime time commercial, or also utilized the weekends, or was waged in a larger media market would quickly escalate the costs. Clearly, the costs of television advertising can be expensive.[37]

In addition to the cost of purchasing time, television involves more elaborate production costs than other media. Some authorities have suggested that a good rule of thumb is to estimate the cost of television production at 20–30 percent the cost of air time. This is substantially higher than the production costs for other forms of media.[38]

A second difficulty with television is one that is a function of geography. In many parts of the nation targeting with television is difficult and candidates may be forced to pay for audiences that cannot vote in their elections. For example, the media markets served by stations in such cities as St. Louis, Kansas City, Philadelphia, New York City, Louisville, Washington, D.C., and Boston, just to name a few, are composed of residents of more than one state. Thus candidates running for any local office, and even state offices, are forced to pay for audiences that cannot participate in their election. While this problem also exists for other media serving communities such as these, the expenses of television heighten the problem.

A third potential problem with television is that many candidates do not project well using television. Though some candidates like Ronald Reagan and Jesse Helms entered politics after first working in radio and television, and others such as former Connecticut Congressman Toby Moffett and former Cincinnati Mayor Jerry Springer had such an affinity for television that when they left elected office they became local news anchors, many candidates are not comfortable with television. This does not by any means preclude the use of television, but it does mean that a realistic assessment of the candidate's abilities must be made and that if the candidate is found wanting the campaign may have to change its advertising strategy.[39]

In sum, just as with any other advertising media, television offers political candidates both advantages and disadvantages. Though campaigns have grown increasingly reliant upon television, the experiences of candidates like Harriet Woods remind us that you cannot win most elections by relying almost exclusively on television. Television commercials often have a strong impact on viewers who must utilize two of their senses as they attend to the commercials. Television can also provide a massive audience for the campaign's messages, contribute to the candidate's credibility, and allow for limited targeting. However, the costs of television are extremely high, especially in many races where candidates find themselves paying for audiences that cannot participate in the election. Moreover, production costs for television are also high and many candidates do not perform well on television. All of these factors must be weighed as the campaign develops its own unique media mix.

CAMPAIGN ADVERTISING STRATEGIES

The circumstances of the campaign normally dictate the use of one of four basic patterns in the purchase of radio and television time. Since radio and television constitute a major portion of the advertising of most campaigns, the strategies used for purchasing radio and television time typically characterize the entire campaign's advertising strategy. With some differences that are reflected in the unique virtues of each form of media, the basic radio and television strategy is often commonly extended to the use of display graphics, direct mail, and print media. In this section we will briefly examine the four most common overall campaign advertising strategies.[40]

The Spurt Strategy

This strategy is often used by candidates who are not well known at the outset of the campaign. The strategy is to "spurt" early in the campaign, often four to six months before the election, purchasing a large amount of radio and television time, for one to two weeks. The use of radio and television is often supplemented with an early round of newspaper advertisements and an early effort at distributing a large number of yard signs, bumper stickers, buttons, and other display graphics. The point of this early spurt is to build name recognition and help establish the candidate as a credible contender for the office.

The campaign, having now utilized a reasonable amount of its resources early, then typically eliminates or drastically reduces its use of radio and television for a long period of time. During this period the campaign may well focus on direct mail efforts, often using direct mail both to target specific audiences for persuasive messages and to help raise funds to replenish the monies spent on the early spurt, deemed necessary to establish name recognition.

Finally, the campaign makes a final "spurt," purchasing considerable radio and television time from the morning of the election backwards as far as it can, hopefully at least a week or more. As with the original spurt, the final radio and television spurt is accompanied by the use of other media. The point of this strategy is to allow the candidate to open strongly and close strongly. While all candidates seek to close strongly, those who start at a disadvantage often utilize the spurt strategy to get them into the race. The candidate who starts out with little name recognition typically has many problems. The initial spurt in advertising spending will hopefully create a spurt in the candidate's standing in the polls, enhance the candidate's credibility, facilitate greater fund-raising, encourage more people to volunteer support, and, in sum, simply get the campaign moving.

The Fast Finish Strategy

This strategy goes by a variety of names, including the Silky Sullivan Strategy, the Miracle Braves Strategy, or the '51 Giants Strategy. Just as the famous California bred race horse and those famous baseball teams started very slowly, only to close with a rush and win at the wire, some candidates choose to start slowly, and close with a rush, expecting to win on election day.

Typically this strategy is implemented by buying a complete schedule of radio and television advertisements for the last portion of the election. Buying backwards from election day, the campaign purchases a complete schedule of radio and television time for as many days as it can afford, normally at least a week, and further back if it can afford it. Then, depending on what the campaign can afford, still buying backwards, the campaign gradually diminishes the amount of commercials it purchases each day. The effect of this type of purchase is that voters see the campaign starting very slowly, with a scattering of commercials. Gradually the advertising increases until voters are completely saturated in the week immediately preceding the election. Similarly, other media efforts are intensified as the election draws closer.

Most campaigns will use some variation of this strategy. Clearly candidates want their messages to have the greatest impact and feel that is best achieved by surrounding the voter with their message in the days immediately preceding the election. Candidates who start from a position of strength find this strategy particularly appealing, since they often feel that their initial strength allows them to husband their resources until near the end of the campaign. By then, concentrating their advertising in a limited time, they can purchase so much airtime in the last days of the campaign that they are confident their messages cannot be missed by voters.

The Really Big Show Strategy

This strategy is designed to capitalize on free news coverage. Named after the expression frequently used by 1950s and 1960s television variety show host Ed Sullivan to describe his show, this strategy is built around several major events that are scheduled periodically throughout the campaign. For example, in a congressional race the candidate holds a press conference and immediately follows it up with several speeches making a major accusation about the shortcomings of his opponent. Second, the candidate has a debate with his opponent. Third, a major national figure comes to town to speak on behalf of the candidate. Each of these three occurrences is a major event in the campaign. Moreover, the candidate has considerable control over their timing.

Using the "really big show" strategy, the candidate will focus his advertising around those events which are likely to receive considerable free media coverage on the news. He will increase his paid advertising at the time of the press conference and speeches, reinforcing through advertising what he is saying in the conference and speeches. He will increase his advertising at the time of the debate, reinforcing positions he takes in the debate or perhaps using cinema verité and testimonial commercials to emphasize how effective he was in the debate and reinforce the points he made during the debate. He will increase his advertising immediately preceding, during, and after the visit by the major national figure, better linking himself to that figure and basking in that figure's prominence and credibility.

By increasing his advertising at the time he is naturally receiving greater free coverage in the news, the candidate turns a campaign event into a "really big show." Often, because of the proximity in timing between the news coverage and the commercials, and depending on how his advertisements are handled, the paid media blends with the free news coverage in the mind of the voter. Candidates using this strategy will generally provide that at least one major event takes place within a few days of the election, so that they can combine elements of this strategy with the fast finish strategy. Moreover, this strategy can also be blended with the "spurt" strategy by coordinating the early media effort with an important campaign event.

The Cruise Control Strategy

This strategy is particularly appealing for candidates who are clearly ahead and are striving to maintain their lead. Just as the cruise control of a car allows the driver to drive at a steady speed, this strategy calls for the campaign to advertise at a steady rate. The campaign makes what the media industry calls a "flat buy," purchasing a constant number of commercials each day during the stages of the campaign when media will be used.

Often this strategy is combined with the fast finish strategy, so that the campaign makes a flat buy for several weeks or a month prior to the last week or two of the campaign, when it then increases its advertising. This strategy allows the candidate who is ahead to remain constantly visible for a long period of time, and then finish strongly.

In sum, the overall advertising strategies of political campaigns can be characterized by the way they purchase radio and television time. Most campaigns utilize one of four strategies, or some combination of them. Factors such as the availability of funds, and the candidates' standing in the polls, enter into the decision about an overall advertising strategy.

MEDIA AND OTHER TYPES OF POLITICAL CONSULTANTS

As part of the 1986 U.S. Senate race in Georgia, an Atlanta television station arranged a debate between Frank Greer and Mike Murphy. Yet neither man was a candidate for the senate. Rather, they were the respective media consultants for U.S. Senate candidates Wyche Fowler, Jr., and Mack Mattingly.[41] This debate dramatically illustrates the growing importance of political consultants, especially media consultants, in contemporary politics. While political consultants provide a variety of services to their candidates, most of those services are advertising and media related. Hence, we will conclude this chapter on the practices of political advertising by briefly examining the rise and growth of political consulting, and the functions of political consultants.

History of Political Consulting

Virtually every political candidate, from Washington's day forward, has turned to a group of advisors for advice on getting elected, and often for advice on governing. However, it was not until Calvin Coolidge turned to Edward Bernays that political figures began to seek the advice of individuals with extensive backgrounds and expertise in advertising, public relations, and polling. Few political figures listened to Bernays, a public relations counselor, who was far ahead of his time in advising candidates to make better use of the media and polling. Nevertheless, his ideas foreshadowed much of what political campaigning has become in the last decades of the twentieth century.[42]

In 1934 Californians Clem Whitaker and his wife Leona Baxter founded the public relations firm of Whitaker and Baxter, which from its very inception took on political clients, normally California Republicans. In that year the firm helped defeat the popular writer Upton Sinclair, the Democratic candidate for governor. From that point forward political candidates sought their services. Whitaker and Baxter was a pioneer firm, and though they eventually diversified to handle a wide variety of accounts, they were still helping candidates as late as 1967 when they handled Shirley Temple's unsuccessful congressional race.[43]

In 1952 television was first used as an advertising medium in a presidential campaign. The 1952 campaigns of both General Dwight David Eisenhower and Illinois Governor Adlai Stevenson made use of television. Although both candidates had reservations about television, both campaigns secured the services of advertising agencies to help produce television commercials and serve in a variety of other functions.[44]

The fact that media consultants, whether in the employ of political consulting firms or advertising agencies, were in politics to stay was evident in 1956 when Stevenson again challenged Eisenhower. Accepting the Democratic nomination Stevenson decried the use of mass media advertising techniques, claiming that "the idea that you can merchandise candidates for high office like breakfast cereal—that you can gather votes like box tops—is I think, the ultimate indignity in the democratic process." Yet, Stevenson made this very remark from a platform that had been redesigned by an advertising agency, to a national convention whose activities were being orchestrated in no small part by that same agency, for the benefit of the television audience.[45]

By the 1960s campaigns were being waged more and more in the media and political consultants were becoming more and more conspicuous in the conduct of those campaigns. Stuart Spensor, Bill Roberts, David Garth, Tony Schwartz, and a host of other consultants began to bring high technology to political campaigning throughout the 1960s.

In the last two decades two factors have combined to make political consultants essential players in virtually every major political campaign. First, getting elected has become a perpetual job. Thus helping candidates has become a perpetual job. In the past it was difficult to work as a political consultant, simply because during nonelection years the political consultant had no clients.

But the 1970s witnessed the advent of the perpetual candidate.[46] In the footsteps of the perpetual candidate has come the perpetual political consultant. As Burdett Loomis has incisively illustrated, since 1974 "new breed" politicians have encouraged the growth of administrative staffs, subcommittee and committee staffs, campaign staffs, political action committees and their staffs, a variety of political caucuses and their staffs, a variety of task forces and their staffs, a host of party organizations and their staffs, as well as the expansion of lobby groups and political action committees. Though the growth of these enterprises is perhaps most evident in Washington, it is also apparent in virtually every state capital as well. These organizations allow candidates to "warehouse" consultants. That is, as Ken Kling, former executive director of the Virginia Republican party and a consultant to a wide variety of candidates observes, candidates, especially incumbents, can find jobs for trusted political operatives that enable those operatives to maintain themselves during off election periods yet allow those operatives to work on behalf of the candidate on a moment's notice during the election cycle.[47] In addition to the increased opportunities for employment of those with the skills of political consultants, political consulting itself is now a longer job. Campaigns have grown in length, thus guaranteeing the consultant longer employment. In sum, since the 1970s political consulting has become a viable career for a large number of individuals.

Second, it has become financially feasible to engage in political consulting as a career. Ten years ago there were 50 members of the American Association of Political Consultants, the principal professional organization for political consultants. As of the summer of 1990 there were over 700 members. Moreover, as a recent article in *Campaigns and Elections* suggestions, this figure is no doubt just the tip of the iceberg.[48]

The rapid growth of the political consulting profession is a consequence of a variety of changes in our political system during the last three decades. From the standpoint of candidates, political consultants provided two big advantages over their own campaign staffs and the efforts of party professionals. First, they provided a bigger bang for the buck, a greater return on the money spent in the campaign. Consultants were specialists in designing media messages and insuring that those messages were transmitted most effectively. Whether it was the consultant who specialized in setting up phone banks, or coaching political debaters, or producing television advertisements, the consultant provided the campaign with a better return on its dollars. Second, political consultants could provide campaigns with public opinion polling designed and executed specifically to help the campaign locate voters and prepare messages for those voters. Hence, the consulting profession grew rapidly in the period 1960–1990 because it provided candidates with highly desired services.[49]

Moreover, during the last decades, the growth of political consulting services has made this field one in which growing numbers of people are able to make a living. Though fees vary from consultant to consultant, by the late 1980s it was not unusual for media consultants to charge a straight fee of $25,000 to $75,000 for a statewide race and receive a 15 percent cut of the money spent on media advertising time. With statewide races, as we have seen, now routinely running $3 million or more, and the majority of that money going into the purchase of media time, some media consultants may make $250,000 to $500,000 for a campaign.[50]

The typical consulting fee for a variety of other types of political service, such as setting up a precinct organization, or a phone bank operation, by the late 1980s had reached $1,000 per day.[51] An all purpose consulting firm that will develop a campaign strategy and offer advice on implementing that strategy will typically charge base fees of approximately $5,000 for a congressional race, and $10,000 for a statewide race. Additional fees will depend on the specific services provided. Most consultants or consulting firms are also available on a monthly retainer fee of $2,000 to $6,000, which allows the candidate and his staff unlimited phone contact with the consultant and also provides that the consultant will be in the campaign several days a month. Though the costs of doing business are often high and these fees are not all profit, for some, political consulting has become a viable way to make a living.[52]

It should be remembered, however, that as with the time of any professional plumber, electrician, lawyer, or doctor, the time of political consultants is limited. Most shy away from taking on more than four to five races simultaneously.[53] Hence, political consulting is no longer the province of enthusiastic amateurs, perhaps occasionally taking leaves from their other positions to help the candidate of their choice. While this type of individual is still a feature of many campaigns and provides valuable services, today political consulting is a fast-growing profession.

Though this discussion has focused on the economic aspects of consulting, because it was not until the field became an economically viable one that people could enter it on a full-time basis, virtually everyone involved in political consulting will note that monetary rewards are a secondary motivation. The primary motivation of most consultants is to make an impact on the political process. Most consultants have strong political beliefs. They work for like-minded candidates. And, invariably, consultants will claim that the most satisfying aspect of their job is to "win one you're not supposed to win."[54]

FUNCTIONS OF POLITICAL CONSULTANTS

Political consultants can provide candidates with virtually any service necessary in the conduct of a campaign, including help in targeting voters, setting up a precinct organization, setting up and utilizing phone banks, polling the electorate, preparing and utilizing direct mail, preparing and utilizing radio and television commercials, writing and preparing to deliver a speech, and preparing for a debate.[55] A full service political consulting firm can provide clients with virtually all of these services, though it may well specialize in a more limited number. Small agencies will limit their work to providing a group of related services. It would be impossible to discuss all of the services provided by consulting firms in the remainder of this chapter. Rather, we will briefly focus on four services that are directly related to the campaign's efforts to communicate through advertising.

Writers

The preparation and communication of messages is at the heart of any campaign. Hence, virtually all consultants are involved in some form of writing. In the chapter on public speaking we discussed political speechwriting. Consultants who specialize in writing can often handle virtually all of the advertising writing chores in the campaign: radio and television scripts, press releases, preparation of copy for all printed materials such as brochures, mailpieces, or newspaper and magazine advertisements. There are techniques unique to writing each of these types of advertisements well, and often in larger campaigns different individuals will handle each. In small and mid-sized campaigns the writer who often serves as the press secretary and speechwriter is generally involved in the preparation of scripts for commercials.

Speech Coaches

One of the basic services frequently provided to candidates at the schools for candidates run by the Republican and Democratic party organizations is speech coaching. Many consulting firms will provide candidates with coaching in public speaking, and, if necessary, in debate. Although much of his early career was spent in television production, and his firm does considerable television work with candidates, Roger Ailes is also among the best known consultants to specialize in coaching candidates for speeches and debates. Based on his experiences, Ailes has identified what he calls the ten most common communication problems. Depending on the individual candidate's strengths and weaknesses, speech coaches will normally work to help the candidate overcome one or more of the ten problems Ailes identifies.

1. Lack of initial rapport with listeners
2. Stiffness or woodenness in use of body
3. Presentation of material is intellectually oriented, forgetting to involve the audience emotionally
4. Speaker seems uncomfortable because of fear of failure
5. Poor use of eye contact and facial expression
6. Lack of humor
7. Speech direction and intent unclear due to improper preparation
8. Inability to use silence for impact
9. Lack of energy, causing inappropriate pitch pattern, speech rate, and volume
10. Use of boring language and a lack of interesting material[56]

Direct Mail Specialists

The preparation of direct mail pieces, and in many instances providing the lists of individuals to whom such pieces are sent, is a specialty of several political consulting firms. Perhaps the best known consultant to specialize in direct mail is Richard A. Viguerie, and his story is highly illustrative of how direct mail specialists operate.

In 1960–1961 Viguerie worked in the Houston campaign offices of Senator John Tower. Soon after, he was employed by Young Americans for Freedom, a group for conservative young people, and was placed in charge of the organization's fund-raising. Recalling his early experiences, Viguerie states,

I'm basically a pretty shy person and I did not feel comfortable asking for money directly. So I began writing letters instead, and they seemed to work. So I wrote more and more letters and before many months, direct mail was my whole focus—for fundraising, subscriptions for *The New Guard* [Young Americans for Freedom publication], YAF membership, everything.[57]

Quickly recognizing the power of direct mail, Viguerie used the simplest of means to begin to develop a mailing list. After the 1964 election he copied the names and addresses of those who had given $50 or more to the Goldwater campaign from the contributor records that, by law, were on file with the clerk of the House of Representatives. This effort provided him with over 12,000 names that became his first mailing list.[58]

Direct mail consultants, like Viguerie, are continually building their lists, adding new names after each campaign in which they are involved. The use of sophisticated computers and printers enable them to handle thousands of pieces of mail quickly, and further enable them to tailor lists to the geographic and demographic needs of a client.

Political consultants who specialize in direct mail typically provide two services for their clients. First, they can provide help in designing and producing the actual mail pieces. Second, they can provide lists of individuals to whom such pieces should be sent. This second service is highly valuable for major national campaigns, and other larger races.

However, in smaller races often the candidate and campaign staff can develop a good mailing list based on their associates, the lists of other candidates who have run in the same area, or the lists of the local party. Candidates who contract to utilize the lists of consulting firms must be certain that the lists are likely to be of help to them and almost invariably will want to supplement those lists. One of the principal ways in which direct mail firms increase the size and value of their lists is by constantly adding names from the campaigns in which they work.

Specialists in Television Commercial Production and Placement

Though modern technology now enables campaigns to produce radio commercials rapidly and inexpensively, because of the larger expense involved, and the technical expertise necessary, today few campaigns will even attempt to produce and air television commercials without the advice of consultants who specialize in such work. Very frequently campaigns will employ local advertising agencies that will work closely with political consultants and members of the campaign staff in the production and placement of television commercials.

This team effort has much to recommend it. Clearly the candidate and campaign staff must make the final decision. Aware of the issues in their particular campaign, they will certainly be receptive to the advice of consultants, but they must make the final decisions on what they want to accomplish with the commercials. Is their goal name recognition, development of the candidate's image, development of the candidate's position on a given issue or group of issues, or responding to an unfair attack by the opponent? Whatever the basic purpose of the commercials, it is the candidate who ultimately must decide. Moreover, the campaign is aware of the local peculiarities of the district, region, or state.

Political consultants can help in a variety of ways. They can suggest types of commercials that can implement the candidate's goals. They may be able to point out how other campaigns successfully, or unsuccessfully, handled similar problems. They are aware of what approaches are working or failing in other parts of the country, and hence might or might not work in this region. Depending on their background they will help script and produce the commercial, utilizing their skills in every phase of production including casting, shooting, and editing. In many campaigns the consultant takes personal control of creating the commercials.

The advertising firm or the consulting firm will also purchase air time. A good advertising firm knows the demographics of the local media market and is experienced with dealing with the local media. They can negotiate the best rates, and place commercials so that they will be seen by target audiences. Some consulting firms will also provide the campaign with these services. Additionally, members of the advertising firm may also be heavily involved in the writing and production teams that create the commercials.

In larger campaigns it is not uncommon to frequently test the commercials before they air. The consulting firm, or the advertising agency, normally utilize a variety of sophisticated techniques in order to establish viewer reaction to the commercials. Time constraints and the added expenses in dollars and labor that this involves often make this impractical. Nevertheless, if pretesting is utilized it often enables the campaign to avoid problems and provides reassurance that effective commercials are being used.

Clearly campaigns can make use of a wide variety of political consultants. In this section we have treated those consultants who we feel impact most directly on political advertising. It is significant to note that although we have not treated such consulting specialties as the public opinion pollster, the fund-raising specialist, or the precinct organizer, it could well be argued that even these consultants impact on political communication and political advertising. We would not dispute that argument in the least, for it gives further credence to the principal thesis of this book, that communication is at the heart of political campaigning.

CONCLUSIONS

This chapter has illustrated some of the practical concerns that must be confronted when using political advertising. We have first noted the importance of advance planning in the development of the campaign's use of political advertising. Second we have examined the five principal advertising mediums used in political campaigns: display graphics, direct mail, print, radio, and television. We have illustrated the virtues and liabilities of each medium for political advertising. Third, we have examined the four principal overall advertising strategies commonly utilized in political campaigns: spurt, fast finish, really big show, and cruise control. Fourth, we have examined political consultants who have, largely because of their mastery of advertising media, become key players in contemporary political campaigns. We have examined the history of political consulting, observing the rapid growth and professionalization of political consulting in the last three decades. Moreover, we have examined the functions of those political consultants who are most directly concerned with political communication and advertising: writers, speech coaches, direct mail specialists, and television specialists.

NOTES

1. The Bond vs. Woods race was commented upon in many national publications as it developed. However, by far the best work on that race, upon which this account relies heavily, is Deborah L. Chasteen, "The Effect of Television Advertising on the 1986 Harriet Woods U.S. Senate Campaign" (Ph.D. diss., University of Kansas, 1989). For background on Woods and Bond including an analysis of Woods's decision to rely heavily on television advertising see pp. 18–20.

2. The figures found in this paragraph are drawn from Chasteen, "Effect of Television Advertising," pp. 26–34. Chasteen was provided access to many of the internal working documents of the Woods campaign.

3. Chasteen, "Effect of Television Advertising," pp. 125–126.

4. Ibid., p. 126.

5. Ibid., pp. 48, 57. The "crying farmer" commercials consisted of a sequence of three commercials that showed Harriet Woods talking with a family whose farm had been foreclosed by Mutual Benefit Life, a company whose board of directors included Kit Bond.

6. Ibid., p. 57. For an excellent analysis of the consequences of these commercials, which focuses on the inability of the Woods campaign to anticipate Bond's response to the "crying farmer" commercials, see Chasteen, "Effect of Television Advertising," pp. 48–64.

7. Ibid., p. 126.

8. Campaign materials, primarily buttons and bumper stickers, using all of these slogans are in the collection of one of the authors, Robert V. Friedenberg.

9. Ibid.

10. All of the price figures cited in this paragraph are drawn from discussions with two of the largest suppliers of display graphic advertising in the Cincinnati area. The authors wish to thank Harry Pallas of A–1 Acme Advertising and Lucy Chagares of Associated Premium Corporation for their helpfulness in providing price figures for a variety of display graphic items.

11. These figures were provided by Tom Hess of Norton Outdoor Advertising, Cincinnati, Ohio, in a phone interview with Robert V. Friedenberg, April 28, 1990. Though there are a variety of ways to purchase outdoor advertising, and the rates vary based on such factors as the size of the boards, and the number of months for which they are being rented, these figures represent the most common way that billboards are currently purchased by political figures in the Cincinnati area.

12. This figure was provided by John Himmelstach of Lithographics Incorporated, Cincinnati, Ohio, in a phone interview with Robert V. Friedenberg, April 28, 1990.

13. Direct mail has often been called a "high interest, low backlash, communications vehicle" in campaign seminars conducted by the Republican National Committee and in the literature that committee has produced for candidates and their staffs. See, for example, Republican National Committee, *Campaign Seminars: Campaign Graphics, Direct Mail, and Outdoor Advertising* (Washington, D.C.: Republican National Committee, no date of publication), p. 5.

14. Richard A. Viguerie, *The New Right: We're Ready to Lead* (Falls Church, Va.: The Viguerie Company, 1980), pp. 125–26. Viguerie, the principal direct mail fund-raiser of the conservative movement, credits the McGovern campaign with making political figures aware of the enormous potential of direct mail as a medium of political fund-raising.

15. Richard A. Viguerie argues that direct mail is exceptionally useful for underdog, nonestablishment candidates. Ibid., p. 124.

16. "The Mailbag," *Campaigns and Elections* (April–May 1990): 46–47. The Yates mailing was the first of six mailings designed to acquaint voters with the congressman's record on a variety of issues and remind them that Yates was "an old friend" who was "doing well" for his district. This brochure, with a large picture of Yates on the inside, cost $273 per thousand. The Helms mailing,

which featured endorsement letters from President Bush, Vice-President Quayle, and Senator Dole, cost $450 per thousand.

17. "Below, Tobe, and Associates, Inc. Price List," provided to Robert V. Friedenberg upon request. Current price lists can be obtained from Below, Tobe, and Associates, Inc., 4745 All Road, Los Angeles, California, 90292 or 7801 Norfolk Ave. Suite 102, Bethesda, Maryland, 20814.

18. Hal Malchow, "10 Ways To Design In-House Voter Mail that Works," *Campaigns and Elections* (June–July 1990): 50–51.

19. Newspaper advertisements played a role in the nation's earliest elections. See Robert J. Dinkin, *Campaigning in America: A History of Election Practices* (New York: Greenwood Press, 1989), pp. 3–4, 14–16. Also see Kathleen Hall Jamieson, *Packaging the Presidency: A History and Criticism of Presidential Campaign Advertising* (New York: Oxford University Press, 1984), p. 5.

20. This information was provided by Deborah Holden of the *Cincinnati Enquirer* advertising sales department in phone interviews with Robert V. Friedenberg, April 27 and April 28, 1990.

21. Studies have repeatedly indicated that Americans usually speak at a rate of between 120 and 150 words per minute. See Stephen E. Lucas, *The Art of Public Speaking* (New York: Random House, 1989), p. 237.

22. This figure is drawn from "Bush, Governors Set Goals," *Facts on File: World News Digest With Index*, March 2, 1990, p. 141.

23. The cost figures used throughout this paragraph were provided by Deborah Holden. See note 20.

24. Republican National Committee, *Campaign Seminars: Media Advertising* (Washington, D.C.: Republican National Committee, no date of publication), p. 12.

25. Dinkin, *Campaigning in America*, p. 167.

26. Mitchell is quoted in Dan D. Nimmo, *The Political Persuaders* (Englewood Cliffs, N.J.: Prentice-Hall, 1970), p. 134.

27. Radio consistently seems to be more popular among Republican campaign professionals than among Democrats. There is no clear explanation of why Republicans tend to like radio to a greater degree than Democratic campaign professionals. Nevertheless, Republican political advisers will, more commonly than their Democratic counterparts, claim that radio is an "important" campaign communications vehicle, and also laud it as especially cost effective. See Republican National Committee, *Campaign Seminars: Media Advertising*, p. 12.

28. These figures were provided by Julene Valitutto of radio WLW's sales department in a phone interview with Robert V. Friedenberg, April 17, 1990.

29. These figures were provided by Mike Evans of radio WCKY's sales department in a phone interview with Robert V. Friedenberg, April 17, 1990.

30. Ibid. This is the practice of WCKY radio in Cincinnati and according to Mike Evans of their sales department this or similar limits are commonplace in Cincinnati and many other large media markets.

31. Cincinnati mayor Charles Luken, quoted in David Wells, "If You Run, Bring Money," *Cincinnati Enquirer*, October 8, 1989, p. B1.

32. While figures such as these are now commonplace for major national and statewide races, David Wells's recent article on campaign expenses in one metropolitan area during the 1988 elections, "If You Run, Bring Money," is especially

revealing. Examining a wide variety of races, including judicial contests, Wells found candidates consistently spending 70 to 80 percent of their money on television commercials.

33. Charles Green, "Congress for Sale?," *Cincinnati Enquirer*, October 8, 1989, p. B1.

34. Ibid. While a variety of other factors including the greater use of polling services, the greater use of direct mail, and the general lengthening of campaigns have undeniably contributed to increasing campaign costs, no authority would deny that the increased use of television is the primary factor causing the dramatic increase in campaign expenses. Moreover, this increase has far exceeded increases in the consumer price index throughout the 1970s and 1980s. Indeed, Montague Kern reports that as of 1984 media consultants testifying at congressional hearings reported that media costs in major markets doubled every four years. See Montague Kern, *30-Second Politics: Political Advertising in the 1980s* (New York: Praeger, 1989), fn. 8, p. 17. On television expenses and their effects also see Dinkin, *Campaigning in America*, pp. 164–68 and Sig Michelson, *From Whistle Stop to Sound Bite: Four Decades of Politics and Television* (New York: Praeger, 1989), pp. 3–5, 16–18.

35. Chasteen, "Effects of Television Advertising," p. 27 claims that the cost of such a commercial in Kansas City during 1986 was $1,400. Between April 26 and May 2, 1990, Robert V. Friedenberg held a series of phone interviews with the specialists in political advertising sales at the three network affiliate stations in Cincinnati. At that time the fixed rate cost for a 30-second spot on the highest rated local new show was $1,800.

All of the cost figures cited in the text and notes reflect fixed rates, which guarantee that the commercial will air. Candidates may gamble and pay lower rates but they run the risk that they will be preempted. Typically, most candidates will not gamble during the last ten days of the campaign, though some will place advertisements at lower rates earlier in the campaign and gamble that they will not be preempted by nonpolitical advertisers willing to pay more.

36. Ibid.

37. The calculation of political advertising rates is highly complex because in addition to the normal variety of rate options, political advertising is also governed by a variety of federal, and often state or local laws. The complexity is such that at each of the three network affiliate stations Friedenberg contacted, only one salesperson was allowed to handle political advertising. That individual was clearly designated as the station's specialist but, as one of them indicated, nevertheless frequently spoke to the station's attorney. For a sense of the complexities involved see the sections on discounted rates and other regulations in Paul S. Hoff *Beyond the 30-Second Spot: Enhancing the Media's Role in Congressional Campaigns* (Washington, D.C.: Center for Responsive Politics, 1988), pp. 69–92.

38. Robert Agranoff, *The Management of Election Campaigns* (Boston: Holbrook Press, 1976), p. 346. In contrast, Agranoff suggests the rule of thumb for radio production should be about 15 percent of time cost and for newspapers about 25 percent of space cost. All of these figures seem somewhat high, based on the author's experience in a wide variety of campaigns. This may be a function of changing technology, which has helped reduce a variety of production costs in

the past 15 years. However, Agranoff's key point remains valid. Television production costs are appreciably greater than those of other media.

39. Typically the change will be to a form of commercial that does not require the candidate to be on the camera. One of the most successful such adjustments was engineered by New York Governor Nelson Rockefeller's 1966 reelection campaign managers. At the outset of the campaign Rockefeller had several major political liabilities, which caused his management team to conclude that putting him on television was counterproductive. Instead they produced a series of advertisements featuring a puppet fish which focused on his many accomplishments as governor. Later in the campaign, when his standing had increased, Rockefeller appeared in his own advertisements. See Edwin Diamond and Stephen Bates, *The Spot: The Rise of Political Advertising on Television*, rev. ed. (Cambridge: MIT Press, 1988), pp. 318–19 for an account of this campaign.

40. These strategies are adapted and in some cases renamed from those presented in Republican National Committee, *Campaign Seminars: Media Advertising*, pp. 21–22.

41. "What's In A Name? For Consultants, Much Cash," *Congressional Quarterly Guide To Current American Government* (Fall 1988): 28.

42. Sidney Blumenthal, *The Permanent Campaign: Inside The World of Elite Political Operatives* (Boston: Beacon Press, 1980), pp. 11–26.

43. Ibid., pp. 143–47.

44. For an excellent discussion of the use of consultants, advertising agencies, and media in the 1952 campaign see Chapter 2 of Jamieson, *Packaging the Presidency*.

45. For a brief discussion of the rise of political advertising and media influence on the 1956 campaign, which includes the quotation from Stevenson, see Stan Le Roy Wilson, *Mass Media/Mass Culture* (New York: Random House, 1989), p. 309.

46. In his remarkably incisive study, Burdett Loomis claims that the huge freshman class of "Watergate" congressmen elected in 1974 changed the face of American politics by combining ambition and entrepreneurship to perpetually work at acquiring resources to guarantee their reelection and to push their favorite policies. Since 1974 the "new breed" politician, Loomis argues, approaches Congress as an enterprise and seeks to develop a group of personnel resources, such as those discussed in this paragraph, that can be relied upon to further their own election and policy aspirations. See Burdett Loomis, *The New American Politician: Ambition, Entrepreneurship, and the Changing Face of Political Life* (New York: Basic Books, 1988), pp. 1–52, 181–208.

47. Ken Kling, in an interview with Robert V. Friedenberg, June 11, 1990, Washington, D.C.

48. Chris Meyer, "Ten Years in the Making," *Campaigns and Elections* (April–May 1990): 39.

49. This paragraph is based largely on the analysis of Charles Press and Kenneth Verburg, *American Politics and Journalists* (Glenview, Ill.: Scott, Foresman and Company, 1988), pp. 155–56.

50. The figures used in this paragraph are drawn from "What's In A Name? For Consultants, Much Cash," p. 25.

51. These figures are based on interviews with a wide variety of political

consultants. Among them, Ken Kling of S.K.C. and Associates, a lobbying and consulting firm, Jim Weber, of Eddie Mahe and Associates, an all purpose consulting firm, and Gary Koops, press secretary and campaign manager in a variety of congressional races, currently press secretary for the Republican Congressional Campaign Committee.

52. Larger political consulting firms who contract to handle a variety of races during a single election period are normally headed by one or more individuals with exceptional reputations. These individuals serve as "magnets" to attract clients. Often they are heavily involved in the formulation of basic strategies, and subsequently turn much of the work over to their associates, and/or the local campaign staff to implement, returning on a periodic basis to help the candidate with major events such as the filming of commercials, or preparing for a debate. Like any business, the consulting firm must judge the often considerable costs of doing business: labor, materials, travel, etc. when establishing fees.

53. Most consultants recognize that if they spread themselves too thin they run the risk of being involved in losing races and hence jeopardizing future employment. Additionally, today most candidates, expecting their consultants to provide them with considerable time and service, shy away from those who have already committed to a large number of other races.

54. This sentiment is constantly voiced when consultants are asked about the satisfactions of their job. It came up in every interview conducted for this chapter.

55. Perhaps the best way to get a feel for the wide variety of services provided by political consulting firms is to simply examine the advertisements such firms run in journals such as *Campaigns and Elections* and *Campaign Industry News*. Virtually every edition brings a new service. Among the more recent services some firms will provide are:

1. Producing (and distributing) video tapes of the candidate to targeted voters that, because of cost, or other factors, cannot be readily reached through the normal use of television

2. Providing a wide variety of software programs to facilitate a campaign developing its own voter surveys

3. Preparing the campaign expense statements

4. Coordinating the scheduling of volunteers

5. Handling a variety of other typical campaign functions.

56. Roger Ailes, *You Are The Message: Secrets of the Master Communicators* (Homewood, Ill.: Dow Jones–Irwin, 1988), p. 9.

57. Viguerie, *The New Right: We're Ready To Lead*, p. 26.

58. Ibid., pp. 26–27.

Chapter Eleven

Political Campaign Communication: An Epilogue

The central thesis of this book has been that communication is the heart of the modern political campaign. It is, as we argued in Chapter 1, the epistemological base. Without it, there would be no campaign. With this as our premise, we explored many principles of contemporary political campaigning including the communicative functions, styles, media channels, and paid television advertising. We have also examined a number of the communicative practices in the contemporary campaign including speechmaking, debating, interpersonal communication, and advertising. Moreover, as we analyzed technological advancements in the modern campaign, we were talking about techniques of communication. While we have not denied the importance of such variables as political parties, voter demographics, philosophical questions, or even economic considerations, we have consistently maintained that understanding the principles and practices of campaign communication is the only way to come to grips with the reality of the modern campaign.

We have striven to present a realistic picture of the way in which candidates and their consultants go about their tasks, implementing the techniques of communication. In so doing, we have attempted to be descriptive. We have not attempted to make judgments, to cast praise or blame on candidates or their methods. We do not intend to do so now. However, we would be remiss (or at the least not very observant) if we failed to acknowledge some of the most important questions or concerns that have been raised regarding modern political campaigning.

Eight years ago, when this book was first written, we raised six questions or concerns about political campaigning. Those concerns remain, and in some instances have become even more disturbing than they were eight years ago. Moreover, those six questions or concerns have, we believe, in the past eight years given rise to an overarching question that both subsumes and transcends our original six concerns. In this epilogue we wish to review our original six questions, examining them in light of recent developments. Moreover, we wish to address a final, and substantially more meaningful question that Americans of all walks of life have been asking with increasing frequency in the past eight years. Finally, while we scarcely presume to be able to resolve many of the questions and concerns generated by contemporary political campaigning, we wish to conclude by examining some of the many proposals that thoughtful citizens, academicians, and practitioners have offered in response to the questions and concerns being raised by contemporary political campaigns.

The first question we and others were asking eight years ago about political communication was simply: Will these trends continue? Will the new techniques of communication continue to play a dominant role in the campaigns of the future? While we do not have the benefit of a political crystal ball, our answer is yes. Eight years ago we observed that it seemed unlikely that the methods of campaigning would revert to those of an earlier day. Today we have no reason to question that judgment. People have seldom turned away from technology, and there is no political precedent for doing so. In fact, just the opposite has occurred. As new methods of transportation and communication were developed, they were incorporated into political campaigns, often before they were widely employed in other situations. We see little prospect that candidates or their staffs will shun current technology or turn their backs on the future. However, the very fact that new tools of communication have changed the nature and methods of campaigning has resulted in more calls to alter campaigns. Every four years political parties, scholars, candidates, and legislators call for such modifications as shorter primary seasons, more stringent finance reforms, providing candidates with free television time, and a host of other changes. Moreover, as we have detailed earlier, changes often take place. But, in the largest sense, the trends we have indicated throughout the books, trends which have made communication the preeminent factor in the waging of contemporary political campaigns, will continue.

A second question that has been raised by many is basic to the thrust of this book. And that is: Does campaigning make a difference? Apparently those who ask the question do so because they see such trends as the steady decline in voter participation and party affiliation and the growth in citizen disinterest and apathy as clear signs that political campaigns have little or nothing to do with election results. Obviously, we disagree with this point of view. Any number of examples illustrate that campaigns have indeed made a difference in winning and losing elections. If we cite only a few contemporary instances, we would have to include the 1988 primary campaigns of Michael Dukakis, the general election campaign of George Bush, the 1990 primary campaign of Dianne Feinstein of California, the 1990 general election campaigns of Senators Jesse Helms of North Carolina, Mitch McConnell of Kentucky, and Governors Peter Wilson of California, William Weld of Massachusetts, Ann Richards of Texas, and George Voinovich of Ohio. Indeed, if campaigning makes no difference to election returns, why then are there more and more candidates, including those on state and local levels, who spend enormous amounts of time and energy, to say nothing of money, planning and implementing campaigns? Political campaigning has become a growth industry. It is difficult to believe this would have happened if the contenders doubted its worth. Finally, and from our point of view, we believe that beyond helping to determine winners and losers, political campaigns serve many useful functions for voters and candidates. While some of these functions are important symbolically, others have instrumental value. Taken collectively, what all of this suggests is that campaigning does make a difference to citizens and candidates alike.

The third question raised by the growing emphasis on political campaigns as communication phenomena is related to the whole area of ethics. This book has dealt with several ethical questions that are conspicuous in contemporary campaigns, including the appropriate use of speechwriters, public opinion polls, and media advertising. Throughout the study we have chosen to describe, not evaluate. But anyone interested in political campaign communication cannot fail to be concerned with its ethical dimensions. "Dirty politics" has been around long before the advent of "unfair" or "unethical" television spot commercials. In fact, it was a part of political life in our nation's first political campaigns. Though campaign principles and practices may change from election to election, practitioners do not. Office seekers and their advisors are human beings. They remain subject to the foibles and temptations that have always confronted people. We see no evidence that contemporary candidates and their advisors are inherently less ethical than those of prior generations. However, the new communication-oriented politics, as well as the greater emphasis on investigative reporting, have doubtlessly brought questions regarding political ethics into sharper focus.

The fourth question raised by the growing emphasis on communication in political campaigns is that of cost. Many have expressed concern about the high costs of political campaigning. In recent years the expenses associated with effective campaigning have increased dramatically. As costs escalate there are those who feel that we have reached, or are fast reaching, the point where access to money will become the chief determinant of a candidate's success. During the past eight years this question has loomed especially large because the cost of campaigning has increased dramatically since we last wrote. Moreover, the inherent financial advantages of incumbency, such as the franking privileges enjoyed by many incumbent federal office holders, and the propensity of political action groups to give to incumbents, means that as campaign costs increase, the advantages of incumbency increase. During the past eight years the financial advantages of incumbency have reached the point where one Washington columnist claims that incumbents have "an almost impenetrable dollar shield against the best possible challengers."[1]

Similarly, campaigns are becoming more expensive in terms of human resources. Candidates and their associates are spending enormous amounts of time and effort to win office. Each of our last three presidents, George Bush, Ronald Reagan, and Jimmy Carter, has made running for president into a full-time job lasting several years, as have many of their competitors such as Governor Bruce Babbitt, Pat Robertson, and Jesse Jackson. Others, such as Senators Robert Dole, John Glenn, and Albert Gore, Congressmen Richard Gephardt and Jack Kemp, and Governor Michael Dukakis found it difficult to campaign and simultaneously hold responsible positions. Though the demands of presidential campaigning are unusually high, these same demands are often placed on those who seek lesser offices. Members of Congress or members of many of the state legislatures, for example, take extended recesses during the election period. Challengers find it necessary to temporarily abandon their professions, often taking leaves of absence. Because time demands are high, it grows increasingly difficult for many citizens to seriously consider running for public office, particularly those who are not financially secure.

Moreover, as we have seen, candidates are not the only individuals who face high costs in money and time when they choose to run. Often responsibilities must be borne by their spouses, children, business associates, and close friends. The use of family and friends as surrogates, fund-raisers, and in other campaign-related activities, places heavy burdens on all. In sum, the length of current campaigns and the demands they make on the financial and time resources of candidates and associates are costs that have grown so dramatically in recent years that many concerned individuals are calling for change.

The fifth question raised by the growing emphasis on communication in political campaigns involves the extent to which public expectations are being affected. Many political observers have commented on the increasing disenchantment and disengagement of the public, evidenced in part by falling voter turnout. Are campaigns fostering an illusion of competency that is at such variance with reality that public disillusionment is an inevitable result? Are contemporary campaigns distorting the public's expectations about officeholders? Are the campaigns a contributing factor to the growing public distrust of government and politicians? In the mid–1960s national election studies consistently found that six out of ten people said they trusted government to do the right thing at least most of the time. In 1988, four out of ten held a similar view.[2] Eight years ago, when we first wrote, we noted that by creating images of enormously talented candidates, campaigns might well be creating public expectations that officeholders cannot fulfill, hence contributing to voter apathy and subsequent dissatisfaction with government.

In many instances that problem still exists. Moreover, it has taken a new turn in the last eight years with the striking growth of negative advertising. Overwhelmingly negative advertising may well create public belief that candidates are unethical and incompetent, hence again contributing to voter apathy and subsequent dissatisfaction with government.

The sixth issue raised by contemporary campaigns focuses on the candidates. The skills of advocacy necessary for election are not necessarily the skills of compromise and deliberation necessary for effective governing. Moreover, today the closest advisors of many elected officials are their pollsters and other communication specialists, not their issue experts or party liaisons. We write this epilogue after experiencing three presidential campaigns in which the two winning candidates and their consultants employed perhaps the most skillful image making techniques ever used in American political campaigns. And yet, during eight years of the Reagan administration and midway into the Bush presidency, there have been numerous instances in which they appeared to have no program or mandate, no consistency between what they said as candidates and did as presidents, and when they and their administrations lost control of the national agenda. Can a nation, even a county, be adequately, much less skillfully, governed by officials and advisors whose skills reflect only the demands of successful political campaigning?

Since we first expressed these concerns eight years ago, none have been remedied. Indeed, many have grown more serious. Like other Americans we sometimes grow exasperated by the effectiveness of modern campaign methods, repeated revelations about campaign and campaigner ethics, the skyrocketing costs of campaigning (which consistently works to the advantage of the incumbent), growing evidence of the public's disillusionment with our political process, and similar evidence of our citizenry's dissatisfaction with the caliber of our national, regional, and local political leaders. These growing concerns all contribute to a fundamental question which both subsumes and transcends the six concerns we expressed eight years ago. Put bluntly: Is contemporary political campaigning failing the nation?

The very fact that a question such as this must be asked, and is being asked, not simply by us, but by countless Americans, both politically sophisticated and politically naive, is disturbing. We would not have asked it 30 years ago, nor would have other Americans. Yet, today it cannot be escaped. Virtually every retiring officeholder laments the election process and celebrates that they will no longer be subject to it. Columnists from across the political spectrum bemoan our election system. Ron Brown, chairman of the Democratic National Committee, and Lee Atwater, before his death, Brown's counterpart at the Republican National Committee, agreed on few things other than the need to reform our election system.[3]

If contemporary political campaigning is failing our nation, what might be done? The list of suggested reforms is lengthy. Among the most frequent suggestions are limiting the number of terms that officeholders such as congressmen and senators can serve, providing candidates for major statewide and federal offices free television time, or providing additional public financing for candidates.

We have reservations about all of these suggestions. This is not to say that they may not have merit. But it is to say that they do not strike at the heart of the question. If contemporary political campaigning is failing the nation it does so because it does not enable the nation to select its best leaders.

Most of the concerns being expressed about our election system and about contemporary campaigning center on congressional, senatorial, and presidential elections. Several observations are in order. First, we have no evidence that the losing candidates in recent years would be better officeholders than the winning candidates. Obviously judgments such as this often reflect the highly subjective and partisan feelings of the individuals making judgment. Second, we have no compelling evidence to suggest that hordes of extraordinary candidates and officeholders are out "there," refusing to run because of the demands of political campaigning. If contemporary political campaigning is failing our nation, presumably it is doing so by providing us with a lesser quality of leadership. It strikes us as virtually impossible to prove such a contention.

Third, the indictments of contemporary political campaigning often seem to miss the point. In one fashion or another, most of the complaints about current campaigning hinge around the charge that campaigns cost too much money. It is this charge that gives rise to most major suggestions for reform: public financing, shorter election periods, free television. But the problem is not that campaigning costs too much money. It is that incumbents have blatant financial advantages over challengers—a fact that was once again demonstrated in the 1990 election when 404 of the 405 House of Representative incumbents running for re-election won their primary contests. In 1988, the last election for which all the figures are available, a total of $459 million was spent in all of the House and Senate elections combined. That is less than the amount of money spent to advertise snack foods and soft drinks on television that year. Again, to put campaign expenses in perspective, we should note that in 1988 over 50 American companies reported advertising budgets in excess of the total combined cost of all of the races for the U.S. Senate held that year.[4] The monies spent on campaigning are not excessive given the importance of the enterprise. What is excessive is the disproportionate share of money that flows to the coffers of incumbents. Frankly, we are not optimistic that incumbents will approve legislation that will diminish their chances of winning. However, any serious attempt at reforming our system of electing public officials must come to grips with this problem.

Questioning political campaign principles and practices is not unique to Americans of our generation. Dissatisfaction has always existed and our system has evolved to accommodate those dissatisfactions that seemed warranted. Concern with methods of campaigning and electing officials have prompted a host of changes over the years, many of which we chronicled in this book. Presumably current questions about political campaigning will prompt changes as well.

Contemporary political campaigning is by no means perfect. It has never been perfect in the past and we see no reason to expect perfection in the future. Critics will always have questions about our election procedures and practices. And they should. Surely no activity is more central to our way of life than the establishment, maintenance, and transfer of leadership through free elections. Political campaign communication is the apotheosis of the democratic experience. It warrants our constant reexamination and reappraisal.

NOTES

1. This phrase was used by Carl T. Rowan in a nationally syndicated column of his that appeared under the headline "Fix Campaign Financing First," *Cincinnati Enquirer*, November 14, 1990, p. A14.

2. Richard Morin, "Is Cynicism About to Take Over?," *Cincinnati Enquirer*, October 8, 1990, p. A10.

3. Both are quoted extensively in Michael Oreskes with Robin Toner, "Free TV Time Could Be Answer: Both Major Parties Agree that Process Needs Drastic Move," *Cincinnati Enquirer*, March 25, 1990, p. H7.

4. William Armstrong, "Campaign Unreform," *Wall Street Journal*, June 8, 1990. William (Bill) Armstrong was, at the time he wrote, completing his second term as U.S. senator from Colorado and had announced that he would not seek a third term. The exact number of companies that Armstrong cited was 52.

Selected Bibliography

Ailes, Roger. *You Are the Message: The Secrets of the Master Communicators*. Homewood, Ill.: Dow Jones–Irvin, 1988.

Alexander, Herbert E. *Financing Politics: Money, Elections, and Political Reform*. Washington, D.C.: Congressional Quarterly Books, 1980.

Bishop, George F., Robert G. Meadow, and Marilyn Jackson-Beeck, eds. *The Presidential Debates: Media, Electoral, and Policy Perspectives*. New York: Praeger, 1978.

Bitzer, Lloyd F., and Theodore Rueter. *Carter vs. Ford: The Counterfeit Debates of 1976*. Madison: University of Wisconsin Press, 1980.

Blumenthal, Sidney. *The Permanent Campaign: Inside the World of Elite Political Operatives*. Boston: Beacon Press, 1980.

Boller, Paul F., Jr. *Presidential Campaigns*. New York: Oxford University Press, 1984.

Brareton, Charles. *First in the Nation: New Hampshire and the Premier Presidential Primary*. Portsmouth, N.H.: Peter E. Randall, Publisher, 1987.

Campbell, Karlyn Kohrs, and Kathleen Hall Jamieson, eds. *Form and Genre: Shaping Rhetorical Action*. Falls Church, Va.: Speech Communication Association, 1977.

Chester, Edward W. *Radio, Television, and American Politics*. New York: Sheed and Ward, 1969.

Denton, Robert E., Jr., and Dan F. Hahn, eds., *Presidential Communication*. New York: Praeger, 1986.

Devlin, Patrick L. *Political Persuasion in Presidential Campaigns*. New Brunswick, N.J.: Transaction, 1987.

Diamond, Edwin, and Stephen Bates. *The Spot: The Rise of Political Advertising on Television*. rev. ed. Cambridge: MIT Press, 1988.

Edelman, Murray. *The Symbolic Uses of Politics: With a New Afterword*. Urbana and Chicago: University of Illinois Press, 1985.

Elder, Charles D., and Roger W. Cobb. *The Political Uses of Symbols*. New York: Longman, 1983.

Foote, Joe S. *Television Access and Political Power: The Networks, the Presidency, and the Loyal Opposition*. New York: Praeger, 1990.

Friedenberg, Robert V., ed. *Rhetorical Studies of National Political Debates: 1960–1988*. New York: Praeger, 1990.

Grossman, Michael, and Martha Kumar. *Portraying the President: The White House and the News Media*. Baltimore: Johns Hopkins University Press, 1981.

Hart, Roderick P. *Verbal Style and the Presidency: A Computer-Based Analysis*. Orlando: Academic Press, 1984.

Hoff, Paul S. *Beyond the 30-Second Spot: Enhancing the Media's Role in Congressional Campaigns*. Washington, D.C.: Center for Responsive Politics, 1988.

Jamieson, Kathleen Hall. *Packaging the Presidency: A History and Criticism of Presidential Campaign Advertising*. New York: Oxford University Press, 1984.

Jamieson, Kathleen Hall, and David S. Birdsell. *Presidential Debates: The Challenge of Creating an Informed Electorate*. New York: Oxford University Press, 1988.

Kaid, Lynda Lee, Dan D. Nimmo, and Keith R. Sanders. *New Perspectives on Political Advertising*. Carbondale and Edwardsville: Southern Illinois University Press, 1986.

Kern, Montague. *30-Second Politics: Political Advertising in the 1980s*. New York: Praeger, 1989.

Kraus, Sidney. *Televised Presidential Debates and Public Policy*. Hillsdale, N.J.: Lawrence Erlbaum, 1988.

Loomis, Burdett. *The New American Politician: Ambition, Entrepreneurship, and the Changing Face of Political Life*. New York: Basic Books, 1988.

Mandel, Ruth B. *In the Running: The New Woman Candidate*. New Haven and New York: Ticknor and Fields, 1981.

Martel, Myles. *Political Campaign Debates: Images, Strategies, and Tactics*. New York: Longman, 1983.

Mayer, Jane, and Doyle McManus. *Landslide: The Unmaking of the President, 1984–1988*. Boston: Houghton Mifflin, 1988.

Mickelson, Sig. *From Whistle Stop to Sound Bite: Four Decades of Politics and Television*. New York: Praeger, 1989.

Nimmo, Dan D., and James E. Combs. *Mediated Political Realities*. 2d. ed. New York: Longman, 1990.

Noonan, Peggy. *What I Saw at the Revolution*. New York: Random House, 1990.

Paletz, David L. *Political Communication Research: Approaches, Studies, Assessments*. Norwood, N.J.: Ablex Publishing, 1987.

Patterson, Thomas E. *The Mass Media Election: How Americans Choose Their President*. New York: Praeger, 1980.

Payne, Gregory J., ed. *American Behavioral Scientist* (March/April 1989).

Pfau, Michael, and Henry C. Kenski. *Attack Politics: Strategy and Defense*. New York: Praeger, 1990.

Press, Charles, and Kenneth Verburg. *American Politics and Journalists*. Glenview, Ill.: Scott, Foresman and Company, 1988.

Reichley, A. James, ed. *Elections American Style*. Washington, D.C.: Brookings Institution, 1987.

Sanders, Keith R., Lynda Lee Kaid, Dan D. Nimmo. *Political Communication*

Yearbook 1984. Carbondale and Edwardsville: Southern Illinois University Press, 1985.

Simons, Herbert W., and Aram Aghazarian, eds. *Form, Genre, and the Study of Political Discourse*. Columbia: University of South Carolina Press, 1986.

Swanson, David L., and Dan D. Nimmo. *New Directions in Political Communication: A Resource Book*. Newbury Park, Calif.: Sage Publications, 1990.

Swerdlow, Joel L. *Presidential Debates: 1988 and Beyond*. Washington, D.C.: Congressional Quarterly Books, 1987.

———., ed. *Media Technology and the Vote: A Source Book*. Boulder, Colo.: Westview Press, 1988.

Valley, David B. *A History and Analysis of Democratic Presidential Nomination Acceptance Speeches to 1968*. Lanham, Md.: University Press of America, 1988.

Viguerie, Richard A. *The New Right: We're Ready to Lead*. Falls Church, Va.: The Viguerie Company, 1980.

White, Theodore H. *The Making of the President 1960*. New York: Atheneum, 1961.

———. *The Making of the President 1964*. New York: Atheneum, 1965.

———. *The Making of the President 1968*. New York: Atheneum, 1969.

———. *The Making of the President 1972*. New York: Bantam, 1973.

Williams, Frederick. *The New Communications*. 2d ed. Belmont, Calif.: Wadsworth Publishing Company, 1989.

Windt, Theodore Otto, Jr. *Presidents and Protesters: Political Rhetoric in the 1960s*. Tuscaloosa: University of Alabama Press, 1990.

Index

ABOUT THE AUTHORS

JUDITH S. TRENT is Professor of Communication and Associate Vice President for Research and Advanced Studies at the University of Cincinnati. She has written and spoken widely on the subject of political campaign communication.

ROBERT V. FRIEDENBERG is Professor of Communication at Miami (Ohio) University. He is the editor of *Rhetorical Studies of National Political Debates: 1960–1968* (Praeger, 1990). In 1989 he received the "Outstanding Book of the Year Award" from the Religious Speech Communication Association for *"Hear O Israel" The History of American Jewish Preaching 1654–1970*. He has served as a communication consultant for the Republican National Committee and has been involved in over 70 political campaigns.